THE LONG LEFT FLANK

By the same author:

Princess Patricia's Canadian Light Infantry
Byng of Vimy, winner of the Governor General's Award

THE LONG LEFT FLANK

The Hard Fought Way to the Reich, 1944–1945

JEFFERY WILLIAMS

Leo Cooper

First Published in Great Britain in 1988 by Leo Cooper Ltd.

Leo Cooper is an independent imprint of
the Heinemann Group of Publishers,
10 Upper Grosvenor Street,
London W1X 9PA.

LONDON MELBOURNE JOHANNESBURG AUCKLAND

Copyright © Jeffery Williams 1988

ISBN: 0-85052-8801

Printed in the United States

CONTENTS

LIST OF MAPS vii

AUTHOR'S NOTE ix

FOREWORD xii

PART ONE — **THE CHANNEL PORTS**

1: PRIDE AND PREJUDICE........................ 17
2: TO THE SEINE 27
3: ESCAPE OF THE GERMAN FIFTEENTH ARMY ... 33
4: THE CINDERELLA ARMY 44
5: DUNKIRK AND OSTEND........................ 50
6: LE HAVRE — OPERATION ASTONIA 56
7: BOULOGNE — OPERATION WELLHIT 61
8: CALAIS — OPERATION UNDERGO.............. 73

PART TWO — **THE SCHELDT**

9: THE FORTRESS 81
10: OUTFLANKING ANTWERP 92
11: WOENSDRECHT 103
12: WATER ENOUGH FOR DROWNING —
     OPERATION SWITCHBACK 114
13: BRESKENS POCKET — THE BRAAKMAN
     APPROACH 122
14: SOUTH BEVELAND — OPERATION VITALITY ...129
15: WALCHEREN ISLAND — OPERATION
     INFATUATE 144
16: THE END OF THE AFFAIR 160

PART THREE — THE RHINELAND

17: WINTER ON THE MAAS 169
18: THE REICHSWALD — OPERATION VERITABLE   181
19: BEYOND THE FOREST 208
20: OPERATION BLOCKBUSTER 221
21: THE HOCHWALD 233
22: THE WESEL BRIDGEHEAD 244

PART FOUR — THE FINAL SIX WEEKS

23: THE RHINE TO THE NORTH SEA 257
24: INTO GERMANY 272
25: 1ST CORPS IN THE NETHERLANDS 280
26: END OF THE WAR IN EUROPE 291

APPENDICES

GLOSSARY 301

MILITARY ORGANIZATION AND ORDER OF
  BATTLE 302

A NOTE ON CASUALTIES 318

ENDNOTES 321

BIBLIOGRAPHY 332

INDEX 335

LIST OF MAPS

Advance to the Somme and Antwerp 38
The Coastal Belt 47
Le Havre: Operation "Astonia" 58
The Capture of Boulogne 68
The Capture of Calais 76
The Battle of the Scheldt 84
North-West Europe, The Front 15 September 89
Woensdrecht 105
The Leopold Canal 117
The Walcheren Causeway 132
The Capture of Walcheren 145
The Northern Front 162
The Nijmegen Island 173
Kapelsche Veer 178
The Rhineland — Operation Veritable 182
Attack by 2nd Canadian Infantry Division 193
Moyland Wood and the Goch-Calcar Road 215
The Battle of the Rhineland 223
The Rhineland — Operation Blockbuster 228
The Hochwald Gap 234
Xanten 248
The Battle of the Rhine — the Left Flank 258
The Advance on the Northern Front 262
Zutphen and Deventer 266
The Western Netherlands 274

AUTHOR'S NOTE

During most of First Canadian Army's operations, I was a staff officer at General Crerar's headquarters, one of the captains and majors who assembled intelligence about the enemy, kept a detailed track of the battle across the Army's front, saw that the right ammunition was available at the right time and place, that replacement tanks and guns went to those who needed them most, that traffic flowed smoothly on inadequate roads and that the Army was fed, housed and cared for to the best of our ability. War being what it is, our performance was seldom perfect. Much of our time was taken in 'plugging holes' — replacing a key signals vehicle which had been blown up or rushing a special unit to where it was needed. Caring for the troops usually came down to such basics as ensuring that they suffered no avoidable discomfort nor walked a mile further than necessary.

In retrospect, I was privileged in that, to do my job, I had to know what was happening each day in every part of the Army and what was planned for the future. In short, I was a witness to its operations and my own part in them is not worth mentioning.

In the autumn of 1944, looking at the situation map one day, I was struck by an uncomfortable sense of déjà-vu. Except in detail, the lines of the opposing forces from the Swiss border to the North Sea bore an ominous resemblance to the Western Front in 1917. But this was 1944 and we were all determined that the mistakes and the poor generalship of the First World War would never be repeated. Now our equipment was better, our men were highly trained and we believed in our generals. That last thought, oddly enough, reminded me at the time of the words of a Canadian veteran, a sergeant in the CEF in the 1918 War, to a clever college boy, 'Say one more word against Haig, you little pansy, and I'll knock you flat!'

I later came to realize that there were many similarities between the Western Fronts and the First and Second World Wars, one of which was the sacrifice demanded of the infantry. The example of my own regiment, The Calgary Highlanders, was typical. If I seem to mention them more frequently than others, it is because I know their story best.

Canadians, British, Poles, Americans, Dutch, Belgians and French all fought together in First Canadian Army. As in any large force only a surprisingly small proportion of its soldiers ever came face to face with the enemy. Those who did not viewed those who did with a certain unadmitted humility which cannot be forgotten. Yet today their achievements are largely unknown to generations who owe them their freedom.

In writing this book which is my own tribute to them, I have been helped by many who served in First Canadian Army and who share my admiration for their former comrades. Among those to whom I am particularly grateful are Lt-Colonel Lawrence Dampier for access to his unique collection of operational documents, the late Lt-Colonel Ronald Kerfoot who gave me his operational maps, and Brig-General and Mrs Denis Whitaker for copies of unit war diaries.

For their personal accounts of episodes of the North-West Europe campaign, I am indebted to the late Major-General J.M. Rockingham, Colonel E.F. Bastedo, Major-General Roger Rowley, the late Lt-Colonel Charles Askwith, Major-General George Kitching, Brig-General W.K. Lye, Major H.J.S. Pearson, Lt-Colonel F.H. Clarke, Lt-Colonel D.G. MacLauchlan, Rt Hon George Hees, Lt-Colonel Vernon Stott, Lt-Colonel Mark Tennant, Major W.L. Lyster, Major W.J. Riley, Colonel Sam Nickle and Major Don Munro; for their advice and their unique views of some of the principal personalities involved, to Commodore William Hayes, Colonel C.P. Stacey, Colonel C.R. Simonds and the late Major-General E.K.G. Sixsmith.

Others who loaned material or who helped with the project

were Lt-Colonel R.G. Woodhouse, Somerset Light Infantry; Lt-Colonel David Ward, King's Own Scottish Borderers; Lt-Colonel and Mrs. E.H. Shuter, Mrs. V.R. Schjelderup; Capt Harold Kenny, Princess Patricia's Canadian Light Infantry; Dr Carl Christie, Dr Jean Pariseau and Mr Paul Marshall of the Directorate of History, Ottawa; Dr Ian McClymont and Miss Barbara Wilson of the Public Archives of Canada; Mr J.W. Hunt and Mr M.G.H. Wright of the Royal Military Academy, Sandhurst; Mr Roger Suddaby and Mr Willis of the Imperial War Museum, London.

The project could not have been undertaken without the assistance of the Canada Council who made a most generous contribution to its cost.

The Directorate of History, National Defence Headquarters, Ottawa, authorized us to reproduce the excellent maps from Volume 3 of *The Official History of the Canadian Army* and where possible, these have been used. Other original maps have been drawn by Captain R.C. Read, former Assistant Hydrographer of the Royal Navy, for whose advice and help during the production of the book, I am especially grateful.

As she did when I have written other books, my wife has walked battlefields in the rain, helped with research and indexing, acted as secretary and typed every word more than once. She knows how grateful I am.

FOREWORD

Canada began mobilizing for war even before the Germans marched into Poland and her 1st Division arrived in Britain before the end of 1939. In the years which followed, the force in England grew to a complete field army of three infantry and two armoured divisions, two independent armoured brigades and groups of medium and anti-aircraft artillery, organized into two army corps with an appropriate mix of Army and Corps Troops. With base and reinforcement units its strength was 232,000 soldiers of all ranks. All were volunteers.

The 1st Division went to France in 1940, after the evacuation of the BEF at Dunkirk, but was withdrawn by the British War Office before it met the enemy. There followed the raid on Spitzbergen, then three years of training, punctuated only by the 2nd Division's disastrous raid on Dieppe in August, 1942. The time soon came when the troops had learned everything that peacetime training could teach. Discipline was good, the men hard and fit. Staleness and boredom became the Army's greatest problems. As time went by it became obvious that First Canadian Army's purpose in life was to defeat the German army in North-West Europe. Lt-Gen A.G.L. McNaughton, its commander, once described his force as 'a dagger pointed at the heart of Berlin.'

In April, 1943, when it was decided that the 1st Canadian Division and the 1st Armoured Brigade would be sent to the Mediterranean to take part in the landings in Sicily, it was understood by both the Canadian and British authorities that they would return to the United Kingdom in time to take part in cross-channel operations, presumably in 1944. Apart from a wish to take a more active part in the War, the primary purpose of the operation was for Canadians to gain battle experience.

Within little more than a month of their departure from Scotland, Colonel J.L. Ralston, the Minister of National Defence, began persuading the British to agree to the force being increased to a full corps, including another division. Given the commitments of the Allies to operations in many parts of the world, there was at first no shipping available and the Allied command in the Mediterranean was not convinced that the additional forces were needed. Eventually it was agreed that HQ 1st Canadian Corps, its Corps troops and the 5th Armoured Division would replace HQ 30 Corps, its Corps troops and the 7th British Armoured Division in Italy which would then return to Britain to bolster the invasion force. The two corps would exchange their heavy equipment — tanks, guns and transport — so reducing the shipping requirement.

The insistence of the Canadian Government in sending 1st Corps to Italy against the wishes of her Allies was perhaps commendable in that it brought more of their troops into battle against the enemy. The part which public opinion in Canada played in the Government's thinking was probably not great. To most people it made little difference whether Canada had one division or two in Italy. Of more consequence was the Cabinet's perception of American opinion. As more and more United States forces were brought into action, it seemed important to Canada's relations with her neighbour that she be seen to be shouldering a relatively larger share of the offensives against the Axis.[1]

Political motives, not military imperatives, lay behind the Government's actions which unfortunately resulted in no veteran division from Italy rejoining the Army before the invasion of Normandy. There the Canadians had to earn their battle experience the hard way, by trial and error — by benefiting from the mistakes of their dead comrades.

In common with every army, some were inadequate to the harshness of the task, others died through inexperience or the failures of others. Casualties were very heavy. But at the end of the Normandy campaign, in every understrength unit was a hard core of battle-tried veterans who now had the experience to put to full use the skills they had polished for so long in Britain.

Part One

The Channel Ports

1

PRIDE AND PREJUDICE

IN AUGUST, 1944, the German armies facing the Allies in Normandy were smashed, their equipment destroyed or captured and the defeated remnants, exhausted and demoralized, made away from the field. Keeping well inland from the Channel coast, British armoured divisions set a furious pace in driving north-east to Antwerp and Brussels, while American tanks thrust eastward toward the Rhine. French troops were in Paris and another Allied army was advancing north from the Riviera. Everywhere ecstatic crowds cheered and feted the liberating armies. Victory was in the air. When rumours spread that senior commanders were saying 'It is all over,'[1] and when so many fervently wished that it was so, who could be blamed for believing that the war would end in 1944?

The bitter realization that more fighting remained to be done came when the airborne operations at Arnhem failed to breach the water barrier of the Rhine and the Allies were brought to a halt before the formidable defences of the Siegfried Line. As British and American armies faced eastward, unable to bring their full strength to bear for lack of fuel and ammunition, the attention of the public, and most soldiers, became fixed on crossing the Rhine and on the Russian armies grinding inexorably into Poland and the Balkans. In Britain and the United States, to a press now accustomed to equate 'fighting' with 'lightning armoured thrusts,' little seemed to be happening. Yet along the long left flank of the Allied Expeditionary Force, a battle was being fought on whose outcome hung not just victory, but the possibility of disaster.

Long before the Allies landed in Normandy, it was planned that First Canadian Army would advance northward from the beachhead to cross the Seine between Rouen and Le Havre. Now, having closed the Falaise Gap and having beaten off the desperate attempts of the enemy to break out of that trap, General Harry Crerar began what was to become one of the most arduous campaigns of the Second World War. Unsung because it seemed unspectacular, it was seen by many to be nothing more than 'mopping-up.' With their eyes looking for a breakout to the east, the world's press saw little of what went on on the left and thereby missed some of the bloodiest infantry battles of the War. At the end of the day, Canadian battalions could claim the dubious honour of having the highest casualty rates in the Allied forces. Not even in those bloodbaths of the First World War, the Somme and Passchendaele, had the average number of casualties per day per battalion matched those suffered along the coast of north-west Europe. (See Appendix — A Note on Casualties)

First Canadian Army was the most international of the Allied formations. Apart from its Army troops, the major Canadian component was its 2nd Corps of one armoured and two infantry divisions. The place of its 1st Corps, which was fighting in Italy, had been taken by 1st British Corps and indeed, until the last two months of the War, it contained more British troops than had Montgomery's Eighth Army at Alamein.[2] The Polish Armoured Division had become almost a permanent fixture in the Army and they were later joined by Belgian, Dutch and Czechoslovakian formations. At various times American infantry and airborne divisions came under command as did commandos of the Royal Marines and the British Army. The Royal Navy participated in many of its operations and it was supported directly by No. 84 Group, RAF, with its British, Polish, Dutch, Belgian, French and New Zealand Squadrons. There were many Canadians in the Group but, curiously, by far the greatest number were in the Royal Canadian Air Force squadrons which made up over half the strength of No. 83 Group supporting Second British Army. The units which served in the Army are named in the Order of Battle page 304; their structure and armament are described in the note on military organization on page 302.

The two British and Canadian Armies were joined in the 21st Army Group commanded by General Sir Bernard Montgomery, one of the finest battlefield commanders of the Second World War. His record of success stemmed in part from a clear, analytical mind, broad experience, years of study of his profession, unwavering resolution and unshakeable self-confidence. Had the fortunes of war not led to his being given command of the Eighth Army before the battle of Alamein, he might have been chiefly remembered as a superb trainer of soldiers. He was prepared to take endless pains in developing the potential of promising officers but was ruthless in getting rid of those he judged to be less than competent. Having once made up his mind about a subject, or an officer, he rarely changed it. In short, he was intolerant, opinionated and often prejudiced. His relationship with Crerar and the Canadians had a long history and was not easy.

It began in 1917. In a letter to his mother, Montgomery told of lunching with his brother Donald, an officer of the 29th Canadian Infantry Battalion from Vancouver:

> I saw Donald. I went over and lunched with his Brigade (sic). The Canadians are a queer crowd; they seem to think they are the best troops in France and that we have to get them to do our most difficult jobs. I reminded them that the Ypres Battle began on 31st July and the only part they have taken part in is the last 10 days. They forget that the whole art of war is to gain your objective with as little loss as possible.
>
> I was disappointed in them. At plain straightforward fighting they are magnificent, but they are narrow-minded and lack soldierly instincts.

To this his biographer added:

> A judgement which in annotations to his letters, Bernard later rescinded, agreeing with Alan Brooke that the Canadian troops were magnificent soldiers, but their leadership poor.[3]

Poor Monty! The officers of the 29th Battalion probably did tease him about their being brought in to finish the Ypres battle and may not have discussed tactics seriously. What they saw was not a future field-marshal but a rather small ferret-faced junior staff officer, not blessed with a particularly engaging personality, who had a comfortable job back at a British corps headquarters. What the Canadians had seen of the battlefield did not enhance their opinion of the staffs who had had anything to do with it. If it were not for the inaccurate impression which Montgomery retained, there would be little point in saying more about it.

The letter was written on 8 November, 1917. Two days earlier the 6th Brigade, of which the 29th was a part, took Passchendaele itself, the ultimate objective of a three-month series of battles which cost the British armies 244,897 casualties. The Canadian success in its final days was a feat of arms whose brilliance has long been concealed in the miasma of gloom which surrounds the wider British experience. The credit for it lay not simply in the fighting qualities of the well-disciplined and highly trained Canadian soldiers but in the imaginative and painstaking efforts of Sir Arthur Currie, their commander, who is acknowledged to have been one of the two best generals in the BEF.

So strong were Montgomery's views about the alleged inadequacies of Canadian leadership that his biographer turned history on its head and referred more than once to the Canadians' 'futile gallantry' at Passchendaele. A more likely basis for Montgomery's prejudice lay in Haig's comment about their behaving more like Allies than fellow citizens of the Empire.

Montgomery's annotation to his letter to his mother was made much later, probably after 1945. While Sir Alan Brooke was dismissive of the abilities of the Canadian Corps artillery commander on whose staff he served in 1917, the remarks on poor leadership attributed to him refer to a much later period.

In the early stages of the Second World War, Brooke, now Chief of the Imperial General Staff became doubtful of the suitability for field commands of some of the senior officers of the 1st Canadian Corps in England. Later he passed on these reservations to Montgomery who had become Commander-in-Chief of the Command in which the Canadians were located.

Lt-General A.G.L. McNaughton, the Canadian commander, soon clashed with Montgomery. He summed up their relationship in simple terms, 'We did not like each other.'[4]

Late in 1941 McNaughton returned to Canada on sick leave and was replaced temporarily as Corps Commander by Lt-General H.D.G. Crerar, who later wrote of his difficulties:

> ... whatever conclusion I might personally reach as to changes in policy, organization and command in 1 Cdn Corps, it was necessary for me to delay action whenever possible until Lt-Gen McNaughton returned and I obtained his approval or otherwise. I was much in the position of a 'locum tenens.'[5]

A few weeks in command was enough to convince Crerar that a good many brigade and unit commanders needed to be replaced. He discussed the problem with Montgomery, explaining that until McNaughton returned, his hands were tied. The C-in-C said that he would be glad to visit each of the Canadian units in turn and give Crerar his *personal* views on their efficiency and that of their commanders as this might help Crerar with his own conclusions. Crerar accepted the offer. In the course of the next several months, Montgomery submitted his views to Crerar in the form of assessments. He pulled no punches. Of one commanding officer, he wrote: 'It is a great pity he was given command of this fine battalion. He is quite unfit for it.' Of a brigade commander, 'A good brigadier. No great training ability; but has a good brain and knows what he wants and is firm and decisive. He inspires confidence.'[6]

In most cases Montgomery's opinions confirmed those which Crerar had already reached, but about which he could do nothing until McNaughton returned. But their patronizing tone was another matter. Crerar tolerated it, but he did not like it.

A more serious cause of irritation was the relationship of the Corps to the Command in which it was located. The Canadians in Britain were an independent national force whose presence was governed by the Visiting Forces Acts of the two countries. The British War Office provided it with accommodation and other services for which Canada paid. In short, the Canadian Corps was a tenant of the British Army. It was not Montgomery's to command nor his responsibility to train. Those prerogatives were retained by the Canadian Government until the Corps embarked on operations, at which point it would be placed under British command. Until Montgomery arrived on the scene, the arrangements were understood by both sides and worked well.[7]

To Montgomery, the idea of a static area 'Command' was anathema. He preferred to see himself rather as the commander of a field army, so, without seeking anyone's permission, he changed the name of his organization to 'South-eastern Army.' He drew up plans to defeat invasion, committing the Canadian Corps which, operationally, was not under his control. When Crerar pointed out that this was not possible without obtaining the approval of the Canadian Government, he accused Crerar of 'bellyaching' and pedantry and, in the words of his biographer, 'his relations with Crerar suffered for the rest of the War.'[8]

Swept along by his egocentricity, Montgomery rode roughshod over Canadian sensibilities, aroused unnecessary resentment by criticizing commanders in front of their subordinates, and treated Crerar like a schoolboy. Crerar looked back on that period January–June, 1941, as 'one of the most difficult and trying periods of my professional life. In the circumstances in which I was placed, this should not be hard to appreciate.'[9]

As was his right, Crerar appealed to his old friend, Alan Brooke, to point out to Montgomery from his own experience, the facts of life when it came to dealing with Canadians. He did so but that only worsened Montgomery's opinion of Crerar. Unfortunately for their future relationship, Montgomery later had Australians, New Zealanders and South Africans under his operational command in Africa and experienced few, if any, of the problems he had with Crerar in England. He chose to forget the difference in circumstances, that as they were about to go into battle, their governments had, in accordance with their equivalent to the Visiting Forces Act, placed them under British control, as Canada did before the invasion of Normandy. Only once when the Canadians were under his command in Europe was there an incident when their national status became an issue.

Crerar's first operational experience in the Second World War was as a corps commander in Italy. Montgomery considered that this did not give him the intimate knowledge of battle that a senior commander should have. Unquestionably experience, say as a divisional commander, would have been valuable to Crerar but to regard it as an essential qualification is to disregard the record of the many successful American and British senior commanders who were denied it.

In July, 1944, in Normandy, on the day First Canadian Army became operational, Montgomery had to intervene in a dispute between Crerar and Lt-General Crocker, of 1st British Corps, who was under his command. In a letter to Brooke later, he conceded that there were faults on both sides but laid the blame on the Canadian. Some two weeks later when Crerar at Falaise was fighting his first major battle, Montgomery reported disparagingly on his understandable anxiety that it should succeed. He told Brooke that with experience and some help from himself Crerar would rid himself of such worries and be much better.[10]

At the end of the war, Montgomery wrote Crerar a fulsome letter of thanks:

> . . . for all that you have done for me since we first served together in this war. No commander can ever have had a more loyal subordinate than I have had in you. And under your command the Canadian Army has covered itself in glory . . .[11]

Commodore William Hayes, the Commandant of the Royal Military College of Canada, had seen the letter at Kingston and, when he met Lord Montgomery at Sandhurst in 1970, he assumed that he and Crerar were friends.

> I met the Field-Marshal with half-a-dozen other people in the Commandant's study. He looked at my new green uniform which gave no hint as to whether I was a soldier or a sailor and said nothing. To break the silence, I said that, though a sailor, I had been a cadet at Kingston when General Harry Crerar was the Commandant. I expected Montgomery to take the conversational ball by saying something about as controversial as 'How interesting,' but instead he fixed me with a look in which there was no trace of a smile, poked me in the chest and to my astonishment said, 'He was quite unfit to command troops.'
>
> He gave me another prod in the chest and added 'And you know it!' I was too indignant to reply at once. Before I could say anything, he poked me again and said, 'You know the best general you Canadians ever had — Guy Simonds, Guy Simonds.'

It was hardly the place for me to enter an argument with a British field-marshal, but I came away with the feeling that I didn't much like the little man.[12]

It was after the war, too, that General Crerar told Colonel Charles Stacey, the distinguished historian, about his relationship with the Field-Marshal. Before he arrived at 1st Canadian Corps Headquarters in 1941, he had never met Montgomery and he asked a British general of his acquaintance what sort of a man he was. 'After a moment's reflection, the general replied, "Well, Harry, all I can tell you about Monty is that he's an efficient little shit." ' Stacey commented that General Crerar, 'all those years later, clearly felt indisposed to disagree with this assessment.'[13]

Another interesting set of relationships were those of Crerar with his corps commanders. After a flaming row in Normandy, Lt-General John Crocker of 1st (British) Corps and Crerar got along well and parted as friends after working together for more than eight months. 30th British Corps was under First Canadian Army during the Rhineland battles and Sir Brian Horrocks, its commander, later spoke of his admiration for Crerar as a commander and of his liking for him.

These two battle-experienced generals were connoisseurs of army commanders, each having commanded corps under at least two, apart from Harry Crerar. This is worth remembering when looking at the relationship between the First Canadian Army commander and the gifted Lt-General Guy Granville Simonds of 2nd Corps.

A major-general at the age of 39, Simonds commanded the 1st Canadian Division in Sicily and Italy where he soon gained a reputation for tactical skill and resolution. But in addition to the hour-to-hour demands of commanding a division in battle, he was also the senior Canadian officer in the theatre with the attendant problems of personnel and supply.

Toward the end of 1943 the Headquarters of 1st Canadian Corps and the 5th Armoured Division began to arrive in Italy under Crerar. In order to widen his experience, Simonds was transferred to the command of the newly arriving division.

At that point Simonds began to show signs of the strain under which he had been working for the past nine months. He chose to misinterpret the reasoning behind shifting him from his successful 1st Infantry Division to the untried 5th Armoured. One or two other relatively minor incidents roused him to write two long letters, each of six pages or more of closely written foolscap, to his new corps commander claiming in effect that Crerar had no confidence in him and was looking for an opportunity to 'take a crack at me.'[14] So far from the truth was this that Crerar had already recommended Simonds for promotion to the command of 2nd Corps.

Alarmed at Simonds' state of mind, Crerar showed the correspondence to two senior medical officers and asked for their professional views on his continuing fitness to command. Both felt that Simonds could probably be relied upon to function as a senior commander though preferably not of an independent Canadian force.

Crerar confirmed his recommendation for Simonds' promotion and locked the file away with the note:

> It is, to me, really a tragic situation because while I continue to believe Simonds to be quite the outstanding Divisional Commander, who will prove to be equally brilliant as a corps commander in the field, I cannot see him going on and up the way and distance I had anticipated.[15]

Simonds was the nearest Canada produced to a military genius in the Second World War. That the obverse of the coin should be a trace of instability, a touch of the prima donna, is not surprising. Finally it focused for the rest of the war in an intense dislike of the man to whom he owed so much. So unreasoning was it that when Crerar used the word 'brilliant' in discussing his future with Simonds, he accused Crerar of sarcasm. There is no doubt that at the end of the war the reservations formed by Crerar about his subordinate's future potential resulted in Simonds' failure to become the professional head of the Canadian Army in 1946.[16] 'Subsequently Guy Simonds hated Crerar to the extent that he was almost irrational about it. I was saddened by the way he never lost an opportunity to run Crerar down.'[17]

In any army it would be difficult to choose a team of generals who were both highly competent and liked each other. The very qualities which make a good general — loyalty to the men he commands, the ability to make up his mind, to choose a course of action and follow it through despite any opposition — applied to such an imprecise endeavour as waging war, makes for disagreement and personality clash. The tensions of battle draw out passions and frailties. Men who are pleasant and friendly at home become withdrawn and aloof — often to shield their emotions from involvement with those they may have to send to their deaths. Add to this the spice of competition for advancement in a small army and the stew becomes rich indeed.

Like the British and Americans, the Canadians had their full share of generals who disliked each other. Crerar, cold and rather withdrawn in manner, was hated by the aloof and introspective Simonds, respected rather than liked by others. Simonds and Major-General Chris Vokes were cadets at the Royal Military College together, got along well subsequently and shared an intense personal dislike for Charles Foulkes who was promoted to command the 1st Corps in Italy, a post which Vokes claimed should have been his. Apparently Vokes never knew that it was Simonds who recommended Foulkes for the job as a result of his performance in the Scheldt battles.[18]

In doing so, Simonds passed one of the more difficult tests of generalship — not to allow personal feelings to stand in the way of doing what he believed to be right.[19]

In their attitudes to each other generals are no different from privates but their relationships can have repercussions which affect every soldier in the Army. The Canadians were fortunate that personal likes or antipathies among generals, their own and their Allies, probably had no effect on military operations. Unhappily that did not necessarily apply to the subject of mutual professional trust.

2

TO THE SEINE

AS THE LAST DESPERATE STRUGGLES of the trapped German armies to break out of the Falaise pocket were coming to an end on 22 August, 1944, General Sir Bernard Montgomery ordered his British and Canadian Armies to pursue their remnants. Freed of the restriction which held them in position until their still-dangerous enemy could fight no longer, they turned eastwards from Normandy toward the Seine.

Three days earlier, General Harry Crerar, commanding First Canadian Army had explained his plans for the advance to his corps commanders. To 2nd Canadian Corps he assigned an axis from Trun through Vimoutiers to Orbec, Bernay and Elbeuf. It was not to move until he gave the order but, in the meantime, it was to begin reconnoitring in that direction. Guy Simonds, its young commander, interpreted the order with imagination. He despatched his reconnaissance units toward the Seine on 21 August, followed by the entire 2nd Division.

Near the coast Lt-General J.T. Crocker's 1st British Corps which had not been involved in the fighting at Falaise, had already begun to move. On the left, paratroopers of the 6th Airborne Division were slogging along the roads toward Honfleur and Pont L'Evêque, while inland, the 7th Armoured Division was fighting in Lisieux. Between them, the 49th (West Riding) Division was shouldering aside stiff opposition on the River Touques.

For the first few hours the advance of the 2nd Canadian Division was slowed by large numbers of Germans surrendering but as they began to shake free from these the 5th Brigade in the lead began to meet enemy who were prepared to resist.

At Vimoutiers on the Trun-Orbec road, the Canadian Black Watch came under fire from an enemy rearguard which could only be cleared with the assistance of Le Régiment de Maisonneuve. Passing through them, a company of the Calgary Highlanders encountered a party of enemy in the process of demolishing a bridge. Racing forward, they drove the German sappers from the bridge. Promptly the enemy demolition guard counter-attacked, supported by a tank. The tank was knocked out by a PIAT and the enemy attack was brought to a halt. As units of the 6th Brigade passed through, the company rounded up a surprising bag of prisoners — two officers and 54 men, having themselves lost one man killed and two wounded in action. The result was uncharacteristic of the Wehrmacht in Normandy. It also was the Highlanders' last inexpensive victory on the way to the Seine.

Next day the Battalion was reminded that the withdrawing enemy had a sting in his tail. Moving through Orbec, they had 18 casualties from shellfire. Ahead, the Fusiliers de Montreal of the 6th Brigade were unable to break through a force of infantry and tanks at St Germain-la-Campagne and the Highlanders were ordered to attack. Flanking the town on the left, B Company was badly mauled by enemy tanks while the Battalion Command Group had to run the gauntlet of a battery of 88mm guns in approaching the town. By the end of the day B Company's normal strength of some 125 was reduced to two officers and 37 men.[1]

Having spent the daylight hours of the 25th in the apple orchards of St Cyre de Salerne near Brionne, the Calgaries were boarding their transport when a brilliant light lit the sky overhead. Captain Mark Tennant dived to the ground.

> Someone had fired a flare right over our area and then the Stukas came in, their sirens screaming. You could have struck a match on their noses they came so close to the ground. As they pulled up, down came their bombs, not the ordinary kind but containers with five to six hundred bomblets a little smaller than a grenade — grass-cutters. One container landed near me and didn't explode, thank God.

There's always been an argument about how many Stukas there were. I think there were three, others say half a dozen, others more. But they only made the one pass. No one had dug in except for Bob Morgan-Deane who was killed next day. He made his platoon dig in and one of those clusters landed right beside them. Not one of them got a scratch. But counting a little skirmish we had next day, we lost five officers and 115 men to those damn Stukas. We all reckoned that it was some 5th columnist who fired the flare that brought them in.[2]

The Canadian Official History states that:

. . . resistance to the 2nd Corps had so far been insignificant; the enemy was chiefly intent on getting away, and such opposition as he offered was merely delaying actions by rearguards which withdrew as soon as strong pressure was applied. Indeed, the most memorable feature of these days was the tumultuous and heartfelt welcome which the liberated people gave our columns. . . . It was an experience to move the toughest soldier.

Generally speaking, the statement was correct and could equally be applied to 1st British Corps. On some routes there was scarcely any resistance, but on the approaches to the three large loops in the Seine, at Rouen, Duclair and Caudebec-en-Caux to the west of the city, it was another matter. Here the enemy was holding a bridgehead to permit the remnants of his armies with their transport, to withdraw beyond the Seine.

From Paris west to the sea the German forces were under the command of Col-General Sepp Dietrich of the 5th Panzer Army. His orders from Field-Marshal Model, Commander-in-Chief West, were 'to stand fast under any circumstances . . . in order to safeguard the crossings of the lower Seine. Elements of the 7th Army not needed and all vehicles to be ferried across the river forthwith at high pressure and without let-up.'

Covering the withdrawal across the Seine in the Rouen area was the 331st Infantry Division, commanded by Colonel Walter Steinmüller, a good division which had not been involved in the disaster at Falaise. Its task was to cover the crossings about Rouen and Duclair at the tops of the Seine bends, while behind it a great mass of armoured and other vehicles stood waiting to cross the river. To support it, armoured groups, one from the remnants of the 2nd and 9th SS Panzer Divisions, the other from the 21st and 116th Panzer Divisions lay across the necks of the great river loops.³

Approaching the enemy positions covering the vital Rouen crossings was the 2nd Canadian Division. Intelligence referred to the enemy facing them as 'nothing more than local rearguards' and Major-General Charles Foulkes, commanding the Division, was led to believe that the enemy had pulled out and little opposition was to be expected. The 4th and 6th Brigades received a rude shock when they attempted to advance toward the strong enemy positions, well concealed in the Fôret de la Londe.⁴

For three days the Canadians tried without success to batter their way through the German defences. Then, during the night of 28 August, the German armour withdrew across the Seine at Rouen and Steinmüller's infantry began to pull back. Early in the morning of the 30th the last elements of the 331st Division crossed the river, their commander claiming that 'no man and no vehicle fell into the hands of the enemy.' They were just in time, for patrols of the 3rd Canadian Division were entering Rouen from the east.

The enemy had fought skilfully and well from commanding positions which were excellently camouflaged. His mortar fire was accurate and he frequently changed the positions of his weapons. In the dense woods, it was difficult for the attackers to keep direction or to pinpoint the enemy's positions. To make matters worse, our maps were inaccurate, our artillery fire ineffective and bad weather limited air support.⁵

But there was another reason for the 2nd Division's lack of success which was more fundamental than a failure of Intelligence or the Germans' ability to fight. It was the lack of trained infantrymen to replace battle casualties.

The 2nd Division had had exceptionally heavy losses in Normandy, and while they had received a large number of reinforcements, on 26 August they were deficient 1,910 'other ranks.'

> The two French-speaking units were worst off, Les Fusiliers de Mont-Royal being 331 men short and Le Régiment de Maisonneuve 246; however, although these were the largest deficiencies, three other units were short more than 200 men each. An attempt had

already been made to improve the situation in the French battalions by 'combing' Canadian units in the United Kingdom for French-speaking personnel.[6]

The 2nd Division was not the only formation suffering in this way. Every Canadian division was affected as were the British, Poles and indeed the Americans. The Allied planners had seriously underestimated the losses of infantry and the armies in the field were having to take emergency measures of their own to fill their depleted ranks.

Already some units, such as light anti-aircraft regiments had been disbanded. Their men had been instructed to take down their artillery badges and replace them with those of infantry regiments; then with little or no further training they were sent to their new units. There they were more of a liability than an asset until, if they survived, they learned the basic skills of the infantry.

Against this background of reinforcement shortages can be judged the shock of the 2nd Division's experience in the Forêt de la Londe. In it the six battalions principally involved lost another 577 men and some were critically under strength. On 29 August the South Saskatchewan Regiment's four rifle companies totalled only 60 men. For those who hoped that, with the War entering a new phase, the demand for reinforcements would diminish, more disappointments lay ahead.

On the left of the 2nd Division, 1st British Corps closed up to the Seine on 29 August, and next day, reconnaissance elements crossed and found that the enemy had withdrawn. On the right, two days earlier, the 3rd and 4th Canadian Divisions crossed the river at Elbeuf and Pont de l'Arche. Casualties were heavy as the Germans did their utmost to block any advance on Rouen from that direction. Then, on the 29th, with the arrival of the 4th Armoured Brigade, the Canadians began to push through. In the afternoon of 30 August, Brigadier John Rockingham, commanding his 9th Brigade from the front, drove into Rouen in his scout car and exchanged fire with a party of Germans in the main square. A patrol of the Highland Light Infantry of Canada dealt with them as the streets began to fill with cheering French.

With its two Corps across the Seine, First Canadian Army

was now ready to carry out the next phase of the operations ordered by Montgomery on 26 August — to take Le Havre, to secure the port of Dieppe and to destroy all enemy forces in the coastal belt up to Bruges.

3

ESCAPE OF THE GERMAN 15TH ARMY

AFTER THE CROSSING OF THE SEINE, the diverging thrust lines of the Canadian and British armies brought a vast increase in the size of the battlefield and in the problems of supply, transport, communications and control. The tasks allotted to him by Montgomery involved Crerar in objectives spread over a distance of 200 miles and for which his resources were far from adequate. To the physical and mental strain which these imposed on him were added those of a nagging, debilitating illness. At a time when all his resources of mind and energy were demanded by the complex military situation, a relatively minor incident arising from his position as a national commander further eroded his relations with Montgomery.

On 1 September the 2nd Division returned to Dieppe where they had suffered so many casualties in their disastrous raid two years earlier. There they were to reorganize and be prepared to pass through the 3rd Division when ordered. When he learned what was proposed, Montgomery signalled to Crerar that he did not consider that this was the time for any division to stop for maintenance. Crerar replied that there was no point in them moving until a crossing had been secured over the Somme and that he considered it essential that this much depleted division, whose infantry had lost a third of their strength, should stop at Dieppe long enough to absorb one thousand reinforcements who were arriving later that day.

Crerar was not a little annoyed. On 31 August Second Army had burst across the Somme at Amiens. Montgomery told him that General Dempsey would send the 11th Armoured Division down the river to Pont Rémy and Abbeville and that he should move immediately to take over the crossings there. In a hair-raising night move, the 4th Canadian Armoured Division drove forward to Abbeville only to find the opposite bank of the river held by the enemy. There was no sign of the 11th Armoured, no possibility of crossing in strength before 3 September and consequently no immediate need to move the 2nd Division.

On the 3rd the 2nd Division held services at the cemetery above Dieppe where 800 of their dead were buried, followed by a marchpast in the town. Crerar took the salute. In the eyes of the Canadian people, Dieppe had become a symbol of gallantry and sacrifice tinged with bitterness. The shock of the casualty figures was fresh in their minds. In their eyes it would have been callous, indeed unthinkable, for the Division not to have remembered their comrades in the way they did. Only an urgent operational reason could have prevented Harry Crerar taking part.

During the afternoon of 2 September a message arrived from Montgomery asking Crerar to meet him at Tactical Headquarters, Second British Army, at 1 p.m. next day. The wording suggested that it would be a personal meeting. Since there had been no unforeseen developments on his front since he last saw the Commander-in-Chief, he replied by outlining what was planned for Dieppe next day and asked that their meeting be postponed until 5 p.m. He added that he would, of course, conform to Montgomery's wishes.

Next day in Dieppe, he received two messages. The first, from the Prime Minister of Canada read, 'I would like you to know I am sharing your joy upon the entry of Canadian troops into Dieppe today. Nothing has so stirred Canada as the rapid series of victories achieved by our forces in recent weeks. My warmest congratulations to you all.'[1]

The second message from his Chief of Staff was handed to him at 2:40 p.m. just as the parade was about to begin. That it had been delayed in transmission was obvious — Montgomery insisted that he should attend the meeting at 1 p.m. It was by now impossible to comply so he completed his part in the ceremonies then flew to Second Army where he learned that, far from a personal meeting, he had missed a formal conference between Montgomery, Bradley and their army commanders. Dempsey told him that its purpose was to discuss the future cooperation of the Second British and First U.S. Armies, and that in his view, it mattered little that Crerar had not been present. Crerar then drove to make his peace with Field-Marshal Montgomery.

Crerar recorded their interview as follows:

On reaching the caravan, the Field-Marshal addressed me abruptly, asking me why I had not turned up at the meeting in accordance with his instructions. I kept myself under control and briefly, with occasional interruptions, gave him the explanation which I have recorded in more detail above. The C-in-C intimated that he was not interested in my explanation — that the Canadian aspect of the Dieppe ceremonial was of no importance compared to getting on with the war, that he had checked through his signals and determined that my Tac HQ had received a message from him at 0615 hrs that morning, instructing me to keep the appointment and that, even if I had not received it, then in default of other arrangements, I should have made it my business to be present.

I replied to the C-in-C that I could not accept this attitude and judgement on his part. I had carried out my responsibilities as one of his two Army Comds, and as the Cdn Army Comd, in what I considered to be a reasonable and intelligent way, in the light of the situation as I knew it, or appreciated it. I had found him, in the past, reasonable in his treatment of me and I had assumed that this situation would continue to prevail. The request in my message, for postponement of the hour of our meeting, had been fully explanatory and, I thought, tactful. I had thought it would have been acceptable to him. I had, as previously explained, a definite responsibility to my Government and country which, at times, might run counter to his own wishes. There was a powerful Canadian reason why I should have been present with 2 Cdn Inf Div at Dieppe that day. In fact, there were eight hundred reasons — the Canadian dead buried at Dieppe cemetery. I went on to say that he should realize, by our considerable association, that I was neither self-opinionated, nor unreasonable, but that, also, I would never consent to be 'pushed about' by anyone, in a manner, or direction which I knew to be wrong.

The Field-Marshal reiterated that I had failed to comply with an instruction issued by him and that such situation could only result in his decision that our ways must part. I replied that I assumed he would at once take this up through higher channels and that, I, in turn, would at once report the situation to my Government.

At once, Montgomery backed down and said that the incident was now closed. Crerar said that he did not wish it to be closed and wanted it aired through proper channels. Further discussion followed. Montgomery gave Crerar a resumé of what transpired at the conference and repeated that as far as he was concerned the matter was closed. General Crerar ended his summary of the affair:

> In conclusion, I must state that I received the impression, at the commencement of the interview, that the C-in-C was out to eliminate, forcefully, from my mind that I had any other responsibilities than to him. The Canadian ceremony at Dieppe was not of his ordering, nor to his liking. It had been the cause of an interference with an instruction which he had separately issued to me — to meet him at a certain time and place. As the interview proceeded, and he found that I would not retreat from the stand I had taken — that I had a responsibility to Canada as well as to the C-in-C — he decided to 'consider the matter closed.' It was not a willing decision, nor one that I can assume will be maintained. However, though our relations have obviously been strained, I trust that the situation is temporary and I shall do what I can to ease them, though without departing from what I consider it my duty to do, or not to do, in my capacity as a Canadian.

In a report to the CIGS that day, Montgomery indicated his displeasure with Crerar by saying that, since crossing the Seine, First Canadian Army's operations had been 'badly handled and very slow.'

A few days later Crerar sent him a detailed explanation of the delays which had occurred in handling the message which had confirmed that he should attend the conference. Montgomery replied: "I am sorry that I was a bit rude the other day and somewhat outspoken. I was annoyed that no one came to an important conference. But forget about it — and let us get on with the war. It was my fault."[2]

In early September intercepted German messages, deciphered at

Bletchley Park in Buckinghamshire and distributed under the codeword ULTRA, made fascinating reading — but not many saw them. They were distributed only to the most senior commanders who were under instructions to take the greatest care in passing on the informaton which they contained. It would be disastrous if the enemy were to discover that their most sensitive signals traffic was being read by the Allies. Within 21st Army Group's two armies, only their commanders were privy to ULTRA, except for Lt-General Guy Simonds. He had been 'indoctrinated' as Crerar's replacement in order that he would be fully ready to assume command of the Army should his commander become a casualty.[3]

A similar arrangement for Second Army was not thought necessary. In the welter of situation reports by retreating German formations and orders from Hitler's headquarters, he saw two related facts which offered both an opportunity for encircling a retreating army and a compelling reason for doing so. The first was that six divisions, nearly one hundred thousand men of the 15th German Army, with their equipment, were falling back on the Scheldt where they intended to cross to Walcheren Island and then eastward, north of Antwerp. The second fact was that Hitler had ordered them to block the seaward approaches to Antwerp, to defend Walcheren, the banks of the Scheldt, the northern outskirts of the city and the Albert Canal as far as Maastricht.

The bulk of 15th Army was still south of the Scheldt. To Simonds the opportunity was obvious. Ignoring the Channel ports for the moment, his Corps should drive with all possible speed to Breskens, the port on the Scheldt opposite Walcheren, then turn to sweep along the south bank to Antwerp. The garrisons of the Channel ports would be masked until they could be dealt with later. Only a few days delay would be involved in opening them, a small price to pay for destroying six undefeated enemy divisions.

After the war he wrote that he had urged his plan on Crerar who declined either to seek Montgomery's approval or to change his own plan to capture the Channel ports. He said that he would have given anything to have had ten minutes with Monty who would have seen the possibilities which it offered.

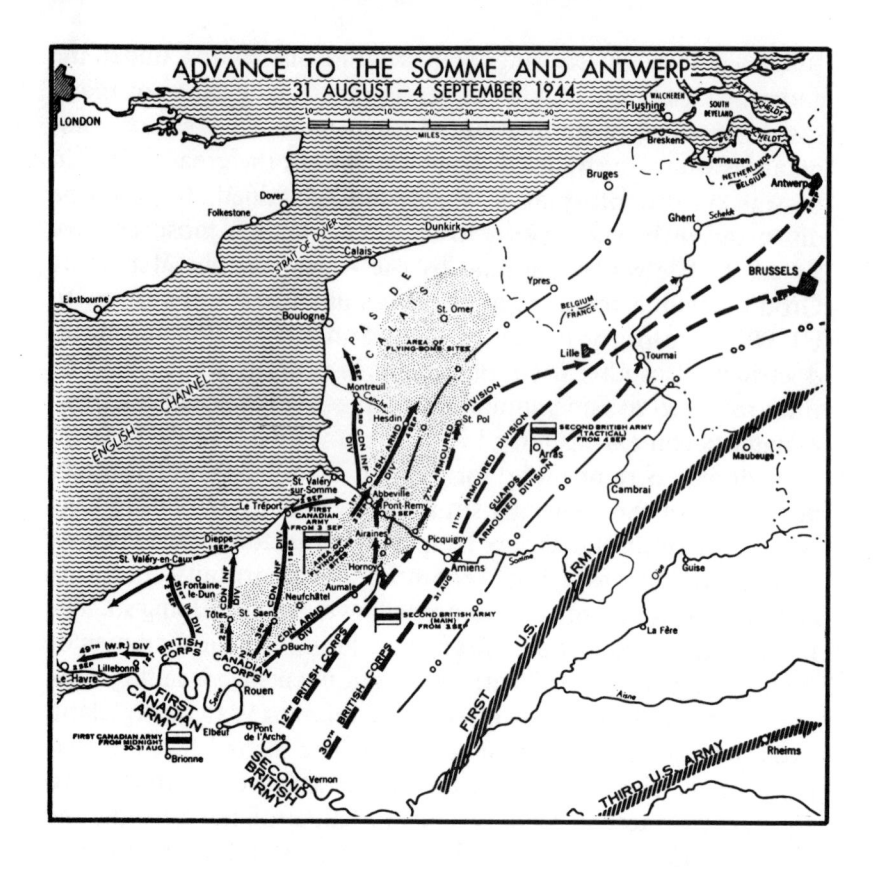

Relations were not very good between Monty and Crerar at the time, and though I protested the order to give priority to the capture of the Channel ports, Crerar refused to raise the issue with Monty.[4]

On the face of it Crerar's reaction indicated a lack of imagination, of that instinct to go for the enemy's jugular which is characteristic of a great field commander. No doubt Simonds believed that what he wrote was true but anything he said about Crerar after the war was bound to be influenced by personal bitterness.

What Simonds did not say was that Crerar knew that Montgomery at the time was little interested in Antwerp. On 6 September his Chief of Staff had warned Crerar's headquarters that the Germans probably intended to hold the Channel ports as long as possible and that the immediate opening of one of the ports north of Dieppe, preferably Boulogne, was essential to the Field-Marshal's plans. Montgomery passionately believed that every possible resource should be thrown into a thrust deep into Germany with the object of finishing the War in 1944. He calculated that with the ports of Dieppe, Boulogne, Calais and Dunkirk he could support a thrust to the Ruhr and even to Berlin without the use of Antwerp. A note on his intentions recorded by his operations staff on 9 September show his calculations which gave the task of clearing the islands blocking Antwerp 'last priority' among the tasks of First Canadian Army.[5]

Montgomery was aware of 15th Army's withdrawal through Walcheren. Not only did he receive ULTRA, but air reconnaissance reported daily what was going on. Eisenhower, too, was aware of the situation. They decided to leave destruction of the retreating Germans to the Tactical Air Force which, though able to cause damage and casualties would, they knew, be incapable of stopping the movement over the Scheldt. Inevitably many would escape, a matter which at the time seemed of little consequence with the collapse of Germany expected to follow the drive across the Rhine.

To Crerar the Commander-in-Chief's intentions were perfectly clear. First Canadian Army was to take Boulogne and the rest of the Channel ports as a matter of utmost urgency to support his drive into Germany. Simonds' proposed 'hook around the Scheldt,' attractive though it seemed, might well take longer than the few days he predicted and would, in any case, delay Montgomery's main operation. Already the Commander-in-Chief had made clear his displeasure at the Army's apparently slow progress after crossing the Seine. He would be unlikely to consent to any further delay for what in the grand scale might be considered as 'mopping-up,' particularly since he had shown that he was aware of the escape of the Germans and was deliberately leaving their destruction to the Air Force.

In refusing to put forward Simonds' plan to Montgomery, Crerar showed, not a reluctance to argue after the Dieppe episode, but that he knew Montgomery's mind and was following the spirit of his orders.

Yet though the Canadian Army could do nothing to block the

escape of the 15th Army, there was a man in position to do so if he were but told that it was taking place.

On 4 September Antwerp fell to the 11th Armoured Division. When its commander, Major-General 'Pip' Roberts, was ordered to capture it, he asked his corps commander, Sir Brian Horrocks, for a specific objective. An armoured division could not be expected to clear an entire city the size of Antwerp. Horrocks well remembered how the Germans' systematic destruction of port facilities along the North African coast had delayed the advance of the Eighth Army. Without hesitation he answered, 'The docks.' Incredibly, Roberts found them undamaged. With the assistance of the Belgian resistance, the *Armée Blanche*, his 159th Infantry Brigade cleared the area and ensured its protection. The Division's success was duly reported and they waited for further orders.

Later Horrocks, who knew nothing of ULTRA, was horrified to learn of the escape of the 15th German Army. He never discovered the reason why their move across the Scheldt, which was observed from the air, was not reported to his headquarters. He later concluded that 4 September was not only the day they captured Antwerp, it was the day they lost the Battle of Arnhem.

> If I had ordered Roberts to bypass Antwerp and advance only fifteen miles north-west, in order to cut off the Beveland isthmus, the whole of this force which played such a prominent part in the subsequent fighting, might have been destroyed or forced to surrender. . . . My eyes were fixed on the Rhine . . .[6]

Horrocks was not the only one whose eyes were so fixed. Eisenhower, Montgomery and almost every other senior commander in the Allied Expeditionary Force believed that if they could cross that river into Germany the war should be finished in 1944.

Since 23 August Montgomery had been pressing his concept of a single massive thrust into Germany on the Supreme Commander. Eisenhower did not agree, considering that the advance into Germany should take place on a broad front. On 1 September a crucial change took place in their relations. Until then Montgomery had been in charge of all operations on the ground. On that day, as planned beforehand, Eisenhower, the Supreme Commander, took direct charge of Allied land operations. On 4 September, as British tanks were entering Antwerp, he directed Montgomery to 'secure Antwerp, breach the sector of the Siegfried Line covering the Ruhr and then seize the Ruhr.'[7]

During the next few days the British and Americans advanced toward the Rhine while Montgomery and Eisenhower exchanged letters on their conflicting views on strategy. On the 10th they met in Eisenhower's plane at Brussels airport and argued the 'broad front' versus the 'single thrust' concepts, in an atmosphere of increasing acrimony. Eisenhower emphasized the importance of opening Antwerp but authorized Montgomery to defer this until after an attempt to seize a bridgehead over the Rhine.

Montgomery believed that the enemy might collapse before Antwerp could be opened. Eisenhower was doubtful of that but was prepared to defer operations to clear the port until after the airborne operation to seize the Nijmegen and Arnhem bridges. Plainly he expected much from it. Both seemed oblivious to the danger developing along their long left flank.

Among Allied generals, only Guy Simonds seems to have recognized at the time the threat posed by those six divisions of the 15th Army. And it was he who eventually had to deal with the consequences of their survival.

When it became obvious to the German High Command that at best only a delaying action could be fought on the Seine, they ordered Field-Marshal Model, the commander of Army Group 'B', to prepare a stop line along the River Somme. Their immediate problem was to save their forces south of that river from encirclement and destruction. On 28 August General Gustav von Zangen, commanding the 15th Army, ordered his two divisions holding the coast south of the river to withdraw to it and prepare it for defence. This they did, blowing all the bridges over which First Canadian Army would have to advance. But early in the morning of the 31st the 11th British Armoured Division caused consternation by overrunning the headquarters of the 5th Panzer Army south-west of Amiens, capturing there the commander of the 7th Army, then bursting across the Somme on a still-intact bridge at Amiens. The defensive line was breached leaving von Zangen's men outflanked and liable once more to being surrounded. They began to withdraw but their rearguards were still holding the north bank when the 4th Canadian Armoured Division reached the river at Abbeville in the early hours of 2 September.

In January, 1944, Hitler had designated certain French ports as 'fortresses' which were to be defended to the last. Among them were Le Havre, Boulogne and Dunkirk. On 4 September, he issued a new directive:

> Because of the breakthrough of enemy tank forces toward Antwerp, it has become very important for the further progress of the war to hold the fortresses of Boulogne and Dunkirk, the Calais defence area, Walcheren Island with Flushing harbour, the bridgehead at Antwerp, and the Albert Canal position as far as Maastricht.
>
> a. For this purpose the 15th Army is to bring the garrisons of Boulogne and Dunkirk and the Calais defence area up to strength by means of full units.
>
> The defensive strength of the fortresses is to be increased by means of additional ammunition supplies from the supplies of 15th Army, especially anti-tank ammunition, by bringing up provisions of all kinds from the country, and by evacuating the entire population.
>
> The commanders of the Calais defence area and of Walcheren Island receive the same authority as a fortress commander.

As Hitler was issuing this order, disaster overtook him at Antwerp. Meeting 'negligible opposition,' the 11th Armoured Division reached the city and by that evening the greatest port in north-west Europe was in Allied hands, its docks and their machinery practically undamaged. To compound the catastrophe, the three corps of 15th Army — 67th, 86th and 89th — were south of the estuary of the Scheldt, west of the city. A note in Field-Marshal Model's diary for that day reads: 'This advance to Antwerp has closed the ring around Fifteenth Army. A thrust to Breda must be expected.'[8]

As we have seen, no such thrust took place and 15th Army began to make its way across the Scheldt. From Terneuzen and Breskens its units were ferried to Flushing on Walcheren Island and to South Beveland. In spite of air attacks, the movement went on until 23 September when it was complete. In its final report on the operation made next day, the 89th Corps which had directed it said that 86,100 men, 616 guns, 6,200 horses and 6,200 vehicles had escaped to continue the war.

Von Zangen had followed Hitler's instructions to the letter. The coastal 'fortresses' were manned and provisioned, and strong forces lay astride the Scheldt to the west of Antwerp.

The consequences of the British failure to mount the 'thrust to Breda' will become obvious later. For the moment First Canadian Army were occupied elsewhere but, in time, they would pay a heavy price to redeem it.

4

THE CINDERELLA ARMY

NORTH OF THE SEINE, German rearguards used small villages as strong points and took a heavy toll of the armoured cars leading the Canadian advance. Withholding their fire until the leading Staghounds were confined in narrow streets, they engaged them at point-blank range with Panzerfausts, their deadly, hand-held anti-tank rockets.

Approaching the farming hamlet of Bierville, Sergeant Ross Bell ordered his driver to move slowly until they reached the church which was marked on his map but which he could not yet see. Carefully he scanned the *château* grounds on his right, then the scattered houses opposite. The only sign that enemy were nearby was the empty street ahead, so unlike Morgny which they had just passed through, where cheering French civilians had waved them on their way.

Past the *château* gates and the new village hall they crawled, alert for any sign of danger.

Around a curve to the right, beyond the duck pond, they saw the church with the road dividing in front of it. There was no one in sight. A few yards further and they would have a clear view of the road they had been ordered to reconnoitre. The driver edged the car forward.

It was then that Bell saw the wreck of Lt. Laird's Staghound and the glint of sunlight off German helmets behind a hedge, too late to reverse out of the ambush.

The gunner too had seen the enemy and the co-ax Browning was firing as Bell ordered the driver to take the left fork at top speed.

He looked back, half expecting to see an anti-tank gun taking them in its sights but there was no sign of life. He swung round to look at the road ahead as they came to a low rise.

Less than fifty yards away, on a curve in the road, was a column of Germans with three anti-tank guns.

Hastily the driver and the bow gunner closed their hatches, as did Bell and his gunner in the turret. Moments later the car crashed into the infantry. With guns blazing it ploughed through them, smashing the anti-tank guns off the road and leaving behind the screams of the crushed and wounded enemy.

At nearly fifty miles an hour, the armoured car was driving deeper into enemy territory and Bell began to search the road ahead for a turn which might lead back to his squadron. Ahead lay another village where a road to the southeast would take him in the right direction. It was as they neared the junction that he saw, coming toward them — menacing, deadly — a Tiger tank with its 88mm gun.

There was no alternative but to keep going, hold their fire and trust to luck. Apparently the driver of the German tank had not yet recognized the Canadian armoured car for the giant fifty-six ton vehicle was beginning to ease over to the right of the road to let it pass.

Bell's eyes were glued on the '88', watching for it to begin traversing toward them. A single round would reduce the Staghound to a flaming wreck. But it did not move and in a few seconds, they were past.

Ahead in the distance lay a wooded hillside where they might find cover and plan their next move.

The road now began to descend in a gentle curve through a steep-sided ravine. The car had just entered its shadows, when Bell and his crew saw coming toward them, a horse-drawn convoy of wagons and anti-tank guns. Again they charged, firing their Brownings and reducing the convoy to a rearing, screaming shambles. Men fled from the wagons and attempted to scramble up the steep, slippery banks, only to slide back into the path of the Staghound chewing its way through the mass of men and horses. Before the carnage was over, the driver's periscope was obscured by blood and debris and Bell was directing the steering of the car from the turret.

At last they broke free from the convoy and a mile further on, came to a halt on a track leading into a wood. Wearily they opened their hatches, in time to see a civilian wearing an armband and a blue beret step from the bush.

It was the young Canadians' first contact with the French Forces of the Interior, the 'FFI', and it could not have been better timed for their ammunition was virtually spent.

Next day, 31st August, they rejoined their regiment, the 12th Manitoba Dragoons, probing ahead of the Army on its way to the north.

Bell and his crew had accounted for nearly three hundred enemy dead or wounded, 70 to 80 horses and several anti-tank guns. In doing so they had proved once more that in war, what is seen as luck, goes most often to him who is skilled and bold enough to seize the fleeting chance.[1]

The days which followed saw the swiftest advances of the campaign as the armoured divisions of Second British Army thrust forward to capture Brussels and Antwerp. Moving with such speed that the Germans were given no time to organize resistance, they swept aside opposition, seized bridges before they could be blown and caught the imagination of the correspondents of Western newspapers who began to tell their readers that the war was all but over.

On their left the First Canadian Army watched their exploits with admiration and not a little envy for it was evident that they were to have no immediate share in any dramatic armoured thrust. Already they had taken Dieppe without a shot being fired and were investing Le Havre. 2nd Corps had crossed the Somme, its divisions heading for Boulogne, Calais and Ypres, carrying out their mandate to clear the Channel coast and a 30-mile belt which lay inland from it.

On 3 September Montgomery, now promoted to the rank of field-marshal, issued a directive to his armies on future operations. His intentions were now 1) To advance eastward and destroy all enemy forces encountered; and 2) To occupy the Ruhr and get astride the communications leading from it into Germany and to the seaports.

On 6 September Second Army was to advance eastwards from the line Brussels-Antwerp toward the Rhine between Wesel and Arnhem. The Ruhr was to be 'by-passed around its northern face, and cut off by a southward thrust through Hamm.' The First U.S. Army, advancing with its two left corps toward Liège, Aachen, Cologne and Bonn, would 'assist in cut-

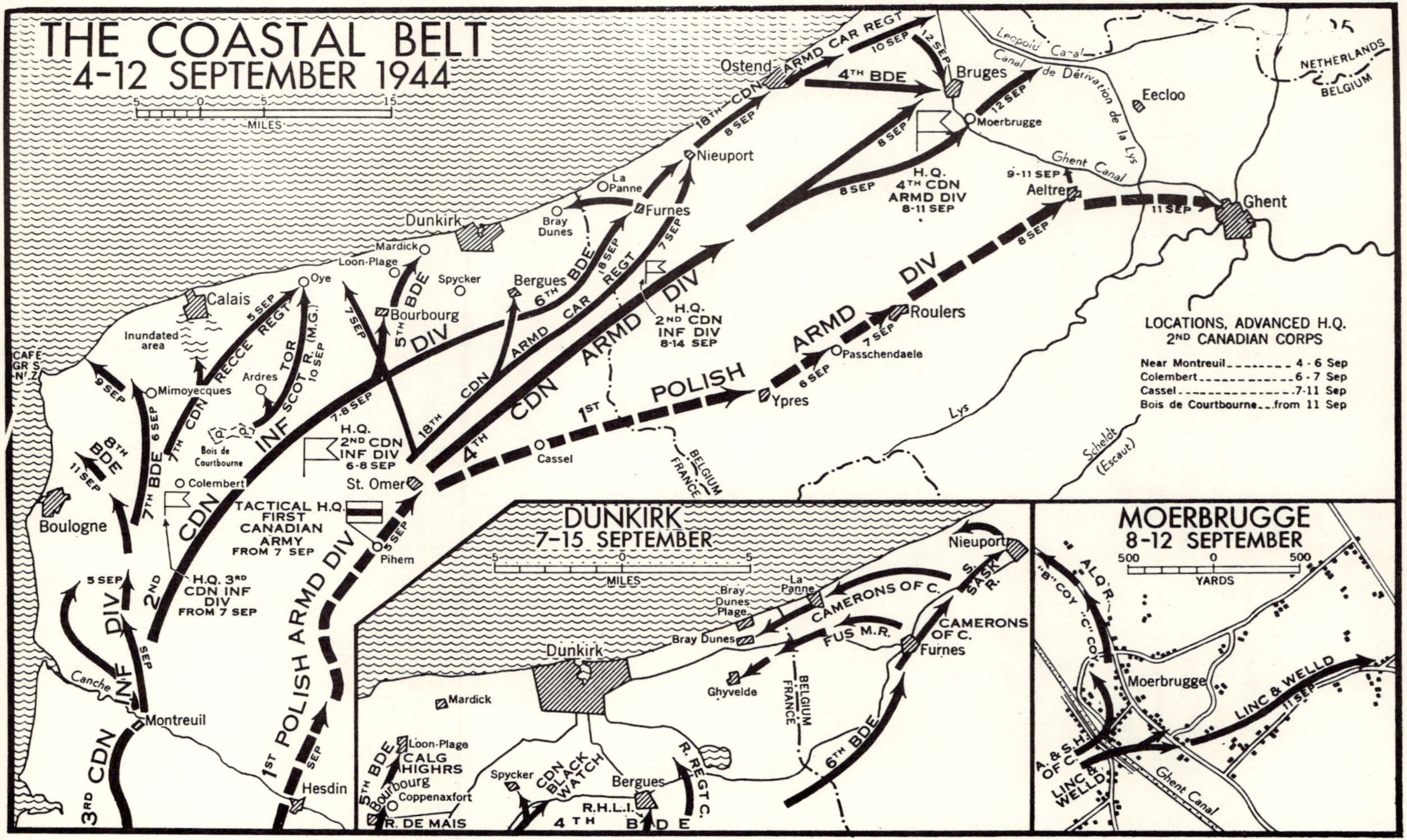

THE COASTAL BELT
4-12 SEPTEMBER 1944
MILES
Ostend
Bruges
Moerbrugge
Eecloo
Ghent
Aeltre
Nieuport
La Panne
Furnes
Bray Dunes
Dunkirk
Mardick
Loon-Plage
Spycker
Bergues
Bourbourg
Oye
Calais
Inundated area
Ardres
Mimoyecques
Bois de Courtbourne
Colembert
St. Omer
Cassel
Ypres
Passchendaele
Roulers
Boulogne
Montreuil
Hesdin
Pihem
Canche
Lys
Scheldt (Escaut)
Leopold Canal
Canal de Dérivation de la Lys
Ghent Canal
NETHERLANDS
BELGIUM
FRANCE
LOCATIONS, ADVANCED H.Q. 2ND CANADIAN CORPS
Near Montreuil 4-6 Sep
Colembert 6-7 Sep
Cassel 7-11 Sep
Bois de Courtbourne from 11 Sep
H.Q. 4TH CDN ARMD DIV 8-11 SEP
H.Q. 2ND CDN INF DIV 8-14 SEP
H.Q. 2ND CDN INF DIV 6-8 SEP
TACTICAL H.Q. FIRST CANADIAN ARMY FROM 7 SEP
H.Q. 3RD CDN INF DIV FROM 7 SEP
4TH CDN ARMD DIV
1ST POLISH ARMD DIV
2ND CDN INF DIV
3RD CDN INF DIV
18TH CDN ARMD CAR REGT
4TH BDE
5TH BDE
6TH BDE
7TH BDE
8TH BDE
CDN ARMD CAR REGT
7TH CDN RECCE REGT
TOR SCOT R. (M.G.)
DUNKIRK
7-15 SEPTEMBER
CAMERONS OF C.
S. SASK. R.
FUS M.R.
Bray Dunes Plage
Ghyvelde
Coppenaxfort
CALG HIGHRS
R. DE MAIS
CDN BLACK WATCH
R.H.L.I.
R. REGT C.
MOERBRUGGE
8-12 SEPTEMBER
YARDS
ALQ R.
"B" COY
"C" COY
A. & S.H. OF C.
LINC & WELLD

ting off the Ruhr by operations against its south-eastern face, if such action is desired by Second Army.'

The Belgian and Dutch contingents were to be transferred from Crerar's command to Second Army which already was in Belgium and was about to enter the Netherlands. As for First Canadian Army, its role was summarized in a single sentence:

> Canadian Army will clear the coastal belt, and will then remain in the general area Bruges-Calais until the maintenance situation allows of its employment further forward.[2]

'Mopping up!' snorted one brigadier. 'So much for McNaughton's "dagger pointed at the heart of Berlin!"'[3]

The 'coastal belt' coincided with the defensive zone which had been manned by the German 15th Army. Many of its units had not been engaged and were well equipped and up to strength. Immediately inland were the V1 launching sites, a security area which the Germans had swept clean of the Resistance. To advance through it meant crossing every river of western France at its widest, and because, unlike Second Army's zone, there were no Maquis to prevent it, every bridge had been destroyed.

On 4 September, the day Antwerp fell, no one in First Canadian Army knew whether the Channel ports would be defended or not. Le Havre was, Dieppe was not. Air reconnaissance reported the Boulogne, Calais and Dunkirk areas 'deserted.'

That evening, General Simonds gave orders to the divisional commanders of 2nd Corps. The primary object of the pursuit to the Scheldt was to destroy or capture all enemy south of that river; the 2nd Canadian Division was to clear the coast from Dunkirk to the Dutch border; the 3rd was to ensure that the 2nd's route was clear and thereafter to reorganize around Calais; his two armoured divisions, 1st Polish and 4th Canadian, were directed toward Ghent and Bruges.

Within 24 hours the 3rd Division's brief prospect of an easy time ahead evaporated when they came up against the landward defences of Boulogne. These were held in strength and the garrison made it plain they intended to fight. Shortly after midnight Major-General Dan Spry, its youthful GOC, gave preliminary orders for the capture of the city and the destruction of its garrison. One of his three brigades, the 7th, was pushed on to seize the high ground south-west of Calais to protect his flank.

The defences of Boulogne were far too strong to be taken without a heavily supported deliberate attack. Heavy bombers, armoured personnel carriers and medium artillery would be needed by Spry's two infantry brigades to overcome the massive defences which were held by nearly 10,000 Germans. But practically all the heavy supporting arms were committed to the 1st British Corps' attack on Le Havre, 135 miles away. There was no hope of capturing Boulogne until Le Havre had fallen. Since Calais too was defended, the 3rd Division would be fully occupied for some time. The 2nd's orders were amended to make it responsible for clearing the entire coast, including Dunkirk, from just east of Calais to the Dutch frontier.

On 8 September the 4th and Polish Armoured Divisions came up against strong opposition on the Ghent Canal which connects Ghent and Bruges. The bridges had been destroyed and it was probable that the enemy would make full use of the meandering waterway to delay the advance to the Scheldt.

In the meantime the 2nd Division, advancing from Dieppe, ran into determined opposition from strongly held outpost positions screening Dunkirk. The garrison of the fortress was estimated to be some 10,000 strong.

With every one of his six divisions engaged with the enemy, on a 200-mile front from Le Havre to Ghent, short of transport and supplies, his infantry battalions suffering from lack of trained replacements for their battle casualties, Crerar's Army was the Cinderella of the Allies. Denied a front seat at the ball, it had been relegated to cleaning up the coastal ports and their hinterland so that its sister armies might be supplied for their advance into Germany. It was not long before their impatience began to show. What was taking Cinderella so long?

5

DUNKIRK AND OSTEND

AFTER REFITTING AT DIEPPE, Maj-General Charles Foulkes' 2nd Canadian Infantry Division moved foward on 6 September to its next task, the clearing of the entire coast from just east of Calais to the Dutch border beyond Ostend. Its 5th Brigade was to take Dunkirk. Approaching from the southwest, they soon ran into determined opposition at Bourbourg. As an attack was being mounted, the Brigade's orders were modified. It was now to 'contain' the garrison of Dunkirk which was believed to be some 10,000-strong, manning well-prepared defences. These were covered by an extensive outpost line from Mardick, west of the port, through Loon Plage, Spycker and Bergues to Bray Dunes on the east.

Much of the area had been flooded by the Germans, severely restricting the attackers' ability to manoeuvre off the roads, most of which were raised above the level of the surrounding fields. Many roads and their verges were mined and registered by the enemy's artillery and mortars — a foretaste of what was to come along the shores of the Scheldt.

The Brigade's first experience of fighting under these conditions was not encouraging. Le Régiment de Maisonneuve's attack on Bourbourg came to a halt in the face of an enemy who showed no inclination to give ground. The Brigade Commander, Brigadier W.J. Megill, believing the town to have been taken, ordered the Calgary Highlanders to pass through and take Loon Plage some six kilometres to the north. Blocked by the Maisonneuve, their column stopped on a dyke road where they were promptly heavily shelled by long-range guns. Darkness brought orders for the Highlanders to clear their own way through the northern part of Bourbourg. By 3:30 a.m. they had done so at a cost of two officers and 30 men killed or wounded.[1]

Early next morning a reconnaissance party of three men led by Captain Mark Tennant set off in a jeep for Loon Plage. In less than an hour they returned with 18 prisoners, nine of whom they captured in an outpost position, others when they forced a German troop carrier off the road, the remainder being the crew of a tank which they knocked out with a PIAT. Tennant reported that Loon Plage was defended by the enemy.[2]

The advance on the village was a slow and costly business. Well-sited enemy machine guns, mortars and artillery took a painful toll of casualties. As the leading companies drew closer, the battalion's six-pounder anti-tank guns succeeded in blowing a German observation post out of the tower of Loon Plage church. In an attempt to break the deadlock imposed by crossfire from camouflaged pillboxes, Lt-Colonel Donald MacLauchlan sent a company to outflank the village from the west. At a considerable cost in casualties, they succeeded in reaching some farm buildings 400 metres from the town centre.

From behind a railway line to the east, German infantry swept the battalion area with machine-gun and sniper fire. An attempt by Le Régiment de Maisonneuve to clear the area failed.

When darkness fell it was plain that no further progress could be made, and the depleted rifle companies were withdrawn a few hundred metres south of Loon Plage. By now they had been without food for 42 hours and had had little if any sleep. Resumption of the attack would have to wait until morning.

That night the Germans evacuated Loon Plage.

An interested witness of the battalion's operations was Earl Wrightman of the 14th Canadian Hussars, (the divisional reconnaissance regiment) who had been ordered to contact the Calgaries and probe forward as far as possible. He came upon a young officer with about 30 men, all that was left of a company, except for a sniper further head.

> We found a small and very brave sniper vigorously firing from two corners of a house (he kept dashing between the two). Corporal

J.A.M. Smith, in the lead car, shouted to him, 'What have you got up there, mate?'

The sniper replied, 'There are about three hundred Germans just over the railroad tracks, but I got one of them.'

'Good,' Corporal Smith told him. 'Then I guess there is nothing to worry about.'[3]

What was written as an example of humour in adversity points a chilling finger at the fighting strength of this most durable of battalions. Three of its four rifle companies, which normally were about 125 strong, had been reduced to less than 30 men each. As one would expect, its headquarters and support companies had not suffered so severely, but the whole battalion could muster fewer than 400 out of an authorized establishment of more than twice that number.[4]

The day after the capture of Loon Plage was a Sunday. A few miles behind the Canadian outposts there was no visible sign of war. Cattle grazed under white puffy clouds in the sunlit fields of a Flemish landscape — windmills turned lazily in the warm and gentle breeze. Along a poplar-lined canal white houses with red-tiled roofs splashed colour on the lush green of late summer.

In villages near the French and Belgian border, families walked to church, men in their best dark suits, older women in severe black, girls in beribboned flat straw hats and flowered dresses. At Roesbrugge, halfway between Ypres and Dunkirk, there was a fair. In the square by the church a merry-go-round moved in time to the music of a steam calliope, a laughing child on the back of every painted horse. No one made the slightest sign of hearing the guns of the field battery a kilometre away near Oost-Cappel which was firing on the enemy outpost at Bergues, or the more menacing sound of German heavy shells from Dunkirk seeking to silence them.

During the next few days the Calgary Highlanders' fighting patrols probed toward Dunkirk and swept the area between their widely separated companies. Far from docile, the Germans reacted aggressively with raids and counterattacks. Early on 14 September an observation post manned by a section of C Company near Mardick watched in fascination as a 20-man German patrol, lit by the moon, approached their position. Holding their fire until the enemy were too close to miss, they opened up with their Bren and a shower of grenades.

From the bottom of a slit trench a signaller was reporting the approach of the enemy by telephone to Battalion Headquarters. Suddenly Major Ross Ellis was startled to hear the signaller scream, followed by silence. Moments later, a sheepish voice said, 'Sorry, sir. A dead Kraut just fell on top of me.'

Next morning two men from A Company, Privates MacDonald and Field, were sent to capture a lone Pole whose presence had been reported by the Maquis. About 90 minutes later they returned, breathless and bathed in perspiration, with 22 German prisoners, including a warrant officer. They reported that they had been unable to bring back the paybooks of two Germans they had shot because they had come under heavy mortar fire. Asked to tell how they managed to make such a 'bag,' MacDonald explained, 'While I gave covering fire, Field outflanked them.'

For two more days the Highlanders continued to harry the enemy and edge forward toward Dunkirk. Little more could be expected of them. Not only were they sorely depleted in strength, their supporting arms could do little to help. Artillery ammunition was rationed to three rounds per gun per day, heavy mortar bombs to five. On the 15th they learned that they were to be relieved by a commando of the British 4th Special Service Brigade and would be moving to the vicinity of Antwerp. As a farewell to an uncongenial area, on the 17th the Calgaries captured Mardick.[5]

To the east the 6th Brigade cleared the coastal towns of Furnes, Nieuport and La Panne in the vicinity of the Belgian border, then turned toward Dunkirk. Under-strength and limited by restrictions on artillery ammunition, its battalions were unable to make any more impression on its defences than had those of the 5th Brigade. Their probes confirmed that Dunkirk could only be taken by a heavily supported major attack.

In the meantime the 4th Brigade took over Ostend from the 12th Manitoba Dragoons, cleared the coast from there to Nieuport, moved to Bruges, which the Germans abandoned without a fight, then returned south to the Dunkirk perimeter. Following an unsuccessful attack by the Royal Hamilton Light

Infantry upon the enemy outpost position at Bergues on the 15th, the Germans withdrew from the village next day.

As the 2nd Division was being relieved by commandos a considerable number of reinforcements arrived for its battalions, though not enough to bring them up to strength. They would soon need many more.

September 8 had found both the 4th Canadian and the Polish Armoured Divisions, which had been directed north-east toward the Scheldt, halted before the Ghent Canal by strong opposition. That night the Argyll and Sutherland Highlanders of Canada attacked across the canal at Moerbrugge, on the south-eastern outskirts of Bruges. No assault boats being available, they used two large punts which they found in the vicinity. Immediately they began to cross, mortar and 88mm fire came down, causing heavy casualties. By midnight it was touch and go in their narrow bridgehead and the Germans were counter-attacking. The Argylls managed to hold them off long enough for the Lincoln and Welland Regiment to join them. Together they defeated the enemy's strenuous efforts to drive them back into the canal.

All next day engineers struggled to bridge the waterway but, 'For the first time since we left the Falaise area the enemy was able to put down a truly effective concentration of fire with the result that the engineers could not get the bridge across in daylight.'[6] That night they succeeded in doing so and by morning a tank squadron of the South Alberta Regiment had crossed to support the hard-pressed battalions.

Closer to Ghent two attempts by the Poles to cross the canal failed. Their operations in the area were abandoned on the 11th when they received orders to relieve the British 7th Armoured Division near Ghent.

On 8 September Lt-Colonel James Roberts of the 12th Manitoba Dragoons near St Omer received orders from General Simonds to head for Ostend and, if possible, take the city. Roaring across the Belgian border, his leading squadrons passed through Poperinghe and swung north, avoiding Dunkirk, on the roads to Furnes and Dixmude. Approaching a canal south of Ostend, two armoured car troops (each of two Staghound armoured cars and a Lynx scout car) commanded by Lieutenants

Charlie Phelps and Ken Jefferson found the road ahead mined with heavy naval shells, their noses upright. The ground on either side of the road was too sodden to bear the weight of their vehicles. Fortunately one Staghound in each troop carried a set of steel trackways and these were brought into play. Using planks and beams which they found nearby to support them, the trackways were laid above the noses of the shells. Then each officer drove one of the small Lynx scout cars across the obstacle.

Beyond, they found bridges over the canal which the Germans had prepared for demolition and removed the charges. But it would take time to clear the minefield beyond and another squadron, guided by the Belgian Resistance, found a safe route into Ostend. Apart from German engineers working on demolitions, the port had been abandoned by the enemy. The rapturous population swarmed over the armoured cars, making it difficult to move without injuring the cheering, singing Belgians.

> As evening fell, it started to rain heavily which did nothing to dampen the enthusiasm and excitement of the citizens. I ordered C Squadron to dismount machine guns and to set up guard posts ... the poor troopers sat all night behind their guns facing a possible enemy counterattack, while countless civilians sat with them, fed and kissed them, asked for cigarettes, and generally distracted the attention of the guard posts. Fortunately no one counterattacked and the wet and dreary night passed. Most of the regiment were given food and beds in hotels and homes and were so well treated that they wished never to leave again.

Roberts set up his headquarters in a large hotel. During the night he received orders to move north and re-establish contact with the enemy. Next morning, as he prepared to leave, the hotel proprietor presented him with a bill for the night's lodging for himself and his headquarters. He signed the account and left. 'Somehow, I have the queer feeling that, sometime later when things settled down, this ingrate may have collected his account.'[7]

6

LE HAVRE — OPERATION ASTONIA

BEFORE THE FIRST CANADIAN ARMY had reached the Seine Montgomery had ordered Crerar to use one corps to clear the Havre peninsula and take the port. No more forces than were necessary were to be used for that task as 'the main business lies to the north, and in the Pas de Calais.' There seemed little doubt that two divisions would be needed. The situation at each of the other Channel ports was so uncertain that no such comfortable allocation of troops could be made.

On 25 August Crerar ordered 1st British Corps to prepare for the task. Since March he and his staff had studied the problems of capturing the port and had concluded that, if the Germans decided to defend it, they would be faced with a major operation. There were formidable defences to be neutralized or destroyed by naval and air bombardment and a large artillery programme and special armour would be needed to support an infantry assault. When, on 2 September, 49th Division advanced on the port and were met by heavy fire, it was obvious that at least a week would be needed to take the city.

Sir John Crocker, the Corps Commander, soon confirmed that he would indeed need considerable support. Crerar provided him with four medium and two heavy regiments of artillery, two armoured brigades including conventional gun tanks, Flails, Crocodiles and Kangaroos, as well as air and naval support. He authorized him to deal directly with Bomber Command and the Navy.

While he and Crocker had had a blazing argument in Normandy a few weeks earlier and he had tried to have him removed from his command, tempers had cooled and Crerar was happy enough to leave the operation in such experienced hands.

In the meantime, whilst the 49th Divisions was moving directly toward Le Havre, the 51st (Highland) Division advanced to St Valéry-en-Caux where its remnants had surrendered to Rommel in 1940. They found it undefended and on 4 September circled back to join the 49th on the outskirts of the city.

The great ocean port, surrounded by water on three sides, was heavily defended by coast artillery batteries, most of which could only fire to seaward. Though the land defences were incomplete, Colonel Eberhard Wildermuth, the fortress commander, had a garrison of more than 11,000 troops supported by 76 field and medium and anti-aircraft guns.

The systematic softening of the enemy's defences began on 5 September with a heavy bomber attack and a bombardment from H.M. Monitor *Erebus*. Her 15-inch shells were landing on the German defences when she herself was hit by a 14.8-inch gun of the Grand Clos battery. Her port after-hold flooded and she withdrew to Portsmouth for repairs.[1] She returned to the attack on the 8th but again was hit and retired. On separate days, Bomber Command struck at three areas of the port's defences dropping some 4,000 tons of bombs. Then on the 10th the naval and air bombardments intensified. Sixty aircraft attacked the Grand Clos battery and later, in two major attacks by nearly 1,000 bombers, the RAF dropped a further 4,900 tons of explosives. Following it, *Erebus* and the battleship *Warspite* engaged casemated guns on the perimeter defences of Le Havre. The Grand Clos battery replied but finally was silenced by *Warspite*'s guns.

All day on the 10th 1st Corps' gunners had been working on the destruction of German artillery and mortars. Then, at 5.45 that afternoon, the infantry and armour attacked.

Crocker's plan was to use both his divisions to take the fortified areas on the northern and eastern outskirts of the city, then, while the 51st Division cleared the coastal fortifications north of the port, the 49th would take the harbour itself.

On the left the 56th Brigade (2 South Wales Borderers, 2 Gloucesters, 2 Essex), preceded by Flails of the 22nd Dragoons

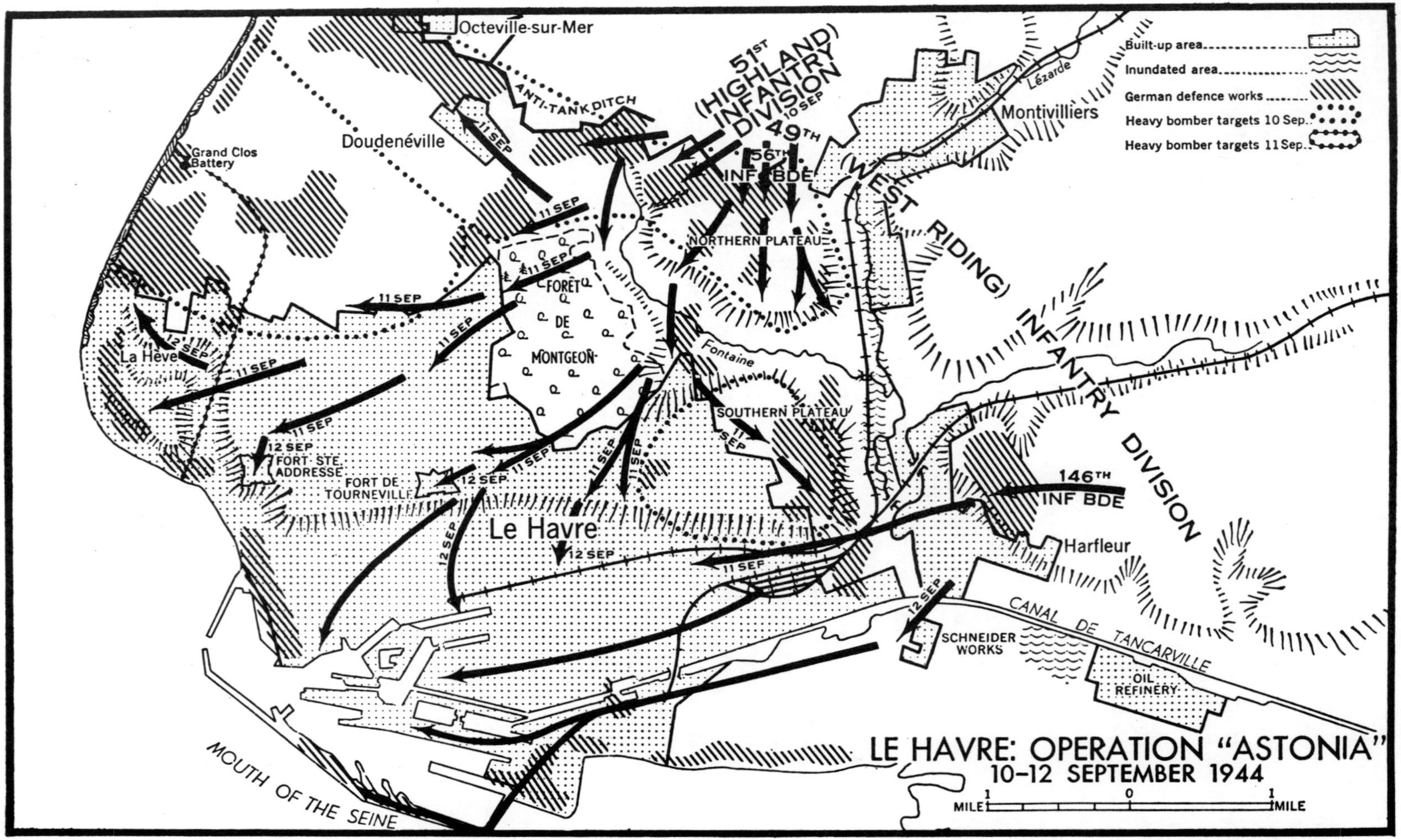

LE HAVRE: OPERATION "ASTONIA"
10–12 SEPTEMBER 1944

which opened a path through a minefield west of Montivilliers, seized the Northern Plateau and crossings over the Fontaine River.

At midnight the 51st Division, on the right, aided by 'artificial moonlight' (searchlight beams reflected off low clouds), began clearing the northern edge of the Fôret de Montgeon. Despite an anti-tank ditch, which caused delays, and several strong points, the Highlanders were through it by morning and began to eliminate the gun areas to the west of the Forêt.

On the 11th, 49 Division took the Southern Plateau on the eastern outskirts of the city while its 146th Brigade (4 Lincolns; 1/4 KOYLI; Hallamshire Bn, Yorks and Lancs) cleared a heavily defended zone at Harfleur which covered the main road into the city. They suffered heavy casualties from mines before tanks and Flails were brought to their assistance. By nightfall the Division reached Fort de Tourneville. Meanwhile the 51st had driven in from the north and had taken the high ground at La Hève overlooking the Channel.

Next morning it was obvious to Colonel Wildermuth, lying wounded in a dugout at his battle headquarters, that the end was near. Fort de Tourneville had fallen to the 49th Division, there was no lessening of the devastating artillery fire, British infantry and armour were closing in and his last anti-tank gun had been lost. When, shortly before noon, a squadron of the 7th Royal Tanks approached, their menace was convincing. Wildermuth surrendered, properly dressed in medals and pyjamas.

The battle continued until late in the day. The 51st Division took Fort Ste Addresse, Octeville and La Hève, the 49th cleared the docks and the Schneider works. The last of the enemy to surrender was a small group on one of the quays.

The battle had taken 48 hours and had cost fewer than 500 casualties; conversely, 11,302 German prisoners were now out of the war. Because they were so well protected, unlike the unfortunate civilian population of Le Havre, the number of Germans killed and wounded was not high.

While more determination on the part of the garrison would have made 1st Corps' task more difficult, they had so systematically destroyed the facilities of the port that it could not be used until 9 October. SHAEF had allotted it to the support of the

American armies. It would have offered no immediate help to Montgomery's 21st Army Group for it was little, if any, closer to their front in eastern Belgium than the Rear Maintenance Area at the Normandy beaches.[2]

7

BOULOGNE — OPERATION WELLHIT

UNLIKE THE PREPARATIONS for capturing Le Havre, which were begun before the Army crossed the Seine, Crerar could make no plans beforehand for capturing the lesser Channel ports. There were too many unknown factors — which would be defended? Which needed? What would his resources and other commitments be? In the event Boulogne, Calais and Dunkirk were each held by garrisons of about the same size as Le Havre. With his two armoured divisions clearing the coastal belt toward Bruges and Ghent and with 1st Corps committed to Le Havre, he had available only the 2nd and 3rd Canadian Divisions. He could expect no help from Montgomery.

Second Army in Belgium and Holland were already overstretched in preparing for the Arnhem operation and for the subsequent hoped-for crossing of the Rhine. Some units were grounded for lack of transport. Practically all of First Canadian Army's heavy and medium artillery and specialized armoured units were committed to the attack on Le Havre.

On 6 September Montgomery gave top priority after Le Havre to the capture of Boulogne. With so few resources Crerar had no option but to allot Boulogne and Calais to the 3rd Division while the 2nd dealt with Dunkirk and the rest of the coast from Calais to the Dutch border.

The 3rd Division's attack could not begin until after the capture of Le Havre and the heavy supporting arms had been moved 160 kilometres north to Boulogne.

As one of Hitler's original list of fortresses, the landward defences of the port had been heavily fortified. On a series of hills running south-east from Fort de la Crèche through St Martin to Mont Lambert, thence south to Herquelingue and from there south-west to St Etienne and Nocquet were the main German defences. Minefields and wire protected well-prepared entrenchments and concrete pillboxes from which machine guns could lay down interlocking belts of fire. At least twenty-two 88mm guns provided the framework of the anti-tank and anti-aircraft defence. Few of the heavy coast defence guns could fire to landward but the garrison was supported by about nine 15cm howitzers. Behind the main defences were strong points on smaller hills, while, well to the north, were further outlying defences around La Trésorerie.

Apart from artillery and engineers from the 64th Division, the 10,000 men of the garrison were mainly low-category fortress troops. It was as well that they were not such experienced veterans as their commander, Lt-General Ferdinand Heim, who had been Guderian's Chief of Staff in Poland and, later, had commanded a corps on the Russian Front. Unfortunately for him, the Russians had chosen his two Roumanian divisions as their target for a major tank thrust. Its success resulted in von Paulus' Sixth Army being surrounded at Stalingrad and in Heim being the scapegoat, imprisoned, then pensioned.

In August 1944, Heim's peaceful life at Ulm ended with orders to take command of the fortress at Boulogne. As a professional officer, he would do his best to defend the fortress but, after his treatment by Hitler, no longer did he feel that this necessarily meant 'unto death.'[1]

Faced with the problem of capturing Boulogne whilst, at the same time, containing the batteries at Cap Gris Nez and the garrison at Calais, General Spry could only allot two of his three understrength brigades to the task. The key to the enemy's defences was Mont Lambert which would have to be taken at the outset. He decided to attack from the east with the 8th and 9th Brigades north and south respectively of the main road from Boulogne to St Omer (N42).

Both brigades would advance to the River Liane, which runs through the city from the south, whereupon the 8th would turn north to Wimereux, some two miles up the coast. The 9th would cross the river and secure that portion of the town lying to the west, including Outreau and Le Portel.

Immediately before the attack, Mont Lambert and the other main enemy-defended areas on the east side of the port would be struck by RAF heavy bombers, while artillery neutralized his guns and positions on the flanks.

To deceive the enemy as to the strength and direction of his attack, Spry formed a 'dummy brigade' from his machine-gun battalion, the headquarters of his anti-tank and anti-aircraft regiments, and an engineers' unit and instructed them to threaten the enemy from the south.[2]

Brigadier John Rockingham of 9th Brigade was dubious about heavy bomber support. It was he who had torn the covers from shell-dressings and had bound Major-General Rod Keller's wounds, suffered when the 3rd Division had been supported by them on the Caen-Falaise road. He had seen the craters of their bombs make ground impassable for armour. But the fortifications on Mont Lambert were so deep and well-constructed that nothing else could penetrate them. With their support there was a chance that Mont Lambert could be taken quickly.

He told General Simonds that if the RAF could not guarantee that they would not bomb his men, he would rather do without their support.

'There's one other thing,' said Rockingham. 'We have to stay 2,000 yards from the objective until the last bomb has fallen. Even moving in Kangaroos it will take ten minutes at best to cover the ground, plenty of time for the enemy to come out and start firing. We could get closer with just artillery support.'

Simonds, who had only obtained approval for bomber support by appealing directly to Air Chief Marshal Sir Arthur Harris, said nothing for a moment as he fixed the brigadier with his cold blue eyes. It was well known that a man had to be very sure of his ground before disagreeing with Simonds, particularly if, in doing so, he implied that an operation might be too risky.

Rockingham was not noted for caution. Large, strong and self-confident, he was the picture of a fighting commander and his face wore the scars of war. In Normandy, while commanding the Royal Hamilton Light Infantry, his headquarters had been practically wiped out. A sniper's bullet killed his signaller, then a second creased the bridge of his nose. Rockingham, who had seen a whiff of smoke from a barn, seized a Sten gun, dived for cover then stalked the sniper and shot him, not the conventional way for a battalion commander to behave. When asked why he had not sent someone to deal with the problem, he replied that there wasn't anyone else and, besides, he knew where the bastard was.

Simonds thought for a moment. 'The enemy goes to ground when the bombers come over, comes up when they go away. After they have dropped their last bombs, we'll have them circle around and do another run over Mont Lambert with their bomb bay doors open while you move forward.

'And if you're nervous about being bombed, I'll give you an RAF group captain to stay with you during the operation. He'll make sure no bombs fall short.'

Later Rockingham recalled,

> Believe me, that fellow stayed with me! I held his hand all the time. Wherever I went, I dragged this poor guy along. When the bombers started to come over he was right beside me and I knew that if they dropped any of those big bombs around us, he'd know what to do.
>
> They had a master bomber controlling the others in the air. First they put down a few marker bombs which were bang on the target and I told the Group Captain to go ahead. He radioed the master bomber. The system which Guy [Simonds] set up certainly worked, as did the trick of the dummy run. The Krauts stayed under cover and we had very few casualties until our troops de-bussed from the Kangaroos.

The shortage of infantry for the attack on Boulogne resulted in plans of some audacity. Rockingham well knew that his primary objective, the crest of Mont Lambert, was a formidable objective for one of his understrength battalions, no matter how heavily it might be supported. Yet it was vital to get into the city to the banks of the Liane River as quickly as possible — another battalion would be required for that. A third would be needed for operations beyond the river.[3]

Early in the morning of 17 September, nearly a hundred spectators — naval, military, air force and press — on the hilltop viewing stand south of Mont Lambert, raised their binoculars as the first Lancasters appeared.[4] Simultaneously air-burst shells fired by the artillery began exploding low over the enemy flak batteries. Ahead a lone Auster slowly circled — the Army Commander himself was watching the attack.

Suddenly fountains of earth and smoke erupted from the broad slopes of Mont Lambert as the first of 692 aircraft dropped their bombs. As they roared overhead, white smoke from a Pathfinder's marker plumed from the peak which minutes later disappeared in a volcano of explosives.

At 9:55 the last bomb fell. Moments later, as another wave of bombers appeared overhead, tanks of the Fort Garry Horse followed by the North Nova Scotia Highlanders in Kangaroos and the AVREs of 87th Assault Squadron, Royal Engineers, advanced on Mont Lambert.

Halfway up the slope, mines and bomb craters brought them to a halt and from then on the infantry had to fight their way forward on foot through a labyrinth of trenches, pillboxes and casemated gun positions, interlaced with wire, mines and booby traps. Most opposition came from machine guns in concrete emplacements which were covered by anti-tank fire. Flail tanks could not be brought into action to clear paths through the mines because of cratering. Before armoured flame throwers of any sort could be used against the machine-gun positions, the infantry had to deal with the enemy's anti-tank guns using 'Lifebuoys,' a man-pack flame gun, to support their assaults. In reaching the crest of the hill, the North Novas overcame 20 separate little fortresses.

Toward evening Crocodiles — flame-throwing tanks — were able to get forward. They proved to be the most effective weapon against pillboxes — their appearance usually being enough to completely demoralize the enemy, who would give up before they could be fired. There were no recorded instances of enemy soldiers being burned. By nightfall most of Mont Lambert had been cleared.[5]

Meanwhile, on the right, the Stormont, Dundas and Glengarry Highlanders, riding in armoured vehicles, had driven forward behind a terrific artillery concentration until forced to debus by mines. Within 45 minutes they had captured their objectives on the northern slopes of Mont Lambert between St Martin and La Cauchèrie and were looking down across Boulogne. Unfortunately they could also be seen by the enemy beyond the Liane, from the peak of Mont Lambert and the high ground north of the road in the 8th Brigade's sector. Artillery and mortar fire now poured into the battalion's position. From whatever cover they could find, the Glengarrians watched with admiration as sappers of the 18th Field Company, Royal Canadian Engineers, cleared a route through the minefields by hand for armoured vehicles to come forward for the next phase of the attack.

With fighting still continuing on Mont Lambert, this was now to begin. Two columns of specialized armour — bulldozers, flame thrower tanks, engineer assault vehicles and Flails, each supported by a platoon of infantry in Kangaroos — would drive with all possible speed to seize two bridges over the Liane which were reported to be undamaged. Because of difficulty in clearing routes, only one column could move initially. By 8 p.m. it had battered its way through the débris-filled streets to the river while the other had come to a halt within the town.

So heavy was the enemy artillery fire that it was dusk before the SDG could move toward the river.

Realizing how vulnerable tanks were in a built-up area at night, Lt-Colonel Roger Rowley sent one of his companies to find them and give them protection.

The city was burning and, with German patrols in the area, the company felt uncomfortably silhouetted as they moved through the unfamiliar streets. After losing their way several times they found the tanks in time to beat off the first enemy tank-hunting teams. The Germans had decided that the tanks must be eliminated before morning.

> They came in on the Glens in hair-raising fashion, their boots covered with cloth so as to be noiseless and their faces and hands blackened. They were familiar with the paths and alleys of the neighbourhood and were able to close in to the attack quickly. The Glens beat them off without losing a tank, though not without a few casualties.

Throughout the night the stillness was broken by shots and the explosion of grenades as Canadians working forward toward the river clashed with enemy patrols.

Early the following morning D Company and the battalion command group headed for the Citadel which was entirely surrounded, like a castle, by a high wall, and at once got into position before the bastion under cover of smoke. Then there appeared, with as nice a sense of timing as an author slipping a character into the plot of a historical romance, a Frenchman who had been living for this hour. He wished to show the officer the entrance to a secret tunnel that led into the heart of the Citadel; would the officer be pleased to follow him? The Company Commander (Major Stothart), who was by this time the only officer in his Company who had not been wounded, took a platoon with him and disappeared at the heels of the patriot. No sooner had he done so than the Churchill tanks rumbled up, raking the ramparts with fire and the Engineers in their armoured vehicles began to place petards against the portcullis. As the gate was blown in, the Company Commander and his platoon dealt the *coup de grâce* to the morale of the defenders by suddenly appearing in their midst out of the tunnel. Scores of dirty white things immediately were seen fluttering from the walls in token of surrender.

Words was sent back to the Commanding Officer, asking him to come and take over the Citadel. About 200 prisoners, including sixteen officers, were captured, all of them delighted to be out of the war.[6]

On the right of the Division, all three battalions of the 8th Brigade were attacking. While the Queen's Own Rifles and Le Régiment de la Chaudière battled their way into the northern outskirts of Boulogne, the North Shore Regiment attacked the heavily fortified positions around La Trésorerie from which the enemy otherwise would have been able to fire into the rear of their sister battalions. Opposition was heavy and it was not until the evening of the next day, the 18th, that the Queen's Own fought their way to the harbour and the mouth of the Liane. The Chaudière had taken the fortified area about the Colonne de la Grande Armée, the monument commemorating Napoleon's preparations to invade England in 1805, and were patrolling towards Fort de la Crèche. The North Shore had

THE CAPTURE OF BOULOGNE
17-22 SEPTEMBER 1944

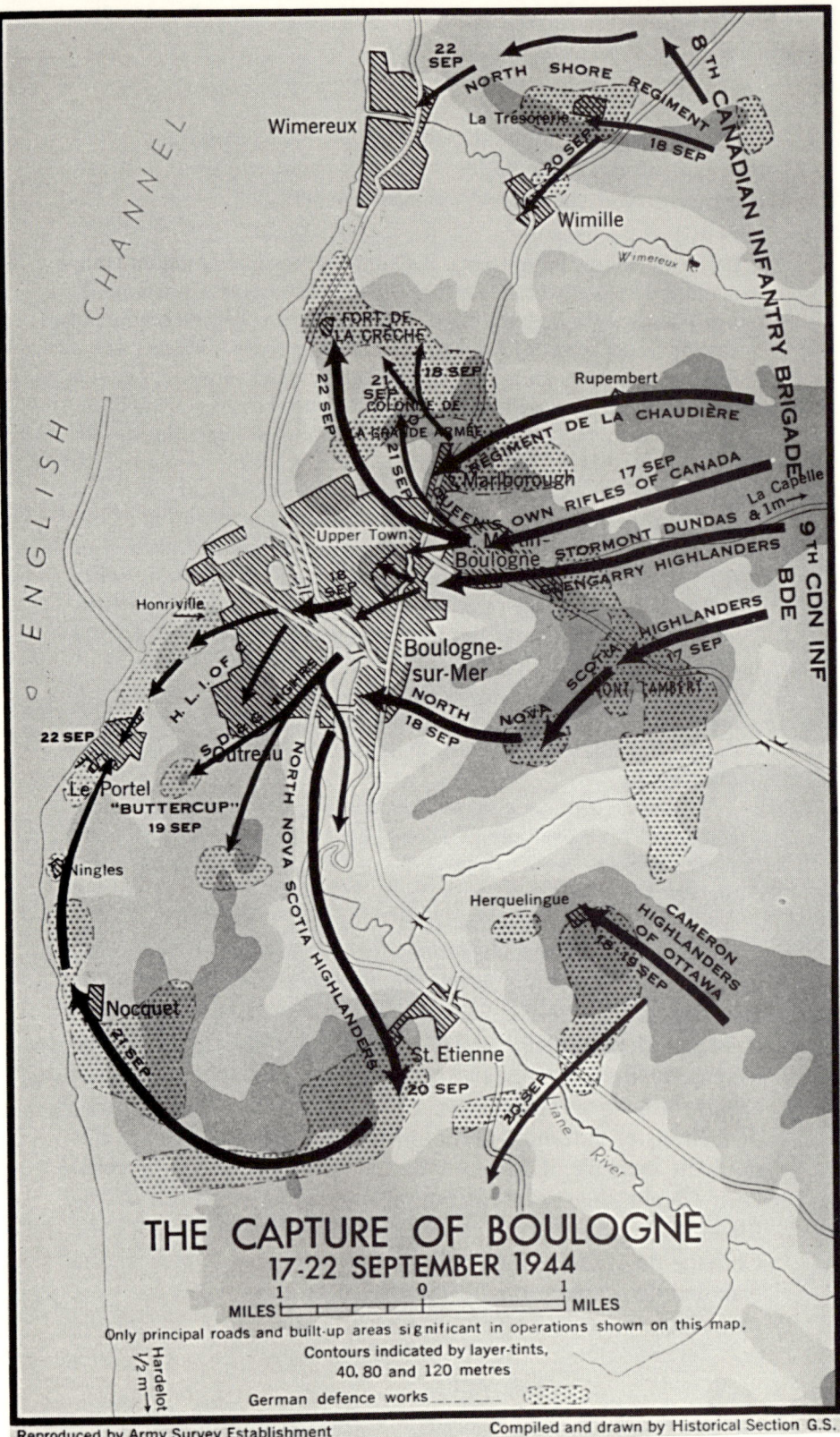

Only principal roads and built-up areas significant in operations shown on this map.
Contours indicated by layer-tints, 40, 80 and 120 metres
German defence works ....

Reproduced by Army Survey Establishment   Compiled and drawn by Historical Section G.S.

taken the pillboxes at La Trésorerie and were mopping up and preparing to deal with the nearby coastal batteries.

Next day they continued to clear the area around Wimereux and Wimille while the Queen's Own and Chaudière mounted an attack toward Fort de la Crèche. It made little progress. 'The enemy was fighting very hard and for the first time was really contesting every yard of ground. There appeared to be no foreign element and the opposition was entirely German.'[7] Next day an attack which was to be supported by medium bombers did not take place when the RAF support was cancelled at the last moment with no explanation.

On the 21st the two battalions succeeded in working forward to the outer defences. Late in the afternoon 77 medium bombers made a very effective attack on the Fort and the infantry were able to move closer to it. After dark the Queen's Own brought forward tanks and anti-tank guns into positions covering the Fort while their riflemen closed up to its protective wire. At first light the armour opened a heavy sustained fire on every visible aperture of the Fort. Taken completely by surprise, the garrison of 500 Germans surrendered, ending resistance in the 8th Brigade's area.

The 9th, which reached the Liane River during the first night of the battle, found all bridges over the river destroyed. The next day for them was spent in mopping up Mont Lambert and the area near the river, while they prepared for an assault crossing that night.

The opposite bank was lined with buildings from which alert enemy machine-gun crews fired at anything which moved on the Canadian side. It would be difficult to cross in darkness, well-nigh impossible by day. And the night was needed for bridging. Rockingham decided to smother the opposition before sending his reserve battalion, the Highland Light Infantry of Canada, over the Liane.

Under cover of darkness he brought every tank and anti-tank gun, every machine gun and PIAT available to him forward to the river line and concealed them in houses and behind garden walls. Their orders were to open fire at H-Hour and 'plaster' the enemy opposite while the artillery fired at targets beyond. While they were moving into position the engineers improvised a footbridge across which the infantry would cross, closed up, at the run.[8]

The supporting weapons were placed under the direct control of the battalion commander who could stop the firing immediately he saw his men moving into a danger zone.

Soon after the bridge was completed, the deceptive quiet of early morning exploded into ear-shattering noise as a sheet of flame flashed across the waters of the Liane. Dust and shards of brick and stone erupted from the buildings opposite as the first HLI platoon dashed across the bridge, their company sergeant-major encouraging them to 'MOVE!'

By 10 a.m. the entire battalion and its supporting arms were over the river and fighting their way through the town toward the sea. 'Murderous fire came from all directions,' costing them 64 casualties and the loss of four Flail tanks. As soon as the HLI were clear of their bridgehead, the SDG crossed and both battalions, under shelling by heavy artillery, 88mm airbursts and 20 and 40mm AA guns, turned south.

During the afternoon the SDG fought their way into the suburb of Outreau, among the prisoners captured being 'thirty black Sengalese complete with fez.'[9]

Between there and the sea was a particularly dangerous and well-protected German battery position on a 250-foot hill which gave them good observation in all directions. On it were 15 artillery pieces including six 88s. Fortunately for the Highlanders, they were so busy shelling the North Novas that they did not see D Company of the Glengarrians forming up in the woods below their position.

As the first shells of their artillery support began to burst on the objective, the infantry swarmed up and over the hill, throwing grenades and bayoneting the defenders. In minutes the first position with three 88s was overrun. A platoon dashed for the next three but the Germans managed to spike them before they were captured. By the time darkness began to fall, the company had rounded up another 185 prisoners.

Next morning their irrepressible commanding officer, Roger Rowley, visited the position with two artillery officers. Together they swung one of the 88s toward one of the strongpoints at Le Portel and opened fire. With the third shot they knocked out one of its 88s. Promptly the enemy opened up with machine guns and 88s from every position from which they could be brought to bear, sending the ad hoc gun crew to cover.[10]

The next two days saw the 9th Brigade involved in clearing the dock area and the outlying defences preparatory to reducing the immensely strong fortifications at Le Portel where it was now known that Heim had moved his headquarters. Like Fort de la Crèche, these were manned by all-German garrisons.

At 2 p.m. on 22 September the attack on the forts began. Within half an hour the northern strongpoint had fallen and its commander was despatched to General Heim with an ultimatum. Just before it expired, a white flag was seen hoisted over the southern fort and Heim emerged to surrender to Brigadier Rockingham. The last fighting ended when the German commander sent a cease-fire order to a lone 88mm gun detachment, isolated on the harbour mole, who seemed determined to fight to the bitter end.

That evening two Canadians stopped at the entrance to one of the docks, arrested by a weather-beaten sign in English. After years of German occupation and in spite of countless raids by RAF bombers and the terrible shelling of the past few days, it stood as a reminder of peaceful ways that surely one day would return — 'All vehicles for embarkation to Folkestone report here.'[11]

Impatient as they were for supplies, the staffs at Montgomery's and Eisenhower's headquarters were critical of the length of time taken to capture Boulogne, contending that, from Crerar down, the Canadians had been too deliberate and methodical in their reduction of the fortress, particularly when compared with 1st British Corps' businesslike seizure of Le Havre.[12] It was an emotional rather than a rational complaint, for Crerar simply did not have the resources at Boulogne which were available at Le Havre — fewer bombers, no naval gunfire, far less artillery ammunition, two infantry brigades as opposed to six, against enemy garrisons of almost equal strength.

The Allies were fortunate that Boulogne was taken as quickly as it was. Given the strength of their defences, if the 9,500 prisoners who far outnumbered the Canadian infantry had all fought as well as the Germans had in Normandy, or, indeed, as the garrisons of Fort de la Crèche and Le Portel, the battle would have lasted longer and cost the 3rd Canadian Infantry Division far more than its 634 casualties, a figure larger than the British losses at Le Havre.

The fall of Boulogne on 22 September brought no immediate relief to the supply situation for so badly were the port facilities damaged that it was not until 12 October that they could receive the first ship. In the meantime none could approach the harbour until the German guns at Cap Gris Nez and Calais were silenced.

8

CALAIS — OPERATION UNDERGO

FIFTEEN KILOMETRES NORTH OF BOULOGNE, at Cap Gris Nez, the line of the Channel coast turns north-east. From there, along the narrow Strait of Dover, to beyond Calais, some twenty kilometres distant, were positioned the 10 batteries of German heavy guns which for four years had periodically shelled the coastal towns of England. On 5 September the 3rd Division's 17th Duke of York's Royal Canadian Hussars cut the landward communications of Calais and the Gris Nez batteries on a front of more than 30 kilometres. Five days later the eastern half of their line of *picquets* was taken over by the Toronto Scottish of the 2nd Division.

In the meantime, south-west of Calais, the 7th Brigade had isolated the garrison from Boulogne and was closing in on Cap Gris Nez. On the 16th two of its battalions supported only by an armoured regiment and some field and medium artillery attempted to take the three heavily fortified batteries at the Cape. Their attack served only to confirm that a far heavier weight of weapons would be needed to capture them. But while the infantry made no progress against the formidable defences, the enemy did not end the day unscathed.

Two observation posts of the 3rd Medium Regiment, Royal Canadian Artillery, directed the fire of its guns in support of the attack and, for once, they had an almost unlimited supply of ammunition. On 15 September they engaged nine of the enemy's batteries. The next day proved equally eventful.

3 Cdn Medium Regiment took on the role of a naval ship today. With dawn, the OPs were away again on their orgy of shooting and harassing fire on enemy batteries. Finally, stung to reply, three guns on the 'Cap' took us on. They were big ones, about 16 inch. After some excellent ranging (5 rds) they got onto the gun positions. There they showed marked impartiality, and threw their rounds into successive troops. Large splinters reached a distance of 1400 yds. Despite the fact that our own fire never lagged, we suffered only one casualty — an arm wound. Capt King rose to the occasion and committed one gun to a duel. He quieted the huge casemates quickly and kept them quiet by intermittent sniping during the day. At dusk, the enemy's nerve revived and one of the guns (which was disappearing-carriage-mounted) reappeared. Capt King promptly landed a shell on the piece, setting fire to the gun pit and destroying the initiative of the crew if nothing else. For the rest of the day, all their guns remained silent.[1]

The landward approaches to Calais were limited by large areas of marsh and inundated ground to the south and east of the city. Except where these were crossed by roads and railway lines radiating from the port, the only practical approach for a combined force of infantry and armour was from the west along the coast where lay the main German coastal batteries. From Cap Blanc Nez and the village of Escalles ten kilometres west of the city, the enemy had constructed a series of strongly defended areas at Noires Mottes, Belle Vue Ridge and the villages of Coquelles and Vieux Coquelles inland from the sea which effectively covered both the road along the coast and that from Boulogne. Minefields and wire had been laid in profusion and these were covered by anti-tank and machine guns in concrete emplacements. Some of the six naval batteries on the coast were capable of firing inland and the defences were supported by field, anti-tank and anti-aircraft artillery. The German commandant, Lt-Colonel Ludwig Schroeder, complained that most of his 7,500 troops were 'mere rubbish,' a fact not obvious to the Canadian infantry until the later stages of the battle.

The city's old fortifications were still formidable in their way. Behind an outer ring of canals and forts a wet ditch and a bastioned wall surrounded most of the built-up area. These waterways divided it into a series of islands at the heart of which lay the old citadel.

General Spry's plan was to clear the coastal defences west of the city with two brigades, close up to its perimeter, then mount a concentric attack on every possible approach. The third brigade, when it had completed mopping up in Boulogne, would capture the batteries at Cap Gris Nez. In the meantime these would be screened by smoke from interfering with the attack on Calais. Each phase of the assault would be preceded by bombardments by heavy bombers and artillery and the infantry would be supported by tanks and the specialized armour, 'the Funnies,' of Hobart's 79th Armoured Division.

The heavy bomber preparations began on 20 September, before the capture of Boulogne was complete, when 600 aircraft dropped over 3,000 tons of bombs on Calais' defences. Bad weather prevented another attack until the 24th. Unfortunately the 3rd Division were told that this attack, like those on the preceding days, had been cancelled and the artillery did not shell the enemy's anti-aircraft batteries. Eight RAF bombers were shot down. The War Diary of the 7th Brigade reflected the frustration and bitterness of the watching soldiers:

> We felt very helpless watching this attack — the casualties to aircraft could have been lowered if someone along the lines somewhere hadn't messed things up. However, one has to expect this sort of thing in war. Patrols were sent out from battalions to try to pick up some of the bomber crews — those we did find were dead.

Next morning, the 25th, following another air attack, the assault began. By that night Le Régiment de la Chaudière and the North Shore Regiment, supported by the Fort Garry Horse on the left, had penetrated to the coast, the former taking the garrison of Cap Blanc Nez — 200 prisoners, most of whom 'were found dead drunk.'[2] Next morning the huge gun emplacements at Noires Mottes and the Sangatte battery surrendered to the North Shore.

On their right the 7th Brigade advanced to clear the western approaches to Calais. The heavy bombers had missed many of the concrete emplacements and the Regina Rifles attacking Vieux Coquelles and the Royal Winnipeg Rifles at Coquelles, both supported by the 1st Hussars, met fierce resistance from pillboxes and in house-to-house fighting. Late in the afternoon,

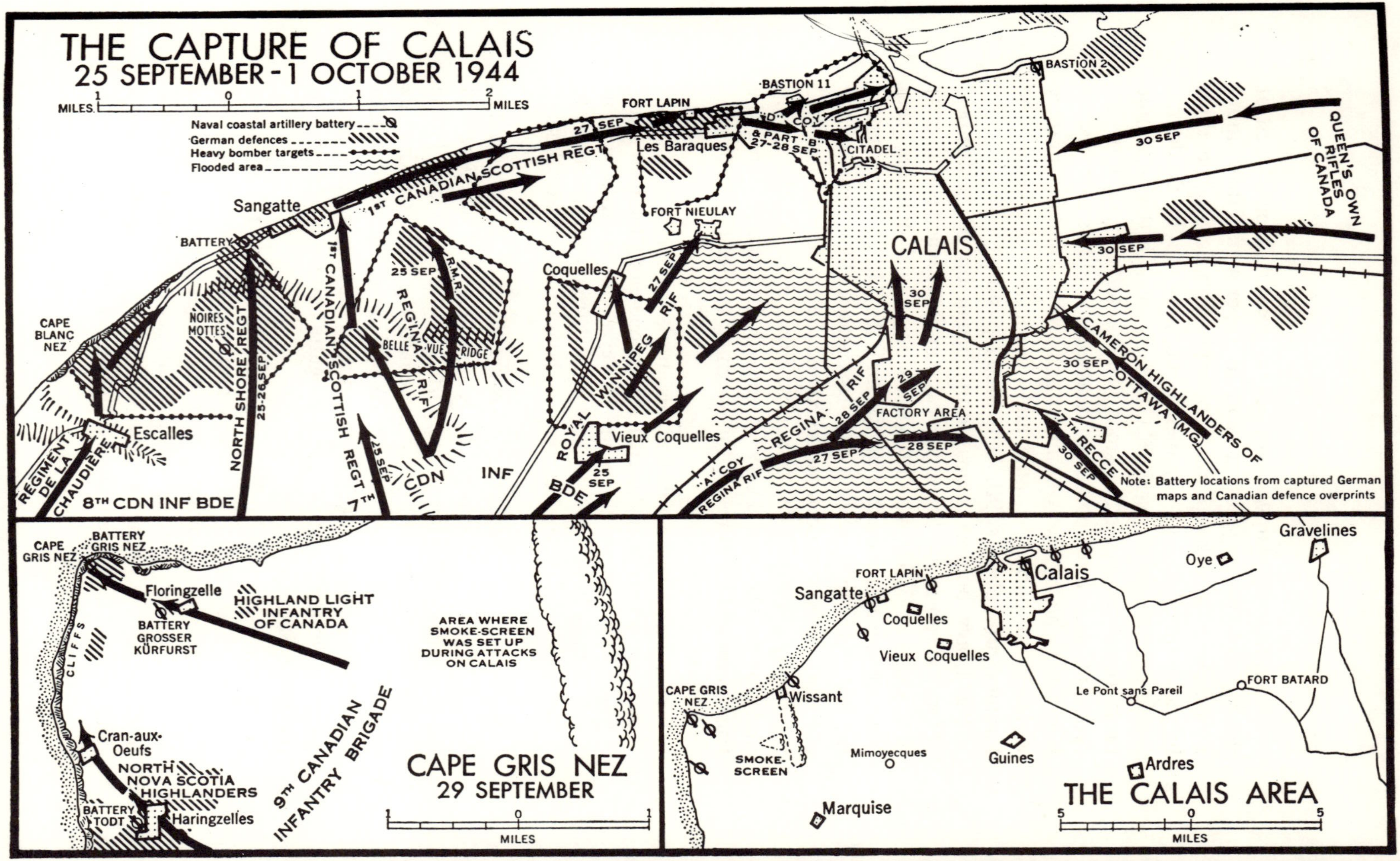

THE CAPTURE OF CALAIS
25 SEPTEMBER - 1 OCTOBER 1944
MILES 1 0 1 2 MILES
Naval coastal artillery battery
German defences
Heavy bomber targets
Flooded area
FORT LAPIN
BASTION 11
BASTION 2
"D" COY
& PART "B"
27-28 SEP
CITADEL
Les Baraques
27 SEP
1ST CANADIAN SCOTTISH REGT
Sangatte
BATTERY
FORT NIEULAY
CALAIS
30 SEP
QUEEN'S OWN RIFLES OF CANADA
CAPE BLANC NEZ
NOIRES MOTTES
NORTH SHORE REGT
25-26 SEP
1ST CANADIAN SCOTTISH REGT
25 SEP
R.M.R.
REGINA RIF
BELLE VUE RIDGE
Coquelles
27 SEP
RIF
WINNIPEG
ROYAL
Vieux Coquelles
25 SEP
7TH CDN INF BDE
Escalles
REGIMENT DE LA CHAUDIERE
8TH CDN INF BDE
"A" COY REGINA RIF
REGINA RIF
27 SEP
28 SEP
29 SEP
FACTORY AREA
CAMERON HIGHLANDERS OF OTTAWA (MG)
7TH RECCE
Note: Battery locations from captured German maps and Canadian defence overprints
CAPE GRIS NEZ
BATTERY GRIS NEZ
Floringzelle
BATTERY GROSSER KURFURST
HIGHLAND LIGHT INFANTRY OF CANADA
CLIFFS
Cran-aux-Oeufs
NORTH NOVA SCOTIA HIGHLANDERS
BATTERY TODT
Haringzelles
9TH CANADIAN INFANTRY BRIGADE
AREA WHERE SMOKE-SCREEN WAS SET UP DURING ATTACKS ON CALAIS
CAPE GRIS NEZ
29 SEPTEMBER
1 0 1
MILES
Gravelines
Oye
Calais
FORT LAPIN
Sangatte
Coquelles
Vieux Coquelles
FORT BATARD
Le Pont sans Pareil
CAPE GRIS NEZ
Wissant
SMOKE-SCREEN
Mimoyecques
Guines
Ardres
Marquise
THE CALAIS AREA
5 0 5
MILES

their Brigadier, Jock Spragge, ordered the 1st Canadian Scottish to help the Reginas shake free by moving around their left flank. By morning they had reached the coast and were advancing eastward.

That morning Bomber Command struck again and the three battalions of the 7th Brigade closed up to the inner line of fortifications in front of Calais. Ahead, barring the coast road, was Fort Lapin with its heavy guns protected by anti-tank ditches and minefields. Both it and Bastion 11 nearby were armed with flame throwers. Inland lay Fort Nieulay and the wide flooded barrier which protected the south of the city.

Once more, on the 27th, Bomber Command came to the support of the 7th Brigade's attack. With the help of tanks, Crocodiles and a smoke screen, the Scottish subdued Fort Lapin and by nightfall were probing for crossings over the old water defences at the western edge of the port. During the night two companies crossed south of Bastion 11 to find, as day broke, that they were under furious machine-gun fire from the bastion and the Citadel. So intense was it that they could neither be reinforced nor withdrawn and there they remained, cut off from food and ammunition supplies for forty-eight hours.

On their right the Winnipeg Rifles, using flame-throwers, subdued Fort Nieulay and the Reginas crossed the floods to the factory area on the southern fringes of Calais.

By now German morale had slumped. The 28th brought yet another heavy attack by Bomber Command and Lt-Colonel Schroeder asked for a truce in order to evacuate the civilian population. Spry gave him until noon on the 30th. Two hours after it expired the attack was renewed and German resistance crumbled. That evening Schroeder surrendered, and by 9 a.m. next morning all resistance had ceased.

During the period of truce on the 29th Rockingham's 9th Brigade captured the huge German batteries at Gris Nez. Two heavy raids by Bomber Command which preceded their attack shook the confidence of the defenders, though they inflicted little material damage. The two battalions involved, the Highland Light Infantry of Canada and the North Nova Scotia Highlanders, had thoroughly reconnoitred the ground. Lt-Colonel Don Forbes, the North Nova's commanding officer, whose reputation for cool nerve became a legend, had himself found a way into the defences of Battery Todt.

At 6:45 a.m. the infantry and armour attacked. Flails cleared paths through the minefields, AVREs dropped fascines into anti-tank ditches for tanks to cross and the artillery kept the enemy's heads down. By mid-morning Forbes' men had taken Battery Todt, about the same time as the HLI, having completed the capture of the four guns of Grosser Kurfurst, began to move on Battery Gris Nez. That afternoon men of the 141st Regiment Royal Armoured Corps (the Buffs), who supported the HLI with Crocodiles, watched as the Germans fired their last shot at Dover.

> One (gun), the last to fire, with Canadian infantry actually on the revolving turret, fired one shell wildly out to sea, another in the direction of Dover and one more inland before sappers could put it out of action with hand-placed charges.[3]

For a loss of 42 casualties the two battalions had taken 1,600 prisoners and had ensured that from that night the people of Dover would no longer suffer shelling by enemy guns.

Two days later, when Calais was finally cleared, it was found that another 7,500 prisoners had been added to the 3rd Division's total. Like those of Le Havre and Boulogne, its port installations had been systematically demolished. The harbour would receive no ships until November.

Part Two

The Scheldt

9

THE SCHELDT — THE FORTRESS

ON 3 SEPTEMBER, 1944, Admiral Sir Bertram Ramsay, Eisenhower's Naval Commander-in-Chief, studied the advance of armoured divisions with as much fascination as did any soldier or airman. Arrows on the situation map marked the thrusts developing toward the Rhine, while reports of demoralized enemy forces suggested that there was little to stop the Allied armies. But, as a sailor, his main concern was the future of naval operations along the coast of North-West Europe. It was this that drew his attention to a long arrow pointing toward Antwerp. It marked the axis of advance of the 11th Armoured Division.

Early in the planning of the invasion the need to capture Antwerp and Rotterdam had been recognized. Now the first seemed likely to fall. With a capacity of 40,000 tons per day, it was the largest port in western Europe and was far closer to the armies advancing into Germany than Cherbourg, Le Havre and the Channel ports. But there was a difficulty — it was sixty miles from the sea. No ship could enter it until its approaches were cleared. Lest others be under any illusion that its capture alone would solve their supply problems, Ramsay sent a telegram to Eisenhower, Montgomery and the Admiralty:

> It is essential that if Antwerp and Rotterdam are to be opened quickly enemy must be prevented from:
> 1. i) Carrying out demolitions and blocking in ports
>   ii) Mining and blocking Scheldt . . .

2. Both Antwerp and Rotterdam are highly vulnerable to mining and blocking. If enemy succeeds in these operations, the time it will take to open ports cannot be estimated.
3. It will be necessary for coastal batteries to be captured before approach channels to the river routes can be established.[1]

Next day the 11th Armoured Division seized the vital dock area of Antwerp and there they stopped. Nothing was done on the ground, either to block the escape of the 15th German Army, or to secure the banks of the Scheldt from Antwerp to the sea. The explanation for this failure was simple. Montgomery saw a gap developing between the 15th German Army retiring north-eastwards and the survivors of the 7th Army moving east to the Siegfried Line. He ordered Dempsey's Second Army to drive forward with all strength and speed to seize the bridges over the Rhine between Wesel and Arnhem before the enemy could establish a defensive line. Airborne divisions would open the way over the main rivers which intervened.

Dempsey's forces would be entirely committed to the main thrust and to protecting its flanks. Crerar's Army was to clear the coastal belt, then remain in the area of Bruges-Calais until there were enough supplies for it to be employed further forward. Montgomery gave neither of his army commanders the task of opening Antwerp.

While Eisenhower, in his discussions with Montgomery, placed somewhat more store on the urgency of opening the port, both appeared to believe that if they made a crossing over the Rhine the problem might solve itself. Such a mortal threat to homeland Germany might bring Hitler's legions scurrying home from Holland. Unlikely though this may seem in retrospect, the disorganization of the German Army at the time appeared so complete, its morale so shattered, that such a withdrawal seemed probable.

On 9 September, the day after the 4th Canadian and 1st Polish Armoured Divisions came up against stiff German resistance on the Ghent Canal, General Crerar reiterated Montgomery's directive that first priority would be given to opening the Channel ports — the destruction of the enemy north-east of the Ghent Canal was of secondary importance, and no important forces were to be committed to offensive action there. At the same time, First Canadian Army's area of responsibility was enlarged to include Ghent and the south shore of the Scheldt to within a few miles of Antwerp.[2]

On 10 September Eisenhower again spoke to Montgomery of the importance of opening Antwerp, but agreed to a delay until the Arnhem operation could take place. Two days later another more potent influence was brought to bear. The Combined Chiefs of Staff, meeting at Quebec, sent Eisenhower a telegram which stressed the importance of opening up Antwerp 'before bad weather sets in.' That same day Montgomery asked Crerar when he thought he would be able to tackle the problem.[3]

At last someone had been given the job. A growing sense of urgency was reflected in a letter from Montgomery on 13 September. Now he stressed the need for speed both in capturing Boulogne, Dunkirk and Calais and in clearing the Antwerp approaches. He hoped that Crerar could carry out all these tasks simultaneously. Given their nature and the size of First Canadian Army, the Field Marshal was being unrealistic.

The day the British captured Antwerp saw Hitler designate Walcheren Island a fortress and issue orders for the defence of the south bank of the Scheldt, the island itself and the land communications to it. As a result, the task facing First Canadian Army bore a resemblance, if on a very large scale, to the reduction of a mediaeval fortress, a comparison which could be extended to the defence problems of the Germans. Like so many, 'Fortress Walcheren' was sited to defend a waterway at a vital crossing. South of the river, its outer defences were protected by a moat — the Leopold Canal. Its central 'keep' was Walcheren itself. The landward approach was a long defended way, the south Beveland Peninsula, with a series of gates, Woensdrecht at the base of the peninsula, the Beveland Canal, and finally the 1,000-metre causeway which joins the island to the mainland. All that was lacking in the latter was a drawbridge and the Germans were to find a substitute for that.

On the face of it Crerar's task was straightforward — cut the fortress's communications, invest it closely, destroy its garrison's mobility and morale by bombardment and flooding, destroy its outer defences, then reduce the keep itself.

THE BATTLE OF THE
SCHELDT
OCTOBER – NOVEMBER 1944
Miles 5 0 5 10 Miles
Kms. 5 0 5 10 15 20 25 Kms.
Flooded areas
Canadian forces
British & Polish
U.S. forces
SCHOUWEN
NORTH BEVELAND
Kampeland
EAST
Zand Creek
WALCHEREN
Westkapelle
Middelburg
Goes
Beveland Canal
Sloe
SOUTH BEVELAND
Gravenpolder
Flushing
Hoedekenskerke
Oudelande
Fort Frederik Hendrik
Breskens
Cadzand
Groede
Zeebrugge
Knocke
Heyst
Hoofdplaat
Schoondijke
Retranchement
Zuidzande
Oostburg
Uitwaterings Canal
Sluis
Sluis Canal
Ijzendijke
Biervliet
WEST
SCHELDT
52nd (L) DIV
3 rd. CDN INF DIV
Terneuzen
Braakman
Leopold Canal
Aardenburg
St Kruis
Watervliet
Isabella Polder
Middelbourg
Moerkerke
Canal de Dérivation de la Lys
7th BDE
Kijkuit
Hulst
Axel
Bruges
Sas van Gent
Canal
NETHERLANDS
BELGIUM
Maldegem
4 th. CDN AMD DIV
Moerbrugge
Eecloo
Canal
Ghent Canal
1st. POLISH AMD DIV
2 ND. CANADIAN
Ghent

OVERFLAKKEE
Maas
River
7th. AMD DIV
Moerdijk
Mark River
Standdaarbuiten
Steenbergen
Welberg
Breda
1st. POLISH AMD DIV
OLEN
Roosendaal
Bergen op Zoom
Wouwsche Plantage
Zundert
Esschen
Korteven
Woensdrecht
Rilland
Baarle Nassau
49th. (WR) INF DIV
Dorn
Ossendrecht
Calmpthout
Wuestwezel
104th. U.S. INF DIV
Kruisstraat
1ST BRITISH CORPS
Santvliet
Putte
Merxplas
St. Leonard
4th. CDN AMD DIV
Brecht
Camp de Brasschaet
Lochtenberg
Turnhout
Brasschaet
Oorderen
Eeckeren
Wilmarsdonck
49th. (WR) INF DIV with 2nd. CDN AMD BDE
Merxem
Wyneghem
Albert Canal
ANTWERP
Scheldt River
St. Nicolas
2 nd. CDN INF DIV
Herenthals
C O R P S

At the same time, General von Zangen, commanding the 15th German Army, had two major problems — the defence of the Antwerp approaches and the extrication of the bulk of his forces still south of the river. Undoubtedly the second was the greater source of anxiety. To his great relief it was completed on 23 September, before First Canadian Army could move to stop him. With them out of the way, the defence of the fortress became much simpler. One well-led infantry division would hold the south bank of the Scheldt, another the Beveland Peninsula and the island itself. Supporting them and protecting the seaward approaches was a very large number of long-range, heavy guns in strong concrete emplacements. There was ammunition, food and stores enough for an indefinite siege.

Following a conference with his Army Commanders on the 14th, Montgomery issued a directive for the forthcoming operations of 21 Army Group. It covered both the Second Army operation directed on Arnhem which would take place on 17 September and clarified the tasks of the Canadians. In the preamble he indicated that their first priority was to clear the mouth of the Scheldt but emphasized that 'our real objective, therefore, is the Ruhr. But on the way to it we want the ports of Antwerp and Rotterdam, since the capture of the Ruhr is merely the first step on the northern route of advance into Germany.'

His detailed instructions to Crerar required him to complete the capture of Boulogne and Calais; then –

10. The whole energies of the Army will be directed toward operations designed to enable full use to be made of the port of Antwerp. Airborne troops are available to cooperate. Air operations against the island of Walcheren have already commenced and these include:
    a) the isolation of the island by taking out road and rail bridges
    b) attacks on coast defence guns
    c) attacks on other artillery, including flak.
11. HQ 1 Corps and 49 Div. will be brought up from the Havre area as early as possible, to the Antwerp area. 51 Div will be grounded completely in the Havre peninsula, and its transport used to enable the above move to take place; the Divi-

sion will remain grounded as long as its transport is required by Canadian Army for maintenance or movement purposes.
12. Canadian Army will take over the Antwerp area from Second Army beginning on 17 September . . .
13. Having completed the operations for the opening of Antwerp, vide para 10, Canadian Army will operate northwards on the general axis Breda-Utrecht-Amsterdam. . . . Task: to destroy all enemy west of the Army boundary, and open up the port of Rotterdam.
14. Subsequently Canadian Army will be brought up on the left (or northern flank) of Second Army, and will be directed on Bremen and Hamburg.

No longer was Crerar required to take Dunkirk. The 2nd Canadian Division would be free to move to the Scheldt area at once but it would be some time before the 3rd Division would be available because of their involvement at Boulogne and Calais.[4]

South of the Scheldt three major canals intersected the area held by the Germans. Dividing it roughly into two equal parts was the Terneuzen Ship Canal running north from Ghent to the Scheldt. From Zeebruge on the coast, the Leopold Canal and the Canal de Dérivation de la Lys run parallel to each other south-eastwards for some 22 kilometres. There they diverge, the Leopold veering eastwards almost to the base of the Braakman inlet from the Scheldt.

On 12 September Simonds, acting on an instruction by Crerar three days earlier, ordered the 1st Polish Armoured Division to clear the area south of the Scheldt between the Terneuzen Ship Canal and the boundary with Second Army which coincided with the Dutch-Belgian border north-west of Antwerp. The 4th Canadian Armoured Division was to sweep the area west of the canal to the sea, its main thrust being from Moerbrugge to Maldegem and Breskens. No one knew better than Simonds that armoured divisions were less than ideal for operating in country so inhospitable to tanks. Any fighting would fall to the infantry, of which each division had only one brigade. He reckoned the task as being about right for two infantry divisions, six brigades, but none was available. Much would depend on the enemy's will to fight. The Intelligence staff opined that the Germans were weak and demoralized with little equipment and no stomach for a fight. After their experience on the Ghent Canal three days earlier, the infantry of 4th Division were not that optimistic.

For the 10th Infantry Brigade the operation began on the 13th with an assault crossing of the Canal de Dérivation de la Lys and the Leopold Canal at Moerkerke by the Algonquin Regiment. Newly arrived reinforcements had raised the average strength of its four rifle companies to 90 men each, about 25 percent short of their official establishment. The crossing itself was physically exhausting. Each company had 10 heavy wood and canvas assault boats which had to be manhandled forward to the Lys Canal, heaved up the steep near bank, launched, then paddled across 90 feet of water to the wide dyke which separates the twin canals, hauled up its near-vertical bank, then dragged across to the Leopold Canal, which in turn had to be crossed.

Though under fire, the four companies succeeded in securing a narrow bridgehead and in beating off several German attempts to dislodge them, while the engineers began to build a bridge. Early in the morning of the 14th, General Gilsa, commanding 89th German Corps, ordered Lt-General Erwin Sander of the 245th Division to eliminate the bridgehead 'at all costs' and placed the corps reserve at his disposal.[5]

A 'storm of fire,' mortars and artillery, rained upon the Algonquins in the bridgehead, on their headquarters and on the engineers bridging the canal. Enemy infantry infiltrated between the rifle companies and their attacks were noticeably well co-ordinated. More than once battalion headquarters moved to escape the heavy and accurate fire which interfered with their control of the battle, but to no avail. Later they learned that a civilian traitor was directing the enemy guns by radio.

As day broke, work on the bridge had to stop. Many of the assault boats had been destroyed and every attempt to ferry ammunition across to replace the dwindling supplies in the bridgehead was halted by intense and accurate fire. By 11 a.m. there was no mortar or PIAT ammunition left and very little for rifles and Brens. The order now was 'One round, one German.'

To Major-General Harry Foster, the 4th Division's commander, it was obvious that, without reinforcement, the

NORTH-WEST EUROPE
THE FRONT 15 SEPTEMBER 1944

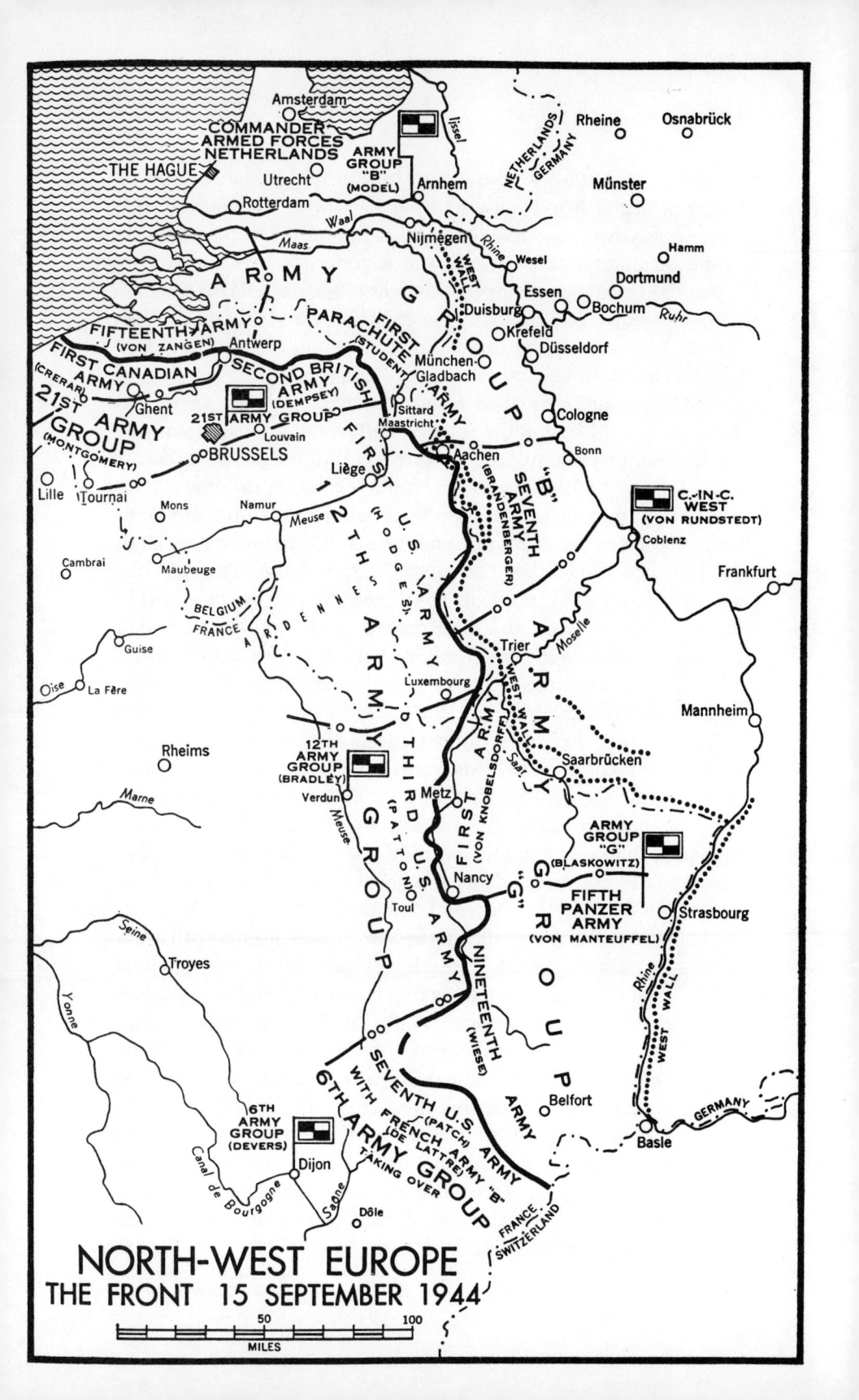

depleted Algonquins could not hold the bridgehead much longer. Despite heavy support by his artillery, the German fire was, if anything intensifying. To send more infantry across would be suicidal. He ordered the Algonquins to withdraw.

For the regiment, the operation was a disaster. There were insufficient boats and many of the survivors had to swim the two canals. In the fourteen hours since the assault began they had lost 148 casualties.

The outcome confirmed Simonds' fears that his armoured divisions would be unable to cope with a determined enemy in polder country. He ordered them to 'maintain contact and exert some pressure without sacrificing our forces in driving out an enemy who may be retreating.' Next day troops of the 4th Division probing across the Lys Canal east of where it diverges from the Leopold found that the enemy were retiring. Though they met considerable opposition south-west of Terneuzen, within three days they were able to close up to the heavily defended Leopold Canal. With the Braakman inlet, it formed the outer boundary of what the Germans called 'Scheldt Fortress South' and the Allies the 'Breskens Pocket.'

To the east, the Poles, after clearing the suburbs of Ghent, drove north-east toward Antwerp. Half-way between the two cities, Major-General Stanislaw Maczek, their redoubtable commander, concentrated his division north-west of St Nicolas preparatory to a systematic sweep of the area between there and the Scheldt. He directed his first probe north-west across the Hulst Canal in the direction of Terneuzen.

On 16 September the 10th Dragoons, his armoured brigade's motor battalion, seized a small bridgehead over the Hulst Canal. The German reaction was as swift and violent as it had been against the Algonquins. A furious counter-attack, supported by armour, overwhelmed the outnumbered Dragoons. Next day the Poles' 3rd Infantry Brigade attacked farther to the west and succeeded in bridging the Canal. On the 20th they captured Terneuzen, where, with Breskens, the enemy had embarked their retreating forces for the crossing of the Scheldt. By nightfall next day all resistance in their area had ceased. In twelve days, they had captured 1,173 prisoners at a cost of 329 casualties, a price they could ill afford.

South of the Scheldt the enemy's outposts had been driven in to the line of the Leopold Canal, the moat to the fortress. In Antwerp and to the east of the city, the next phase of the operation had begun — the cutting of the land approaches to Walcheren.

10

OUTFLANKING ANTWERP

ON 19 SEPTEMBER Crerar ordered 2nd Corps to 'thrust northwards to Roosendaal and Bergen op Zoom, in order to establish a firm base on the mainland to the east of Zuid Beveland, and from which a landward thrust along the island from the east can be developed.' Both the Canadian and Polish Armoured Divisions were to take part. 1st British Corps would move up to the right flank of the army by the 24th, to form a link with Dempsey. It was to 'keep its main strength on the left in order to assist the 2nd Corps.'

Three days earlier, when the 2nd Division relieved the 53rd Welsh in Antwerp, they found that the Germans were holding the line of the Albert Canal from its outlet in the northern outskirts of the port, south-eastwards to Herenthals. In the dock area itself an air of unreality hung over the war. For the soldiers of the 4th Brigade every day brought vicious skirmishes with the enemy. The villages of Wilmarsdonck and Oorderen were taken and lost several times. The Germans could and did shell the harbour locks and on the 20th attacked with the intention of destroying a railway bridge in the Merxem area but were beaten back. Yet, though that suburb was in German hands, civilians regularly came through it to the Canal by tram, alighted, crossed on foot, then caught another south of the bridge and continued into Antwerp.

Every day a few men from the Canadian battalions were given leave and would catch a tram close to the front line for a few hours in downtown Antwerp. The transition from the dangers of the bullet-swept streets of the dock area to the bright lights of a city, apparently untouched by war, was so dramatic as to be almost beyond belief. Beer and wine flowed in the many bars and cafés, pretty girls were happy to dance with the soldiers, there were English-language movies showing in modern cinemas. Department stores were well stocked and the barrows in the open-air markets were heaped high with vegetables and fruit which many of the men had not seen for years. There was none of the austerity of wartime Britain. Remembering that, some resented the affluence but could not harbour it long in the face of the open-hearted hospitality of the Belgians. It was difficult for most Canadian soldiers to pay for a drink and even more difficult to tear themselves away and catch the last tram back to the front.

Desirable though it would have been for the Division to gain more elbow room around the Antwerp docks and clear up the security problems of 'line crossers' in the city, it did not have the strength. The cost of an attack across the Albert Canal followed by a house-to-house battle to clear the other side would be high. Major-General Foulkes, its commander, decided to outflank the German defences in the city and open the way for an advance to the north by sending the 5th Brigade across the Canal beyond the eastern suburbs.

Early in the morning of the 21st scouts of the Canadian Black Watch attempted to cross to the north bank but found every likely crossing-point closely guarded by the enemy. There was no obvious alternative to a full-scale assault. But such an operation would demand overwhelming fire support and the artillery was almost out of ammunition. There was plenty in dumps in the Normandy beachhead but no transport to move it forward. The odds against a successful crossing were all too obvious to Brigadier W.J. Megill of the 5th Brigade, but cross they must. He ordered the Calgary Highlanders to take the lead.

The Algonquin Regiment's disaster on the Leopold Canal was well known and the Highlanders approached their task with care and no little trepidation. Their company commanders were unanimous in preferring stealth and speed to a storm crossing. Every foot of the Canal in the Brigade's area had been examined for possibilities. Only at one point did the operation seem even remotely possible — a partially intact lock gate just east of the village of Wyneghem.

The plan which evolved was simple and appallingly hazardous. A fighting patrol would steal across and take out the sentries covering the lock gate. Immediately a rifle company would follow to form a small bridgehead. Hot on their heels, two more companies would race across and the Engineers would begin building a bridge. The risks were obvious, but at least the weather favoured it. 'Black as the inside of a cow's belly' muttered the signal sergeant to the Intelligence Officer as he prepared for an anxious vigil by a radio set.[1]

At 1:30 a.m. on 22 September Sergeant Clarence Crockett of C Company led the eight volunteers of his patrol across a semi-demolished footbridge to an island in the centre of the canal. With darkened faces and carrying only weapons, ammunition and grenades, they moved in complete silence across the narrow strip of land to the lock gate.

With infinite care the patrol inched their way along the narrow top of the 90-foot-wide gates, knowing that at the least sound machine-gun fire would sweep them from their path. As they drew close to the far bank Crockett was appalled to discover that the last eight feet of the gate was missing. The only connection to the shore was a six-inch pipe above which the Germans had strung a single taut strand of wire as a hand grip. Moving sideways, Crockett edged his way along it to the bank. Then with every sense alert, he began to crawl forward.

'Halt!'

Crockett saw the German sentry almost as he spoke. In an instant he had him on the ground and despatched him with his knife. As his men moved up on either side of him, two enemy machine guns began lacing the south end of the lock gate and the island in the centre of the Canal. Crockett could see that any delay in dealing with them would be fatal to the battalion's crossing. Without hesitation he and his men stormed the first gun in its concrete emplacement, killed its crew then destroyed the second with one round from a PIAT. Moments later the leading platoon of C Company arrived to help.

All day the Highlanders fought to expand their bridgehead, beating off German counter-attacks which were supported by accurate shell fire, which their frustrated artillery observers could do nothing to suppress.

By 7 p.m. the Engineers had completed a bridge and crossed to fight alongside the Highlanders. During that night the Germans attacked again, but by morning Le Régiment de Maisonneuve were also over the Canal and the bridgehead was secure.

Their failure to stop the Canadians crossing convinced General Otto Sponheimer of the 67th Corps that he must pull back without delay to the next main obstacle, the Antwerp-Turnhout Canal. When the newly arrived 49th Division crossed the Albert Canal at Herenthals, they were unopposed.

Sergeant Crockett's gallantry was the key to the success of an operation which enabled two divisions to advance up to 16 kilometres. The Regiment recommended him for a Victoria Cross but Montgomery turned it down, commenting that it was a 'very good Distinguished Conduct Medal.'[2]

On the right the 49th Division's reconnaissance regiment found a place where the Antwerp-Turnhout Canal could easily be bridged. Major-General E.H. Barker, the Divisional Commander, ordered a diversionary attack some two kilometres away from the site which absorbed the enemy's attention while a bridge was being built. Next day six of his battalions were across the Canal and were enlarging the bridgehead in spite of heavy enemy counter-attacks in which some 800 prisoners were taken.

To the west, the 2nd Division had not fared so well. Two attempts by the 6th Brigade to cross the Antwerp-Turnhout Canal in the area of Lochtenberg were unsuccessful. 2 Corps Headquarters could do nothing to help. Indeed, with its four divisions fighting at separate places as far apart as Boulogne and Antwerp, it was well-nigh impossible for them to influence all their operations.

On 26 September, at Simonds' suggestion, Crerar made 1st British Corps responsible for operations in the Antwerp area and placed the 2nd Canadian and Polish Armoured Divisions under their command. With the 49th, Crocker now would have three divisions to drive the last of the enemy from Antwerp and to cut the base of the South Beveland Peninsula.

Like most of his troops, Crerar had been attacked by dysentery — 'the Normandy Glide' — but his had not responded to the usual drugs. After weeks of fighting this debilitating affliction, the Army Commander bowed to the advice of the Medical Corps and agreed to return to England for diagnosis and treatment. He left on 27 September, having appointed General Guy Simonds to replace him during his absence. Charles Foulkes took command of 2nd Corps while Brigadier Holley Keefler, in turn, became the acting commander of the 2nd Division. These changes had no small influence on the subsequent operations on the Scheldt.

The day that Crerar left, Montgomery issued new orders to his army commanders. 'The major task of the (Second) Army will be to operate strongly with all available strength from the general area Nijmegen-Gennep against the N.W. corner of the Ruhr.' Of First Canadian Army he wrote, 'The right wing of the Army will thrust strongly northwards on the general axis Tilburg-Hertogenbosch and so free the Second Army from its present commitment to a long left flank facing west. This thrust should be on a comparatively narrow front and it is important that it should reach Hertogenbosch as early as possible.'

The British Official History commented:

> Gen Crerar had intended to seal off South Beveland by pushing two divisions of I Corps up to Bergen op Zoom and to Roosendaal, a short distance east of Bergen. But as 's-Hertogenbosch was some forty miles east of Roosendaal, Montgomery's new orders would result in the I Corps divisions being sent off at a tangent and, as will be seen, the operations due north from Antwerp suffered accordingly.[3]

Simonds had no alternative but to order Crocker to direct the Poles and the 49th Division to the north-east. Montgomery was still giving the operations to open Antwerp a low priority in 21st Army Group. Even First Canadian Army could not bring all its resources to bear on the task for now one of its corps was directed from the scene. The Poles would not take Bergen op Zoom — the 2nd Division alone would seal off the South Beveland Peninsula.

To understand what happened next, it is necessary to look outside the boundaries of First Canadian Army.

When Antwerp fell to the British on 4 September, Hitler ordered his forces in the West to hold 'Walcheren Island... the bridgehead at Antwerp and the Albert Canal position as far as Maastricht.' East of Antwerp there was no organized force ready to respond to the Führer's call, only the remnants of defeated units in full retreat toward the Fatherland. It is doubtful that General Kurt Chill knew of the order to hold the Albert Canal when he made up his mind to defend it but he recognized its strategic importance. Of more immediate significance, it offered an easily recognizable obstacle along which retreating units could be halted to regain their cohesion and to delay the Allied advance. At bridges over the Canal, he posted staff officers backed by military police to sort the weary and bewildered survivors of the Normandy battles into units which then were turned to face their advancing enemy. So was born 'Battle Group Chill.'[4]

On 6 September Second Army resumed its advance north-east from Brussels and Louvain toward Arnhem and immediately ran into stiff resistance along the Albert Canal. In the days which followed, the Guards Armoured Division, leading the advance, was slowed by stubborn rearguards and counter-attacks as they forced their way forward to cross the next main obstacle, the Escaut Canal. It was soon evident that Chill's improvised battle group had won enough time for units of the 15th and 1st Parachute Armies to organize a shaky defensive line running east from Antwerp to the Maas. Their headlong retreat had ended.

On 17 September the German front was shattered. American and British airborne divisions landed behind it at Eindhoven, Grave, Nijmegen and Arnhem whilst Horrocks's 30th Corps drove north-eastwards through them, bound for a crossing over the Rhine. Ten days later this bold thrust was brought to a halt just short of complete success when the gallant remnants of the British 1st Airborne Division were overwhelmed by German tanks at Arnhem.

By then the bulk of Second Army had moved forward to give weight to the thrust and to protect the two 55-mile-long flanks of the salient which had its apex north of Nijmegen. From both sides the Germans attacked to cut off the British and American divisions but were thrown back. Montgomery's spearhead was close to the Rhine. To cross it and advance into Germany remained his primary objective.

On 26 September, when John Crocker's 1st Corps was made responsible for operations in the Antwerp area, the 2nd Canadian and 49th (West Riding) Divisions were fighting along the Turnhout Canal. Their right joined the 53rd Division of Second Army east of Turnhout. Ten miles further to the east, that division's front turned to the north at the base of the Nijmegen Salient.

Opposite them von Zangen's 15th Army which had escaped across the Scheldt, faced the Canadians and British from Antwerp to Nijmegen. Many of its units had been nearly destroyed but its brain and nervous system — commanders, staffs and communications — were largely intact. With desperate efficiency, they strove to counter the threat to the Rhine, whilst holding grimly to their fortress of the Scheldt.

By now no one in First Canadian Army was under any illusions about the enemy's capacity to fight. Though short of equipment, under strength and often with untrained boys in their ranks, many German units showed a determination and willingness to press home a counterattack which could be disconcerting. The War Diary of the 5th Brigade, speaking of the battle for the Albert Canal, noted 'This was the first time our troops had met the enemy using bayonets.'

The first result of the new command arrangements in the Antwerp area came when Crocker ordered the 2nd Division to stop its attacks near Lochtenberg and cross the Antwerp-Turnhout Canal through the bridgehead established by the 49th. Swinging westward, the Black Watch took St Leonard on 28 September but attempts to advance further through the sandy heathland were met by accurate shell and mortar fire and by well-concealed machine guns. When Le Régiment de Maisonneuve and the Calgary Highlanders attacked in the direction of Brecht, they encountered 88mm fire, and, for the first time in recent weeks, a German tank.

But Canadian tanks too had appeared on the scene. The Fort Garry Horse, with whom the 5th Brigade had trained for years in England, moved into the bridgehead. They had worked together in Normandy but that close *bocage* country had precluded the intimate cooperation which they practiced so often on the Sussex Downs. The Germans were in for a shock.

Captain Sandy Pearson of the Calgaries described what happened:

> The fighting strength of the Company was about thirty or forty. Every man carried an automatic weapon. They gave me a troop of tanks from the Fort Garry Horse and we did one of the first "Infantry-cum-Tank" attacks. It worked so well that the combined force seemed unstoppable. We got a lot of prisoners with few casualties. We ended up at a deserted distillery near the Canal for the night.[5]

Directing the supporting artillery and mortars from the bow-gunner's seat of a tank was Captain Mark Tennant.

> Ahead of us, a German was running away and I decided to let him go. I didn't want to shoot the poor devil but then he turned back and picked something up. I thought that it must be pretty valuable and that if he was that serious about it, we probably needed it more than he did. I gave him the works and told the tank commander to stop. In the German's hand was a tin can with a swastika on it, used to collect coins for the war effort. And that had cost him his life!
>
> When I met Sandy in the distillery, we found tables set for the German officers' dinner.[6]

But the battle was not over. In Brecht the Black Watch finally drove the enemy from the town on 1 October and the Maisonneuve held it for the next two days, while being constantly shelled and mortared and beating off several counterattacks.

The Poles and the 49th Division, which Crocker had ordered to break out of the bridgehead to the north-east, immediately ran into heavy opposition. Three kilometres west of Merxplas the attack of the 146th Brigade got off to a bad start. Its right-hand battalion was late in crossing the start line for an attack on the Dépôt de Mendicité, enabling the enemy to concentrate his full fire on the troops attacking on the left. This was C Company of the Hallamshire Battalion of the York and Lancaster

Regiment who were protecting the left flank of the main assault.

Unaware of the strength of the enemy, the company was advancing with one platoon forward, it in turn being led by a section of six men commanded by Corporal John Harper.

The Depot was a natural defensive position being surrounded by an earth wall about 12 feet high backed by a wide road and a moat about 30 feet wide. Before it there was not a vestige of cover for more than 300 metres on the dead flat ground.

There was no sign of life from the enemy until the leading section came within 50 yards of the wall. Suddenly a hail of mortar bombs and small arms fire burst upon the advancing troops. Harper's section rushed the enemy on the near side of the wall and there were pinned down by fire from both flanks and by grenades thrown from over the wall. His platoon commander, attempting to get forward, was badly wounded and Harper took charge of the platoon. Looking back, he could see the rest of his company pinned to the ground. The attack was on the point of failure. Looking up the steep slope of the wall, he could see spurts of dust where a machine gun was raking the top. A stick grenade flew across and exploded a few yards away. He could at least reply to that.

Angrily he pulled the pin from a 36 grenade, tossed it over the wall, then followed it with two more. By the time the third one had burst, he had scrambled up the wall and was firing at the enemy on the far side. Three of them dropped, four threw up their hands in surrender, while several ran and dived into the moat and began swimming to the far side. Harper dropped his rifle, picked up an enemy light machine gun and shot them as they swam.

He brought his prisoners over the wall, which was still under heavy fire, then returned across it to look for a way to cross the moat. Not finding one, in spite of bullets ricochetting from it, he crossed the wall again, gave orders to his section, climbed back on to the wall and covered them across with fire from a Bren gun, then occupied the abandoned enemy position.

Corporal Harper then left the comparative safety of a German weapon pit and once more walked alone along the moat for about 200 metres in full view of the enemy to find a crossing place. Eventually he made contact with the battalion attacking on his right and found that they had located a ford. Back he came across the open ground and on the way to report to his company commander he was hit by a rifle bullet and died on the bank of the moat.

Later it became obvious that the battalion on the right were only able to cross the ford with the help of fire from Harper's platoon.

His citation for the Victoria Cross acknowledged that the success of his brigade's attack on the Dépôt de Mendicité 'can thus fairly be attributed to the outstanding bravery of Corporal Harper.'[7]

The Poles now spearheaded the 1st Corps advance up the railway line from Turnhout toward Tilburg with the West Riding Division supported by tanks of the Sherbrooke Fusiliers, keeping pace on both their flanks. Ahead of them, Typhoons and Spitfires of 84 Group RAF criss-crossed the axis of advance looking for targets.

On 3 October Field-Marshal Gerd von Rundstedt received one of those reminders from above which field commanders find so irritating. The Chief of Operations at OKW, Col-General Jodl, wrote that if the early opening of the Scheldt, which was obviously vital to the Allies, was to be prevented, the line Antwerp-Tilburg-'s-Hertogenbosch must be held to the last. The British, Canadians and Poles could attest that Rundstedt had already reached that conclusion. That day he cancelled a projected attack by Battle Group Chill on the Nijmegen salient which he considered less important than holding Tilburg. Instead he ordered it to join the 67th Corps and drive back 1st Corps who had now taken Baarle Nassau. The battle group, formed around the nucleus of Chill's depleted 85th Division, now contained remnants of the 8th and 89th Divisions, the Hermann Goering Replacement Regiment and the highly trained and well-equipped 6th Parachute Regiment.

Like other formations of First Canadian Army, the Poles were suffering the effects of the heavy casualties to their infantry earlier in the campaign. The few replacements which came forward were poorly trained. When, on the 6th, Chill's battle group and the 719th Division made a concentric attack, the

Poles gave no ground but they lost heavily in both tanks and men. Later, trying to advance against von der Heydte's paratroops, their infantry and tanks seemed to have lost their earlier skill in working together. Without mutual support, Polish tanks were knocked out by German 88s at close range while their unsupported infantry were cut down by Spandau fire.

On 7 October 1st Corps was halted for a reorganization of the front. The 2nd Canadian Division returned to 2nd Corps, whilst Crocker gained the British 7th Armoured and 51st Highland Divisions, together with a considerable extension to his overlong 15-mile front.

The early hours of 2 October saw the beginning of the end to the fighting in Antwerp. At 3 a.m. two companies of the Royal Regiment of Canada crossed the Albert Canal into Merxem where they were joined later in the morning by the Essex Scottish attacking from the west. Further north-east, beyond the city, the South Saskatchewan Regiment led the 6th Brigade's advance south-west along the Canal. By the afternoon, they had taken Lochtenberg. Next day, with the Queen's Own Cameron Highlanders from Winnipeg, they took Brasschaet on the Breda road north of Antwerp. Continuing their sweep westward, they reached Appeln on the 4th, the 4th Brigade were north of Eeckeren, and Antwerp and its suburbs were free of the enemy.

The 4th Brigade now had the bit in its teeth. On the 5th, the Essex Scottish, despite fairly heavy casualties, drove the enemy from the village of Putte on the Belgian-Dutch border. Passing through them, the Royal Hamilton Light Infantry and the Royal Regiment swept forward another eight kilometres to within four and a half kilometres of Woensdrecht. The 2nd Division's first main objective was almost within their grasp.

11

WOENSDRECHT

EARLY ON 7 OCTOBER the 5th Brigade passed through the 4th with the object of sealing off the South Beveland Peninsula. Despite the warm October sunshine which lifted men's spirits, a sense of foreboding was reflected in the unsmiling faces of the leading companies of Le Régiment de Maisonneuve and the Calgary Highlanders. There was something menacing in the atmosphere — the glistening, flooded polders rising inland to silent dunes and heathland, the orderly plantations of pine and spruce, all seemed to hold an ominous secret. No birds sang. Up the roads ahead lay villages with unpleasant names — Woensdrecht, Hoogerheide and Zandvoort. One soldier remembered his father speaking of a Zandvoort near Ypres in the last war and hoped that there was no similarity. There was almost a sense of relief in B Company of the Calgaries when at 0820 they came under rifle and machine-gun fire. That they understood.

On the right the Maisonneuves were stopped short of their objectives while the Calgaries battled their way into Hoogerheide. Casualties mounted as house-to-house fighting began and the enemy showed no inclination to surrender. 'Contrary to what we had expected, they were not all old, sickly men but rather young, fairly well-built . . . some spoke English and informed us that it was the first battle for many of them.'[1]

During the evening, battalion headquarters moved forward to Jansen's Farm on the outskirts of the village. Approaching it, following their reconnaissance party, they could hear 'the sound of rifle and Bren mixed with Schmeisser from the area of the farm. The convoy reached the farm amid a crackle and thump of small arms and the crump of mortar. For a while it looked as if we would have to fight on into the night to hold our H.Q. position.'[2]

Pockets of enemy were holding out behind the leading companies and counterattacks were launched at each of them during the night. Sixty-one prisoners were taken that day.

With morning, came orders from brigade to double the battalion's frontage by taking the objectives of the Maisonneuve on the right. Operations began with an attack by a platoon supported by Wasp flamethrowers and a tank to take out a concrete pillbox within 75 metres of battalion headquarters.

Brigadier Bill Megill, of the 5th Brigade, had a well-earned reputation for being a hard driving commander and he was putting pressure on the Calgaries to 'get on.' Their C.O., Lt-Colonel Donald MacLauchlan, had much the same reputation, and a caustic tongue to boot. Both were needling Charlie Doré, the adjutant. The following radio conversation took place between him and Win Lasher, a company commander, who was 'mouseholing' or blowing his way through the walls of adjoining houses toward a key crossroads in the village:

'Hello, Peter.' (A Company's call sign). 'Have you made any progress?'
'Hello, Peter. No. Out.'

(Ten minutes later)
'Hello, Peter. Have you made any progress yet?'
'Hello, Peter. No. Out.'

(Ten minutes later, voice of adjutant, heavily sarcastic)
'Hello, Peter. Have you made any progress *yet*?'
'Hello, Peter. Yes, Five minutes ago I was in the dining room. Now I'm in the kitchen. Out.'[3]

During the morning two civilians came out of a wood opposite C Company, holding white handkerchiefs in the air. They were soon giving Company Sergeant-Major 'Swede' Larson some disturbing news. South of Bergen op Zoom 2,000 German infantry, supported by eight tanks, had assembled and were preparing to attack.[4]

It was the advance guard of 'Battle Group Chill,' specifically von der Heydte's 6th Parachute Regiment, shifted from opposing the Poles to the more critical threat which was developing near Woensdrecht. Their orders: 'To reoccupy Hoogerheide and then to push on southwards to Ossendrecht.'

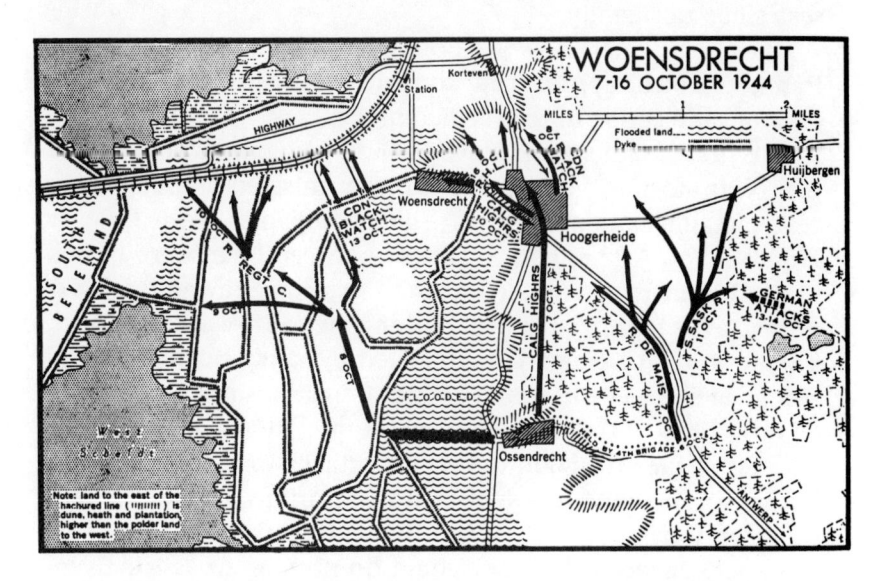

Already there was plenty of evidence that the 2nd Division would have no easy task in cutting the neck of the Beveland Peninsula. The Black Watch, attacking toward Korteven, ran into a storm of artillery and machine-gun fire in which the characteristic unsettling crash of 88mm high-velocity shells could be heard. Their advance was soon halted. Le Régiment de Maisonneuve, on their right, fared little better. The Division's right flank which extended back twenty miles to the Turnhout Canal near Brecht was thinly held by the 6th Brigade, assisted by the divisional reconnaissance and light anti-aircraft regiments. The 4th Brigade were still clearing the rear areas. When Air OP and RAF aircraft confirmed the presence of von der Heydte's battalions, Keefler ordered his division to prepare to meet an attack. They had no more than enough time to draw into defensive positions before the first enemy probe began.

Major Ross Ellis, of the Calgaries, described his first sight of the enemy they were now facing. 'Striding down the street was a husky-looking Boche paratrooper wearing a jump smock and carrying an MG42, its belt thrown over his shoulder, a stick grenade in each of his jackboots. Five others followed, hugging the edge of the road. Our men waited until he was within crossfire then cut him down.'[5] Here was the archetypal *Fallschirmjaeger*, bold to the point of foolhardiness, his like not seen since Normandy.

During the afternoon the Fort Garry Horse knocked out a Panther which approached too close, its presence another ominous indication of the forthcoming attack.

The first assaults took place in the evening and were beaten off. Next morning von der Heydte concentrated the full weight of his Regiment against the left flank companies of the Calgary Highlanders. Attempts to infiltrate between them were beaten off and the Germans pulled back to regroup, leaving the hulks of two tanks burning in a field. During the pause which followed, a platoon of the Calgaries supported by tanks cleared a wood from which the enemy could overlook their positions, capturing an officer and thirty men, not from the 6th Parachute Regiment.

Later in the afternoon the enemy attacks were resumed. The left forward company, which had a precarious grip on the outskirts of Woensdrecht, was surrounded, while the others were so closely engaged that they could do nothing to assist. Eventually the remnants of the company fell back to the next in rear and the battalion prepared to regain the position.

The German official report on the fighting in Hoogerheide tells what happened:

> In the following days attack and counterattack alternated. Three times the vanguard unit, Combat Group v.d. Heydte, succeeded in thrusting through the southern edge of Hoogerheide. Every time, the position gained had to be given up again, for lack of force against the enemy counterattack.
>
> In a vigorous attack the paratrooper combat groups succeeded, in spite of stubborn resistance of Canadian troops, in pushing through to the edge of Hoogerheide. By counterattacking, the enemy regained, in the late evening hours, part of the village.
>
> On 9 October several enemy armoured vehicles driving up on the embankment west of Hoogerheide, pushed onto the Woensdrecht-Flushing railway line. They were beaten back. The connection with

the 70 Infantry Division along the railway embankment continued to exist.[6]

Soon, more than the vanguard of paratroops was engaged. 'The enemy is thick on the ground with some tanks and SPs. There are some German Air Force Troops — even some flying personnel — and generally they are better troops than we have met for some time.'[7] They were from the Hermann Goering Replacement Training Regiment, part of 'Battle Group Chill.'

The German attack had succeeded in keeping open the gate to the Scheldt fortress and their link with the 70th Division in Beveland and Walcheren. On the ground they more than matched the infantry strength of the 2nd Division and for the moment there was little that Keefler could do to tip the balance. On the 9th he was given an infantry battalion and an armoured regiment of the 4th Division to help protect his open right flank, enabling him to increase the forces attacking the neck of the Peninsula, but the odds were still not in his favour.

On the 10th the Royal Regiment of Canada picked their way across the sodden polder land south-west of Woensdrecht and reached the railway line which runs along the isthmus, but were unable to cut the highway beyond and parallel to it. Since the ground there was impassable for a further advance, Keefler ordered the 5th Brigade on the right to block the road and rail lines near Woensdrecht station. The operation was nicknamed 'Angus.'

Brigadier Megill's plan for the attack involved The Black Watch (Royal Highland Regiment) of Canada attacking in daylight across a thousand metres of water-soaked polder with no more cover than the beets which grew there. They would have considerable tank, mortar and artillery support but the plan involved several objectives and one company passing through another in an exposed position. The enemy situation was not clear.

At first light on Friday, 13 October, two under-strength companies of the Watch advanced into a hail of enemy machine-gun, mortar and artillery fire. Tanks could not move with them because of flooding and could not see to fire in their support because of fog. Enemy heavy machine guns dug into the sides of the dykes which flanked the advance and kept up a steady and accurate fire on fixed lines, despite attempts to blind them with with smoke.

Two and a half hours after the attack began, the remnants of the two companies, their commanders wounded, struggled back to the start line. One of them, reduced to 25 men had managed to work forward to within 50 yards of the objective but the enemy moved in behind them and few returned.

Brigadier Megill, with the commanding officer, Lt-Colonel Bruce Ritchie, went forward to one of the forward companies to see for himself what had happened. On their return to battalion headquarters, he ordered Ritchie to make another attack that afternoon, this time using Wasp flame-throwers to neutralize the enemy. With that exception, the plan was little changed from its disastrous predecessor.

Again the Watch attacked and again they were massacred. In Major Bill Ewing's company of ninety men, only four were not killed or wounded.

In the pitch black of the night men searched the sodden fields for their wounded comrades. At 1 a.m. on the 14th Megill ordered the battalion to withdraw.

> The men were given a hot meal upon their return to their company positions and then they slept the sleep of the utterly exhausted. It was thought best to have them forego lunch and sleep right through until 1600 hrs, when supper was served. The K. of C. [Knights of Columbus, a Catholic welfare organization] showed a movie tonight. That originally scheduled was entitled *We Die at Dawn* but this was hurriedly changed and the film substituted therefor was in much lighter vein.[8]

Captain Ron Kerfoot, the mortar officer of the Calgary Highlanders, was horror-struck when, 'Later, after we had taken the area, I walked down one dyke and their dead were so thick that you could not walk over them, you had to walk to one side.'

The price in blood was fifty-six killed, ninety-one wounded and thirty-six missing — 183 lost in a predictably futile action.

Those who knew the story were outraged. The day became known as 'Black Friday' to the infantry of the 2nd Division. It marked the nadir of their fortunes, an unwelcome contribution to an already high casualty record.

To add to the bitterness, it was obvious that the attack had made no impression whatever on the Germans. They had begun counterattacking the 4th Brigade the previous day and continued on the 13th. Tanks and SP guns closed in to point-blank range and attempted to 'shoot in' their infantry who followed. Most of the attacks were beaten off but two companies of the Brigade were forced to change their positions. Losses were heavy.

The German road link to the garrison of the Scheldt fortress remained open. It was now blindingly obvious that if the 2nd Canadian Division were to break it, they must take the high ground on which stands the village of Woensdrecht. From those low hills in daylight the enemy could see everything that moved on the bare fields which formed the neck of the Peninsula.

Three days after Operation Angus, the Royal Hamilton Light Infantry, known as the Rileys, supported by 168 guns, a squadron of tanks and the heavy mortars and medium guns of the Toronto Scottish took Woensdrecht. Their attack had begun in the dark, at 3:30 a.m. Within an hour their leading companies had reached their objectives and were beginning to prepare for the inevitable enemy counterattack.

The first came in at 10:30, von der Heydte personally leading his paratroops and their supporting tanks and assault guns. Within minutes they had overrun the right forward company of the Rileys. Major Joe Pigott of C Company first saw them when they were within fifty metres of his position. There was only one way to stop them. He called for the heaviest possible concentration of artillery fire upon his own position and shouted to his troops to take cover.

Lt-Colonel Dennis Whitaker, the battle-wise CO of the Rileys, called for a 'Victor Target' — the fire of every gun in the Corps which could be brought to bear — centred on Joe Pigott's headquarters. Moments later an earth-shaking concentration of high explosive was bursting on the position.

Caught in the open, the attacking paratroops could not escape the terrible storm of shells. In five minutes it was over and for a moment nothing could be heard but the screams of wounded men and the crackle of flames from burning tanks. Then the men of C Company climbed from their slit trenches, each man astonished to find that he was not the sole survivor, and drove the shocked remnants of the paratroops from their position. Incredibly, only one soldier of the Rileys was slightly wounded in the bombardment.[9]

For five days the RHLI continued their battle in Woensdrecht, beating off counterattacks and ferreting out snipers who lurked in the ruins of the village. The War Diary of the 19th noted that, that day, they 'experienced the heaviest and most concentrated shelling and mortaring since Caen'.

Their casualties in the battle were only slightly less than those of the Black Watch — 167. But they had won.

At times, during those five days, Denny Whitaker wondered how much longer his sorely depleted companies could hold onto their gains. It was not simply that their numbers were so depleted. Of those left, so few were trained or experienced infantrymen. On the 17th he reported that his four rifle companies totalled no more than 170 and were very low in officers and NCOs. 'Nearly all reinforcements reaching the battalion of late have been men transferred from other arms, armoured corps, artillery, ordinance and service corps. They have had very little infantry training and are difficult to control. . . . The Hun is battling most bitterly and seems to have no shortage of weapons. It is close, hand-to-hand fighting — the enemy is not giving up here the way he has in the past.'[10]

Every battalion in First Canadian Army suffered from this lack of trained infantrymen. Given time, the 'converts' from other arms could be taught battlecraft, but there was no available time for the understrength units engaged in these intensive operations. The new men knew nothing of battlefield survival and as a result were needlessly killed or wounded. Knowing this, the old hands tried to protect them, often by taking on the most hazardous jobs and thereby decreasing their own chances of survival.

For the moment the 2nd Division could do little more than

improve its positions and wait for the help which they now knew was coming. As for the Germans, von Rundstedt recognized on the 16th that he could no longer hope to keep open the land connection with Walcheren. He authorized the flooding of South Beveland.[11]

Gradually the emphasis on opening the approaches to Antwerp was increasing. On 9 October Montgomery ordered First Canadian Army to give priority above all other operations to opening the port, though it was still to protect Second Army's flank. Two infantry divisions, the 52nd (Lowland) and the American 104th, which were due to arrive in the theatre shortly, would be available to help. Though they would speed the process, the Scheldt operations had still not been given absolute priority in 21 Army Group over the projected attack on the Ruhr.

A few days later, Eisenhower recognized that 21st Army Group could not deal with both operations and gave the responsibility for the Ruhr to General Omar Bradley's 12th Army Group. Immediately Montgomery told his army commanders that henceforth the opening of Antwerp would have 'complete priority over all other offensive operations in 21 Army Group, without any qualification whatsoever.'

No longer would First Canadian Army be responsible for Second Army's flank but would use all its forces to free Antwerp. Moreover, Dempsey's Army would now close down its other offensive operations and drive westward toward Breda both to take the weight of the enemy off Simonds' right flank, and, with the Canadians, attempt to trap the enemy south of the River Maas.

Freed of his commitment to Dempsey, Simonds now directed 1st British Corps to change its axis of advance to the north and west. The 4th Canadian Armoured Division would cut off the enemy facing the 2nd Division by taking Bergen op Zoom. The 49th Division and the Poles, joined by the 104th U.S. Infantry Division, would drive northward to the Maas.

In the grey early light of 20 October General Crocker watched the 49th Division starting from Brecht toward Wuestwezel. The men of this veteran formation, which had been fighting since D-Day in Normandy, looked surprisingly youthful — and many were — young soldiers who had replaced the casualties of earlier battles and now were moving into danger. Inevitably some would die, though few of them believed that they would be among that number. But their commanders knew, and, having done their best to ensure that the number would be as small as possible, tried to put the thought from their minds. They seldom entirely succeeded. Yet it was their duty not to show openly the inward price they paid for their responsibility.

That day to John Crocker's emotional account as a commander was added the price of being a father when his own son was killed in action.

On the right of the Corps, the 49th Division advanced steadily through Wuestwezel toward Breda. As they approached the historic Dutch city, they were strongly attacked by the German 245 Division. The attack was beaten off with heavy casualties to the enemy. But so strong had their reaction been that it was apparent that the Germans saw the northward advance as a dangerous threat.

And so they did. With the failure of the Arnhem operation, Rundstedt's intelligence staff predicted that the Allies would now thrust north across the Maas into Holland, then eastwards into Germany.

Crocker ordered the 49th to change its next objective from Breda to Roosendaal, further west, thereby helping the 4th Armoured Division which had run into heavy opposition and making room for the Americans to be brought into the line.

Early on 22 October the 10th Canadian Infantry Brigade took Esschen in a night attack which so surprised the enemy that twenty-two of their vehicles drove into the town next morning believing it still to be theirs. But the Canadians' intentions were now clear to the Germans, who moved to keep open an escape route for their troops around Woensdrecht. It took the 4th Armoured Brigade four days to advance the three miles from Esschen to Wouwsche Plantage.

On the 23rd, the day after the 4th Division took Esschen, the 2nd Division attacked again in the Woensdrecht area. On the right, the 6th Brigade drove north toward the high ground south of Korteven, while, to the west, the Calgary Highlanders advanced to cut, at last, the neck of the Beveland Peninsula. The enemy fought hard and it was not until the following day, the

24th, that they succeeded in reaching the northern sea dyke. They then swung east, driving back strong enemy rearguards from positions north of Woensdrecht. Behind them the 4th Brigade moved in the opposite direction, west into Beveland toward Walcheren Island.

On the 27th opposition in front of the Calgaries crumbled and their patrols thrust forward almost to Bergen op Zoom. The same day the 10th Brigade fought their way into the town in the face of the redoubtable 6th Parachute Regiment. For three days the battle went on in its northern outskirts before the enemy finally pulled back on the 29th.

With the town securely in its hands, the 4th Armoured turned to the north to join 1st British Corps' advance toward the Maas. The 2nd Division, having severed the land link to the Fortress Scheldt, was moving toward its 'keep,' the island of Walcheren. Across the river, the battle to clear the south bank had been going on for more than three weeks, against an enemy described as 'the best infantry division in the German army'.[12] It had been a bloody and miserable business.

12

WATER ENOUGH FOR DROWNING — OPERATION SWITCHBACK

FIFTEENTH ARMY is to ensure that everything is done to put Northern Belgium under water by blowing locks and dykes, as soon as the bulk of our forces have been withdrawn behind the sector to be flooded.
OKW instruction of 7 September.

Mention the desert to a veteran of the Eighth Army and he recalls dust, sand, wide horizons, flies, burning days, chilling nights and, perhaps, beauty in the stark landscape and in the colours of the sunset. *Bocage, the jungle, island-hopping*, all evoke their particular memories and those moments when beauty, unexpected in war, lifted the spirit or roused an unbearable longing for home and peace. *Polder country* is such a term, etched forever in the minds of those who fought in the Scheldt campaigns but, for them, it held little beauty.

Flat, dyked country, much of it polderland reclaimed from the sea, borders both banks of the Scheldt. Roads and a sprinkling of houses are built on some of the dykes, villages on islands of higher ground. Small orchards and the trees lining roads and canals offer some vertical relief to the landscape but can, in themselves, be monotonous in the regularity of their planting. But dykes had been opened and water glistened on the polders, not deep enough to float an amphibious vehicle but sufficient to drown a wounded man.

There were days of bright sunshine during the Scheldt battles, usually after morning mist and fog, but these have been forgotten. The abiding memory is of grey skies, rain, fog, bone-chilling dampness, boots, battledress and blankets soaking wet, cold food, matches that wouldn't light, the soldier's weariness that is as much fear as lack of sleep, and everywhere, mud and water.

By the end of September all the Channel ports but Dunkirk had been captured and the enemy south of the Scheldt had been confined to the 'island' formed by the deep water barrier of the Braakman inlet, the Leopold Canal and the sea. Only at one place was there a land entry to their position — between the eastern end of the Leopold Canal and the Braakman where, in a narrow gap, lies the Dutch-Belgian frontier. Known as 'Isabella,' it had been fortified before the War and was strongly held by the Germans.

The 'island' itself was flat polder country, most of it saturated. A Belgian military geography describes it even before it was flooded as *'généralment impropre aux operations militaires.'*

Facing the 4th Canadian Armoured Division, who were picqueting the Canal, was the German 64th Infantry Division, commanded by Major-General Kurt Eberding. It had been raised hurriedly during the summer from experienced soldiers on leave from the Russian front and from Norway, too late to intervene in the Normandy battles. Being nearly at full strength, it was especially selected by Hitler to defend 'Scheldt Fortress South.' As the remnants of the Fifteenth Army withdrew through it, it collected all the weapons, ammunition, stores and food it could possibly need for a protracted defence. It mustered about 11,000 officers and men, more than 500 machine guns and mortars, 200 anti-tank and anti-aircraft guns (including twenty-three 88s) and 70 field guns. In addition, it could call on the support of guns which could be brought to bear among the five coast artillery batteries in its area, as well as those on Walcheren Island.

The task of clearing the Breskens Pocket, as it came to be called, was now given to Dan Spry's 3rd Division. Because of its special training for the Normandy landings, many, particularly in the Press, referred to it as an 'assault division,' crediting it with qualities which made it specially suitable for an attack across water obstacles. In fact, as with other D-Day Divisions, its concentration on preparing for amphibious operations meant that training for other types of warfare had sometimes suffered. It was no better prepared than any other division of First Canadian Army for fighting in polder country.

After the 4th Armoured Division's experiences, no one expected anything but a hard battle in crossing the Leopold Canal. The disastrous attack of the Algonquins had been followed by patrols which had been met by accurate machine-gun and mortar fire. Every possible crossing place was held by the enemy. For him to do this so effectively suggested to Simonds that much of the strength of the German garrison was committed to guarding the crossings, either along the Canal itself or poised behind ready to counterattack. He reasoned that Eberding would accept the possibility of a seaborne attack to outflank the Canal on the North Sea coast near Knocke, but this he could counter with his immensely strong coastal defences. A landing on the shore of the Scheldt opposite Walcheren and Beveland was not worth considering — where would the boats come from and how would they be launched? The only practical approach for the Canadians would be across the Leopold Canal and it was on that waterway that his eyes would be fixed.

What Eberding could not know was that Simonds had enough tracked amphibious vehicles to negotiate the difficult approach to his river flank.

Simonds' plan was for the 3rd Division to attack with one brigade, where Eberding thought they would, across the Leopold Canal. A second would then follow. Two days later, when the enemy's attention and reserves were committed to defeating that thrust, a third brigade would cross the Braakman in amphibians and land in his rear.

The two battalions of the 7th Brigade which were to make the initial assault had little time for preparation. The 1st Canadian Scottish Regiment and the Regina Rifles finished clearing the enemy from Calais on 1 October. They were to attack across the Leopold Canal, 145 kilometres away, at first light only five days later.

The Canal itself, 90 feet wide and confined between dykes, was a formidable obstacle. The enemy positions on the far side were known to be dug in on the reverse bank of the Canal dyke, hence very difficult to neutralize with artillery or direct-fire weapons. An experiment carried out on a similar stretch of canal with Wasps showed that, if flame was aimed at the near edge of the dyke just below the crown, the blazing fuel would ricochet and splash into trenches on the far side.

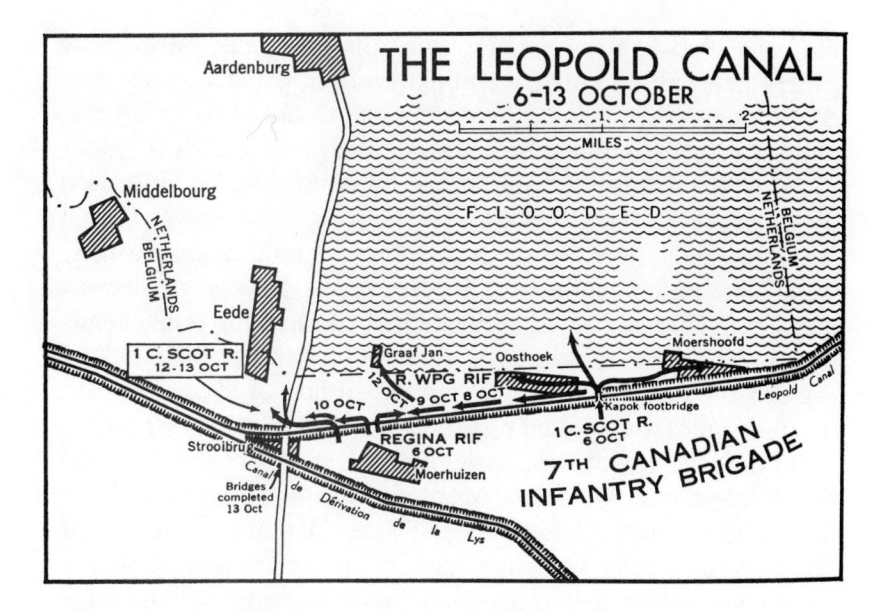

Early on 6 October, 17 Wasp carriers were positioned behind the south bank of the Canal near the crossing sites — the Division's 317 guns would remain silent until the assault began to improve the chances of surprise.

Shivering in the chill of early morning, men of the North Shore Regiment carried the sixteen assault boats for each assaulting battalion forward from their trucks to the southern dyke of the Canal and there waited for H hour. There would be little enough time for troops to cross — a Wasp could empty its tanks of fuel in 20 seconds and the demoralizing effect would last no more than two or three minutes.

Just before 5.30 a.m., a line of flame splashed along the opposite bank. The carrying parties, with a supreme burst of energy, hauled boats up the dyke to the water's edge. Into each scrambled a section of infantry who dug their paddles deep into the water as they raced for the far bank. On the right two Canadian Scottish companies landed unopposed near Oosthoek, as did the left-hand company of the Reginas, north of Moerhuizen. But their right company had hesitated. Before they could launch their boats, the enemy had returned to their posts and a hail of machine-gun fire made the open stretch of water impassable. Eventually, the whole battalion had to be ferried over on the left.

Immediately, the enemy began to counterattack. Mortars, small arms and machine-gun fire from the front and flanks was incessant. Though the 7th Brigade had two narrow bridgeheads across the Canal, it was impossible to link them. Only on the right of the Scottish was there any possibility of expansion and this they quickly exploited by taking the village of Moershoofd.

On the left, one of the classic bad-luck stories of the War was being played out. The Royal Montreal Regiment, a proud Canadian Militia unit, had been made the Defence Battalion of Headquarters First Canadian Army. In three months on the Continent it had seen no action. To give it some battle experience (and some Regina Riflemen a well-earned rest), a company from the RMR was doing a temporary exchange with one from the Rifles. They were the company which made the successful assault across the Canal and attempted to expand inland. By afternoon, barely a handful survived.

The scene in the bridgeheads was one of unparalleled violence and misery. For much of their length, troops were confined to the Canal bank. Except in the walls of the dykes, slit trenches could be dug little more than a foot deep — in the waterlogged ground, they filled with water and their walls collapsed. Men were soaking wet and coated with mud, matches and cigarettes unusable. So intense was the enemy fire that it was virtually impossible to organize co-ordinated actions even within platoons. So many enemy counterattacks were launched against them that the defenders lost count. The German lines of advance toward the bridgeheads were confined to a few narrow approaches and were accurately registered by the Canadian guns which took a heavy toll in casualties. To the almost incessant artillery fire was added the noise of more than 200 fighter-bomber sorties flown that day.

But artillery and air support could not break the deadlock. For five days the Reginas were pinned to the Canal bank, separated in places by only ten yards from the enemy. It became almost a grenade war, with each rifleman throwing as many as twenty-five No. 36 grenades every night.

The Germans replied in kind.

As night fell after the first day, it was obvious that the two battalions across the Canal could do little but hold on to their precarious positons. To those listening to the fury of the battle and to the reports from the far bank, it was a miracle that they were able to do even that. The bridgehead would not be secure until tanks could cross to reinforce the infantry. Before that could happen, a bridge must be built and the only feasible site lay nearly a kilometre west of the Regina Rifles' left flank. Brigadier Jock Spragge, commanding the 7th Brigade, decided to send the Royal Winnipeg Rifles into the Canadian Scottish position on the right with orders to link up the two battalion bridgeheads preparatory to attacking to the west.

Well before daylight, about 4:45 a.m., as they were crossing, a strong German counterattack fell upon C Company of the Scottish which was holding the left of the Battalion's position in the village of Oosthoek. Using covered approaches and leaping from slit trench to slit trench of abandoned German positions, enemy infantry overran the three platoons of C Company and surrounded both the Company Headquarters and that of No. 14 Platoon which were in buildings. Sergeant Armando Gri, commanding the platoon, with four men continued to fight 'and eventually was the only survivor, having killed or wounded twenty of the enemy. His ammunition expended, the building on fire, Sergeant Gri, with his clothes burning from the intense heat, was overwhelmed and taken prisoner.'[1]

Now the enemy were able to concentrate on the destruction of Company Headquarters, commanded by a cool, boyish-looking captain named Roger Schjelderup who had won a Military Cross in Normandy. For another two and a half hours he and his men fought on with the enemy throwing grenades in the windows and firing tracer bullets into the building in an attempt to set it on fire. Eventually, with the building burning to the ground around them and with their ammunition exhausted, Schjelderup and the remnants of his headquarters could hold off the attackers no longer and were captured.

Had they not held out, the enemy counterattack could have reached the Canal close to the footbridge over which the Winnipeg Rifles were crossing.[2]

During the day, attacks by the Winnipegs and the Scottish succeeded in capturing many of the previous night's attackers and freeing some survivors of C Company but not Gri or Schjelderup. But their war was not over.

When capture was inevitable, both men had concealed knives but there was no opportunity to escape until two weeks later when they were on a train bound for a prisoner-of-war camp in Germany. Together they opened a hole in the side of the goods van in which they were confined as it was standing in a siding. When the train moved off, they broke out. Seventy-five days later, on 6 January, 1945, after many adventures, desperate illness and an exhausting journey over ice and snow, Schjelderup and Gri returned to the Allied lines bringing valuable information about the enemy and the Dutch Resistance movement. They were both decorated, Schjelderup with an immediate Distinguished Service Order, a rare decoration for a captain, and Armando Gri with an immediate Distinguished Conduct Medal. They were in good time for the beginning of the Rhineland battles.[3]

The progress of the Royal Winnipeg Rifles west along the canal dyke and through the sodden polders beside it was painfully slow. Each success of a few yards was met by a counterattack. Casualties on both sides were heavy and before long 'the ground was littered with both German and R Wpg Rf dead.' Casualty evacuation was 'slow and difficult as wounded had to be carried for over a mile over flooded fields and roads blocked by fallen trees.'[4]

Early in the morning of the 9th, 48 hours after crossing the canal, the Winnipegs reached the left flank of the Regina Rifles. For three more days the 7th Brigade struggled to clear a bridge site. 'Shelling and small-arms fire continued to make it impossible to move about in forward areas except by crawling on the semi-flooded ground or in water-filled ditches, both of which were littered with German and Canadian dead.'[5]

During the night of the 13th Engineers succeeded in bridging the canals at Strooibrug and, next day, tanks of the British Columbia Regiment moved across. The enemy continued to fight hard but his artillery fire slackened. To the north-east the 9th Brigade had landed and were making their presence felt.

13

BRESKENS POCKET — THE BRAAKMAN APPROACH

EARLY IN OCTOBER, Rockingham's 9th Brigade arrived in Ghent from Cap Gris Nez and began training for their next operation with Landing Vehicles, Tracked, of the 5th Assault Regiment, Royal Engineers. Each 'LVT,' as the soldiers called them before the War Office dubbed them 'Buffaloes,' carried 24 men or a Bren carrier. Neither the infantry nor the engineers had used them before. There were two days for training before the force set out in the late afternoon of 7 October, to swim 20 miles down the Terneuzen Canal to the Scheldt. There they were to enter the river, turn left across the mouth of the Braakman inlet and make a surprise landing on the north-east corner of the Breskens 'island' at 2 a.m. on the 8th.

At last light the column moved off, only the LVTs' tail-lights showing in the dark. At Sas van Gent there was trouble getting through the locks for the amphibians were hard to manoeuvre at slow speed. Near the end of the Canal, at Terneuzen, a set of locks had been jammed shut by the enemy and ramps had to be cut for the vehicles to bypass the obstacle. It was a slow and laborious process and several craft were damaged as they were being winched from the water. With these unexpected delays disappeared the possibility of a surprise landing that night. To attack in daylight would be suicidal. Rockingham had no alternative but to delay the operation for 24 hours.

It was not an easy decision to take. The pressure on 7th Brigade in their tenuous bridgehead would continue unabated for yet another day and the enemy might discover the assault force lying in wait in the flat countryside around Terneuzen. Already the noise of the LVTs' aeroplane engines had sounded so much like approaching bombers that German anti-aircraft guns on Walcheren Island had thrown up a curtain of fire.

With only a few hours of darkness remaining, the Brigade concealed both men and their vehicles in nearby farms, camouflaged the ramps with nets and confined the local population to their homes.

Shortly after midnight on 9 October the LVTs took to the water and formed into two assault groups, each carrying an infantry battalion. The North Nova Scotia Highlanders were bound for 'Green Beach,' three kilometres east of Hoofdplaat, while the Highland Light Infantry of Canada, on the left, headed for 'Amber Beach,' closer to the Braakman. Both flotillas were led by a motor boat, that on the right carrying the Naval Liaison Officer at Army Headquarters who had volunteered to navigate. As they neared the shores of the Breskens island, artillery fired coloured marker shells onto the landing beaches, scattering others widely to confuse the enemy. Both battalions landed with little difficulty. Apart from a few shots fired against the HLI, there was no enemy reaction until after dawn when the coastal guns near Flushing opened fire.

Within eight hours the LVTs had returned with The Stormont, Dundas and Glengarry Highlanders, the heavy mortars and machine guns of the Cameron Highlanders of Ottawa and Brigade Headquarters. Soon the whole brigade was advancing.

Eberding had been completely surprised, but he reacted swiftly, sending his divisional reserve to block Rockingham's advance. Soon the heavy guns at Breskens and Flushing were inflicting casualties on the Canadians. From Walcheren, two companies of infantry and some engineers from the 70th Division sailed to reinforce the 64th, their passage screened by a low-hanging mist.

Faced with mounting opposition in the difficult polder country, the Canadian advance slowed. Hoofdplaat fell to the SDG on the 10th but the HLI were unable to take Biervliet until the following day. Yet the situation here was far more promising than in 7th Brigade's bridgehead on the Leopold Canal. General Spry decided to cancel the 8th Brigade's crossing by that route and land them instead behind 9th Brigade. The main thrust of the 3rd Division would now be from east to west instead of from south to north. First, though, the western shore of the Braakman would have to be cleared.

The first reinforcement to land was the 17th Duke of York's Royal Canadian Hussars, the divisional reconnaissance regiment, fighting as infantry. They struck out towards the southwest. By the 12th, the 8th Brigade had landed and the entire 3rd Division began to advance through the polders.

The dykes which bordered them intersected to form a gridiron pattern. Their junctions were defended by the veterans of the 64th Division who fought with skill and tenacity. As so disastrously demonstrated by the Black Watch near Woensdrecht, it was impossible to cross sodden fields in the face of the interlocking fire of machine guns sited at the corners. Yet anything which moved along the dykes themselves was a sitting target.

For the Canadians there was no alternative but to take out each enemy machine-gun position in turn, a series of platoon battles, helped where possible by artillery and Wasp flame throwers. Being restricted to the dykes meant advancing on a 'one-man front.' Usually this man was a junior officer or NCO and the casualty rate among leaders mounted alarmingly.

By 15 October the North Nova Scotia Highlanders had lost every lieutenant and most of their NCOs. 'Almost every company commander that went into that Breskens battle became a casualty — not wounded, killed.'[1]

Captain Jock Anderson, the much-decorated padre of the HLI, commented that in other battles, mortar fire caused most of the casualties, about twenty percent of which were fatal. But on the Scheldt the majority were caused by machine-gun and rifle fire and the percentage of fatalities was much higher — close to fifty percent.[2]

During the first few days of the battle, the weather prevented air attacks, but, as the 8th Brigade joined the fight, the skies lifted. In four days the RAF flew 1,300 sorties against targets in the Breskens Pocket. Heavy bombers dropped 1,150 tons of bombs on the batteries at Breskens and Flushing which continued to fire in Eberding's support.

On the 14th, south of the Braakman, the 4th Armoured Division attacked in the Isabella area and met the 8th Brigade advancing from the north. Swinging to the west, by the 18th, the 8th was only ten kilometres from Oostburg at the centre of 'Scheldt Fortress South,' while the 9th was about three from Breskens on the coast.

That day the weary 7th Brigade, which had fought its way out of the confines of its restricted bridgehead, was relieved by the 157th British Infantry Brigade which had come under command of the 3rd Division. (Its parent division, the 52nd Lowland, specially trained in mountain warfare, was about to fight its first battle — below sea level.) On the 19th, the 157th occupied Aardenburg without opposition and there were joined by the 17th Hussars advancing from the east. By now the enemy had withdrawn to a shorter defensive line from Breskens to Schoondijke thence south-west through Oostburg and Sluis and along the Sluis Canal to the Leopold.

On the right the 9th Brigade had the unenviable task of capturing three of the strongest positions on the Scheldt which Rockingham allotted to his three battalions in turn. First the Stormont, Dundas and Glengarry Highlanders would capture the port of Breskens, then the Highland Light Infantry of Canada would take Schoondijke, the key to the new German defence line, and the North Nova Scotia Highlanders would assault the formidable Fort Frederik Hendrik whose guns control the entrance to the Scheldt opposite Walcheren. The Glens would attack first whilst the remainder of the brigade attempted to hold the enemy's attention with diversionary attacks. Ten regiments of artillery, heavy bombers and rocket- and cannon-firing aircraft would support them.

Breskens promised to be the most awkward objective of the lot. Surrounding it were a 20-foot anti-tank ditch full of water 12 feet deep, minefields and belts of wire. All were covered by anti-tank and machine guns. To cross them, the Glens had been allotted a squadron of special armoured vehicles of the 79th Armoured Division — flail tanks to clear paths through the mines and wire, AVREs to destroy concrete emplacements and flame-throwing Crocodiles to neutralize covering weapons and to help in clearing the town.

The afternoon before the operation, the AVREs and Flails were lining the edge of a field, loading ammunition and fuel, when disaster struck. A delayed action mine detonated under an ammunition truck, setting off a chain reaction which blew the squadron to pieces. Not a man in the field survived who was not deaf or blind.

Within an hour of learning of the tragedy, Roger Rowley, the Glens' commanding officer, received a message that he would have no bomber support. The weather in England was so bad that they could not take off. As he contemplated the problem of taking Breskens without support, a message from Brigade Headquarters at 9 p.m. postponed the operation for 24 hours. For the moment it appeared that the battalion might relax. Then, at about 10.30 p.m., came the news that the proposed delay was unacceptable at the highest level. It was claimed that Churchill himself had intervened to insist that Breskens be taken next day. Rowley had fewer than 12 hours to plan and mount a completely new operation.

At 10 a.m. on 21 October two companies of the Glens left their forming-up positions and began moving toward the anti-tank ditch. Soon the enemy was firing on the left-hand company which was advancing up the main road to the town, their whole attention directed upon them. What they did not see was C Company on the right racing in single file along the sea wall. 'It never occurred to them that we'd be so stupid,' Rowley later claimed.[3] Eight men of the company followed, carrying a light Kapok floating bridge. In little more than an hour they crossed the anti-tank ditch, cleared the enemy from their immediate area and began advancing into the town.

The enemy's heavy guns, only five kilometres away on Walcheren, now opened fire at what was point-blank range on the Canadian infantry. They in turn were engaged by the 9-inch guns of the Army's heavy artillery followed by rocket-firing Typhoons. By noon the harbour area had been cleared of the enemy and Rowley was using his considerable powers of persuasion and energy to encourage his men to open a route for Crocodiles to move into the town. By midnight Breskens was captured and Eberding had lost his last port of contact with Walcheren.[4]

Next day the HLI's attack on Schoondijke met fierce opposition and the town was not finally cleared until the 25th. The North Novas met an equally hot reception when two companies attempted to take Fort Frederik Hendrik. Nothing short of a full-scale attack supported by bombers held much hope of success and one was planned for the 25th. But German morale was crumbling. A deserter was sent back to the garrison warning them of destruction if they failed to surrender. They soon emerged carrying a white flag.[5]

9th Brigade's immediate task was done and Spry decided to withdraw them completely from action, not only to rest but to worry the enemy as to where they would be used next. Already the 7th Brigade had reentered the battle and were clearing the enemy defences westward along the coast. Further south, the Queen's Own Rifles of 8th Brigade attacked Oostburg, the remaining bastion of the enemy line. In a brilliant manouevre, they outflanked the formidable defences of the town and broke into it from the south leaving the Germans with no choice but to withdraw.

An enemy attempt to form a new defensive perimeter around Cadzand and Zuidzande was disrupted by the speed of 7th Brigade's advance along the coast. By the 30th the 8th Brigade had reached the enemy's new position along the Uitwaterings Canal at Retranchement and Sluis.

The 9th Brigade now were given the task of finishing off the enemy, whose remnants were concentrated around Knocke, whilst the 8th protected their southern flank. On the 31st the SDG Highlanders, the HLI and Le Régiment de la Chaudière seized bridgeheads over the Canal. The Chaudières, typically, solved the problem of a bridge to replace one blown by the enemy by driving a Bren carrier into the narrow canal and piling earth, steel beams and wooden planks on top of the almost submerged vehicle. Next day the HLI fought their way into Knocke and the North Nova Scotia Highlanders captured General Eberding in a concrete bunker on a nearby golf course.

In the door of the operations van at Headquarters 3rd Canadian Infantry Division, Dan Spry read the reports which had come in from his brigades, glanced up at his staff and said, 'That's over. Tell everyone to stand down.' Captain Mac Reed bent over the operations log and wrote '0950 hrs Op Switchback now complete.' Major Larry Dampier, the GS02 Operations, reached across and took the log sheets, interleaved with carbon from him. Beside the last entry he added, 'Thank God!'[6]

'Every day after the battle started, Crerar would fly over the front (a somewhat dangerous operation) in a small aircraft. . .' (Gen. Horrocks) (Photo by Major L.A. Audrain / Public Archives of Canada / PA129048)

An infantry rifleman killed by mortar fire. His chances of surviving the North-West Europe campaign, uninjured, were less than his father's in an equivalent period of the First World War.

Advance to the Seine: Headquarters of Le Régiment de Maisonneuve and an armoured car pass a knocked-out Panther. (Photo by M.M. Dean / Public Archives Canada / PA 132813)

The memorial service at Dieppe which caused a rift between Crerar and Montgomery — Lt-General H.D.G. Crerar, Major-General Charles Foulkes, Lt-General Guy Simmonds. (Photo by Lt. G.K. Bell / Public Archives Canada / PA 116584)

Lifebuoy manpack flamethrower. (Harold G. Aikman /Public Archives Canada / PA 143951)

Canadian armour blocked by mud and mines in 'The Neck' — South Beveland, October, 1944.

'Water enough for drowning'. Flooded polder country. (Harold G. Aikman / Public Archives Canada / PA 143943)

The sea pouring into Walcheren Island through gap blown by RAF — Westkapelle village, lower right. (Imperial War Museum)

The assault at Westkepelle: 'So long as the Germans made the mistake of concentrating their fire on the Support Squadron, close action was justified and losses acceptable.' The crew of a 'Landing Craft Gun' abandons ship. (Imperial War Museum)

The Supreme Commander's only visit to First Canadian Army. General Eisenhower and Major-General S. Maczek inspecting the 10th Polish Mounted Rifle Regiment near Breda, 29 November, 1944. (Photo by Lt. B.J. Gloster / Public Archives Canada /PA 12805)

Icy roads near Nijmegen, January, 1945.

A Canadian 25-pounder in action near Groesbeek, January 1945.

Canadian canoes flown to Holland to enable infantry to make silent approach to enemy positions. Men of the Lincoln and Welland Regiment rehearsing for the attack on Kapelsche Veer. (Photo by J.H. Smith / Public Archives Canada / PA 114067)

4.2-inch mortar of 2nd Princess Louise's Kensington Regiment supporting 49th British Division on Arnhem Island, January 1945. (Photo by Michael Dean / Public Archives Canada / PA 143944)

2nd Battalion, Argyll and Sutherland Highlanders, 15th Scottish Division, advancing with Churchill tanks into the Reichswald, 8 February, 1945. (Imperial War Museum)

The German border at the village of Wyler, captured by The Calgary Highlanders, 8 February, 1945. (Photo by Michael Dean / Public Archives Canada / PA 143945)

14

SOUTH BEVELAND — OPERATION VITALITY

ACROSS THE WEST SCHELDT the 2nd Division, too, had completed its part in the battle.

On 24 October the 4th Brigade began its advance up the South Beveland peninsula toward Walcheren Island, 40 kilometres to the west. Like the Breskens 'island,' it was polder country. For the first 12 kilometres their route led up a narrow three-kilometre-wide neck which abruptly doubled in width at the Beveland Ship Canal which gives access from the Rhine to Antwerp. Beyond that it widened again to some 18 kilometres. About halfway between the Canal and the near end of the causeway to Walcheren Island, was Goes, the largest town. Simonds recognized that the 'neck' and the Beveland Canal were the key obstacles to be surmounted in clearing the peninsula. He decided to turn them and speed operations by landing the 5th Brigade on the southern shore, west of the Canal.

While their battalions were completing the clearance of the Woensdrecht area, the brigade staff prepared detailed plans for the landings with the 79th Armoured Division.

By the 22nd it had become obvious that the 5th would not be free of its commitments in time for the operation. Simonds decided to replace it by 156th Brigade of the 52nd Lowland Division and the 5th Brigade's plans were handed over to them.[1]

At that time it was forecast that the 4th Brigade would seize the causeway onto Walcheren over which the other two brigades would cross to clear the Island.[2] While amphibious attacks were being planned against the south and west coasts of the Island, they might be foiled by the uncertain weather of late October, if not by the enemy. The land route might prove to be the only entrance to the Island fortress and its capture now was vital and urgent.

Leading the 4th Brigade, the Royal Regiment of Canada soon overran the defences in the narrowest part of the neck. Brigadier Fred Cabeldu then ordered a column of tanks, armoured cars and infantry to press forward to the ship canal. Mud, mines and anti-tank guns soon put paid to that venture and the battle, as elsewhere in the polders, became one for the infantry. Real progress could only be made at night. In a series of small outflanking attacks which obviously shook the confidence of the enemy, the Brigade reached Krabbendijke by the 26th. There its weary battalions halted and the 6th Brigade took up the advance.

Early that morning the 156th Brigade of the 52nd Division began landing on two beaches near Hoedekenskerke. They had sailed from Terneuzen in 176 LVTs of 79th Armoured Division and 24 Assault Landing craft of the Royal Navy which had been brought by train from Ostend to the canal at Ghent. Leading the flotilla, as in the Breskens assault, was Lieutenant Commander Franks, the naval liaison officer at First Canadian Army Headquarters. At 4:30 a.m. artillery began firing on the landing beaches, and 20 minutes later, the leading troops touched down. On the right the 4/5 Royal Scots Fusiliers were met by some ineffective shellfire but the 6th Cameronians were unopposed.[3]

During the day the British expanded their bridgehead in spite of a strong counterattack from the north which made a temporary penetration. By nightfall the 6th Cameronians had taken Oudelande, the 7th Cameronians had landed and the bridgehead was securely held. That afternoon the 6th Canadian Infantry Brigade attacked toward the formidable Beveland Canal which now had been outflanked.

Each of the Brigade's battalions was directed toward possible crossing places. In the centre the South Saskatchewan Regiment headed for the main road and rail bridges. On the right the Queen's Own Cameron Highlanders of Canada had two bridges and the vital canal locks at the northern terminus as their objective, while Les Fusiliers de Mont-Royal had the equally important southern locks to capture.

During the advance the Brigade lost its dynamic commander, Brigadier Guy Gauvreau, seriously injured when his jeep struck a mine. That bullets are no respecters of rank had already been shown on the 16th when Lt-Colonel T.A. Lewis, commanding the 8th Brigade, was killed by machine-gun fire south of the Scheldt. The deputy commander of the 156th Brigade and his batman were luckier. They were the only survivors of a direct hit on their LVT.

As dawn broke on a wet and windy 27 October, the Camerons saw that all bridges over the canal had been blown and that the enemy were holding the far bank. Quick crossings were defeated by German mortar fire and when they attempted a boat crossing, eight of their nine assault boats were sunk. In the centre, after initial setbacks, the South Saskatchewans managed to scramble across broken bridges and seized a foothold which they held against two counterattacks. Eventually the Fusiliers too were successful. Wading through waist deep water at night, they reached the locks which they crossed hand-over-hand, and fell upon the rear of a surprised enemy, 120 of whom they took prisoner. By noon, a bridge had been completed on the SSR front and the 4th and 5th Brigades began advancing through the 6th.

On the right the 8th Reconnaissance Regiment worked westward along the north coast. On the 31st members of the Dutch Resistance told Major Dick Porteous, commanding the leading squadron, that there was a small German garrison on the island of North Beveland which lies some 400 metres away across a channel of the Scheldt called the Zand Kreek. Through it the enemy still kept open a line of communications to their troops on Walcheren.

That night Porteous and his squadron, with a company of heavy mortars and machine guns of the Toronto Scottish, commandeered boats and barges near a ferry station and crossed to the island. They found the German garrison concentrated in the town of Kamperland near its western end and demanded their surrender, which was refused. The Canadians responded with 4.2-inch mortar bombs.

By this time, Porteous had been joined by Lt-Colonel Mowbray Alway, his commanding officer, who called for air support. 84 Group was completely committed by this time to operations on Walcheren but agreed to direct a squadron across North Beveland in a show of strength. Alway warned the enemy that his supporting aircraft would make one pass over Kamperland without firing but that on the next they would blow them off the face of the earth.

On schedule, 18 Typhoons roared across the island at 50 feet. The sound of their engines had not faded before the first Germans were seen emerging from the town carrying a white flag. In all, over 450 prisoners surrendered to the 8th Recce on North Beveland.

By the 29th it was obvious that South Beveland would soon be clear. Two brigades of the 52nd Division were ashore and their artillery had joined them by the land route through Antwerp. The 4th Brigade had met them near Gravenpolder and was advancing to the west. The 5th had liberated Goes. The weary 2nd Division was nearing the end of its task.

Ahead lay only the causeway which carried a road, a railway and a bicycle path and a thin line of poplars to Walcheren Island. Across it in the past few days, the retreating remnants of the German garrison of South Beveland had been withdrawing.

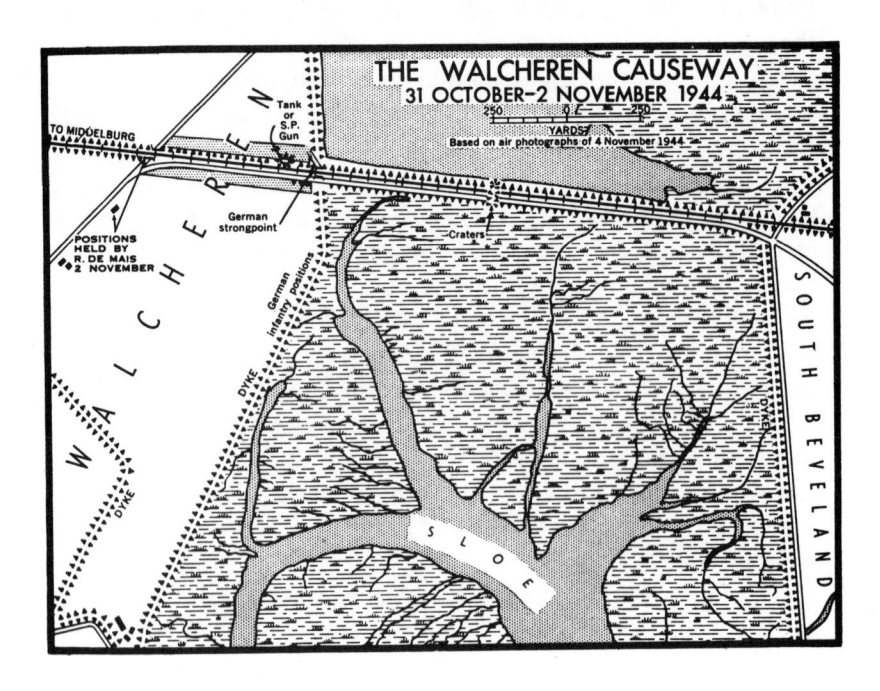

THE WALCHEREN CAUSEWAY
31 OCTOBER–2 NOVEMBER 1944
Based on air photographs of 4 November 1944

They had fought well enough but since the crossing of the Beveland Canal, their resistance had faltered. An increasing number of prisoners were surrendering and their casualties in dead and wounded had been heavy.

Within the 2nd Division, little was known about the enemy on Walcheren. A large-scale map with an overprint issued on 23 October showed in some detail the German defences east of the Causeway but indicated none at its western end.[4]

Yet, if the enemy continued to retreat as he had been doing in the past few days, there was a possibility that the Causeway could be 'bounced' — taken by a swift, bold stroke — at little cost. And if it were, the opportunity of taking Middelburg, the island's main town, only four kilometres distant, could not be ignored.

Late on the 30th the Royal Regiment were within 800 metres of the east end of the Causeway. They expected to take the enemy positions covering it by morning. Earlier that afternoon, Brigadier Keefler, the acting commander of the 2nd Division, asked Brigadier Cabeldu 'to try and exploit further and push a bridgehead over the causeway to enable another brigade, possibly of the 52nd Division, to pass through.'[5] At the same time he ordered Brigadier Megill of 5th Brigade to make a plan for clearing the eastern part of Walcheren Island presumably in the event that the 52nd Division was not available.[6]

Cabeldu did not like the idea. A glance at a large-scale map showed what a daunting task it was likely to be. Rising a few feet above sodden mud flats, the bare 40-metre-wide causeway led 1,000 metres straight across the gap from the mainland. There was not a vestige of cover on it to shield troops from the enemy guns which must surely be trained upon it. And it was mined. On either side the mud flats were bare at low tide but were hidden at high water. He reckoned that a direct assault across the causeway had a slim chance of success if it were carried out by fresh troops. Otherwise a major water crossing would be involved such as that rehearsed in England before the invasion by some units of the Division in anticipation of an assault-crossing of the Seine. It would take some time to mount, and he knew that 5th Brigade had already made plans for it. He discussed the problem with his battalion commanders who agreed with him, then drove to divisional headquarters at Goes to see Keefler. He put the case that given the tired state of his troops — and of the other brigades — an attempt to force a direct passage over the causeway had little chance of success. It would be better to try a storm-boat crossing. In the interests of speed, 5th Brigade, who had done some planning, should be given the task. The Calgary Highlanders of that brigade were one of the two units in the Division who had the necessary training.

Keefler agreed.[7]

Shortly after the advance onto Beveland began, the task of planning an assault across the Causeway had been shifted from the 4th to the 5th Brigade. On the 29th, the 5th Brigade's diarist noted: 'Our job has not changed — we are still to go on as fast as possible to secure the causeway'; words which imply taking its western end.

Few tried to hide their disappointment when their brigadier told them on the 30th, without any suggestion that it was a contingency plan, that they were not to 'bounce' the Causeway but to prepare to clear the unflooded part of Walcheren Island. Preliminary orders had been issued to battalions who had briefed their men when word was received that the operation was 'off.' The 52nd Division would clear the island. The Brigade was ordered to 'stand down' and it was now widely believed that they were to be withdrawn for rest. After a peaceful night they learned that Keefler had changed his mind. 5th Brigade were to secure a bridgehead on Walcheren Island for the 52nd Division.[8]

The changes of plans, the disappointment inflicted on weary troops and what was to follow gave rise to bitterness and rumour. It was said that Keefler had set a race for the 4th and 5th Brigades. The one which failed to reach the causeway first would have the task of assaulting across it — a cynical way to avoid a commander's responsibility for selecting men for a hazardous mission. The official history states that he had indeed said that, but, in fact, he had selected the 5th Brigade for the task early in the advance. Later he contemplated giving the job to 4th Brigade but decided against it after Cabeldu's representations. Nonetheless, before the operation began, officers and men of the 5th Brigade gained the impression that indecision and chance, or both, were playing an undue part in their fate.

Simmering beneath the surface, especially in the Black Watch, was a sense of outrage at the way they had been handled in the past. For them, it had begun when their rifle companies had been practically wiped out in their first major battle in Normandy and had flared up after the disaster of Operation Angus near Woensdrecht only two weeks earlier. In four months they had had more than 1,400 casualties, a rate far in excess of that of infantry battalions in the First World War. The Calgary Highlanders' casualties were only slightly lower, while those of Le Régiment de Maisonneuve were considerably less, a reflection not of lack of aggressiveness on their part, but of a chronic shortage of reinforcements even worse than in the English-speaking regiments. Any operation about to be undertaken by troops who had been subjected to such severe strains would have to be carefully handled indeed.

So serious was the situation in the Black Watch that Bruce Ritchie, their commanding officer, appended a note to the War Diary of 31 October, 1944, describing the critical situation which had arisen from the shortage of officers, and NCOs and from the lack of training of private soldiers who came to replace their casualties. He added these chilling lines:

> The morale of the Battalion at rest is good. However it must be said that 'Battle Morale' is definitely not good due to the fact that inadequately trained men are, of necessity, being sent into action ignorant of any idea of their own strength, and after their first mortaring, overwhelmingly convinced of the enemy's. This feeling is no doubt increased by their ignorance of fieldcraft in its most elementary form.

On the morning of the 31st at 10 a.m. Megill broke the news to his commanding officers that the 5th Brigade was to form a bridgehead on Walcheren Island. The Black Watch would lead the attack by sending a company across the Causeway to determine whether or not a crossing by that route was feasible. The Calgary Highlanders would, in the meantime, prepare to cross the water gap by storm boats at high water, about midnight, when the tide would measure 14 feet. They would be followed by the Maisonneuve.

If the Black Watch were successful in crossing, the Brigade

would follow them over the Causeway.[9] Few thought that there was much likelihood of that happening. On past form, the Germans would have every inch of it covered by fire, and the gallant old militia regiment from Montreal was heading for another disaster.

While the Watch made ready for their advance to the Causeway, Major Ross Ellis of the Calgaries prepared for the storm-boat assault. Only a pitifully small number of those who had trained in England for the Seine crossing survived, there were no covered approaches to the launching sites and practically nothing was known of the German defences. Having explained his reservations to the brigade commander and being told to 'get on with it,' he ordered Captain Francis H. Clarke to run a 'crash' training programme.

> I couldn't believe the storm-boat idea. When I got the order from Ross Ellis, I presumed to say that he had to be kidding. He wasn't. With my veteran platoon commanders, John Moffat and Walt LeFroy, and one or two NCOs, we drew boat outlines on the ground pending the arrival of the Engineers with the real thing, and proceeded with loading and off-loading drills. All the time I, and I believe others, were praying that sanity would return to someone in a position and prepared to stop it before too late.[10]

Close to midday, C Company of the Watch, commanded by Captain H.S. Lamb, stepped onto the Causeway as enemy shell and mortar fire burst about the approaches. As they advanced, machine guns began a cross-fire whose effect was limited by poor visibility but snipers located in the marshy flats beside the Causeway, were deadly. Beyond the halfway mark, the company found a huge crater or furrow filled with water which effectively destroyed any hope that tanks would be able to follow them. Beyond it, the leading platoon worked forward to within 75 metres of the far bank. Then all forward movement halted as a constant hail of shell, mortar and machine-gun fire drove the company to dig in. One very heavy enemy gun sought out the men on the Causeway sending plumes of water 200 feet high when its shells dropped short. At least one high-velocity gun was firing down the road from close range, ricocheting armour-piercing shells off the road, close to the much-depleted company. Later, even with darkness to shield them, it was impossible to evacuate their casualties since the slightest sound of movement drew a storm of enemy fire.[11]

The Black Watch had found the expected answer to the strength of the German opposition. And while they occupied the enemy's attention, engineer officers discovered something else — even at high tide there would be insufficient water for boats to cross to Walcheren and the mud flats would not support amphibious vehicles. There was no other route forward for the 5th Brigade but the Causeway. Megill ordered the Black Watch to hold the position near the far end and the Calgary Highlanders to pass through them and establish a bridgehead. Once they had done so, the Maisonneuve would follow and expand it.[12]

Major Ellis's plan was for his leading company to seize an arc about 200 metres deep around the end of the Causeway. His following companies would extend this to a depth of about 1,000 metres, each being centred on a key road junction. Supporting them would be field and medium artillery, 40mm Bofors AA guns, 4.2-inch mortars and medium machine guns. Co-opting the mortar platoons of other battalions, he arranged for each of his companies to be supported by six three-inch mortars whose high angle of fire could reach an enemy close by on the far side of a dyke.[13]

At midnight Captain Nobby Clarke with B Company began to cross, while artillery concentrations were directed at suspected enemy positions. But they were not all covered. The Germans had moved in more close-support weapons which poured a withering fire into the advancing Highlanders. The leading platoon soon practically ceased to exist. Clarke coolly assessed the situation and asked for permission to withdraw his men to the crater in the centre of the Causeway, while a new fire support plan was made. It was granted and he and Ellis went to Megill's tactical headquarters to explain the situation.

Ellis told the brigadier that, with a new fire plan, he reckoned that the Calgaries could establish a bridgehead but that, because their strength was so depleted, they would be unable to hold it for long. He recommended that the Maisonneuve should be sent over early to help.[14]

It was 6:05 a.m. when D Company of the Calgaries set out to cross the Causeway. This time the barrage extended well onto the mud flats to take care of snipers. Forty-five minutes later the leading platoon commanded by Sergeant 'Blackie' Laloge had inched their way to within 25 yards of a road block covered by concrete positions at the western end. There they were pinned down by machine-gun and 20mm cannon fire.

Major Bruce MacKenzie, the company commander, examined the block with distaste. There was no clever alternative to a direct assault. He announced his conclusions in pure western Canadian, 'Shit!'[15]

Huddled in a shell hole with Laloge, he radioed for a two minute artillery concentration at 'intense rate' to pound the German positions ahead. As the last shell burst, D Company were on their feet and charging the road block. Men fell in the withering cross-fire of MG42s but speed protected others who, within seconds, were in the German position, spraying the defenders with automatic fire. Fourteen prisoners surrendered and MacKenzie's men began fighting their way toward their objectives, unaware that they had stepped foot on Walcheren Island at almost the same moment that British commandos had landed at Flushing.

At 9:33 MacKenzie reported that his small bridgehead was secure but casualties had been heavy. Ellis ordered A and B companies to cross and move out to the north and south respectively but to be wary of the high-velocity gun which was still bouncing shells off the roadway. When both were near their objectives, enemy fire on the Causeway once more became so hot that C Company following them was forced to take cover.

Probing south from the western end of the Causeway, B Company was strung out along the bottom of the dyke which marked the edge of the tidal mud plain, their objective a group of farm buildings some 50 metres inland from it. The top of the dyke and the intervening ground were devoid of cover and raked with automatic fire. They needed mortar and artillery support to keep the enemy's heads down. With both his radios knocked out, Nobby Clarke sent back two runners with requests for fire support but neither reached battalion headquarters.

> I clearly recall my despair and exasperation at our position because we could actually see battalion observers across the flood plain on the far dyke. We prayed that they would appreciate our position and act . . . a ridiculous and foolish hope.[16]

A Company too were under such heavy fire that they could not move. A determined German counterattack nearly penetrated to the end of the Causeway but stopped and fell back before a furious Sergeant Laloge of D Company hurling grenades practically into their faces. Brigade headquarters asked Ellis when he would be clear of the Causeway so that the Maisonneuve could cross. He replied, 'Not before 13.30.'

At 3:45 p.m. Ellis, accompanied by George Hees, the brigade major, crossed the Causeway to see the situation for himself. They returned but set out for the other side once more when they learned that Captain Win Lasher, the only officer in A Company, had been wounded for the third time. Hees volunteered to replace him and another artillery officer, Captain Bill Newman, offered to serve as his second-in-command.[17]

The German fire and counterattacks mounted in ferocity until there was imminent danger of A and B Companies being cut off. There was no alternative for the few who were left but to pull back behind D Company.

With communications destroyed, no orders for the withdrawal were received by Nobby Clarke:

> I became aware that . . . 'D' were moving back along the Causeway toward the crater. When I went to ascertain the situation at my rear, I found Sgt Laloge swearing something fierce and returning Gerry grenades as fast as they arrived over the dyke. Unfortunately he didn't get them all because the handle from one of them struck one of my lads and broke his leg. I put a rifle splint on it and we lowered him into a slit trench, remembering to prop him up because, with the tide, the trench would partly fill with water.
>
> I was now in danger of being cut off. I simply had to maintain contact with 'D' at my rear so we began working back. You can believe me that this was the last thing I wanted to do.[18]

Ross Ellis now ordered A and C Companies to dig in near the cratered area and reported to Megill for orders. He was told to hold fast until instructions were obtained from divisional headquarters. Hours went by while the Highlanders waited under constant heavy fire. It was past midnight when they learned that Megill had ordered Le Régiment de Maisonneuve to pass through them on the Causeway and establish a small, tight bridgehead which 157th Brigade could exploit.[19]

The War Diary of the 5th Brigade on 2 November reflected one facet of the uncertain direction of the Causeway battle.

> During the early hours of the morning the plan was changed by Div HQ once more. Now the **R DE MAIS** are to be relieved at 0500 hrs by 157 Bde, only one hour after they start their push. This will result in a one company bridgehead only. CALG HIGHRS are to pull out as soon as the **R DE MAIS** company have gone through in order to make way for 157 Bde's leading battalion (Glasgow Highlanders).
>
> ... at 0400 hrs they started over. Once again they received the same type of reception as the other two battalions and had great difficulty in getting over the causeway and were held up temporarily by shell and mortar fire.

By the time Captain Camille Montpetit's D Company had struggled onto Walcheren it had been reduced to less than 40 men. Charles Forbes, commanding the leading platoon, captured an anti-tank gun which had been firing down the Causeway and pressed on to a house which was their objective. The remnants of the company soon were fighting a confused and hair-raising battle in the dark, uncertain either of their own or the enemy's locations. Somewhere close by, three 20mm automatic AA guns were pumping a mixture of high explosive and armour-piercing shells into the Canadian positions.

Dawn broke grey and dirty for the Maisonneuve on Walcheren and there was no sign of the British troops who were to relieve them. But there were Germans aplenty. A column of them, withdrawing toward Middelburg, came down the road toward Forbes' position from the *east*. Nearby, across a dyke, Guy de Merlis watched, PIAT ready, as a tank moved toward his position. Then suddenly that menace was no more, as rockets from an RAF Typhoon lifted the turret from its hull. Then Private J.-C. Carrière took the PIAT, crawled down a ditch full of water and destroyed one of the 20mm guns which had been making life difficult for the platoon.[10]

At 5th Brigade Headquarters, an imperial row had blown up. The progress of the battle for the Causeway had been watched with keen interest and mounting disbelief by officers of the 52nd Division as Megill sent three battalions in succession along that road of death. Their military instincts were revolted by this violation of a cardinal principle — never to reinforce failure. They did not question the need to take a bridgehead on Walcheren and they could not at the moment suggest another way to cross. But given time, they would find one. Of one thing they were certain — there had to be a better way to fight this battle.

Major-General Edmund Hakewill-Smith, commanding the 52nd, who now was to command all the operations on Walcheren Island, had been opposed to the concept of the 5th Brigade's frontal attack from the outset. When on 1 November, Charles Foulkes, the acting commander of the 2nd Canadian Corps, ordered him to send his men across the Causeway, he refused, saying he would find another route. In an atmosphere of mounting acrimony, the discussion ended with Foulkes threatening to sack him if the 52nd Division failed to attack within the next 48 hours.[21]

Brigadier J.D. Russell of 157th Brigade was already urgently looking for an alternative to the Causeway for his troops to cross, when Megill demanded that he relieve the Maisonneuve. Russell was unwilling to commit his brigade to the operation but finally agreed to send over as many men as the Maisonneuve had on the opposite side of the Causeway. It was accepted that there were no more than forty.

The history of the 52nd Division described the scene:

> It was at six o'clock on the morning of November 2, 1944, that No. 10 Platoon of B Company of the Glasgow Highlanders started to lead the battalion into hell. That conventional phrase does not exaggerate the horrific situation. The Germans had . . . the Causeway completely taped and plastered. The smoke of continual explosions eddied always over the embankments. The noise and incessant shocks tried the stoutest of nerves. The whole of the dam, sides and surface, was pockmarked with craters. The trees were splintered parodies of green growth. To move a foot in daylight was nearly impossible; to advance a yard in the darkness was an adventurous success.[22]

Behind them, three companies of the regiment moved onto the Causeway to take over the Canadian positions.

When the Scots reached the Maisonneuve, the enemy fire was so intense that it was impossible for anyone to move. Two hours later, covered by a smoke screen, both pulled back to the Causeway.

During the night of 1 November, two young men, Lieutenant F. Turner, MC, and Sergeant Humphrey of 202 Field Company, Royal Engineers, embarked on one of the most dangerous and technically challenging reconnaissances imaginable. After carefully studying airphotographs, they set out to cross the Slooe channel three kilometres south of the causeway. Picking their way through the quicksand-like mudflats, where more than a hundred Germans were lost in 1940, they found a path which might be followed by infantry and returned to report to a relieved Brigadier Russell. Next night Turner, with three sappers, returned to Walcheren marking the path with tape.

In the cold hours before dawn next day, the 6th Battalion of The Cameronians picked their way across, following the tape, and were ashore on the sea-dyke before they were seen by the enemy. Their reception was typically violent. Counterattacks threatened to engulf the left flank of the bridgehead while the crossing area was heavily shelled. But the build-up of strength continued until the 5th Highland Light Infantry were ashore and able to attack. The going was not easy but next day, in a headlong assault, the HLI broke through the German ring and linked up with their comrades in the Glasgow Highlanders at the Causeway.[23]

What happened to them later belongs in the account of the battle of Walcheren Island.

The soldiers of the 2nd Division left South Beveland with a feeling of relief that they had seen the last of polders and of the Scheldt. They put the past behind them and gave little thought to the future, determined to make the most of a week's rest in the outskirts of Antwerp.

They did not know, nor would they have been much interested to learn, that not enough had been done to even the odds against them at Woensdrecht and that the responsibility for that was shared by Montgomery and Eisenhower. But the battle for the Causeway was a different matter. In the words of one soldier, 'It was a bad deal.'[24] By coincidence, the 5th Brigade's numbers who fought there were almost the same as the 600 of The Light Brigade at Balaclava. Like them they have left us a rare example of discipline and gallantry. And those who came back from that Causeway of death believe to this day that they were ordered across by the military heirs to Lords Lucan and Cardigan.

15

WALCHEREN ISLAND — OPERATION INFATUATE

AT LAST the assault had begun against the strongest concentration of defences the Nazis had ever devised — the main bastion of Fortress Scheldt — Walcheren Island.

Nowhere on the Atlantic wall, in Normandy, Dieppe or in the Pas de Calais, were so many heavy casemated guns trained on the sea approaches. Beaches were mined and bristled with obstacles. A full infantry division, the 70th, stood ready to counter any breach of the defences while batteries of anti-aircraft guns covered the skies above.

Intelligence reports had spoken disparagingly of Lt-General Wilhelm Daser's troops as an 'ulcer' division — a sort of convalescent unit where soldiers suffering from stomach complaints were fed on milk, eggs and white bread. So it was, but as the 2nd Division, who had met them on Beveland could attest, they were veteran soldiers and their intestinal complaints had remarkably little effect on their willingness or ability to fight.

The island, roughly square in shape, sits at the mouth of the Scheldt, its southern corner with the town of Flushing directly opposite Breskens. Much of it is below sea level. Except for some higher ground in the east and north it is rimmed by dykes which hold back the sea.

On 13 September Montgomery asked Crerar to begin planning for the island's capture, saying that parachute troops would be available and that bombing to destroy the forts on the island was to begin at once. 'On the day concerned we can lay on for you the whole weight of the heavy bomber effort from England, both Bomber Command and 8th Air Force.'

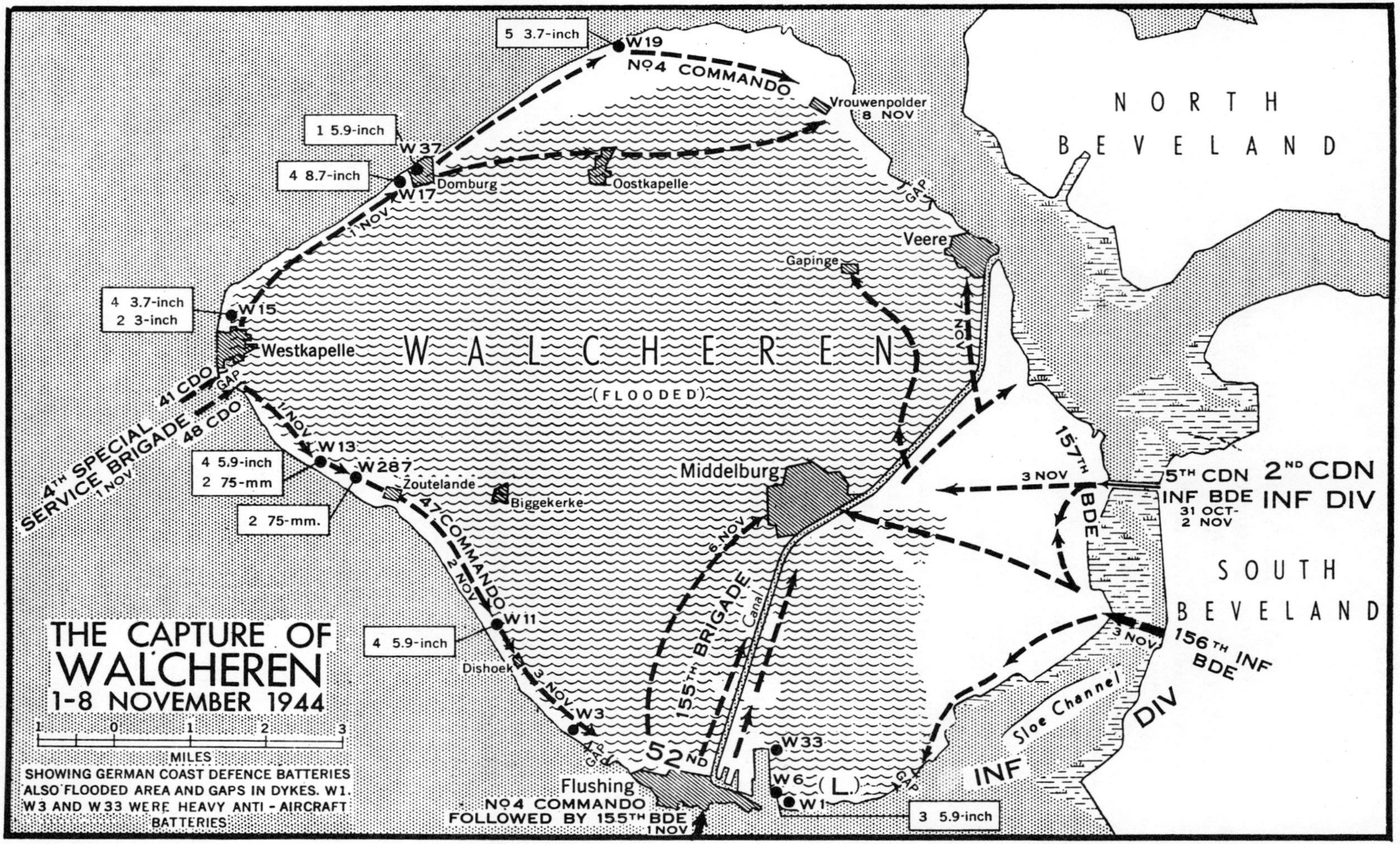
THE CAPTURE OF WALCHEREN
1-8 NOVEMBER 1944
MILES
SHOWING GERMAN COAST DEFENCE BATTERIES ALSO FLOODED AREA AND GAPS IN DYKES. W1. W3 AND W33 WERE HEAVY ANTI - AIRCRAFT BATTERIES
NORTH BEVELAND
SOUTH BEVELAND
WALCHEREN
(FLOODED)
5 3.7-inch
W19
No.4 COMMANDO
Vrouwenpolder 8 NOV
1 5.9-inch
W37
4 8.7-inch
W17
Domburg
Oostkapelle
1 NOV
GAP
Veere
Gapinge
7 NOV
4 3.7-inch
2 3-inch
W15
Westkapelle
41 CDO
48 CDO
4TH SPECIAL SERVICE BRIGADE
1 NOV
4 5.9-inch
2 75-mm
W13
W287
2 75-mm.
Zoutelande
Biggekerke
47 COMMANDO
2 NOV
Middelburg
157TH BDE
3 NOV
5TH CDN INF BDE
31 OCT-2 NOV
2ND CDN INF DIV
4 5.9-inch
W11
Dishoek
3 NOV
W3
6 NOV
155TH BRIGADE
Canal
52ND (L.) INF DIV
W33
W6
W1
3 5.9-inch
Flushing
No.4 COMMANDO FOLLOWED BY 155TH BDE
1 NOV
156TH INF BDE
Sloe Channel

General Guy Simonds' plans for taking Walcheren were conceived when Crerar assigned 2nd Corps the responsibility for clearing the Scheldt estuary on 21 September. Some details were altered later to reflect developments as the Scheldt battles progressed but his original concept remained unchanged.

His proposals were revolutionary:

I consider that the technique for the capture of Walcheren Island should be as follows:
a) Bombing operations should be undertaken to break the dykes and completely flood all parts of the island below high water level.
b) Those parts of the island which remain above water should then be systematically attacked by heavy air bombardment, day and night, to destroy defences and wear out the garrison by attrition. RDF (radar) stations should have an early priority as 'point' targets.
c) Whenever possible, heavy bombers proceeding to or from targets in western Germany by day or night should be routed over Walcheren so that the garrison can never tell whether the approach of large numbers of aircraft indicates attack or not. This combined with heavy bombing attacks will drive the enemy to cover on approach of large aircraft formations and will help to cover eventual airborne landing.

He went on to describe the conditions under which airborne and waterborne assaults should take place and the arrangements for the necessary training. The 2nd Canadian Division was to 'exploit the land approach along South Beveland as far as practicable.'[1]

Originally he planned to use a brigade of the 3rd Canadian Division to assault the beaches on the north and west of the Island, while the 2nd Division crossed from Beveland. When the 4th Special Service Brigade became available on 23 September, they were given the amphibious role. It was not until late October that he could be sure that the 52nd Division would be able to take over the main responsibility for clearing the Island from the 2nd Division, a fact which caused some uncertainty in that formation immediately before the Causeway battle.

Crerar agreed with his proposals but when he was taken ill a few days later and Simonds replaced him as Army Commander, two key questions had not been answered — would airborne troops be available and was it practicable or desirable to breach the Walcheren dykes by bombing?

Undoubtedly parachute or glider landings on Walcheren would have been hazardous. Taking the advice of General Brereton, the American commander of 1st Allied Airborne Army, Eisenhower decided against it. Later, on 21 October, when Simonds asked for a parachute brigade to be dropped at the western end of South Beveland, he was told that all allied airborne forces had been placed in support of General Bradley who was planning to make full use of them.[2] Their next drop did not take place until March, 1945.

Predictably the proposal to flood Walcheren by bombing met with immediate opposition. Experts, including army engineers and officers of Bomber Command, thought it could not be done. The dykes were immense. That near Westkapelle was 25 to 30 feet high and in places, over 300 feet wide. It had withstood the ravages of the sea since the fifteenth century. Even the most accurate bombing was unlikely to create a breach, and if it did so, it would probably silt up. Others thought the proposal immoral or politically undesirable. To visit ruin upon the rich farm lands and orchards of a close friend and ally was a terrible step to take. But flooding Walcheren offered the hope of speeding the opening of Antwerp, of saving the lives of allied soldiers, of shortening the war and of an earlier rescue of the Dutch people held under Nazi yoke.

At first Crerar accepted the judgement of the experts but Simonds persisted. If they did not flood the island, he feared that the Germans would let in water enough to soak the polders and create another 'Breskens pocket': 'So many military advantages to us would result if flooding could be achieved that it should be done if it's technically possible.' To him the advantages were obvious. The enemy would be restricted to a limited area where it would be easier to attack them. Their reserves would be immobilized or destroyed. Communications would be cut. It might be possible for amphibious troops to enter the island through breaches in the dykes and attack the fixed German defences from the rear. Bomber Command consented to make the attempt providing the Supreme Commander agreed. His approval was received on 1 October.

In the meantime, Simonds, now Army Commander, had directed Brigadier Geoffrey Walsh, the Chief Engineer, to look again at the proposal and recommend where the dykes should be breached. He, in turn, summoned one of his staff, an untidy-looking captain with a moustache like Bairnsfather's 'Old Bill.' Noted amongst his colleagues for being unimpressed by the near-legendary irascibility of his brigadier, Capt R.C. West was a brilliant engineer intelligence officer. For two days and nights, he studied air photographs, charts and tide tables, then reported his conclusions. Breaches should be attempted at three precise points, near Westkapelle, Weere and Flushing, at specific times when the force of the tides was greatest. 'Spot' West's recommendations were forwarded to Bomber Command and formed the basis of their plan.[3]

On 3 October 243 heavy bombers dropped 1,263 tons of high explosive on the Westkapelle dyke. That evening aerial photographs showed the sea flowing in through a 75-yard gap which was widening. Later the dykes at Flushing and Veere were struck. By the end of October, the island resembled a saucer filled with water.

When Eisenhower turned down Simonds request for airborne troops, he promised to call on Bomber Command and the 8th U.S. Air Force 'for the complete saturation of the targets you select. All medium bombers will also be made available to assist.' That did not happen and many soldiers, sailors and marines died as a result.

There were a number of small attacks by Bomber Command on Walcheren during September, chiefly against coast defence batteries. In all they dropped 616 tons of bombs, nothing like the amount used in support of the Canadian Army in Normandy or against the Channel ports. At the end of that month Air Chief Marshal Sir Trafford Leigh-Mallory, with Eisenhower's approval, asked Montgomery to agree to limiting the amount of air preparation at Walcheren in favour of concentrating on oil and industrial targets in Western Germany. He proposed that the attacks on Walcheren should 'take the form of a limited number of attacks on specially selected objectives to commence forthwith, followed by an intensive preparation by all bomber resources available during the three days prior to the assault, this to be followed by the maximum assistance to the assault itself.' Montgomery agreed. First Canadian Army had lost both its fight for airborne troops and its high priority for bomber support. The U.S. 8th Air Force was never seen over Walcheren and the RAF Bomber Command's attacks were inadequate, not only because of Leigh-Mallory's restrictions, but because of bad weather at the time of the assault.

It later became clear that the Air Force simply did not understand the problem. They ruled 'that heavy bomber support should be provided only when ground troops are going to assault the bombed positions immediately afterwards' — a principle sound enough for operations in the open field. But at Walcheren the targets were permanent defences, concrete positions which could only be destroyed by a heavy weight of bombs, and once hit, could not be repaired.

In previous operations, Crerar had dealt directly with Bomber Command. A good relationship had developed between the Canadians and Air Chief Marshal Sir Arthur Harris. On 21 September 'Bomber' Harris sent a personal message to both Crerar and Simonds thanking them for their messages of appreciation for his crews' work at Boulogne: 'Will be interested to hear your casualties and any new suggestions for next chapter. Suggest that where no allied civilians are involved we dig out final objective for you in addition to outer approaches.'[4] It reinforced one he had sent three days before: 'You can count on maximum support from Bomber Command whenever you are convinced that it is necessary.'[5] But now Eisenhower's staff insisted that all requests for support be channelled through them.

As is so often the case in war, the commanders immediately responsible for fighting a battle are eager to help each other uninfluenced by service politics. If Simonds had been able to explain his problems directly to Harris, there is little doubt that he would have risen to the challenge of destroying the deadly German fixed defences.

During October Bomber Command dropped 5,306 tons of bombs on factories and oil refineries and 51,312 tons on cities, but 'army support and tactical targets received only 9,728 tons.'[6]

In the same month 2nd Tactical Air Force made several rocket and bombing attacks on radar stations and ammunition stores, and, with Bomber Command, attacked the batteries near Flushing which were firing on the 3rd Division in the Breskens pocket. In the three days beginning on 28 October the Tactical Air Force and Bomber Command concentrated on the enemy's batteries, but there was no flying on the 31st.

By this time the impression had grown among senior air officers that First Canadian Army was relying on Bomber Command to do their job for them. One air marshal is reputed to have said that after the weight of bombs delivered to Walcheren, he could have taken the place with his batman. The Deputy Supreme Allied Commander, Air Chief Marshal Tedder, thought the Canadians had been 'drugged with bombs.' They were all too ready to misinterpret any request. When Simonds' staff asked that Bomber Command should attack four pinpointed targets in order to 'destroy defences, disrupt communications and demoralize the enemy' in Flushing, an air officer at SHAEF translated this as a request for area bombing. Tedder asked why the army was asking that Flushing should be flattened, which was not the case. The request was refused. An appeal was made saying that the Germans were reinforcing Flushing and strengthening the defences on its outskirts. Because the first refusal had been reported to Churchill and the Combined Chiefs of Staff, the Air Force now felt it necessary to obtain their approval for engaging this tactical target. Eventually it was agreed that it might be attacked, but only by Mosquitoes of the 2nd Tactical Air Force — a niggardly response which again was to cost men's lives.

In the meantime, preparations for the assault on Walcheren were under way. Naval Force T, commanded by Captain A.F. Pugsley, was training with Brigadier Leicester's 4th Special Service Brigade at Ostend. Assault landing craft and Buffaloes sailed from Terneuzen to Breskens under cover of smoke to join the 52nd Division for the assault on Flushing. More than 300 guns controlled by Brigadier Bruce Matthews, the artillery commander of 2nd Corps, were deployed near Breskens and Fort Frederik Hendrik. They would lend formidable support to the landings at Flushing but only a few heavy and super heavy guns could reach the batteries north of Westkapelle. Operating with them was a new unit, an experimental rocket battery armed with 12 projectors developed as a Canadian project in the United Kingdom and known by the code name of 'Land Mattresses.' For 'Infatuate' they were manned by the 112th Light Anti-Aircraft Battery, Royal Canadian Artillery.

Two seaborne assaults by 4th Special Service Brigade were to be launched against Walcheren on the same day. The first by No. 4 Commando would be against Flushing. Four hours later the remainder of the Brigade would land on the western side of the Island near Westkapelle. The 155th Brigade would be in reserve at Breskens, ready to follow through at Flushing if the initial assault was successful. If it failed, it was to move overland to Ostend and then land at Westkapelle. The attacks from South Beveland would be scheduled to coincide with them. D Day would be 1 November.

At 4:45 that morning the soft bubbling of the exhausts of 20 assault landing craft rose to a full roar as they set out from Breskens harbour for Flushing, five and one-half kilometres across the Scheldt. Simultaneously the artillery opened fire on the port defences and on the enemy batteries nearby. Overhead the last of No. 2 Group's Mosquitoes were returning home, leaving behind a fire burning ashore which silhouetted a windmill — a useful guide to the landing beach.

At 5:40 the artillery switched to targets on the flanks of the beach. Five minutes later, in the darkest hour of the night, the leading Commandos landed and swiftly overran anti-tank guns and pillboxes before their occupants could fire a shot. Then the German defences came to life. 20mm cannon and machine-gun fire swept the beach and the main group of landing craft as they came in, but none were stopped. In the grey early light Commandos began to work into the town, closely followed by the 4th Battalion, King's Own Scottish Borderers while behind them landed the remainder of the 155th Brigade. A fierce battle developed for the port and its ship building yards and for the fortifications which covered them. As visibility improved Typhoons of 84 Group came to the help of the infantry.

In the dock area enemy suicide squads in the cranes and gantries swept the area with machine-gun fire. They gave the

Lowlanders a unique opportunity to put their specialized training to use. 452 Mountain Battery was equipped with 3.7-inch guns which could be broken down for carrying on pack animals. Two of these were dismantled and taken to the upper floors of nearby houses where they were reassembled and engaged the Germans at point-blank range, the boxes of the cranes dissolving in smoke. As one fired a final satisfying shot, the weight of the gun and its recoil proved to be too much for an old house. The floor caved in and the gun with its crew crashed through the next floor to the ground. From the debris, Bombardier John Walker was heard to exclaim, 'Saves us hauling the bloody thing downstairs!'[7]

Four hours after the first landing at Flushing, Royal Marine Commandos were due to touch down on the west coast of the Island near Westkapelle. The odds against Infatuate II, as the operation was called, were high but so were the stakes. Success would speed the opening of Antwerp and shorten the war. With failure would go any hope of a swift capture of Walcheren and the 52nd Division would be faced with a costly piecemeal reduction of the enemy's defences.

Around the rim of the Island, the Germans had constructed a series of coast defence batteries armed with weapons ranging from 22cm guns capable of engaging a battleship to captured British 3.7-inch anti-aircraft guns deadly to landing craft. Smaller guns covered the beaches while many of the anti-aircraft batteries could also fire against surface targets.

Unless these were neutralized, most of the assaulting landing craft would be sunk before they reached the beach. Much depended on the effectiveness of the RAF's preliminary bombing, on the naval bombardment during the landings, on close air support and the fire of the Army's heavy guns from Breskens.

The whole operation depended on the weather, which, on the North Sea Coast at the end of October, was at best uncertain.

Brigadier Leicester's plan was for No. 41 Commando to land on the north shoulder of the gap in the dyke and capture Westkapelle. No. 48, followed by No. 47, would sail through the gap, land in rear of the German defences, then advance south to Flushing. Twenty-four Flails, AVREs and armoured dozers from 79th Armoured Division would land with them.

Close fire support would be provided by the 25 ships of "Support Squadron, Eastern Flank' — so named because it had been formed to operate opposite the eastern landing beaches in Normandy. Its ships were landing craft manned by the Navy, armed with guns and rockets served by Royal Marines.

The heavy guns of the battleship *Warspite* and the monitors *Roberts* and *Erebus* would engage the main German batteries. These were also to have been attacked by Bomber command during the three days preceding the assault but because of bad weather, no bombing took place on 31 October. Fighter bombers would attack the beach defences for twenty minutes immediately before the landings.

Shortly after 6 a.m. on 1 November, Leicester and Pugsley in HMS *Kingsmill*, the headquarters ship, received a chilling message from First Canadian Army — 'Extremely unlikely any air support spotting or air smoke possible due to airfield conditions and forecast.' To proceed now would mean a heavy loss of men and ships.

Alternatively they could postpone the operation — the sea was calm and the sky appeared to be clearing. Conceivably, air support might be possible later in the day. But there was no assurance that the sea would remain so placid. If it turned rough, it might be days before it calmed. Both knew the importance and urgency of the operation.

They signalled their reply by a pre-arranged codeword — 'Nelson.' They would attack.

Shortly after 8 a.m. the first German guns opened fire — at a motor launch which marked the position where the headquarters ship was to anchor. Others joined in. *Warspite* and the monitors replied. Without their spotting aircraft, accurate shooting was difficult but they silenced two of the enemy guns. Army air observation post planes tried to help but their radios could not transmit on the ships' frequencies.

Without air bombardment or fighter bomber attacks before H hour, the responsibility for supporting the landing fell to Commander K.S. Sellar and his support squadron.

In two columns, one on either side of the approach area, the little ships headed for the shore, guns blazing. Twenty-five ships on a flat sea in broad daylight were a dream target for the German coast artillery and they lost no time in concentrating every weapon upon them.

Zig-zagging in an attempt to get in under the enemy guard, the Squadron found it impossible to avoid the deadly fire of the German guns. Every ship was hit; some sank, others beached and fought it out with the enemy until they blew up; others were so badly damaged they could no longer fight.

As H hour approached the survivors of the Squadron kept up their fire on the beaches near the gap. Determined to help in what they realized was a desperate situation, 84 Group RAF ordered 183 Squadron to take off, despite the fog which closed their airfield. They reported as a 'cab rank' to the Air Controller in HMS *Kingsmill* minutes before the assault was to go in. Their twelve Typhoons swept in firing rockets over the heads of the tank landing craft just as they were about to beach.

At 10:10 a.m. the first Commandos touched down and the Support Squadron continued to engage the enemy until 12:30. By that time all the Commandos were ashore, Westkapelle village had been taken and the nearby battery which had done so much damage was captured. Captain Pugsley ordered Sellar to break off action and return to Ostend. Only seven of his 25 craft remained fit for action.

> '... the battered remnants of his gallant squadron slowly withdrew, carrying with them 126 badly wounded officers and men and those of their 172 dead who had not already found graves in the sea.'[8]

Sellar later reported that, during the action, casualties to the Commandos were reported as light. 'I therefore considered that so long as the Germans made the mistake of concentrating their fire on the Support Squadron, close action was justified and losses acceptable.'[9]

Operational research after the battle revealed that the landings would have failed but for two circumstances. One was the enemy's mistake in engaging the support craft instead of those carrying troops. The other was that the four 150mm gun batteries south of the gap in the Westkapelle dyke ran out of ammunition just as the first troops were landing. They had fired heavily on the Canadians in the Breskens pocket and flooding prevented them from being re-supplied.

No. 41 Commando's landing on the north shoulder of the gap and the operations which followed were carried out with textbook precision. Their first troops touched down at 10:10. Twenty minutes later, the remainder negotiated the gap in Buffaloes, dismounted and attacked Westkapelle supported by Flail tanks of the 1st Lothian and Border Horse. In an hour they had cleared the village and found two nearby batteries unoccupied and under water. At 12:00 a troop attacked a six-gun battery north of the town and captured it with 120 prisoners. There Brigadier Leicester halted them.

South of the gap, 48 Commando suffered casualties from artillery fire as they came ashore. Swiftly they captured a radar station, then attacked the 120mm battery which had run out of ammunition. Its garrison was in no mood to surrender and beat off the first assault with machine-gun fire. A second attack which followed air strikes, shelling by *Roberts* and the artillery at Breskens, convinced the enemy to change their minds. The battery surrendered with about 100 prisoners.

At 3 p.m. No. 48 Commando advanced through the sand hills north-eastwards towards Domburg and its battery of immense 22cm guns. About fifty Spitfires bombed and strafed the enemy positions ahead, eventually attacking the battery itself. On the way the Marines collected an embarrassment of prisoners. That evening the Domburg battery surrendered but, when they reached the outskirts of the village, the Commandos were met by determined rearguards. There they were ordered to halt and part of No. 10 (Inter-Allied) Commando consisting of British, Norwegian, Belgian and Dutch troops relieved them. (Their 100 French soldiers were with No. 4 Commando in Flushing).

During the morning of the 2nd No. 48 Commando captured Zoutelande where No. 47 passed through them to assault the final major battery on that shore, the four 150mm guns four kilometres west of Flushing. The only approach was over an anti-tank ditch, then across some 2,000 metres of open country. They suffered heavy casualties. Two troops managed to work forward toward the battery but enemy near the anti-tank ditch cut them off from the remainder of their unit. By nightfall the position by the anti-tank ditch had been cleared but every troop leader in the Commando had been wounded.

Next morning the Commando captured the battery, silencing the last guns which had made the landing beaches at Westkapelle a misery for the unsung members of the supporting services who worked there. Among these, units of the Royal Canadian Army Medical Corps cared for the casualties under appalling conditions. The two landing craft which had been prepared as hospital ships were sunk by mines. Another, pressed into service to evacuate casualties to Ostend also struck a mine and burned, killing many of the wounded. After that the weather turned so bad that evacuation became impossible.

Driving sand and the violence of the gale made the care of casualties a work of ingenuity as well as devotion. At best there was barely enough canvas to shelter them. Tents blew down and generators failed while doctors carried out life-saving surgery in the cramped interior of a tent nine feet long by six feet wide.

And for three days enemy guns probed the area for targets. On the second, a shell struck three Buffaloes loaded with ammunition. For forty-five minutes the crowded beach was raked by exploding mortar bombs and small arms ammunition, killing stretcher bearers and wounded, German prisoners and their guards.

Two surgeons, Major J.B. Hillsman and Captain Lew Ptak, spent the longest half-hour of their lives on their bellies on the sand 'dressing wounds, stopping haemorrhages and splinting fractures. Constant explosions were blowing sand over us as we worked.'[10]

When the last German battery was silenced, weather became the enemy for the Canadian units. For twelve days they worked around the clock until the last casualty had been taken from the Island. They themselves had paid a price in killed and wounded in what had been the most hazardous medical action of the North-west European campaign.

Meanwhile, on 3 November, 47 Commando pushed on south, clearing the enemy defences until they reached the gap in the dyke near Flushing.

In the town and elsewhere on the eastern side of the Island, the 52nd Division were fighting a bitter uncompromising battle with the Germans. 156 and 157 Brigades had linked up at the Causeway and were clearing the unflooded area east of Middelburg.

The street fighting in Flushing itself was a severe test for the Lowlanders of 155 Brigade in their first battles. West of the dock area, the magnificent boulevard with its hotels stands high above the water. At the western end, the large Britannia Hotel had been converted into a fortress. Trenches, bunkers, wire and encroaching flood water isolated and protected it.

Wading waist to shoulder deep through the icy floodwater with a five knot current, three companies of the 7/9th Battalion, Royal Scots, laden with weapons and equipment, struggled toward the hotel. As dim moonlight gave way to dawn they saw for the first time the extent of its defences. Pillbox after pillbox had to be cleared before the hotel itself was entered. By the time the first troops had charged into the building, two company commanders had been killed, Lt-Colonel Melville, their commander, was severely wounded and the number of casualties had mounted alarmingly.

A flanking German strongpoint swept the approach to the hotel with such heavy fire that it was impossible to reinforce the few who gained an entry. It had to be destroyed. But with its rear protected by the high, nearly vertical sea wall, it was almost impregnable. And so it would have been if its attackers had not been mountain troops. Led by Major Hugh Rose, the only surviving company commander, a party scaled the wall and stormed the position from the rear.

Under fire, one young officer, Lieutenant Beveridge, scaled the outside wall of the hotel to its flat roof and drove the defenders from it. Inside the Scots probed the cellars where they came upon an unexpected prize. In a heavily reinforced concrete shelter, more than 600 apprehensive Germans waited with no alternative but to surrender. Among them was a badly shaken Colonel Reinhardt, the commander of 1019 Grenadier Regiment and of the Flushing garrison.[11]

Brigadier J.F.S. McLaren now directed his 155th Brigade north toward Middelburg. About a mile south of it, on the canal to Flushing, an anti-tank ditch barred the way. As the leading infantry approached they were met by Spandau fire. When they raced to deploy they found the only possible cover had been mined. There mortars searched them out. This enemy was experienced. When the position was taken, they found it manned by 40 veterans of the 64th Division who had escaped being trapped by the Canadians south of the Scheldt.

By now the main enemy force on the Island was concentrated in Middleburg under Lt-General Daser. Behind the old city walls, with every approach but the canal banks flooded, they were confident they could hold out indefinitely. The presence of a large Dutch population guaranteed them immunity from bombing. That the civilians were suffering from hunger, disease and the effects of flooding did not affect the military equation so confidently calculated by Daser.

Alarmed by the situation, a local surgeon, Dr. E.L. Nauts, escaped from the town and rowed toward Flushing in a small boat. There he was taken to McLaren's headquarters, where he implored the British to go to the rescue.

About noon on the 6th, a company of the 7/9 Royal Scots, commanded by Major R.H.B. Johnston, set out for Middelburg in eight Buffaloes. Moving around the town, across flooded fields to the west, they entered unseen behind the German defences. Mistaking the huge tracked amphibians for tanks, the startled Germans, unprepared for an armoured attack, gave up.

Major Johnston sent a demand for Daser to surrender — the General declined to submit to an officer so junior. Johnston borrowed four pips and promoted himself to the 'local and temporary rank' of colonel which satisfied Daser's sensibilities. He then ordered the German to parade his 2,000 men in the town square where they laid down their arms.

A few tense hours ensued with the Germans guarded by fewer than 120 British, not only against escape but for their protection from an aroused Dutch population. Late in the day the HLI arrived from the Causeway, followed shortly afterwards by 4 KOSB from Flushing.

Early on 10 November the last Germans on Walcheren Island surrendered and the approaches to Antwerp were clear of the enemy.

The damage wreaked on Walcheren by flooding resulted in serious hardships for the population. Indeed, after the surrender, it appeared to be calamitous. Fortunately it was not irreparable and after the war the farms and orchards were soon restored to prosperity.

The Germans on Walcheren admitted that it was the flooding which had made their situation impossible. Though few batteries were flooded, many were isolated and could not be resupplied. Ammunition was damaged, communications broken, garrisons immobilized.

And it helped the attackers. It was possible to use amphibious vehicles which in both Beveland and the Breskens pocket could not move across the saturated ground. There the infantry had no option but to struggle forward on foot and the battle lasted far longer than on the Island. Simonds' insistence on flooding Walcheren resulted in Antwerp being opened at least two weeks before it otherwise would have been.

On 26 November the Royal Navy announced that the approaches to Antwerp had been swept free of mines. Two days later a convoy of eighteen ships entered and on 1 December, 10,000 tons of stores were landed.

There was a ceremony to welcome the first ship to arrive, appropriately enough the Canadian-built *Fort Catarqui*, manned by a British crew. Admiral Ramsay, the Naval Commander-in-Chief, was there to meet her with representatives of SHAEF, 21 Army Group, British and American port authorities, the Belgian Government and Army. Curiously, no one from First Canadian Army was invited to attend.[12]

16

THE END OF THE AFFAIR

ON 23 OCTOBER, the United States' 104th (Timberwolf) Division joined First Canadian Army for the balance of the Scheldt operations. Simonds assigned it to 1st British Corps to help in clearing the enemy from south of the River Maas.

Rarely in the War did the Americans place one of their divisions under the command of an ally for its initiation into battle. Simonds was conscious of the implied compliment and that the Americans might not be too happy about fighting their first battle under a foreigner. He was determined to give them all possible help and encouragement. While they were in Belgium, he visited every regiment in the division to brief the troops on the operations which were to come. No senior general had ever before taken the trouble to tell the men what the future held in store, let alone take them into his confidence about operational plans. They liked the experience.

The Division had arrived fresh from mild weather in the States into a cold damp Belgian autumn. With only their standard issue of one blanket per man, they were feeling the cold. Simonds learned of this during his visit and that night 18,000 grey Canadian Army blankets were delivered to the troops. There was no mistaking them for the GI version.

The result of these two actions was that the Americans went into their first battle feeling that they were among friends and that the Army Commander was personally concerned about their welfare. Major-General Terry Allen, their commander, was one of the most experienced officers in the U.S. Army, having commanded their 1st Division in North Africa. In 1962, he recalled:

> Simonds made sure that our first mission was well within the capacity of a new division — enough opposition to teach the boys that war is a serious business but not so much that they'd get a bloody nose. They came out of it with a nice balance of prudence and confidence. The next battles were tougher, more of them got hurt but, like with the first one, they won. Before long they were veterans.[1]

With four divisions under command, Crocker's 1st Corps now had sufficient strength to clear the enemy from south of the Lower Maas. On 27 October the Polish Armoured Division and the 2nd Canadian Armoured Brigade advanced toward Breda. The 104th U.S. Infantry Division, on their left, in their first battle, took Zundert, and the 49th Division was approaching Roosendaal while the 4th Canadian Armoured Division had entered Bergen op Zoom. Two days later the Poles were clearing Breda in house-to-house fighting and the 4th Division had captured Bergen.

The German Fifteenth Army, operating under instructions from Hitler, was again in danger of being destroyed. Second British Army, advancing to the west, had taken Tilburg and the enemy's line from Bergen op Zoom to Breda and 's-Hertogenbosch had been broken. Von Rundstedt asked for permission to withdraw behind the River Waal, the main stream of the Lower Rhine. Hitler ordered him to stand fast but the old field marshal was determined not to lose the Fifteenth Army if he could avoid it. He ordered them to pull back to the line of the River Mark and its canal.

Crocker now instructed the Poles, with 2nd Armoured Brigade under command, to drive hard for the vital Maas bridges at Moerdijk, the Americans to swing north-west to the River Mark at Standdaarbuiten, the 49th Division to secure the route northward from Roosendaal and the 4th Armoured to advance through Steenbergen to the coast of the estuary.

By the end of the month, despite hard-fought actions, neither the Poles nor the Americans had succeeded in securing a bridge-

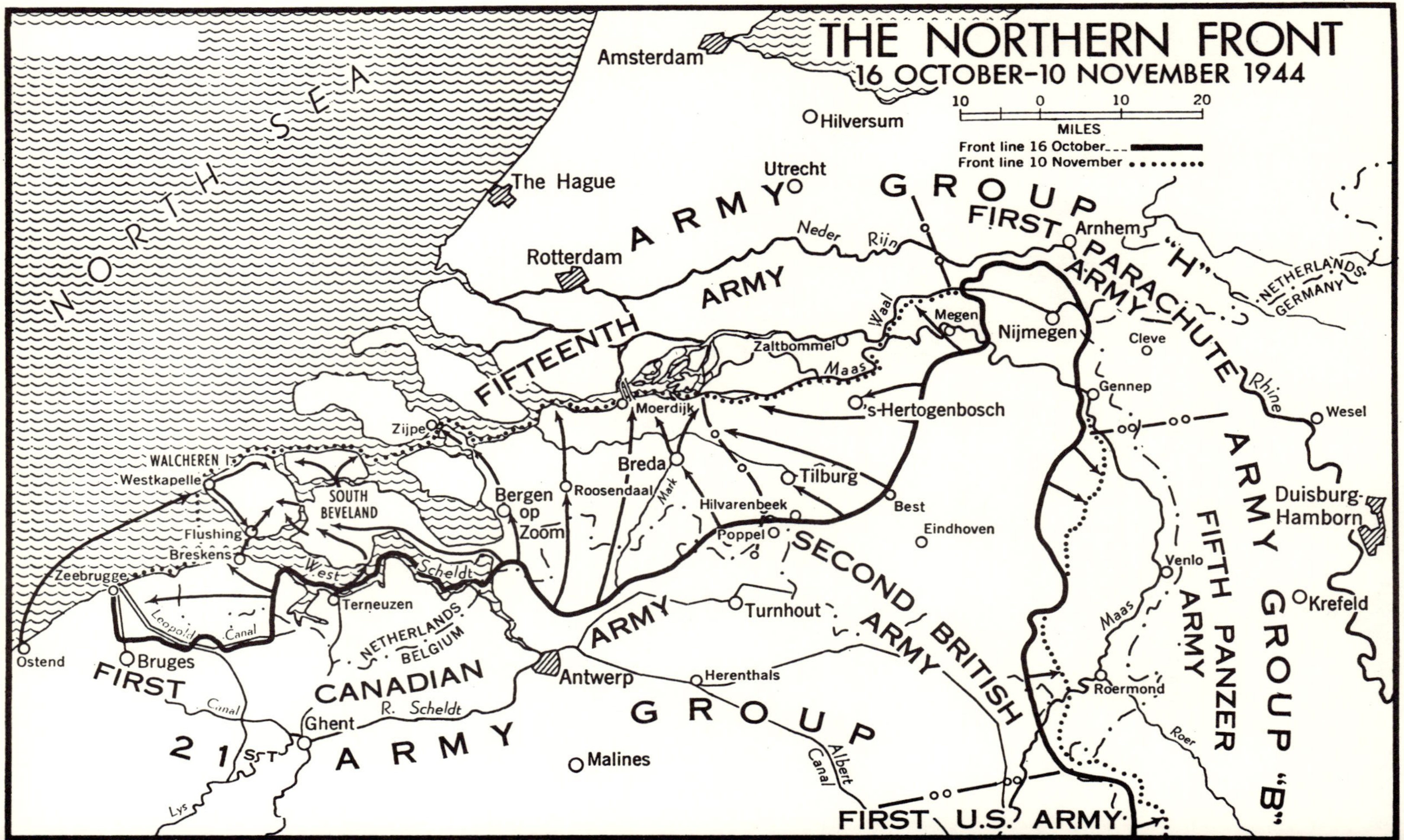

THE NORTHERN FRONT
16 OCTOBER–10 NOVEMBER 1944
10 0 10 20
MILES
Front line 16 October
Front line 10 November
NORTH SEA
Amsterdam
Hilversum
Utrecht
The Hague
Rotterdam
ARMY GROUP
FIRST PARACHUTE ARMY
"H"
Arnhem
Neder Rijn
NETHERLANDS
GERMANY
FIFTEENTH ARMY
Waal
Megen
Nijmegen
Cleve
Zaltbommel
Maas
Rhine
Gennep
Wesel
Moerdijk
's-Hertogenbosch
Zijpe
WALCHEREN I.
Westkapelle
SOUTH BEVELAND
Breda
Tilburg
Bergen op Zoom
Roosendaal
Mark
Hilvarenbeek
Best
Eindhoven
Flushing
Breskens
Poppel
SECOND BRITISH ARMY
ARMY GROUP "B"
Duisburg-Hamborn
FIFTH PANZER ARMY
Zeebrugge
West
Scheldt
Venlo
Terneuzen
Turnhout
Krefeld
Leopold Canal
NETHERLANDS
BELGIUM
Ostend
Bruges
FIRST CANADIAN ARMY
Antwerp
Herenthals
Roermond
Canal
Ghent
R. Scheldt
21 ST ARMY GROUP
Malines
Albert Canal
Roer
Lys
FIRST U.S. ARMY

head over the Mark. Every attempt to do so had been met by prompt and effective counterattacks. But by now Hitler had authorized the Fifteenth Army to make a 'deliberate' withdrawal adding that if the Moerdijk bridges fell intact into Allied hands the commander of its strong covering forces would pay with his head.

On 2 November the 49th and 104th Divisions, supported by bomb and rocket attacks of 84 Group, crossed the Mark. On the 6th, as the Poles and Americans closed in on Moerdijk, the Germans blew the great road and railway bridges across the estuary. The Poles finally cleared the last Germans from south of the River on 9 November.

To the west the 4th Division's advance ran into strong opposition at Welberg. Two companies of the Algonquin Regiment entered the town but were immediately counterattacked by members of the Hermann Goering Replacement Regiment supported by a Tiger tank and two SP guns. By first light the Algonquins had pulled back to their start line having lost half the strength of two companies, including their commanders. Patrols identified the 6th Parachute Regiment in Welberg.

Next day, in an attack by the 10th Brigade, the Algonquins took the town while the remainder of the Brigade closed on Steenbergen under very heavy shell-fire. During the night the shelling suddenly stopped. The enemy had departed. Troops entering Steenbergen found the population 'none too friendly; whether their animosity stemmed from pro-German sentiments or from antagonism over the damage done by our Typhoons we were unable to ascertain.'[2]

The last action for the 4th Division in the Scheldt campaign took place when tanks of the British Columbia Regiment and a company of the Lake Superior Regiment (Motor) opened fire across a channel of the sea on German naval vessels in the harbour of Zijpe at the eastern end of the island of Schouwen. Three were sunk and a fourth damaged.

The Argyll's War Diary described 6 November as 'the most peaceful and uneventful day the Argylls had spent in many a month. Even the weather turned in our favour and the troops enjoyed a real day of rest. They were physically refreshed by bath-parades, mentally rejuvenated by "Sally Anne" movies and internally cleansed by the cognac which the good people of Steenbergen bartered for a few cigarettes or chocolate bars.'

The Battle of the Scheldt was over and thousands of tons of stores would now flow through Antwerp. The British Official History comments:

> Sixty days had elapsed between its capture on September 4th and the winning of the land defences of the Scheldt on November 4th. In those sixty days the First Canadian Army had been wholly responsible for the land operations in the coastal area, culminating in the seaborne assault on Walcheren Island, the clearance of both banks of the Scheldt estuary and the freeing of Antwerp's port. During those two months they had advanced from the Seine to the Scheldt and the Maas, capturing the ports of le Havre, Dieppe, Boulogne, Calais and Ostend. In that time they had taken 68,000 prisoners and killed an unknown number. They had also bottled up in Dunkirk the German garrison. In this achievement they had themselves suffered some 17,000 casualties of whom 3,000 were killed in action or died of wounds. The part they played in the Allied actions of those months was outstanding.[3]

Casualty statistics convey little to most people except perhaps, a sense of horror and revulsion at the evil of war but sometimes comparing them can prove enlightening. Twenty-seven years before the Battle of the Scheldt, at the same time of year, 18 October to 15 November, 1917, sixty miles south-west of Antwerp, the Canadian Corps fought a series of battles which culminated in their capture of Passchendaele. The name still strikes horror into the hearts of those who know of the appalling conditions under which the battle was fought and of its terrible casualties. In 29 days the four Canadian divisions lost 15,654 men killed, wounded or missing, 3,914 per division. On the Scheldt the 2nd Canadian Division lost 3,650 in 33 days.

But in the First World War each division had twelve battalions, in the Second, only nine (in both cases, disregarding machine-gun units which were similar in size). At Passchendaele the average loss per battalion was 326 men. On the Scheldt the losses of the 2nd Division were 405 per battalion in much the same length of time.

Without attempting to compare the muddy swamps of Passchendaele with the sodden polders of the Scheldt or to make other than this rough comparison of casualties, it is fair to say that the soldiers of First Canadian Army who fought to free Antwerp had endured much and needed no instruction from their fathers in the horrors of war.

Unlike Passchendaele, no one afterwards would claim that the Battle of the Scheldt had been fought for no good purpose. But there were mistakes. Field-Marshal Sir Alan Brooke noted on October 5, 'I feel that Monty's strategy for once is at fault. Instead of carrying out the advance on Arnhem, he ought to have made certain of Antwerp in the first place.'[4] In his *Memoirs*, Montgomery wrote:

> I must admit a bad mistake on my part — I underestimated the difficulties of opening up the approaches to Antwerp so that we could get the free use of that port. I reckoned that the Canadian Army could do it *while* we were going for the Ruhr. I was wrong.[5]

But Eisenhower had approved the Arnhem operation and had given Montgomery the task of seizing the Ruhr as well as securing Antwerp. He allowed matters to drift until 9 October before expressing dissatisfaction about progress at Antwerp and making a definite request that more be done. He denied the Canadian Army the use of airborne troops and agreed to the Air Forces' refusal of the great bomber effort needed to overwhelm the Walcheren defences.

Both underestimated the enemy. When Montgomery overrode Crerar's plan to have 1st Corps secure Bergen op Zoom, he opened the way for the Germans to send a strong force to counter the 2nd Division's advance near Woensdrecht, to commit that Division to protecting its flank — in effect, to fighting with one arm tied behind its back.

That he was little interested in the Antwerp operations until required to be by Eisenhower is reflected in his biography which makes only passing reference to them. It is plain that before and during them his concerns were Arnhem, the Ruhr and his disagreement with Eisenhower over who should command land operations. Too late, he did put his weight behind them. But Eisenhower, the Supreme Allied Commander who had assumed control of ground operations himself, never visited First Canadian Army to see for himself what was going on or what was needed in a battle which he considered to be of vital importance to the future of his forces.

During the last weeks of September, when the German's every effort was concentrated on countering the Allied airborne operations in Belgium and Holland, Crerar could not use the grounded 51st Division for lack of transport. With it he could have attacked the Breskens pocket before the enemy consolidated their positions on the Leopold Canal. Yet during this time Eisenhower was reinforcing the Allied right wing, even to the extent of allowing Bradley to move a division from Belgium to Lorraine. Patton's Moselle offensive was mounted at the expense, not only of the attack on the Ruhr, but of the operations to open Antwerp.[6]

Since the First World War Field-Marshal Lord Haig has been criticized for not visiting the Passchendaele front. When General Kiggell, his chief of staff, did so after the battle, he exclaimed 'My God! Did we send men to fight in that?' and burst into tears.

Montgomery came to realize his mistake. It is doubtful if anyone ever pointed out to Eisenhower the price paid by First Canadian Army for his neglect. Certainly the Canadians would not have done so. They were far too polite.

Part Three

The Rhineland

17

WINTER ON THE MAAS

WHILE THE SCHELDT BATTLES WERE IN PROGRESS, the staff at Army Headquarters were preparing for future operations. The Army was soon to take over the entire line from south-east of Nijmegen to the sea. It would be fighting a winter campaign in snow and frost with all that that entailed in the way of tactics and training, special clothing and equipment, vehicle maintenance, accommodation and camouflage. But first its exhausted divisions would have to be brought up to strength in men and equipment and trained for the hard fighting which lay ahead.

Fortunately Canadian losses in the next three months were relatively light and infantry battalions were restored to full strength. But by this time it was apparent that the Army could not be sustained by volunteers alone. Since 1940 men had been conscripted for service in Canada and by late 1944 thousands of them, trained as infantry were guarding the country against a threat which had disappeared. It took months of persuasion before the Government in Ottawa could be convinced that the only solution to the problem of the rifle company of thirty exhausted and increasingly embittered soldiers was to send these conscripts overseas. In early 1945 they began to arrive and were accepted gladly, with no discrimination, in the ranks of First Canadian Army's veteran battalions.

It was not only the three Canadian divisions which had been worn down. The Polish Armoured Division lacked reinforcements of any kind and was in even worse shape. The shortage of infantry in British divisions was so serious that two had been disbanded. It was a problem shared by all the Allies. Eisenhower complained in November that the American planners had miscalculated the number of infantry units needed in a balanced army, a deficiency compounded by a shortage of replacements for casualties.

On 7 November Lt-General Crerar, now restored to health, returned to his Army. A week later he was promoted to the rank of General, a rank never held before by a Canadian officer in the field. Simonds returned to the command of 2nd Corps, whilst Major-General Charles Foulkes, who had taken his place during the Scheldt operations, left to take command of 1st Corps in Italy. His replacement as commander of the 2nd Division was Major-General Bruce Matthews.

For exactly three months from the end of hostilities on Walcheren Island — 8 November to 8 February — there were no major operations on the front of First Canadian Army. The respite was put to good use and by the time its next offensive was launched, the Army was at full strength, trained and confident.

Before the Allies could advance into Germany and bring the War to an end, they would have to cross the Rhine. Lying before it, except in the south near Switzerland, lay the formidable defences of the Siegfried Line. The euphoria of the headlong advances across France and Belgium disappeared when the Allies realized the price they were going to have to pay to reach the river.

On 2 November, as the Scheldt battles were ending, Montgomery issued a directive to his army commanders which outlined some immediate tasks. The next operation to be undertaken by Second British Army was to drive the enemy to the east side of the River Meuse (as the Maas is known in Belgium and France). First Canadian Army was to prepare plans for offensive operations:

a) South-eastward from the Nijmegen area, between the Rhine and Meuse;
b) Northwards across the Neder Rijn, to secure the high ground between Arnhem and Apeldoorn with a bridgehead over the Ijssel river.

Planning began at once while the Army took up its new positions. Sir John Crocker's 1st British Corps now held the line of the lower Maas as far east as Maren, north-east of 's-Hertogenbosch, with, as Crerar ordered, 'the minimum strength necessary, maintaining a reserve of mobile and armoured troops in suitable positions to deal with any enemy attempt to cross the river.'

Simonds' 2nd Corps was to take over the Nijmegen salient from 30th British Corps on 9 November, their forward positions extending from Cuijk, opposite the Reichswald, across the 'Arnhem island' to Maren. The Army would then be responsible for a front of over 225 kilometres from the Rhineland forests to the tip of Walcheren. Its most vital defensive task was the protection of the Nijmegen bridge, the only crossing of the Rhine in Allied hands.

Opposite them was Army Group H, commanded by General Kurt Student, with his 15th Army's front roughly coinciding with that of 1st British Corps, and 1st Parachute Army opposite Simonds.

Before the last shots were fired on Walcheren, 2nd Corps began moving to the Nijmegen area where it took command of two divisions already in position, the 50th (Northumbrian) and the U.S. 101st Airborne on the so-called island between the Waal and Arnhem. On the right the 2nd Division moved into the line opposite the Reichswald between Cuijk and Groesbeek. Between them and Nijmegen, the 3rd Division relieved the U.S. 82nd Airborne on the night of 12 November.

It was the first time that General Spry's men had had direct dealing with Americans. They were intrigued by their language which was familiar but seemed non-military — torches were flashlights, petrol was gasoline. They were fascinated by their equipment, their robust 'deuce-and-halfs' and four-wheel drive 'threequarters' ($2^1/2$ and $^3/4$ ton trucks), their weapons and their rations. They liked the U.S. .30 calibre carbine but wouldn't swap a Browning automatic rifle for a Bren. In fact, there was little that the Americans had that they envied, certainly not their rations nor their clothing. Everyone shivered in that damp November but the Americans 'looked' colder. As one battalion commander put it, 'They were great guys, good soldiers who had fought well. We gained a great respect for them but their ways were not our ways.'[1]

Too many visitors can be a problem to a headquarters in the field. That of the 82nd Airborne had to be approached on foot along clearly marked paths because of the danger of mines. Major-General James Gavin was said to be the source of a widely spread rumour that close proximity to the fluorescent tape, which marked them, made men impotent.[2]

On the right of the Army's line the two Canadian divisions each held their positions opposite the Reichswald with two brigades. After two weeks in the line, each brigade would spend one in reserve, training.

From positions on high ground both they and the Germans opposite had good observation over the open undulating ground west of the Reichswald. Much of it was strewn with the remains of gliders wrecked in the airborne assault of the previous September. Some were booby-trapped, some were used by the enemy to observe the Canadian positions, as some were used by our patrols. Both sides made strenuous efforts to control this no-man's land. Almost every night patrols clashed as they tried to gain information or capture prisoners.

As in the First World War, the Canadians kept the enemy on edge with frequent raids. These were carefully planned and rehearsed and were supported by artillery, machine guns and mortars. Though they achieved some valuable results, they could be expensive.

On 20 December B Company of the South Saskatchewan Regiment, commanded by Major Bill Edmondson, raided enemy positions in front of Groesbeek to obtain information for a future attack. The assault was swift, efficient and lucky. One frightened prisoner was hustled to the rear — a staff car driver, who had been sent into the line as a disciplinary measure. But one platoon had mistaken its objective and had left a strong enemy post in action. Casualties mounted as Edmondson, in a wrecked barn, strained to keep contact with his platoons over a crackling radio net and extricate them under enemy machine gun and artillery fire.

At that point a sergeant, obviously upset, said to Edmondson, 'I've got five wounded men in the barn. How am I going to get them back?'

Edmondson rounded on him and shook him into action by saying, 'I don't give a damn about your wounded. It's your job to get them out. Mine is to get those sixty men out there back without any more of them getting hurt.'

The South Saskatchewans lost three men killed and 20 wounded and the sergeant learned an unforgettable lesson in the realities of war. As for the German staff car driver, disgruntled at the Wehrmacht for his punishment, he named every senior commander known to him and gladly shared his unique knowledge of the location of enemy units and headquarters.[3]

2nd Corps' primary task was the defence of the Nijmegen bridgehead and of the bridges themselves. On the Arnhem island the 50th (Northumbrian) and 101st Airborne Divisions held soggy positions opposite an enemy equally determined to protect the Arnhem bridge. At this time the Germans were not capable of mounting a large-scale attack, but both sides patrolled aggressively.

At Nijmegen bridges for road and rail, captured intact, span the Waal, the main stream of the lower Rhine. Beside them the British had laid a third across a row of barges. Almost every day

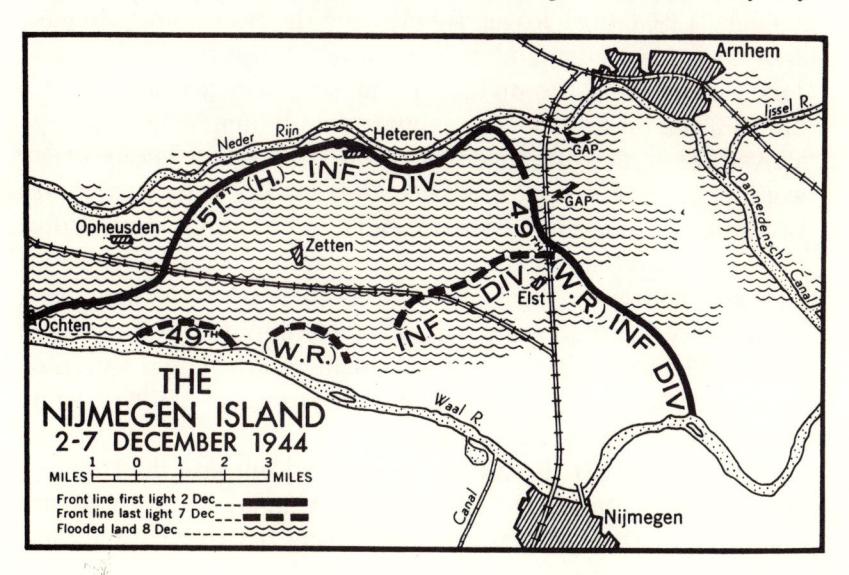

THE NIJMEGEN ISLAND
2-7 DECEMBER 1944

Front line first light 2 Dec
Front line last light 7 Dec
Flooded land 8 Dec

the Germans attempted to destroy them by shelling or air attacks. At the end of September enemy frogmen, using mines, blew a gap of 80 feet in the road bridge which was soon repaired, and destroyed a span of that carrying the railway. In November and December they damaged the barge bridge by floating mines down the stream.

At the end of November the 49th (West Riding) and 51st (Highland) Divisions relieved the troops on the Arnhem island. A few days later the Germans blew the river dyke and the railway embankment south of Arnhem, allowing water of the lower Rhine and the Waal to flood the low-lying farm land. Within two or three days much of the island was under three feet of water. As the floods extended, the few remaining civilians and livestock were evacuated, while the British withdrew to defensible positions closer to Nijmegen. Before dawn one morning, while this movement was in progress, units of the 6th Parachute Division attacked the 49th about three miles upstream from Nijmegen. At first they made some progress but a counterattack drove back the enemy who left behind 60 dead and more than a hundred prisoners.

In January, 1945, the Germans made another attempt to destroy the Nijmegen road bridge. Late in the evening of 12 January Lt-Colonel Roger Rowley, of the Stormont, Dundas and Glengarry Highlanders, was called forward by Captain Jake Forman of C Company who mysteriously asked his C.O. not to bring his artillery representative with him. When Rowley arrived forward, Forman led him to the river where, alongside a warehouse, on the opposite bank, they made out the shapes of two midget submarines. Men appeared to be loading them. Forman explained that he was moving two anti-tank guns into position and had given them instructions that, on his order, they would open fire with armour-piercing ammunition, followed by high explosive shells. He was confident that he could sink the two boats and didn't need any help from the artillery who would only claim the credit for it.[4]

When eventually the submarines moved out into the stream, the anti-tank guns ended their part in what was a much larger enterprise. Other submarines were engaged that night by the

12th and 14th Field Regiments, Royal Canadian Artillery, but the scale of the operation only became known after the War. The Germans had launched 17 midget submarines, or 'Biber.' None of them reached the Nijmegen bridge. Eight members of their crews were lost.[5]

Further west, 1st British Corps held the south bank of the lower Maas with the 4th Canadian and 1st Polish Armoured Divisions on the right and left respectively. The 12th Manitoba Dragoons patrolled the 25 miles of the Maas from its mouth opposite Schouwen to the canal just west of Moerdijk. The 52nd Lowland Division continued to occupy Walcheren.

Generally the front was 'quiet.' There were frequent artillery duels and 1 Corps and German patrols probed across the river.

Since early November the planning staff at Headquarters First Canadian Army had been studying the problem of an attack south-east from Nijmegen to clear the west bank of the Rhine. On 7 December Montgomery telephoned Crerar and gave him the responsibility for carrying out the operation. For it the Army would be reinforced by 30th British Corps including one armoured and four infantry divisions. The target date for 'Veritable,' as it was to be called, was 1 January, or as soon as possible thereafter.

By the time Montgomery issued a written instruction for the operation on 16 December, preparations were in full swing. Army and Corps staffs had completed their initial plans and the tremendous task of building roads capable of supporting the operation had begun.

On that same morning, 16 December, 1944, in poor visibility, von Rundstedt launched the 5th and 6th Panzer Armies against the thinly held American front in the Ardennes forest. Its primary aim was the encirclement and destruction of 21 Army Group. It achieved complete tactical and strategic surprise. In the days that followed, the German spearheads penetrated more than 80 kilometres. Some American units were completely overwhelmed, but others held their ground tenaciously.

The Allies regrouped and, when skies cleared, the air forces attacked the Panzers. The Germans were halted within two miles of the Meuse.

The enemy's Ardennes offensive was to have a profound effect on Crerar's battles in the Rhineland. In the meantime First Canadian Army was not much involved.

On 19 December 30th Corps was taken away, temporarily, to prepare to counterattack if the Germans crossed the Meuse. Two days later the Intelligence Section at Army Headquarters detected some disquieting activity on the part of the enemy north of the Maas in Holland. Four to five divisions were concentrating in preparation for an attack.

Von Rundstedt had ordered Army Group H to be prepared to cross the lower Maas once the Ardennes thrust reached the Meuse. The initial thrust would be conducted by 88th Corps whose pedestrian commander was replaced by Lt-General Felix Schwalbe, a man more suitable for a difficult and dashing operation. His force of two infantry and two parachute divisions would be supported by 150 tanks.

Crerar regrouped 1st British Corps on whose front the attack would fall and positioned divisions ready to counterattack. All administrative units were ordered to prepare for their own defence while continuing their preparations for 'Veritable.'

Between Headquarters First Canadian Army in Tilburg and the Maas, 18 kilometres to the north, stood one platoon of infantry and an armoured car troop. For the first time it looked as if the staff might have to defend themselves. Officers, clerks, drivers, cooks and signallers drew extra ammunition and grenades, dug slit trenches and manned guard posts. The Armoured Corps section crewed two armoured cars, the artillery some anti-tank guns. All were told of the alarm signal — a Bofors AA gun firing bursts of four rounds across the town.

About 10 o'clock one night, just such a series of bursts was fired. For a time all was silence then suddenly came the unmistakable sound of a Bren from the direction of the nearby Ordnance Field Park. More machine guns opened up.

Inside a school which housed some of the staff, an officer found his young clerk shaking, speechless and near to tears. A sergeant explained that the boy had been on duty as a sentry on a vehicle park and had shot an Army Service Corps officer who had failed to halt when challenged. Fortunately he had just winged him and it was questionable which of them was in worse shape. After half an hour an officer of the Defence Battalion arrived and reported that it had been a false alarm.

Later they discovered what had happened. Two Dutch civilians selected that night to rob the Ordnance Field Park. Armed to the teeth with machine guns taken from stores, the Ordnance unit had never been so alert or so well guarded. When a sentry saw two figures crawling under the wire of the boundary, he opened up with his Bren along the line of the fence. With bullets cracking over their heads, the next post beyond the intruders believed themselves to be under attack and fired back. Others eagerly joined in. Soon a full-scale fire fight developed.

Apart from the two Dutchmen, no one was hurt, but the officer commanding the Field Park noted that there was a marked decrease in pilfering after that.[6]

With the end of the German offensive in the Ardennes, 30th Corps returned to First Canadian Army. Preparations for 'Veritable' which had been continuing, now took top priority. Even before operational plans were finalized, a tremendous amount of work had been done.

In early February the ground was likely to be snow-covered — tons of white sheeting, camouflage suits and paint were distributed. To concentrate some fifteen divisions with thousands of tracked vehicles, guns and a vast quantity of wheeled transport would be far too much for country roads. New ones were built and the others reinforced. Thousands of tons of ammunition, of POL (petrol, oil and lubricants), of engineers' stores and rations were brought forward and concealed in readiness.

One painful result of the Ardennes offensive was the battle of Kapelsche Veer. There the Germans held an outpost on an island which lies in the river Maas, north of Tilburg. Army Group H had named it as one of the crossing places for their projected attack across the river. On 21 December its garrison was increased to one company, plus an advanced observation post supported by medium artillery, self-propelled guns and mortars from north of the Maas.

Both Crocker and Crerar were very concerned at the condi-

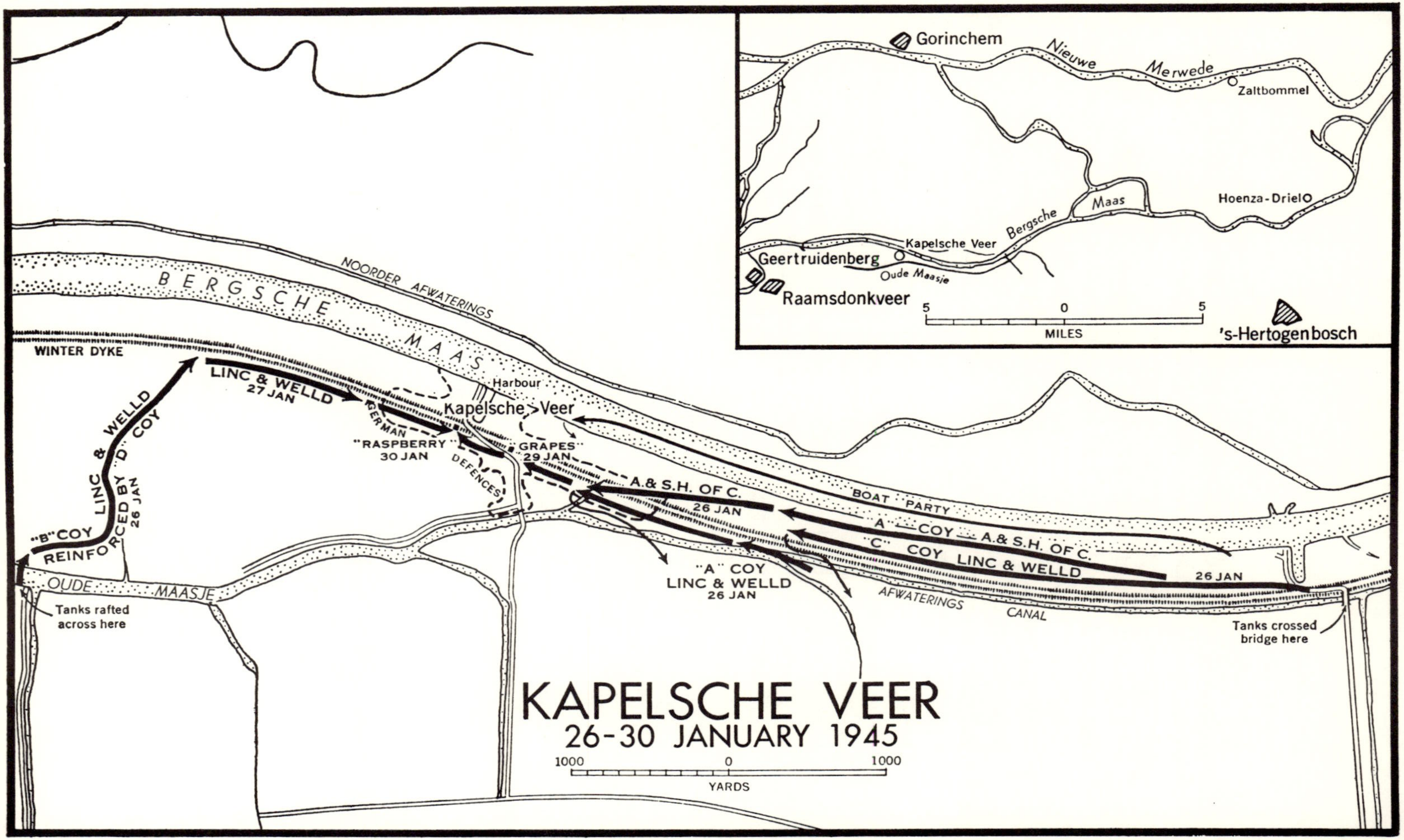

KAPELSCHE VEER
26-30 JANUARY 1945
1000
0
1000
YARDS
Gorinchem
Nieuwe
Merwede
Zaltbommel
Maas
Hoenza-Driel
Bergsche
Kapelsche Veer
Geertruidenberg
Oude Maasje
Raamsdonkveer
5
0
5
MILES
's-Hertogenbosch
BERGSCHE
MAAS
NOORDER AFWATERINGS
WINTER DYKE
LINC & WELLD
27 JAN
Harbour
Kapelsche Veer
GERMAN
"RASPBERRY"
30 JAN
DEFENCES
"GRAPES"
29 JAN
A.& S.H. OF C.
26 JAN
BOAT PARTY
"A" COY — A.& S.H. OF C.
"C" COY LINC & WELLD
26 JAN
"A" COY
LINC & WELLD
26 JAN
AFWATERINGS
CANAL
Tanks crossed
bridge here
"B" COY LINC & WELLD
REINFORCED BY "D" COY
26 JAN
OUDE
MAASJE
Tanks rafted
across here

tion of the Polish Armoured Division. Its ranks now were filled by ill-trained men who only a few months before had been serving under compulsion in the German Army. Ideally the Division should be taken out of the line for reorganization and training but this was not possible. By the end of December the likelihood of a major German offensive from across the river had faded. Yet it would have been foolish to leave such an active enemy bridgehead on the front of such a weakened formation.

On the night of 30 December Polish infantry attacked. They made little progress against a well dug-in enemy, supported by effective artillery. After suffering 46 casualties, the Poles were withdrawn, taking with them a few prisoners from the 6th Parachute Division. A week later, the 9th Polish Infantry Battalion attacked again. By noon they had cleared the harbour area but could make no progress against the paratroops dug-in on the nearby dykes. After a fierce enemy counterattack and a loss of 120 men killed and wounded they were ordered to withdraw.

Crocker judged that the Poles could do no more and called on 47 Commando Royal Marines to eliminate the bridgehead. On the night of 13/14 January the Marines, attacking from both flanks over the open polder country, made little progress. With a high proportion of their officers casualties and ammunition nearly exhausted, they were ordered to break off the attack.

The struggle for Kapelsche Veer now assumed an importance far beyond the value of the ground or the threat posed by the German bridgehead. To abandon the fight after three failures would be to concede superiority to the enemy, an example to the shaken Polish Division which could not be afforded. Crocker ordered the 4th Canadian Armoured Division to destroy the German position.

On the morning of 26 January the Lincoln and Welland Regiment, supported by almost every gun in 1st British Corps, launched a pincer attack on the German paratroops. The enemy held their fire until the Canadians were virtually on their objective, then opened up so effectively that within minutes all the officers of the two companies attacking from the east were hit. After a fierce German counterattack, they were withdrawn from the island. On the west, despite all its platoon commanders being killed, the leading company gained a foothold, beat off enemy counterattacks and held its position until it was reinforced. By nightfall, on the opposite flank, the battalion's anti-tank platoon had fought their way onto the island and there were relieved by a company of the Argyll and Sutherland Highlanders of Canada, supported by two tanks of the South Alberta Regiment.

The island was as featureless as the polder country of the Scheldt. The only practical line of advance was along a high dyke, 300 metres in from the edge of the river. A few Shermans crossed to the island by raft or a rickety bridge, but the sodden tracks were virtually impassable for armour.

From east and west the Argylls and Lincoln and Wellands worked toward the German positions, digging in after each short move. For four more days of acute cold and misery, they clawed their way forward while the artillery pounded the stubborn German paratroops. The 15th Field Regiment fired more than 14,000 twenty-five pounder rounds during the operation.

Early on the morning of the 31st the two Canadian battalions met in the ruins of the hamlet. They had captured 34 prisoners and counted 145 German dead on the battlefield. In the final action, the Canadians suffered 234 casualties, of whom 65, including nine officers, were killed. After the War the commander of the 6th German Parachute Division said that the defence of Kapelsche Veer had cost him between 300 and 400 'serious casualties,' plus 100 more men disabled by frostbite.

In all, nearly 1,000 men of both sides were killed, wounded or went missing in the snows of Kapelsche Veer.

18

THE REICHSWALD — OPERATION VERITABLE

LYING ACROSS ITS WESTERN APPROACHES, a barrier of mountains and great rivers form the historic natural defences of the Reich. Buttressed by them, inside its borders, lay the 'West Wall,' built by Hitler before the war. From the Swiss frontier to the northern border of Belgium, in places three miles deep, a defensive zone of mutually supporting fortifications, anti-tank obstacles, minefields, wire, protected command posts and troop shelters blocked the Allied advance. In 1944 the Siegfried Line, as it was known in the West, had been extended northward along the Dutch frontier.

Into it shattered units of the Wehrmacht had tumbled after their long retreat from Normandy, exhausted and bewildered.

Reacting with admirable speed and decisiveness, the German General Staff set about rebuilding fighting organizations and ensuring that defences were manned. Reinforcements and equipment were brought forward from depots in Germany and, within days, the whole frontier once more was guarded. Behind it, new recruits, boys and old men, were armed and trained and the Army's striking force, its panzer divisions, began to receive new tanks.

Soon the Allies were faced with the unpalatable and unavoidable prospect of attacking a German army entrenched in defences as strong as any they had faced on the Western Front in the First World War. Montgomery's bold attempt to outflank them had failed just short of success at Arnhem. There was no alternative now but to smash through. Then, beyond them, the

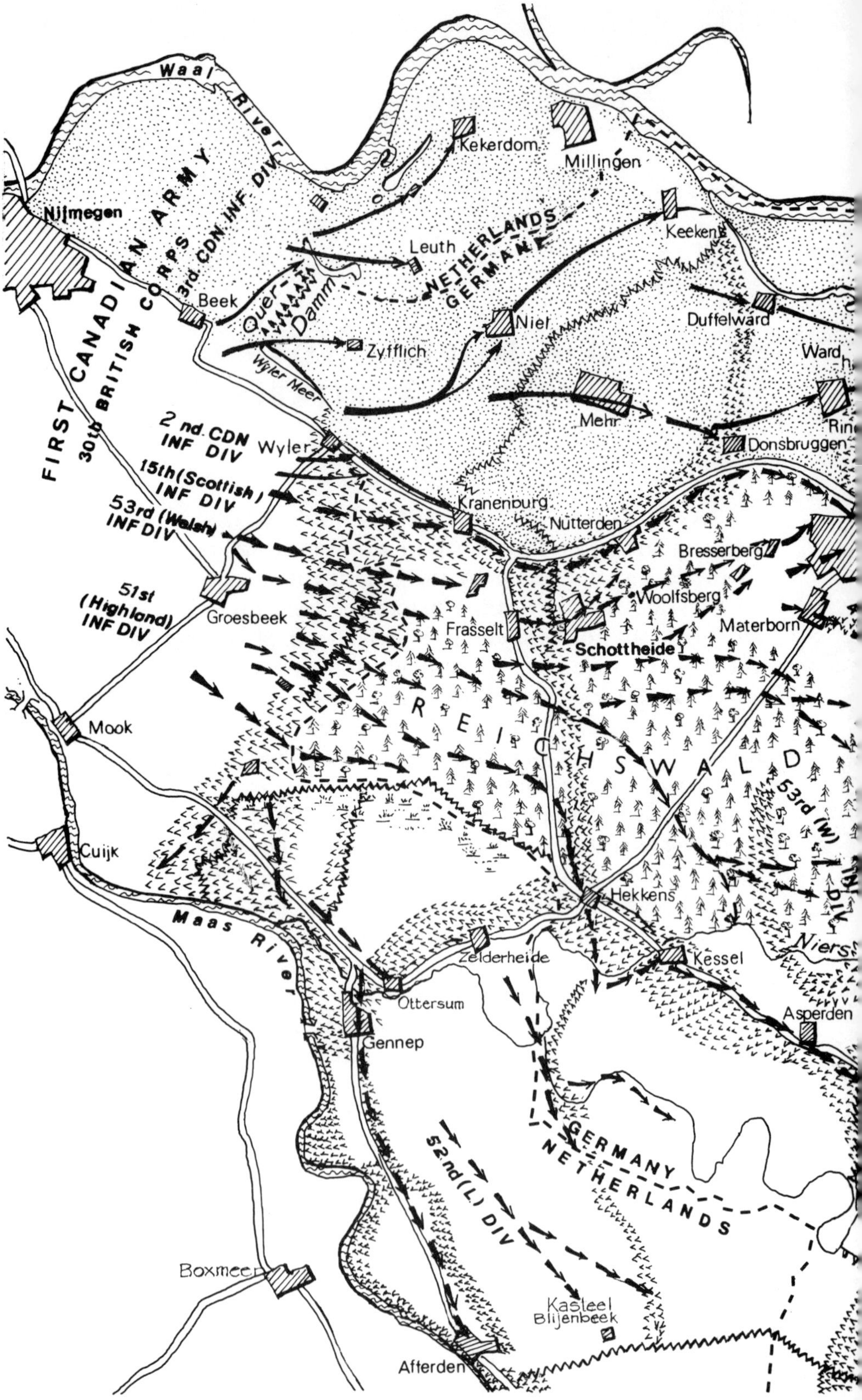

Waal River
FIRST CANADIAN ARMY
30th BRITISH CORPS
3rd. CDN. INF. DIV
Nijmegen
Kekerdom
Millingen
Leuth
NETHERLANDS
GERMANY
Keeken
Beek
Quer-Damm
Niel
Duffelward
Zyfflich
Wyler Meer
Ward
Mehr
Wyler
Donsbruggen
2 nd. CDN INF DIV
15th (Scottish) INF DIV
53rd (Welsh) INF DIV
Kranenburg
Nütterden
Bresserberg
51st (Highland) INF DIV
Groesbeek
Woolfsberg
Frasselt
Materborn
Schottheide
REICHSWALD
Mook
53rd (W) INF DIV
Cuijk
Hekkens
Maas River
Niers
Zelderheide
Kessel
Ottersum
Asperden
Gennep
GERMANY
NETHERLANDS
52nd (L) DIV
Boxmeer
Kasteel Blijenbeek
Afterden

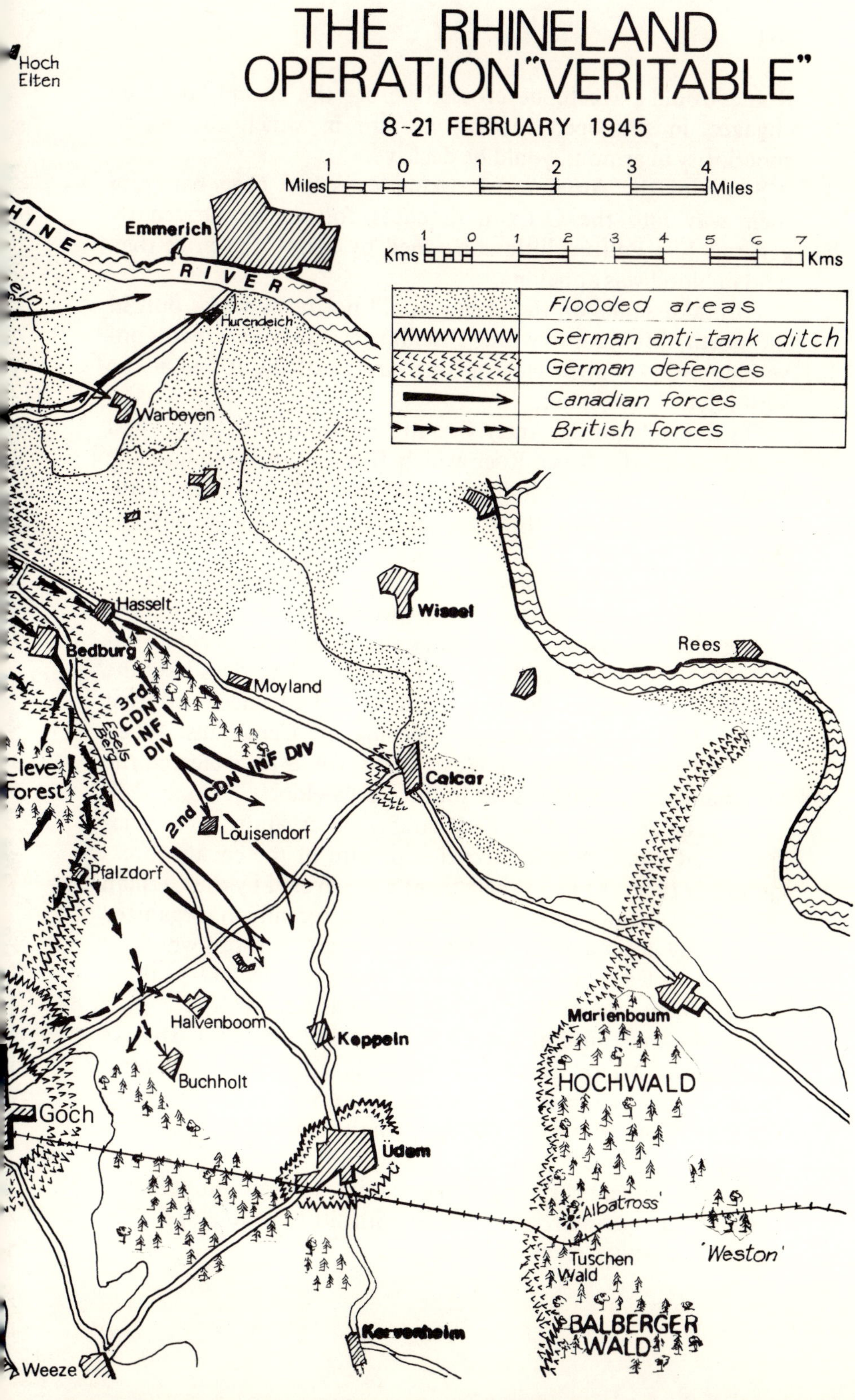
THE RHINELAND
OPERATION "VERITABLE"
8-21 FEBRUARY 1945
Miles
Miles
Kms
Kms
Flooded areas
German anti-tank ditch
German defences
Canadian forces
British forces
Hoch Elten
Emmerich
RHINE RIVER
Hurendeich
Warbeyen
Hasselt
Bedburg
Moyland
Wissel
Rees
Calcar
3rd CDN INF DIV
2nd CDN INF DIV
Esels Berg
Cleve Forest
Louisendorf
Pfalzdorf
Halvenboom
Keppeln
Buchholt
Marienbaum
HOCHWALD
Goch
Üdem
'Albatross'
Tuschen Wald
'Weston'
BALBERGER WALD
Kervenheim
Weeze

Rhine would have to be crossed before the enemy could be engaged in the open mobile warfare in which the Allied superiority in armour would be decisive.

South of the Ardennes the Americans had been battering their way into the German defences for weeks. Driven by generals like Patton, little concerned by losses, the price they paid in blood was appalling.

Frontal assaults on the enemy could not be avoided, but, in the north, Montgomery and Eisenhower saw where two converging attacks might clear a long stretch of the Rhine at the least relative cost in lives.

On the right of 21 Army Group the Ninth U.S. Army had closed up to the River Roer which flows north-west into the Maas. From there Second British Army held that river northwards to where their front joined that of the Canadians opposite the Reichswald.

While Second Army blocked this line, the western edge of the battlefield, First Canadian Army, with almost every British division under command, would attack south-eastward from its six-mile front between the Maas and the Rhine. Two days later the Ninth U.S. Army would cross the Roer and advance north-east across the rear of the enemy opposing the Canadians. When they met in the vicinity of Wesel, they would have cleared the west bank of the Rhine as far south as Düsseldorf.

By constant patrolling and careful observation, the Canadians had established an accurate picture of the enemy forces opposing them. Most of their front was covered by the German 84th Division, a second-rate formation recently re-organized after being decimated in Normandy. The green troops who held the line at least had the virtue of being young and healthy. Behind them, one of the two units in immediate reserve was the 276th Magen (stomach) Battalion, formed of men with digestive complaints. Major-General Heinz Fiebig, the divisional commander, said that he had chosen them in preference to an Ohren (ear) battalion 'who couldn't hear even the opening barrage of an attack.'

A swift, violent thrust in overwhelming strength should burst through such a ramshackle outfit with little trouble and that, sensibly, is what Crerar planned.

But he was aware that other factors, not so easy to assess, would affect the operation. For one thing, the total opposition should not be judged by the example of the 84th Division. They formed part of the Fifth Parachute Army led by General Alfred Schlemm, one of the best and most experienced of German field commanders. He had been Student's chief of staff in the airborne assault on Crete, he had commanded a corps in Russia and had performed a near miracle of military improvisation in containing the Allied landings at Anzio in Italy in January, 1944. He could be relied upon to react with embarrassing speed and effectiveness. Crerar's intelligence staff reckoned that he had two divisions close enough to intervene in the battle within six hours of an assault.

And there was the ground and the weather. The battle would be fought between the Rhine and the Maas, both of which were prone to flooding, now likely after a winter of excessive rainfall. The extent of it would be limited by rising ground near the Maas but, if the Germans blew the winter dykes along the Rhine, it could in places cover half the battlefield.

Between the flood plains, higher gently rolling ground broadened toward the south-east, much of it open farmland suitable for armoured operations. But at its western end and again a dozen miles to the east were large state forests, inhospitable to tanks. They were mostly of young pines planted in regular rows about six feet apart. Within them narrow sandy rides, forming a grid pattern, gave access to the depth of the forests. From the Canadian positions near Groesbeek, the lowering black mass of the Reichswald could be seen rising up abruptly from the hillsides opposite. The others to the east were as yet known only by their names — the Hochwald and the Balberger Wald. But that each was defended there was little doubt.

Three main belts of defences faced First Canadian Army, each anchored on the Rhine. A formidable system of trenches, minefields, anti-tank ditches, fortified villages and houses lay across the western face of the Reichswald, then down the east bank of the Maas. Then came the Siegfried System itself, its main positions about five kilometres inside the Reichswald with a secondary belt east of the forest. These came together at the heavily fortified town of Goch from which they ran south, roughly parallel to the forward line along the Maas.

Ten kilometres to the east was the Hochwald 'layback,' two and sometimes three lines of trenches, 500 to 1,000 metres apart, belts of wire and anti-tank defences, running from the Rhine opposite Rees across the face of the Hochwald to beyond Geldern.

Because of the initial narrow frontage, Crerar decided that his attack would be led by 30th British Corps. As its divisions moved forward, the battlefield would widen and 2nd Canadian Corps would come in on the left. The strength of the successive German defensive lines would probably require him to mount deliberate well-supported attacks on each in turn. This would result, he concluded, in the operation taking place in three phases.

Phase 1. The clearing of the Reichswald and the securing of the line Gennep-Asperden-Cleve.

Phase 2. The breaching of the enemy's second defensive system east and southeast of the Reichswald, the capture of the localities Weeze-Üdem-Calcar-Emmerich and the securing of the communications between them.

Phase 3. The breakthrough of the Hochwald layback defence lines and the advance to secure the general line Geldern-Xanten.[1]

But, he stressed, any opportunity for a breakthrough must be exploited with speed and vigour.

For the first phase, 30 Corps would have seven divisions under its command, some 200,000 men. It came to First Canadian Army with a record of success which dated back to Alamein and its commander, Lt-General Sir Brian Horrocks, cool, urbane, experienced, was treated by the press as a star.

The Canadians did not know Horrocks, nor he them, but they were prepared to be impressed. He did nothing to disappoint them.

At the initial conference at Crerar's headquarters, he arrived in a shiny, flagged and starred, khaki-painted, open-topped Bugatti, escorted by immaculate motorcycle outriders and radio jeeps. Ostentatious perhaps, but no one was in any doubt that here was the commander of 30th British Corps. And Horrocks well knew that soldiers like to see their generals, especially near the front.

Next day the staff received an order to find an open touring car for General Simonds.

The 2nd and 3rd Canadian Divisions were to be under Horrocks for the attack. Brigadier James Roberts of the 8th Brigade described his first impression of the corps commander:

> On 25 January, commanders down to brigade level were called to a conference held by General Horrocks. I was deeply impressed by this fabulous character, a born leader such as I had never met before. Horrocks was brief, strictly to the point, but so overwhelmingly confident and amusing that most of the Canadian commanders felt like cheering when the general completed the outline of his plan and his intentions.

Ten days later, Roberts took General Horrocks to a position held by a standing patrol of the Queen's Own Rifles of Canada.

> Horrocks walked up to the group and spoke to its commander, enquiring about the state of the enemy, the amount of activity, and the best place to view the enemy's forward lines. Then Horrocks suggested we move forward but, before leaving the patrol, he turned to a Queen's Own corporal and asked for the loan of his dark rifle-green beret. The corporal obliged and the general took off his scarlet cap with general's rank badge and plopped it on the corporal's head. The whole Queen's Own patrol stood with open mouths as we moved off.
>
> We moved forward quietly on foot and finally, on our bellies, until we found a reasonable position from which both General Horrocks and I could view the enemy forward lines and the terrain before we pulled out and returned to the QOR patrol. Here General Horrocks exchanged his rifleman's beret for his own magnificent staff cap and, with a cheery word of thanks from Horrocks, we returned to the jeep and to my HQ.
>
> After the general had departed, I sat a few moments, thinking of the impact of his personality. Here was one of the finest officers in the British army, with a magnificent record of service and of personal gallantry. Here was a man who really led, a general who talked to everyone, down to the simplest private soldier. He called his of-

ficers 'Joe', 'Peter', 'Reggie', 'Mike', or whatever. I was 'Jim' before we crawled back to the Queen's Own patrol. By his personal qualities of leadership he brought out a respect and an affection which made better soldiers of his officers and men. Why, I wondered, rather guiltily, were our senior officers not of the same personality; and we were supposed to be Canadians, less stiff and formal than the British. Our own army commander was a good soldier, a very nice man personally, and, I am sure, a man loyal to his troops as a whole. But his personality was not that of a leader of men. He addressed his officers as 'Smith', 'Jones', and 'Roberts'. So did Guy Simonds and so, if I remember correctly, did Field-Marshal Montgomery. Some of them were, indeed, leaders, but none like Horrocks.

While preparations were being made for the battle, Horrocks set about discovering the Canadians. To him, they 'seemed bigger than our men . . . tough, battle-experienced troops.

'I also saw quite a lot of their commander, General Crerar, who, in my opinion, has always been much underrated, largely because he was the exact opposite to Montgomery. He hated publicity but was full of common sense and always prepared to listen to the views of his subordinate commanders. Every day after the battle started, he would fly over the front (a somewhat dangerous operation) in a small aircraft, and then came to see me wherever I might be.'[3]

Crerar was an artilleryman and as a young officer had served on the staff of the Canadian Corps in the First World War. From its two brilliant commanders, Byng and Currie, he had absorbed one cardinal lesson about attacking prepared defences — use guns instead of men.

For the attack on the 84th German Division, 1,034 guns would put down the largest concentration of fire ever seen on such a narrow front in the war in Western Europe. Nine tons of shells would burst on each of 268 targets. On the front of each attacking division, a 'Pepperpot group' — every available tank gun, mortar, medium machine gun, anti-tank and anti-aircraft gun — would sweep the area continuously with carefully coordinated short-range fire. To this would be added salvoes of 'Land Mattress' rockets.

Air support was to be on a massive scale — heavy bombers of

the RAF Bomber Command, and the United States Eighth Air Force, mediums of 2nd Tactical Air Force and fighter bombers of Nos. 83 and 84 Groups and the U.S. Ninth Air Force. Before D Day, railways, bridges and ferries leading to the battle area would be hit, particularly those across the Rhine. The towns of Cleve and Goch were to be completely destroyed whilst other towns where cratering was not acceptable would be hit by incendiary and anti-personnel bombs.

Careful arrangements were made for the control of 84 Group's fighter bombers which would provide close support for the attacking troops. No. 83 Group, which was largely made up of Royal Canadian Air Force squadrons, and usually supported Second British Army, would deal with the Luftwaffe and continue the interdiction of the battle area after D Day.

Daily the Canadians opposite the Reichswald kept a careful watch on the Germans to detect any sign of the 84th Division being reinforced. Only a small increase of enemy strength on such a narrow front would greatly increase the price which would have to be paid in lives in this frontal attack. Surprise was essential.

To achieve it, the obvious precautions such as concealment of tanks, guns and dumps, no movement by day and restriction on the use of radios were strictly enforced.

But a major problem was reconnaissance. Literally thousands of British officers and NCOs had to see the ground over which they were to attack. So much movement near the front, if unrestricted, would soon be discovered by the Germans. The activity of all reconnaissance parties was carefully scheduled and controlled. All were dressed in the darker Canadian battledress without formation patches, and travelled in Canadian vehicles escorted by officers of the 2nd Division. They carried passes valid only for the time needed for their reconnaissance which had to be produced at Military Police check points.

To deceive the enemy and distract his attention 1st British Corps along the lower Maas went through the motions of preparing for an attack aimed at liberating northern Holland.

On 5 February, three days before the battle, Rundstedt's intelligence staff predicted that the next major British attack would take place at the bend in the Maas north of Roermond.

Their situation map showed 30th British Corps as 'whereabouts unknown.'

General Schlemm was sceptical. He thought that the Allies might well be attracted to an attack through the Reichswald but he could not sway his superiors. They attempted to reassure him by saying there was no sign of a large Allied concentration in the Nijmegen area. Schlemm was not convinced, but, without the approval of his army group commander, he could make no significant change in the layout of his army. He did, however, obtain a reinforcement — a regiment of the 2nd Parachute Division which he placed in the line on the left of the 84th between the edge of the Reichswald and the River Maas.

Even greater help came to Schlemm from another quarter. December and January had been cold, the ground frozen and snow-covered. Roads could carry heavy traffic and tanks could move fairly easily across country. If it continued, Crerar and Horrocks were in little doubt that they could burst through the enemy defences into the open plain beyond the Hochwald in two or three days. But February brought thaw instead of hard ground suitable for armoured formations and they were faced with that great enemy of mobility — mud. Later Horrocks wrote: 'Fortunately for my peace of mind, I did not realize just how soggy it could become.'[4]

To the troops of 30th Corps nightfall on 7 February brought the sound of aircraft, followed by the distant rumble of bombs. Soon the horizon to the east glowed red with fires of burning towns. Then, precisely at 5 o'clock in the morning, the artillery opened fire. The whole sky to the west was lit by a flashing wall of light, and overhead came the rushing sigh of a thousand shells. Moments later, on the enemy positions opposite, orange flashes marked their explosion followed by a mounting, echoing roar of sound as the crump of their bursts merged into a continuous monstrous bellow. For two-and-a-half hours it continued, then suddenly stopped. High above the ground, puffs of grey appeared in the air as 25-pounder base-ejection shells, spewed out a shower of canisters which fell to the earth trailing white smoke. Soon a cloud blanketed the enemy, blinding their view to the west. To them, it meant that the attack had begun.

Immediately every German gun within range put down a screen of fire in front of their infantry positions.

For ten minutes the British and Canadian artillery lay silent as survey teams plotted the positions of enemy guns and mortars now in action for the first time and added them to the target list. Then the guns resumed their work.

At ten o'clock, half an hour before H Hour, the full force of the artillery and the Pepper Pot groups fell upon the German forward defences. To the almost unimaginable noise now was added the sound of aircraft overhead and of tanks grinding forward to their attack positions.

To avoid giving any hint to the enemy that other troops were present, the start lines of the attack were held by seven battalions of the 2nd Canadian Division. Behind them, ready to advance, were the 51st (Highland) Division, the 53rd (Welsh), the 15th (Scottish), the 3rd Canadian and the remaining two battalions of the 2nd.

At 10:29, a line of yellow smoke shells marked the last minute before the barrage was to lift. In tanks of the 6th Guards, 8th and 34th Armoured Brigades, the quiet order 'Driver, advance' was given, platoon commanders waved their lead sections forward and the infantry, pulling the brims of their helmets lower on their foreheads, began to walk eastward into Germany.

Instead of the expected hail of Spandau bullets, mortar bombs and shells, almost everywhere they met what commentators like to call 'patchy resistance' — a few brave riflemen or machine-gunners — and 'sporadic shell and mortar fire' — nasty concentrations of deadly high-explosive. They killed and wounded a few unfortunate infantry but did little to stop the tide of the advance.

Prisoners testified to the devastating effect of the bombardment. Dazed, disoriented, isolated, their communications shattered, opposed by what seemed overwhelming force, they had lost their will to resist.

From the crossing of the startline, it was plain that this was to be an infantry battle. Opposite the Reichswald, on the front of the 53rd Division, mud bogged the flail tanks which were to clear paths through minefields for the infantry and armour.

Some of the broader-tracked Churchills managed to get through. But after the 71st Brigade had seized control of the north-west corner of the forest, the 160th's advance eastward was virtually unsupported. Shortly after midnight its leading battalions were fighting in the main defences of the Siegfried Line, east of the Hekkens-Kranenburg road.

On their right, the 51st Division, attacking the southern shoulder of the Reichswald, ran into unexpected resistance from a battalion of the 180th Division which had been hurriedly thrown into the line the previous evening. The Highlanders outflanked it and, by early next morning, had advanced beyond the high ridge at the south-west corner of the forest.

On the low ground on the northern edge of the Reichswald runs the main road from Nijmegen through Cleve and Xanten, giving access to the Rhine bridges at Emmerich, Rees and Wesel. Between it and the river much of the land was flooded. Rising above the water, the buildings of drowned farms and villages formed islands joined by the trees which lined submerged tracks and roadways. As far as Cleve, the road itself was threatened by rising water but was usable. It was the only practicable route for moving tanks and guns beyond the Reichswald, a fact which was as apparent to Schlemm as it was to Crerar. The need for the road became a near obsession to Horrocks.

At the Nijmegen end two battalions of the 5th Canadian Infantry Brigade were to clear the enemy from it as far as Kranenburg. From there it would be the axis of advance of the 15th Scottish Division.

In the Canadian sector the road passed through the village of Wyler, the northern hinge of the enemy's forward defences, protected in depth by road blocks, dug-in anti-tank guns, minefields and stretches of anti-tank ditch. That the garrison was alert had been proved in raids by the 3rd Division in January. Later that month officers and NCOs of the Calgary Highlanders were briefed for a battalion raid on the village, made detailed reconnaissances and rehearsed the operation. Then, early in February, the battalion was withdrawn from the line and learned of the importance of their forthcoming attack. If they failed to take Wyler quickly, the advance of 30 Corps on Cleve might grind to a halt.

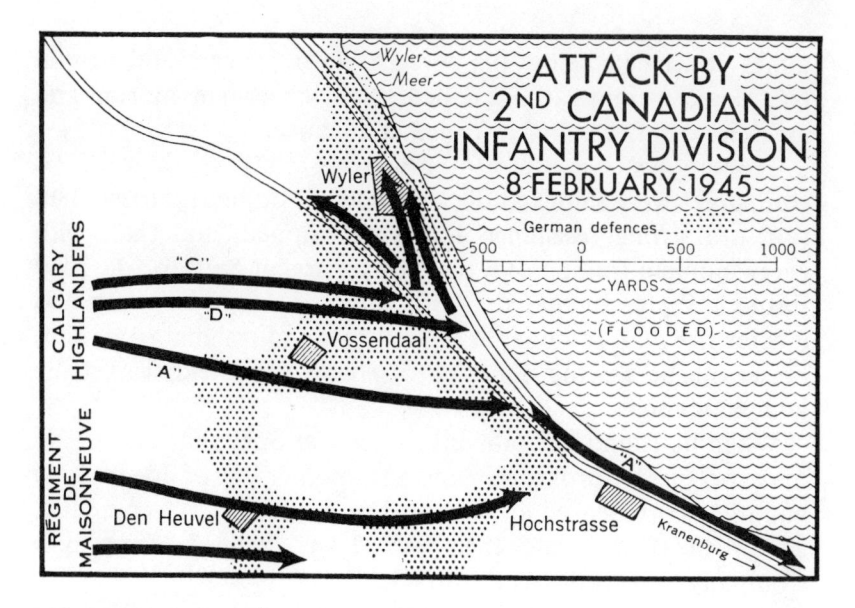

They would have massive artillery support and their right flank would be protected by the advance of Le Régiment de Maisonneuve through the hamlets of Den Heuvel and Hochstrasse.

Despite the support he was promised, the prospect of a frontal attack held no appeal for Lt-Colonel Ross Ellis. Instead he decided to cut the main road south-east of the town. Then, having severed the garrison's escape route, he would turn back northwest and clear it.

Leaning on the artillery barrage, the Calgaries moved steadily eastward through Vossendaal. By noon, despite losing several casualties in a minefield, A Company had reached the main road and advanced a mile and a half down it to meet a battalion of the 15th Scottish Division near Kranenburg. Behind them, two companies reached the road and turned toward Wyler. Almost immediately C Company met with disaster in a minefield. The Germans had laid several rows of Schu-mines on the surface. Gingerly, the leading troops picked their way safely past the first row, but in trying to avoid the next, men stepped on mines concealed below the surface. Two officers and several NCOs were among those killed. Heavy German mortar and machine-gun fire halted any further advance.

To complicate matters for Ellis, the radios of three of his companies were knocked out. He knew little but that they had run into strong resistance and were stopped, and that, with every moment that passed, the Army's urgent need for the road through Wyler increased. Arranging for a new artillery and mortar fire plan to be set in motion by a radio signal from him, he set out across the bullet-swept enemy minefields to get the attack moving.

When he found C Company, he saw at once that they could make no further progress. Choosing another line of advance, he and his escort cleared a new start line for his reserve company, gave them their orders, then walked and crawled across to D Company to co-ordinate the attack.

As soon as the artillery and 4.2-inch mortars opened fire, the two companies raced forward into Wyler, clearing snipers from houses and ferreting the enemy out of strongly built bunkers. By 6:30 p.m. the last resistance had ended, the battalion capturing 287 prisoners, including a regimental commander and his staff and detailed information about the Siegfried defences. It had cost the Calgaries sixty-seven casualties.

The final note in the battalion's war diary for the day recorded that one company had sent in an unusual prisoner. When the Intelligence section began their usual careful physical searches for documents and concealed weapons, they discovered that one German soldier was a girl: '. . . a member of the I section is going around with a very flushed expression.'[5]

To the west of Cleve and the village of Materborn, two kilometres to the south-west, a range of hills looks down on the road from Nijmegen and onto the open country to the east. No advance beyond the Reichswald would be possible until the enemy was driven from them. The 15th Scottish Division was ordered to take this 'Materborn feature' with all possible speed, having breached the main Siegfried defences on the way.

Major-General 'Tiny' Barber's plan was in the best blitzkrieg tradition but outdid the original in the range of equipment he was able to use. Tanks he had aplenty, the 6th Guards Armoured Brigade, and the full range of 'special' armour, the 'Funnies' of the 79th Armoured Division. Flail tanks would beat paths through the minefields for infantry of the 46th and 227th Brigades to assault the German forward positions. Once these were taken a Special Breaching Force of the 44th Brigade in 300 heavy armoured vehicles would smash through the main Siegfried defences. Again Flails would open routes through the covering minefields, then AVREs carrying folding bridges and fascines would lay crossings over the next obstacle, a wide anti-tank ditch. The first to cross them would be the weapons the Germans feared the most, Crocodiles, whose long tongues of flame searched out and incinerated machine-gun crews in their bunkers. Then would come the infantry, 8th Royal Scots, 6th Royal Scots Fusiliers, 6th King's Own Scottish Borderers, and 2nd Gordon Highlanders, every man mounted in Kangaroos of the 1st Canadian Armoured Personnel Carrier Regiment. With them would be the Churchills of the 4th Grenadier Guards and their own artillery observation officers mounted in tanks.

As on the front of the Welsh Division, rain and flooding produced quagmires. Only one Flail was able to reach the start line, and the 46th and 227th Brigades suffered more casualties from mines in the first hours than they did from enemy fire. But, by keeping close to their artillery barrages, by 6:30 p.m. they had driven through the forward enemy defences and captured Kranenburg on the Cleve road and the village of Frasselt two kilometres to the south.

Behind them, a route forward from Groesbeek had been opened along secondary roads and farm tracks for the vehicles of each brigade. Under the weight of tanks, carriers and heavy trucks these were soon reduced to mud. Sweating soldiers, too breathless to swear, heaved ammunition lorries, ambulances and command vehicles past the worst stretches. Early in the afternoon 227th Brigade's route in the north broke down completely and the entire traffic of the Division was thrown on to the 46th Brigade's. That night, when 44 Brigade's Breaching Force attempted to follow it, they were brought virtually to a standstill as tanks and Kangaroos crawled belly-deep, their tracks churning the mud into viscid black porridge.

Lt-Colonel C.W.P. Richardson of the 6th KOSB went forward during the afternoon to a hill overlooking Frasselt to make final arrangements for his attack, scheduled to begin at 9 p.m. on the Siegfried positions beyond the village. The day for him, as for every commander concerned with the advance, ended in frustration. As it had in so many battles, mud had brought progress to a crawl. There would be no attack on the Siegfried Line before morning.

The northern flank of the battle area, between the Nijmegen-Cleve road and the Rhine, was virtually polder country. When in January, the 3rd Canadian Division was given the task of clearing it, its unpleasant resemblance to the shores of the Scheldt was obvious but there was a significant difference. So long as it remained frozen, they would be able to advance across its open fields in Kangaroos supported by tanks. Then came the early thaw and heavy rain. Daily the ground grew soggier. On 3 February the level of the Waal began to rise. On the 6th water started to flow through gaps blown by the Germans in the main river dyke. On the 8th the mile-long Quer Damm collapsed and by that evening, when the 3rd Division's attack was to begin, most of their area was under water. Instead of using tanks and Kangaroos, they would ride to their objectives in Buffaloes. It did not take them long to realize that, while the Germans had delayed the advance of 30 Corps by flooding its main supply route, they had, in the process, drowned their own minefields, anti-tank ditches, wire entanglements and trenches. Most of the three belts of the Siegfried defences near Cleve were under water and the enemy's forward positions north of Wyler, apart from a short stretch, were confined to the flooded villages of Zyfflich, Leuth and Kekerdom and to the crests of a few dykes which remained above water.

H Hour for the 3rd Division's two attacking brigades was 6 p.m. Ahead the floodwaters gave off an eerie metallic sheen under 'artificial moonlight,' created by searchlight beams reflected from the low clouds above. Dykes and buildings were dark shadows on the surface.

After a ten-minute 'Pepperpot,' the assault began. Only on the extreme right were the infantry, The Regina Rifles, able to advance on foot. Supported by tanks of 13/18th Royal Hussars, in two hours they had seized the southern end of the Quer Damm and captured the village of Zyfflich, a mile to the east. In the meantime, other battalions of the 7th and 8th Brigades were learning new lessons in the strange art of Buffalo fighting.

Two companies of the Canadian Scottish, setting out in the ungainly craft to take the village of Niel, soon discovered how difficult it was to keep direction in the dark when crossing relatively shallow water. When one track of a vehicle touched ground, the craft would swerve violently, sometimes making a complete circle before coming under control. Knowing that they were vulnerable to enemy fire, the Scottish gave a wide berth to Zyfflich 'whose numerous blazing buildings lit up the surrounding water-covered fields like a lighthouse.'[6] Confused by the very number of burning villages, they mistook another hamlet for their objective.

That night atmospheric interference made radio communications almost impossible. At his tactical headquarters, Lt-Colonel Desmond Crofton had heard nothing from his leading companies since they embarked for Niel. After allowing what he judged to be sufficient time for them to reach their objective, he and his command group boarded two Buffaloes and followed. As they approached the village, some if its buildings afire, they could see no sign of their men and could hear nothing over the roar of the Buffaloes' aircraft-type engines. As the leading craft eased between the first buildings, there was a blinding flash and an appalling explosion as the rocket of a panzerfaust burst inside, leaving the officers commanding the Buffaloes and the supporting artillery dead and eight others wounded or dying. Crofton, his right arm smashed, led a blinded lieutenant to cover in a nearby barn where they remained until rescued some twelve hours later.

The crew of the second Buffalo now under fire replied with their heavy Browning machine gun and their 20mm Polsten cannon as they backed away.

By this time, about 5 o'clock in the morning, the two missing companies were moving in to attack. In little more than an hour the village and nearly 100 prisoners were in their hands.[7]

On the left the 8th Brigade's initial objective was a defended dyke which lay some 300 metres in front of a similar position held by them. Two companies of the North Shore Regiment were to cross the flooded polder in Buffaloes. Once ashore, a light signal would summon Le Régiment de la Chaudière who would cross in canoe-like skiffs to the southern half of the enemy dyke.

Immediately the first shells of the 'Pepperpot' exploded on the Germans, at exactly 6 p.m., the Buffaloes' engines roared and their tracks began to dig them deeper and deeper into the soaking earth of the dyke. They did not move.

Brigadier Jim Roberts' immediate reaction was concern that the attack would be delayed long enough for the enemy to recover from the effects of 'Pepperpot.' He radioed for a ten-minute extension, then ordered Major Marks, commanding the Buffalo squadron, to reverse the vehicles off the dyke and climb it diagonally. Slowly, one by one the huge machines clawed their way over the crest and plunged into the water. Only half of them reached the enemy dyke, not one of which carried an officer of the North Shore Regiment nor the means of signalling the Chaudière to follow.

Major Marks' responsibilities to the infantry had ended with the landing of his Buffaloes' load of soldiers. Fortunately he had initiative and courage. In his amphibian, he learned, before any of the men ashore, that they were without officers. Immediately he jumped from his vehicle, rallied the men nearby and set about capturing the dyke.

So swift was his action that, with only about one quarter of the men originally sent to take the position, he cleared it from end to end. Stunned by twenty minutes terrific bombardment, the aged 'Volkssturm' defenders, mostly veterans of the First World War, emerged from their dugouts, holding their ears, rolling their heads and drooling at the mouth.[8]

At headquarters of the Fifth Parachute Army, General Alfred Schlemm listened to Crerar's guns on the morning of the 8th and could imagine that he was hearing once more one of 'Koniev's symphonies' on the Russian front. Despite the lack of other indications, it could only mean the beginning of the long-expected Allied offensive. Before any report arrived from the front, he telephoned Col-General Johannes Blaskowitz, the commander-in-chief of Army Group H, to ask for reserves to reinforce the 84th Division. His request was refused.

By this stage of the war, German intelligence had been so discredited in the eyes of the generals that they preferred to make up their minds about Allied intentions by imagining what they would do if they were the opposing commanders. Blaskowitz and Rundstedt, his superior, had both concluded that the main attack would be launched toward the Ruhr by the Second British and Ninth U.S. Armies, from the great bend in the Maas north of Roermond. Any attack by Canadian formations opposite the Reichswald could only be a subsidiary 'to deceive us regarding the real centre of gravity of the attack.'[9]

Wedded to their misconceptions, Schlemm's superiors grudgingly permitted him to commit the 7th Parachute Division on the evening of 8 February. In their opinion, the attacks had been launched by the Canadian 2nd and 3rd Divisions and 2nd Armoured Brigade. Next day, though they had identified both the 51st and 53rd Divisions, they persisted in believing that the main blow would be delivered by Second Army from the Maas bend.

Further south, General Simpson's Ninth U.S. Army were poised to begin their attack across the Roer on the 10th. The day before, while Schlemm raged at the collective stupidity of Blaskowitz and his staff, Montgomery was agreeing with Simpson that Operation Grenade would have to be postponed for 24 hours to allow the unusually high level of the Roer to subside. At almost the same time a unit of the First U.S. Army had reached one of the key dams on the Roer to find that the Germans had jammed open a sluice gate, unleashing more than a hundred million tons of water into the river. Within hours, the level of the Roer rose by another five feet, overflowing its banks across the whole of Ninth Army front and causing the Maas to flood in First Canadian Army's area. By wrecking the sluice gate, instead of blowing up the dam, the Germans had created, not a short-lived torrent, but a flood which would last for at least eleven days.

On the 10th, when satisfied that any advance by Second and Ninth Armies had been blocked by floods, Rundstedt gave Schlemm the Headquarters of 47th Panzer Corps to take control of the battle and moved his armoured reserve — 15th Panzer Grenadier and 116th Panzer Divisions — closer to the scene. That he was becoming concerned by events on the Reichswald front can be seen from his signal to Blaskowitz at noon that day which emphasized the disastrous consequences of a break-through to the Rhine and the necessity of holding Cleve at all costs.[10]

The ancient and historic town of Cleve lies below the slopes of the Reichswald at its north-east corner. From it roads splay out to the east and south, into the heart of the Rhineland. If holding it was vital to Rundstedt, capture of the town and the hills above which dominate the road network was crucial to 30 Corps.

In the early hours of the 9th, General Horrocks listened to the rain driving against his caravan with the noise of a firehose playing on a window. With mounting frustration he learned of the rising flood waters and impassable roads which slowed the advance of the 15th Scottish Division. Behind, poised to move the moment. Cleve was taken, were the 43rd (Wessex) and the Guards Armoured Divisions — the breakout forces which would fan out to disrupt the German rearward defences.

To the east the 44th Brigade's Armoured Breaching Force had struggled through the night toward the minefields and the anti-tank ditch which covered the Siegfried Line. In the darkness and the sheeting rain, a nightmare of traffic jams, diversions, bogged vehicles and mud broke up the planned order of advance. To make matters worse, trees on either side of the narrow tracks fouled the girder bridges being carried by the AVREs. Their supports snapped and the bridges fell forward into the lowered position making the vehicles virtually unmanoeuvrable. When the head of the Force reached the start line for the attack at 4 a.m. Brigadier H.C.T. Cumming-Bruce, its commander, decided that, despite disorganization, the attack could not be delayed. An hour later, Flails and AVREs reached the ditch, laying a bridge over it at one site and making a rough fascine crossing at the other. Only one rifle company of the leading battalion, Richardson's 6th KOSB, had reached the crossing sites at Frasselt in their Kangaroos. Immediately they began to cross but an anti-tank gun towed by a Kangaroo fouled the bridge and blocked it. Using only the fascine crossing, the company soon established a bridgehead where they were joined by the other three companies of the Battalion who had been diverted via Kranenburg.

On the left the 2nd Gordon Highlanders attacked astride the main road to Cleve and, within an hour, reported that they had seized the main road bridge over the anti-tank ditch. Meeting little resistance, they reached Nutterden by 10 a.m.

So little sign of fight had the enemy shown that Cumming-Bruce ordered the KOSB to continue the advance rather than wait for another battalion to pass through them. Climbing into their Kangaroos, they drove eastwards to the next objective, the Wolfsberg, a hill which air photos showed was heavily fortified. With only a few casualties, the Borderers overran its defences, capturing four 88mm guns, the headquarters of an infantry battalion and an artillery regiment for a total 'bag' of 240 prisoners.

The main defences of the Siegfried Line had been breached, albeit some eleven hours behind schedule, a task which might well have exhausted a brigade. It had been achieved so cheaply that General Barber cancelled his plan for two brigades to move through the 44th for the final advance on Cleve and ordered Cumming-Bruce to press on. It was about noon on 9 February, the second day of the battle.

At that time Schlemm was the only senior German commander to recognize that First Canadian Army's thrust was no diversion. He was well aware of the weakness of the Siegfried Line and its defenders but there was little he could do to prevent a breakthrough. The situation was deteriorating far too quickly for him to use the 7th Parachute Division, which had been grudgingly released to him, for a counterattack. As its battalions arrived, he placed them in rear of the 84th Division between the Reichswald and the Maas, and ordered a battle group to move with all possible speed to occupy the two hills of the Materborn feature which block the approaches to Cleve from the south-west.

When the 6th KOSB once more mounted APCs and, with a tank

squadron of the 1st Grenadier Guards headed for the Bresserberg, the hill closest to Cleve, they did not know that they were in a race but their instincts and their orders left no doubt about the need for speed. Heading through forest tracks, they reached the hill about 3 p.m. to be met by bursts of machine-gun fire and the crump of mortars. Without dismounting, they drove forward almost a mile, incinerating pillboxes and raking a double line of trenches with fire. Within minutes the straggling hamlet of Bresserberg was aflame and grey figures with hands held high began to appear. As the leading company reached the slopes above Cleve they saw moving toward them the vanguard of the 7th Parachute Division. In the gathering dusk the Borderers beat off every attempt of the aggressive paratroopers to gain a foothold on the hill. That evening patrols of the 15th Division's reconnaissance regiment found strong enemy resistance on the roads south and east of Cleve, but in the town itself the Germans seemed disorganized.[11]

That night Barber issued orders for the 227th Brigade to clear Cleve in the morning and for mobile columns of tanks, infantry and guns to drive south-east down the road to Calcar and north-eastwards to seize the ferry across the Rhine to Emmerich. But, as the divisional history notes, 'Floods, mud and traffic congestion — these three were to defeat all plans.' Indeed they were — with some inadvertent help from Horrocks.[12]

All day the commander of 30 Corps had been waiting for news that the Materborn feature had been taken. When it had, the 43rd Division was to move forward from Nijmegen to advance across it and capture Goch, Üdem and Weeze. Having learned that the 15th Scottish Division were on the hills above Cleve and were advancing into the town, Horrocks

> . . . unleashed my first reserve, the 43rd Wessex Division. . . . This turned out to be one of the worst mistakes I made in the war. The 15th Scottish had not reached as far as had been reported and one of their brigades had not been employed at all. The chief enemy at this time was not the Germans but the congestion caused by the flooding which almost precluded cross-country movement. The arrival of this fresh division bursting for the fray caused one of the worst traffic jams in the war. . . . My only excuse is that all too

often during the war I had witnessed a pause in the battle when one division was ordered to pass through another, which allowed the enemy time to recover. In this case, speed was absolutely vital and I was determined that our attack should flow on.[13]

It was well after midnight when the leading brigade of the Wessex Division, the 129th, riding on their supporting tanks reached Nutterden. There they learned that the main road ahead was blocked and that Cleve had not yet been cleared. Lt-Colonel J.E.L. Corbyn of the 4th Wiltshires led his battalion by a secondary route around the north edge of the Bresserberg toward the town. As they neared it, bursts of Spandau fire raked the leading scout car. The infantry were off their tanks in a flash and swung out on either side of the track to outflank the road block. Having eliminated it, the advance continued on foot with the tanks firing into every house, their progress slowed by gigantic craters. As dawn was breaking, the Wiltshires reached a park on the southern outskirts of Cleve and could hardly believe their eyes at the scenes of devastation. Scarcely a house was standing. 'Bomb craters and fallen trees were everywhere, bomb craters packed so tightly together that the débris from one was piled against the rim of the next in a pathetic heap of rubble, roofs and radiators. There was not an undamaged house anywhere, piles of smashed furniture, clothing, children's books and toys, old photographs and bottled fruit were spilled in hopeless confusion into gardens from sagging, crazy skeletons of homes.'[14]

There their brigade commander ordered the 4th Wiltshires to halt and protect the northern flank, whilst his other two battalions by-passed them and advanced due south. In doing so, they began to move between the German main defences which were on the slopes above Materborn and the 6th Parachute Division which was moving to reinforce them. There followed a battle of such violence and confusion that the aim of both sides became simply to kill or be killed. All day the fighting raged and everyone in the vicinity was involved. 129th Brigade Headquarters fought off a German attack. Major-General Fiebig, commander of the German 84th Division, was caught up in a battle around his headquarters.

The history of the 4th Somerset Light Infantry tells what happened when the head of their column reached the eastern exits of Cleve.

> At this point a German counterattack, in the form of S.P.s and paratroopers, came in from the South. No one can fully describe what happened. Small groups stood and fought where they were, forming a thin line with the general direction facing South. German S.P.s picked off vehicle after vehicle, and we certainly 'bought it.' The head of the column was blocked by huge craters in the road and it was impossible to move forward until bulldozers could be got up to fill in the craters and clear the way.

The action of one private soldier, typified the fighting spirit of the men involved.

> [The carrier platoon] was attacked by a Panther, an S.P. gun and some infantry. The Panther came within 25 yards of the platoon position and the situation began to look desperate. Pte H.A. Tipple armed with a PIAT took up a position on the lip of a bomb crater but before he could bring his weapon into action, the tank spotted him and, firing a round of H.E. at point blank range, blew Tipple and his PIAT into the bottom of the crater. Undeterred, Tipple ... crawled up again to the lip of the crater taking up another fire position, engaging the tank and scoring direct hits. Unfortunately he was unable to knock the tank out but the blast effect of the bombs on the hull of the tank so discomforted it that it beat a hasty retreat and was not seen again.[15]

To the acute frustration of General Barber, the presence of 129th Brigade on part of his objective meant that artillery could not support the advance of his 227th Brigade into Cleve on 10 February. Instead the day was spent by the Scottish Division in clearing the remaining hills above. Then, next morning, they relieved the 129th Brigade on the outskirts of the town and proceeded to clear it. As they were doing so, the 214th Brigade of the Wessex Division cleared Materborn village and advanced east and south to capture Hau which lies at the eastern edge of the Reichswald. Here they found their advance blocked by German infantry and S.P. guns.

Schlemm had moved swiftly to contain 30 Corps' advance,

preparatory to a counterattack by 47th Panzer Corps to recapture Cleve. He ordered the 84th Division to hold the prepared defences of the Siegfried Line's rear position along the Eselsberg ridge between Hasselt on the Cleve-Calcar road and the rectangular Forest of Cleve which stands east of the Reichswald. But while the two divisions of the 47th Corps were concentrating near Üdem, General Heinrich Freiherr von Lüttwitz, their commander, learned that Hau had fallen and that the 53rd Division was threatening the Cleve-Goch road in the eastern Reichswald. Instead of advancing directly on Cleve, he decided to move west into the Reichswald then swing north with all his forces to capture the Materborn heights.

The attack began at 9:30 a.m. on the 12th and immediately ran into the 43rd Division. Three efforts to break through the British failed and at nightfall Lüttwitz' Corps pulled back to take up defensive positions.

Mud, floods and traffic congestion were still restricting 30th Corps' operations but now the full effects of the flooding of the Roer began to be felt. With that barrier thrown across the front of the Ninth U.S. Army, Rundstedt began to reinforce Schlemm with some of his best divisions. The soldiers of First Canadian Army would meet no more halfhearted resistance from shell-shocked troops west of the Rhine.

As the 43rd Division prepared to advance down the east side of the Forest of Cleve, the 51st (Highland) Division was driving eastwards south of the Reichswald. On the 9th their 152nd Brigade reached the Siegfried Line north of Hekkens and the 153rd, driving south, cut the road from Mook to Goch. Next day they advanced along it. That night the 5th Battalion, Black Watch crossed the Niers River in assault boats to take the town of Gennep in a surprise attack from the north-east, overwhelming its defences which faced the west.

> There is one strange story of this village of Gennep. It has been told again and again, but always with a sense of wonder. Capt Donald Beales of the 5th Black Watch was standing in the doorway of a house in Gennep, where he had established the headquarters of his company. He sent his runner, Pte Smith, on a message, who, as he moved down the roadway, shouted back to his officer: 'I'll see you

in twenty minutes, sir.' The next minute Beales was killed, as Smith was exactly twenty minutes later.[16]

The way was now open for Second Army to begin bridging the Maas. Further east Hekkens was taken by the 154th Brigade after bitter fighting, and on the 13th, the Highland and Welsh Divisions met two miles to the east on the fringes of the Reichswald.

Fighting their way eastward through the dank, dripping depths of the forest, the 53rd (Welsh) Division broke through the Siegfried defences and reached the heights above Materborn on the 9th. The advance was far from easy and the Germans mounted several well planned counterattacks by infantry and SP guns against the East Lancashire Regiment on the Hekkens-Frasselt road. Only tracked vehicles could be used on the sodden forest tracks and frequently even these bogged down. Opposition was fierce. SP guns firing down the rides were difficult to destroy. On the 12th and 13th the Panzer Corps' counterattack was met head-on by the 6th Royal Welch Fusiliers and the 1/5 Welch Regiment. They stopped the advancing Panzer Grenadiers dead about 300 yards from their positions with artillery and machine guns — then continued their clearance of the south-east bulge of the Forest.

To the north the attacking brigades of the 3rd Canadian Division had reached their initial objectives in the drowned flood plain of the Rhine by afternoon of the 9th only to find that they were virtually cut off by rising waters. Vehicles which had been ordered forward were caught in the floods and drowned. Rations began to run short. Nonetheless, infantry fighting patrols swept the area east of Mehr to ensure that 9th Brigade's start line for their attack next morning suffered no enemy interference. That day most men in the division learned they had a new nickname:

9 Feb 45

1. The Army Comd, Comd 30 Br Corps, Comd 2 Cdn Corps are all extremely pleased with the excellent work done by THE DIV in Op VERITABLE. In view of ops SWITCHBACK and VERITABLE Comd 2 Cdn Corps now refers to us as 'THE WATER

RATS.' I have accepted our new nickname and I am sure that all ranks will agree.
2. Good luck, God bless, and keep splashing!

(DC SPRY) Maj-Gen
GOC 3 Cdn Inf Div

There were now more than 17 inches of water on stretches of the Nijmegen-Cleve road and it was still rising.

With their artillery marooned out of range, the leading battalions of the 9th Brigade moved forward in Buffaloes ('Schwimm Panzers' according to the Germans), across the watery wastes. In Donsbrüggen on the Cleve road, the Stormont, Dundas and Glengarry Highlanders made contact with the 2nd Gordons of the 15th Division. By midnight they were fighting through the fortified houses of Rindern, a key bastion of the Siegfried Line.

Farther north, the Highland Light Infantry of Canada were held up by machine guns in fortified houses and pillboxes on the outskirts of Duffelward. Next morning they took the town and captured Wardhausen. By midnight the two battalions held the whole line of the Spoy Canal which joins Cleve to the Alter Rhein. On the 14th Brigadier John Rockingham sent the North Nova Scotia Highlanders to probe eastward and by nightfall they were in possession of the submerged road from Cleve to Emmerich on the Rhine.

While headquarters of the Glengarrians was being set up in a house in Rindern, a photograph of an ice hockey team caught the eye of Lt-Colonel Roger Rowley. It was of the victorious English Olympic team of 1936 with their German escort, an officer in uniform. Most of the players were Canadian students at university in Britain, its captain known to everyone in the 9th Brigade as its DAA & QMG, Major Don Dailley.[17]

19

BEYOND THE FOREST

SIX DAYS AFTER OPERATION VERITABLE BEGAN, the three divisions on the left of 30 Corps were east of the Reichswald. In the centre the 53rd was nearing the southeastern corner of the forest opposite Goch, while the 51st was closing on the town from the west. On its right the 52nd (Lowland) Division was taking over part of the widening front between the River Maas and the forest.

The logistic situation was a nightmare. The Corps' main axis road was under water near Kranenburg. Such transport as could get forward had to be carried past the floods by ferries, while amphibious DUKWs of limited capacity carried essential supplies and evacuated casualties. Rations were late in getting to the forward troops and the guns, ever hungry in the offensive, were often down to their last few rounds of ammunition before fresh supplies arrived. Plans to open new supply routes over the Maas were laid aside until the flood waters subsided enough for it to be bridged.

Still the rains continued, miring tanks and APCs as well as the infantry's tracked carriers which they relied upon for bringing ammunition, food and heavy weapons across bullet-swept ground. The mechanized might of First Canadian Army was being neutralized by mud, just as it was shaking free of the confines of flood and forest.

Protected by the flooded Roer from the Ninth U.S. Army, and by bad weather from attacks by the Allied air forces, the Germans had raised their strength opposite First Canadian Army to nine divisions, four of them Parachute formations, and these were fighting with a skill and valour which the enemy had not shown during the first days of the battle.

Before Veritable began, Crerar told his commanders that if progress was slow he intended to bring Simonds into the battle on Horrocks's left to take over the thrust to the south-east. The Cleve road would be his main supply route, but an essential prelude to any takeover by 2 Canadian Corps would be the capture of Goch and the opening of adequate maintenance routes for 30 Corps south of the Reichswald.

Those conditions had not been met on 14 February, but neither was the Ninth U.S. Army attacking and drawing upon itself its share of the German reserves. In Crerar's view, unless he kept the enemy off balance by keeping up the momentum of his attack, there was a danger of stalemate. He determined to stretch the enemy to breaking point by attacking on a broad front with every fresh division he could lay his hands on.

At noon that day he ordered Simonds to move in on the left and advance south-eastward from Cleve to Üdem, whilst Horrocks sidestepped to the right to thrust down a new centre line from Goch to Weeze and Kevelaer. Initially the Canadian Corps would consist of its 2nd and 3rd Divisions and 2nd Armoured Brigade plus the 46th Brigade of 15th Scottish Division. Waiting in the rear, ready to be launched were the 4th Canadian, Guards and 11th Armoured Divisions.

Before either Corps could advance, 2nd Corps had to clear its flank by driving the enemy from Moyland Wood and secure an attack position on the Goch-Calcar road, while 30 Corps had to open their new main supply route by taking the heavily fortified town of Goch.

The problems which had to be overcome in bringing more troops into battle were daunting but there was one hopeful sign — the sun was shining. It was doubtful if anyone foresaw that day, that three bitter actions would have to be fought before the two corps were in a position to advance and that these would take a week to complete.

When the 43rd (Wessex) Division broke free from Cleve, it began to advance south-eastward in order to gain elbow room before turning due south toward Goch. Halfway between the two towns, the main road and railway which connect them pass between the eastern face of the Reichswald and the mile-square Forest of Cleve. Rather than attempt to pass through this dangerous defile, Major-General Ivor Thomas directed his division around the Forest to the east. His intended axis of advance would involve rolling up the rearmost line of Siegfried defences from the north. Immediately in front lay a ridge of high ground which extended westward from Bedburg to Hau.

On the left flank of the division the 4th Somerset Light Infantry of 129th Brigade came upon a huge sanatorium, the Bedburg Institute, and found that the patients had been abandoned by their doctors and left in the charge of a medical ('med') warrant officer. The message received at Army Headquarters reported their capture of '500 lunatics and a mad sergeant-major.'[1]

From Bedburg the attack was taken up in succession by the 4th and 5th Battalions of the Wiltshire Regiment. Each was met by heavy and accurate shellfire, SP guns firing point blank and hand-to-hand fighting with men of the 15th Panzer Grenadiers. A vicious counterattack overran one of the 4th's companies. All senior officers but one of the 5th were casualties and, by the time they had secured a position on the ridge, that battalion had lost no less than 200 men.

Next morning the 130th Brigade took up the advance with the 4th Dorsets leading. Almost at once they met a fresh German battalion, Battle Group Hutze, who fought to the last. Casualties were heavy and few prisoners were taken. The 7th Royal Hampshires passed through to be met by von der Heydte's paratroops who fought as determinedly as they had at Woensdrecht. Withering machine-gun fire from the Forest of Cleve poured into the Hampshire's right flank. All night the battle went on with mounting casualties and little progress.

The weight and accuracy of German artillery fire now was matching that of the British.

During the prolonged and vicious fighting on the 15th, Ivor Thomas concluded that, if he kept up the pressure, the enemy would reach the limit of his endurance by about noon next day. Then would be the time to launch his reserve, 214 Brigade, in an all-out attack to gain the escarpment which overlooks Goch.

His plan was for two battalions to break through to seize the high ground east of the village of Pfalzdorf. A third, mounted in Kangaroos, would then drive on to capture a row of villages along the Goch-Calcar road. Following them a fourth battalion would pass through at night and seize a commanding position on the escarpment which looks down on Goch from the north.[2]

Next morning, the 5th Dorsets went forward to secure the start line for the attack. They had barely reached it when the 1st Worcestershires and 7th Somerset Light Infantry arrived and began to deploy under heavy shellfire. Despite suffering severe punishment, the attack went forward on time, the infantry crowding close to the bursting shells of their artillery. Each leading section had with them a tank of the 4/7th Dragoon Guards and, this being Germany, they were not inhibited in using their guns to set fire to any house which might harbour enemy.

Again casualties were heavy but, by late afternoon, the 7th Somersets had advanced nearly 3,000 metres and had captured 413 prisoners.

With both battalions on their objective, Brigadier Hubert Essame ordered the APC-mounted 5th Duke of Cornwall's Light Infantry with their supporting squadron of the 4/7th Dragoon Guards to advance. In the fading light five columns of armour roared forward, smashing through the opposition to cut the Goch-Calcar road.

Now followed one of the most difficult operations an infantry battalion can be called upon to perform. The 4th Somerset Light Infantry were to move forward in the dark to attack across ground they had never seen and seize an objective 2,000 yards distant. Night attacks can either be 'noisy' — taking advantage of the covering fire of artillery and of tracer ammunition to keep direction — or they can be 'silent' in the hope of achieving surprise. The great difficulty in the latter is in keeping direction, particularly in a dark night but that is what the 4th Somersets chose to do.

Their C.O., Lt-Colonel C.G. Lipscomb, with his intelligence officer, went forward before nightfall to see what they could of the country and to mark start lines for the rifle companies. They arrived as their 7th Battalion were still mopping up the objective and, ignoring shelling and the fighting going on around them, they laid their white tapes.

A few hours later, the battalion filed into their attack positions, then at 3 a.m. they began to walk forward. Steadily and deliberately, keeping direction by compass, they moved ahead, scarcely believing their luck with each yard that went by without a challenge.

Then just before A Company reached its objective, the attack 'went noisy.' A challenge in German was followed by a burst of Spandau fire. At once a sergeant silenced the gun with a PIAT. Along the front, automatics opened up and the company went to ground.

Major V.W. Beckhurst, their commander, called for artillery fire. As it came down, silencing the enemy, he and his company crawled forward. The moment it stopped, they charged, shouting at the tops of their voices. Within minutes, the enemy position was overrun and 71 prisoners taken.

Beckhurst later reported: 'The German company commander, who spoke good English, said to me that in all his six years of soldiering he had never known the British to attack by night and that it was most unfair as he thought we were only a patrol. I told him that he still had a lot to learn.'[3]

By dawn the 4th Somersets held 1,000 yards of the escarpment above Goch and the remainder of 214 Brigade were moving up to widen their hold. Behind, the defenders of the Cleve Forest were devastated by the 'Land Mattress' of 1st Canadian Rocket Battery and by Typhoons. Few were left to meet 130 Brigade's sweep of the woods.

Now all attention turned upon the capture of Goch. With its observers on the ridge above it, the divisional artillery began a ruthless and unremitting bombardment of the town. Patrols of the 7th Somersets crossed the two anti-tank ditches surrounding it and the Battalion moved forward to protect the engineers constructing crossings. By dawn on the 18th seven had been completed. To the west, the 53rd Division had moved up the escarpment and the Highlanders of the 51st had reached the anti-tank ditches south of the town.

Early that afternoon, the 15th (Scottish) Division's armoured assault brigade, the 44th, mounted as they had been for the attack on the Siegfried defences, burst across the first anti-tank ditch and flamed and blasted their way to the second. A brigade of the Welsh Division began clearing the factory area north-west of the town while, on the other side of the River Niers which divides it, the 51st Division were fighting their way through the streets. By next morning the town north of the river had been cleared and the garrison commander surrendered. For two more days, confused fighting continued to the south but by the evening of the 21st, Goch was free of enemy troops.

Far to the right, along the Maas, the 52nd (Lowland) Division took the town of Afferden but were brought to a standstill on flooded ground dominated by an ancient Dutch frontier bastion, Kasteel Blijenbeek. So solid was it that artillery had no effect and its paratroop defenders had every approach covered. Every subterfuge, every attempt to close on it by night or covered by smoke, failed. Tanks as well as infantry were knocked out the moment they left cover. Finally, on the 18th it was subdued by bombs placed with great accuracy by 84 Group RAF.[4]

By nightfall on the 20th brigades of the 15th and 43rd Divisions had advanced across the Goch-Calcar road to take the towns of Buchholt and Halvenboom. By doing so, they closed the gap between 30 Corps and the Canadians who were fighting a vicious battle on their left.

On 13 February, while the 4th Somersets were taking Bedburg and the unfortunates in the 'Institute,' the 46th Brigade of the 15th Scottish Division advanced along the Cleve-Calcar road as far as Hasselt. Next day their objective was the village of Moyland with its ancient castle three kilometres further to the east. South of the road which now lay across flooded fields rose a low four kilometres long ridge covered by a narrow pine wood.

Immediately the Brigade entered Moyland Wood they met fierce opposition. When they left, five days later, their numbers sadly depleted, 'All were to agree that it had been the worst experience they had endured since the campaign began.'[5] And only half the wood had been cleared.

Unfortunately for them and for the Canadian brigades who followed, the enemy regarded the Cleve-Calcar axis as the key to the defence of the Rhineland. Against it he concentrated an unprecedented weight of artillery and mortars and some of the best troops in the German Army.

The 2nd Glasgow Highlanders were the first to discover the kind of opposition which the Wood concealed, followed later by the 9th Cameronians and 7th Seaforths. Every foot of the way was contested by a determined enemy, every success was met by counterattack, every halt by a hail of mortar and artillery fire made the more deadly by shells bursting in the tree tops. Supply carriers could not get through the intense fire, adding hunger and thirst to the misery of the cold and wet being endured by the forward companies.

After three days they reached the lateral road which crosses the ridge near Moyland. So heavy was the enemy fire which swept it that no patrol could cross into the woods beyond.

Since the 15th, the Brigade had been under the command of the 3rd Canadian Division which once more was part of 2nd Corps. So narrow was the front between the boundary with 30 Corps and the floods to the north, that Simonds could only feed in one new brigade at a time. The first to enter the fray was the 7th, its task to pass through the 46th and open the way to Calcar.

On its right the Royal Winnipeg Rifles, mounted in Kangaroos, with two squadrons of the 3rd (Armoured) Battalion of the Scots Guards, swept forward from the Cameronians' positions south of the woods to seize Louisendorf three kilometres to the south-east. On the left the Regina Rifle Regiment came under such heavy fire from the woods that they were brought to a halt and had no alternative but to attempt to clear them. They were soon embroiled in the same kind of fighting that had proved so costly and frustrating to 46 Brigade.

The Reginas spent most of the first day of their attack, 16 February, fighting in the woods west of the lateral road from Moyland which had earlier been cleared by the Scots. The Germans allowed one company to advance east of the road then moved in behind it, counterattacked and overran its forward platoon. Next day every attempt to enter the woods was met by such heavy fire, particularly by deadly 'tree-bursts,' that no progress could be made. But to the south the Canadian Scottish,

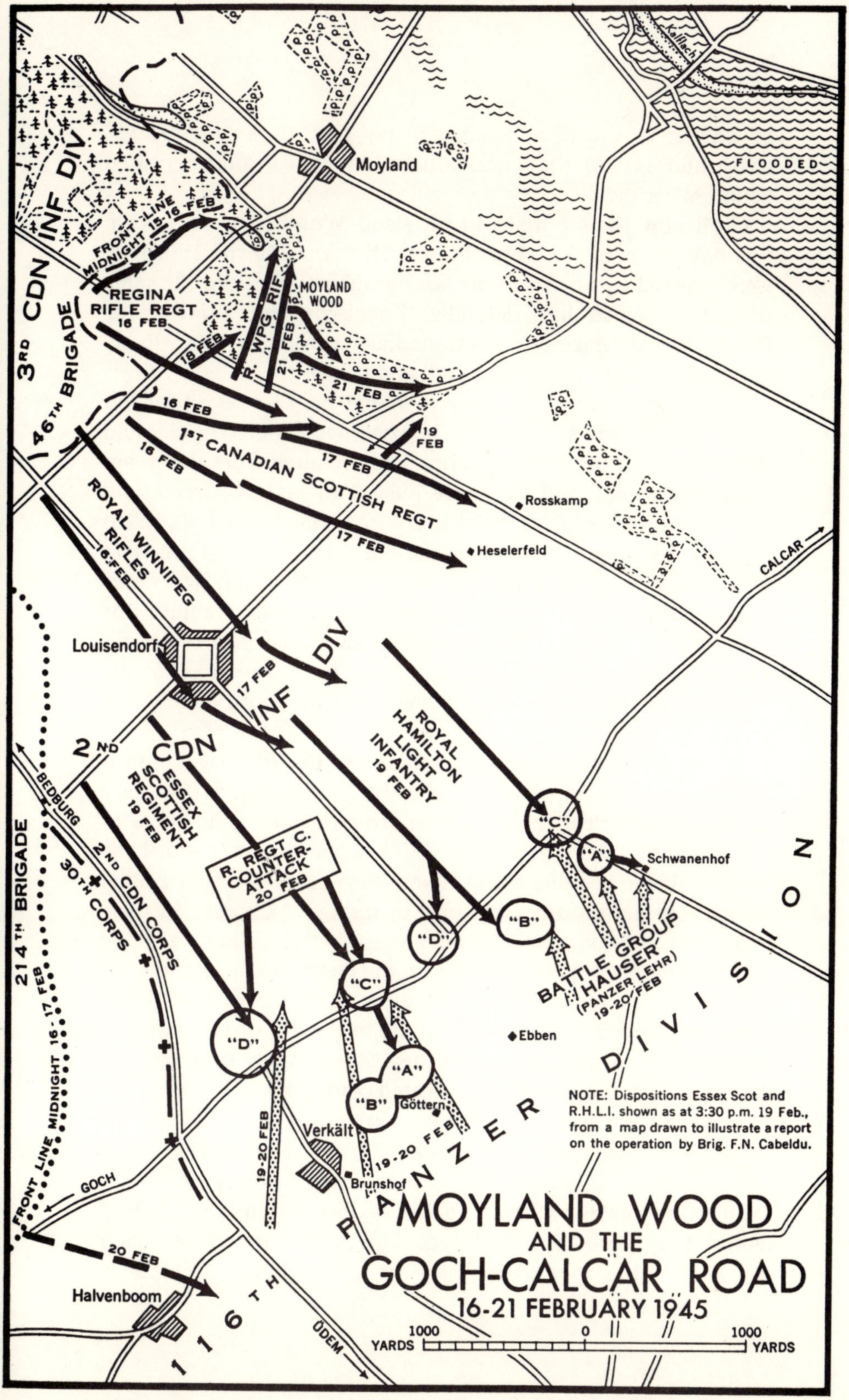

MOYLAND WOOD AND THE GOCH-CALCAR ROAD
16-21 FEBRUARY 1945
Moyland
FLOODED
Kalflach
MOYLAND WOOD
3RD CDN INF DIV
FRONT LINE MIDNIGHT 15-16 FEB
REGINA RIFLE REGT 16 FEB
46TH BRIGADE
R. WPG RIF
18 FEB
21 FEB
21 FEB
16 FEB
16 FEB
19 FEB
1ST CANADIAN SCOTTISH REGT
17 FEB
17 FEB
Rosskamp
Heselerfeld
CALCAR
ROYAL WINNIPEG RIFLES 16 FEB
Louisendorf
17 FEB
2ND CDN INF DIV
ROYAL HAMILTON LIGHT INFANTRY 19 FEB
ESSEX SCOTTISH REGIMENT 19 FEB
R. REGT C. COUNTER-ATTACK 20 FEB
"C"
"A"
Schwanenhof
"D"
"B"
BATTLE GROUP HAUSER (PANZER LEHR) 19-20 FEB
"C"
"D"
"A"
"B"
Göttern
Ebben
Verkält
Brunshof
19-20 FEB
19-20 FEB
116TH PANZER DIVISION
BEDBURG
2ND CDN CORPS
30TH CORPS
214TH BRIGADE
FRONT LINE MIDNIGHT 16-17 FEB
GOCH
20 FEB
Halvenboom
ÜDEM
NOTE: Dispositions Essex Scot and R.H.L.I. shown as at 3:30 p.m. 19 Feb., from a map drawn to illustrate a report on the operation by Brig. F.N. Cabeldu.
1000 YARDS 0 1000 YARDS

advancing in the open against heavy fire, took two villages south and east of the wood which they held against repeated counterattacks.

Until now the Germans in Moyland Wood had come from two battalions of the 116th Panzer Division. On the 18th they were relieved by one from the 6th Parachute Division, the same formation which had defended Kapelsche Veer against the Poles, Royal Marines and Canadians earlier in the winter. Again they were to fight with skill and ferocity.

They were *Fallschirmjaeger* in name only — very few had ever jumped from an aircraft. They belonged not to the German Army but the Luftwaffe. Goering had recruited from the cream of German manhood far more men than his air force could possibly use. Late in the War these were formed into divisions to fight as infantry. The men of the 6th, 7th and 8th Parachute Divisions now coming into action in the Rhineland had never experienced defeat nor the morale-sapping traumas of disorganized retreat. Thoroughly indoctrinated into the tradition of the German fighting man, they were convinced of the rightness of their cause and of their own superiority over their enemies.

Brigadier Jock Spragge, commander of the 7th Brigade, now decided to attack the wood from the south, gain a firm base across it, then clear the remainder from the west. Shortly after noon on the 18th, the Regina Rifles again moved toward the woods, this time using Wasp flame-throwers. Soon they gained a foothold among the trees but, in trying to advance further, were met by counterattacks from their right flank. Despite devastating machine-gun fire from the enemy in the woods and continuous shelling by heavy artillery from across the Rhine, they clawed their way forward. Late in the afternoon they had reached the central crest where they were brought to a halt, exhausted. There they beat off repeated counterattacks.

General Guy Simonds was not a patient man and nothing annoyed him more than being told by Harry Crerar that his Corps was not advancing as quickly as it should. Each day more German troops were arriving and he was burning to attack them before they were fully deployed. The failure to take Moyland Wood was the root of his problem and he made it clear to

General Spry of the 3rd Division that he expected it to be cleared with no further delay. In the meantime a single brigade of the 2nd Division would be brought into action and drive south-west through the Royal Winnipeg Rifles to the Goch-Calcar road.

Spry arranged for the relief of the Winnipegs on the 19th so that they could be used later in Moyland Wood. In the meantime Spragge ordered the Canadian Scottish to clear it but also told them to improve their positions east of the wood by taking more of the high ground overlooking Calcar.

On the 19th C Company of the Scottish, barely 68 strong, advanced toward the south-east corner of Moyland Wood.

> The enemy allowed them to approach close to the objective before opening fire. The result was deadly. The CSM, on orders, withdrew with eight men, one or two others later made good their escape; the rest were either killed or captured.[6]

There was no doubt that the German strength in the woods had been seriously underestimated. Next day the 7th Brigade had a new commander.

The attack of the Royal Winnipeg Rifles on 21 February was planned with great care. The uncleared portion of Moyland Wood east of the lateral road was divided into belts some 250 metres wide. From the west, each in turn was to be saturated by the divisional artillery and mortars, while anti-tank guns and medium machine guns laced them over open sights from the south. Four tanks of the Sherbrooke Fusiliers and twelve Wasp flamethrowers were to go forward with the leading companies. For the first time in days 84 Group's Typhoons were able to take to the air. Attacking at ground level, they rocketed machine gun and mortar positions and helped prevent the enemy from reinforcing his troops in the woods.

At 10 a.m. the advance began. Methodically, the Winnipegs cleared each belt, their casualties from airbursts and machine guns mounting alarmingly. But the German paratroops were not prepared to stand and fight in the face of the Wasps. A well-thought-out 'drill' enabled these to be refuelled in turn so that at all times three of them were with each forward company.

By the time the fourth of the six belts had been cleared, C Company of the Winnipeg Rifles had only two officers and 40 men left while in A only 25 men commanded by an NCO remained. D Company now took up the attack and finally won through to the eastern tip of the woods.

At noon on 19 February, the day of the disastrous attack by the Canadian Scottish, the 4th Brigade passed through the 7th's positions at Louisendorf headed for the high ground beyond the Goch-Calcar road. They had not underestimated the strength of the enemy. The companies which led the attacks of the Essex Scottish and the Royal Hamilton Light Infantry were mounted in Kangaroos. Each battalion had with it a squadron of Shermans of the Fort Garry Horse and the Brigade was supported by 14 field and seven medium artillery regiments, two batteries of heavy guns and the mortars and machine guns of the Toronto Scottish.

A rolling barrage moving at 'tank pace,' 200 yards in two minutes, led the Shermans and the APCs of the infantry toward their objectives nearly 3,000 metres ahead. Almost at once the sodden fields they were crossing began to take their own toll as tanks and Kangaroos ground their tracks belly-deep into the clinging mud and stopped. Mines and a screen of 88s along the Goch-Calcar road knocked out eleven tanks and seven APCs. Both battalions succeeded in crossing the road, the RHLI to within 200 metres of their final objectives. On the right the Essex met a strong counterattack by tanks and infantry on their front and right flank, but by 4:30 in the afternoon had beaten it off and their two leading companies were digging in on their objectives. More than 100 prisoners were taken from the 12th Parachute Reconnaissance Battalion, a fresh unit new to the battle.

German shelling now increased in intensity, playing havoc with communications. During the afternoon, the Essex Scottish' commanding officer's radio, linking him to Brigade headquarters, was destroyed by a direct hit as was a second set a short time later.

As dusk fell the Royal Regiment of Canada had arrived at

their reserve positions some 750 metres behind the Essex and the RHLI, the tanks of the Fort Garrys were drawing back to refill with ammunition and fuel, and recovery vehicles were winching bogged-down Shermans to firmer ground. Within the forward battalions, soldiers needed no urging to dig as shell and mortar fire pounded their positions.

During the previous night von Luttwitz's 47th Panzer Corps had been reinforced by the Panzer Lehr Division. At 8 p.m. on the 19th battle groups from it and from the 116th Panzer Division were launched against the 4th Brigade along the Goch-Calcar road.

For Lt-Colonel Whitaker and his 'Rileys' on the left, the fighting soon bore an unpleasant resemblance to their epic defensive battle at Woensdrecht. That they would be attacked was obvious and Whitaker had worked strenuously throughout the afternoon overseeing preparations to meet it. The sheer momentum of the German attack carried it into the centre of the battalion area and two companies on the left were overrun. Major J.M. Pigott repeated his tactic of calling down artillery fire on his own headquarters after which Whitaker sent his own small counterattack force to drive out the enemy.[7] As they were advancing, enemy tanks penetrated to within 25 yards of battalion headquarters where one was knocked out. All night the enemy continued to attack but by morning none were left in the RHLI positions and the numbers of their dead and seven knocked-out tanks bore witness both to their determination and to the quality of the defenders.[8]

On the right the Essex Scottish fought an equally furious battle. Before midnight German armour and infantry had driven through to the rear of the battalion position. By 11 p.m. three tanks supported by 40 infantry had surrounded the farmhouse containing battalion headquarters and levelled it with their guns. In the cellar Lt-Colonel John Pangman continued to give orders to his companies and to direct his supporting artillery.

At Brigade Headquarters, Brigadier Cabeldu asked for and got the help of an additional battalion, the Queen's Own Cameron Highlanders of Canada, and then ordered the Royal

Regiment to reinforce the Essex Scottish. A company sent forward in the dark found Pangman's headquarters 'held by enemy tanks and infantry.'[9]

At 9:30 next morning the Royals attacked to recover the Essex' positions. Within an hour they made contact with Pangman but, because of the deadly enemy fire, it was not until 2 p.m. after a further attack that carriers could get forward to bring out the wounded. Next morning when the leading company of the Royals reached it, they found Major Kenneth MacIntyre and the remnants of A Company of the Scottish, 35 men and their wounded, still holding the battalion's final objective which they had taken 48 hours earlier.[10]

The Riley's battle had not ended with the restoration of their position on the morning of the 20th. During the afternoon an attack by tanks and infantry was beaten off. Then, that evening, Panzer Lehr made a final attempt to drive them from it. They made little progress. As soon as Cabeldu learned of its strength he sent the reserve squadron of the Fort Garry Horse and every available man of the Cameron Highlanders to Whitaker's assistance. Two hours later the Germans broke off their attack.

> For the time being both 116 Panzer and Panzer Lehr had had enough. The field was strewn with their dead, and at least 11 of their tanks and six of their 88mm self-propelled guns had been destroyed. In those two hard-fought days the casualties of the 4th Brigade's battalions alone totalled 400.[11]

No less than seven of the enemy tanks, all Panthers, had fallen to the 17-pounder self-propelled guns of Lieutenant David Heaps' troop of the 18th Canadian Anti-Tank Battery during Panzer Lehr's attacks on the afternoon and evening of the 20th.[12]

To the north the 5th Brigade of the 2nd Division, having relieved the weary Scots of the 46th, occupied Moyland village. The woods were clear and at last the road to Calcar was open.

20

OPERATION BLOCKBUSTER

THE CONSEQUENCES of flood and foul weather were now to be felt to the full.

It had taken two weeks to breach the Siegfried defences and capture Cleve and Goch. Given that gift of time and freed by the raging Roer from the threat of attack by the Ninth U.S. Army, the Germans had developed their rearward defences and had concentrated nine divisions against Crerar on a front which now was 20 miles in length.

Barring his advance was the so-called 'Hochwald layback,' known to the Germans as 'the Schlieffen Position.' From the Rhine opposite Rees it extended across the western face of the Hochwald and Balberger Wald due south to Geldern. Manned by the best German troops on the Western Front and backed by a mass of artillery, it could not be breached by other than a full-scale attack.

Crerar decided to make his main assault in the north with Simonds' 2nd Corps. In addition to its three Canadian divisions, the 2nd and 3rd Infantry and 4th Armoured, it would have two British divisions, the 43rd (Wessex) and the 11th Armoured. On their right, Horrocks' 30 Corps with the British 15th, 51st, 52nd and 53rd Divisions, plus the 3rd Infantry and Guards Armoured in reserve, would protect Simonds' right flank while clearing the country bordering the Maas. The Canadian attack would be known as 'Operation Blockbuster.'

On the 22nd Simonds conferred with his divisional commanders, then gave his orders for the attack which was to be launched on the 26th — no written operation order was issued. His aim was to assault across the ridge which lies between Calcar and Üdem, smash through the Hochwald defences and exploit to Xanten and Wesel. Each of his divisions would enter the battle on the first day, attacking on narrow fronts to bring the maximum pressure to bear on the enemy.

The overriding importance of a good main supply route was obvious after the experience of Veritable. Simonds thought it likely that the enemy would expect him to make a major drive to open the Cleve-Xanten road — a view later confirmed by captured German intelligence reports. Instead he chose the comparatively undamaged Goch to Xanten railway line which runs through the gap between the Hochwald and the Balberger Wald. As the advance progressed, his engineers would tear up the track and develop it into a major road.

To attract the enemy's attention and possibly his reserves, the attack would begin in the north. There the 2nd Division would secure the north end of the Calcar-Üdem ridge opening the way for the 4th Armoured Division to advance south along it toward Udem. As the tanks began to move, the 3rd Division on the right would attack the strongly held village of Keppeln and Udem itself, the southern anchor of the German forward position, while the 11th Armoured Division would drive south of that town to seize the southern tip of ridge near Kervenheim. Finally the two armoured divisions would attack eastward, the 4th through the Hochwald gap and the 11th south of the Balberger Wald toward Xanten and Wesel.

In the next three days, while 2nd Corps prepared for Blockbuster, the 15th and 53rd Divisions attacked southwards toward the Weeze-Üdem road. They met strong opposition from Panzer Lehr and the 6th and 8th Parachute Divisions but forced their way ahead and, at the cost of some 900 casualties, reached the outskirts of Weeze on 25 February. The 15th was then relieved by the 3rd British Division and moved into reserve to prepare for the Rhine crossing.

But the best news came from the south. On the 23rd Simpson's Ninth U.S. Army crossed the Roer against light opposition and began its long drive toward the Rhine.

On the eve of Blockbuster the forward troops of Schlemm's

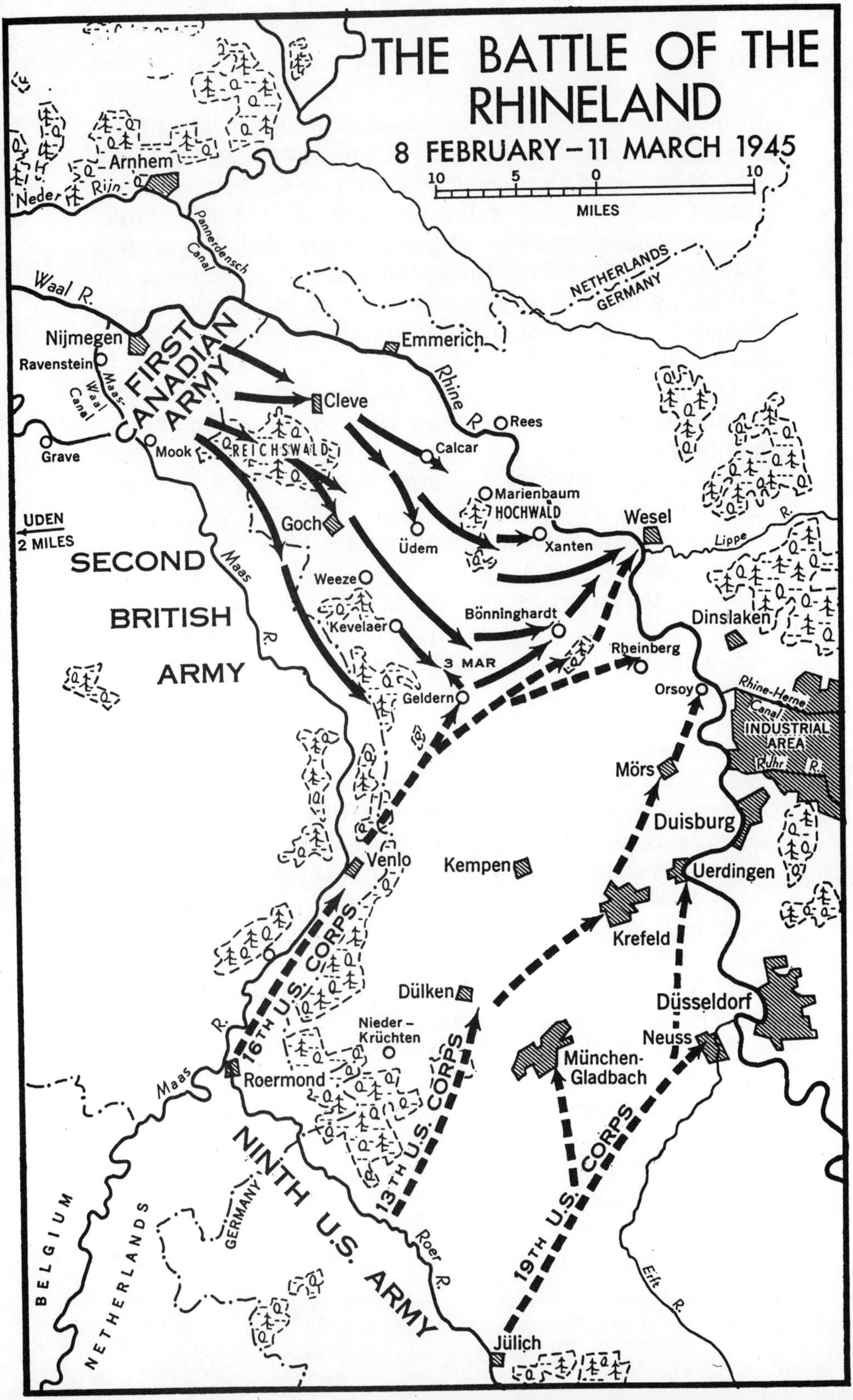
THE BATTLE OF THE RHINELAND
8 FEBRUARY – 11 MARCH 1945
10 5 0 10
MILES
Arnhem
Neder Rijn
Pannerdensch Canal
Waal R.
NETHERLANDS
GERMANY
Nijmegen
Emmerich
Ravenstein
Maas-Waal Canal
FIRST CANADIAN ARMY
Cleve
Rhine R.
Rees
Grave
Mook
REICHSWALD
Calcar
Marienbaum
HOCHWALD
Wesel
UDEN
2 MILES
Goch
Üdem
Xanten
Lippe R.
SECOND BRITISH ARMY
Maas R.
Weeze
Kevelaer
Bönninghardt
Dinslaken
Rheinberg
3 MAR
Geldern
Orsoy
Rhine-Herne Canal
INDUSTRIAL AREA
Ruhr R.
Mörs
Duisburg
Venlo
Kempen
Uerdingen
Krefeld
16TH U.S. CORPS
Dülken
Düsseldorf
Nieder-Krüchten
Neuss
München-Gladbach
Roermond
Maas
13TH U.S. CORPS
19TH U.S. CORPS
NINTH U.S. ARMY
BELGIUM
NETHERLANDS
GERMANY
Roer R.
Erft R.
Jülich

First Parachute Army were well forward of the Schlieffen Position. In the north von Lüttwitz's Panzer Corps held the high ground between Calcar and Üdem, with the 6th Parachute and 116th Panzer Divisions, and Udem itself with the independent 7th Parachute Regiment. Between there and Weeze was Meindl's 2nd Parachute Corps composed of the 7th and 8th Parachute, 15th Panzer Grenadier and 84th Infantry Divisions. South of Weeze, the 86th and 63rd Corps extended the line to beyond Roermond.

The strongest sector of the Schlieffen Position was in the north where Schlemm had deployed fifty 88mm guns to cover its anti-tank minefields.

Behind the Goch-Calcar road for which the 4th Brigade had paid such a heavy price, the remainder of the 2nd Division now formed up for their assault. On the left two battalions of the 5th Brigade were to take the ground above Calcar itself, while, on the right, the three battalions of the 6th, mounted in or on armour and with tanks in support, were to drive the enemy from the rolling farmland which looks down on the Hochwald from the west.

H hour for the attack was set for 4:30 a.m. 'Artificial Moonlight' would give some visibility, while 40mm Bofors guns, firing tracer ammunition toward the objectives, would help guide the tanks and Kangaroos. During the whole of a long night the enemy shelled the only possible forming-up areas in which, chilled by a steady rain, the 2nd Division waited to attack. Then suddenly at 3:30 a burst of shellfire exploded on the right flank company of the RHLI holding the start line, while at least six Panther tanks with infantry came storming toward them. Immediately they called for artillery and tank support while every Bren and rifle opened fire. In little more than half an hour the attack was beaten off and all again was quiet except for the crackle of flames from a burning panzer. Fifteen minutes later, 600 guns opened fire on the German positions between Calcar and Üdem. Brigadier Holley Keefler, commanding the 6th Brigade, later admitted that the German attack had 'caused some tension' until it was defeated.

His unconventional plan of attacking with his three battalions 'up' was designed to clear the way for the 4th Armoured Division as quickly as possible. The South Saskatchewan Regiment on the right and the Cameron Highlanders on the left each were mounted in Kangaroos while the rifle companies of Les Fusiliers de Mont-Royal in the centre were carried forward on the tanks of two squadrons of the Fort Garry Horse. Supporting each battalion was a tank squadron of the Sherbrooke Fusiliers.

With only a few casualties, the two battalions on the left reached their objectives before dawn but the Camerons' attack ran into trouble within a few hundred yards of their start line when they found that a combination of heavy mud and mines along the Calcar-Üdem road made the way ahead virtually impassable for armour. There was no alternative but to follow Les Fusiliers de Mont-Royal on their left on to the high ground before attacking their objectives. After the battle Major David Rodgers of the Camerons was recommended for the Victoria Cross but was awarded the Distinguished Service Order. The following extracts from the citation give an impression of the intensity of the action:

> In spite of the difficulties of such a manoeuvre in darkness and under extremely heavy fire and without the full benefit of the timed artillery programme, Major Rodgers in the leading vehicle pushed on to within a hundred yards of the final objective only to find it infested with snipers concealed in houses and slit trenches, determined to make a last stand. . . . Major Rodgers, ignoring the hail of fire which swept the intervening ground, leaped from his vehicle alone and dashed forward to the nearest house, completely clearing it before the first man of his leading platoon came up to him. Alone he also quickly cleared a second house. So inspired were his men by this gallant act that, emulating his example, they pressed the attack with such vigour that the fierce enemy resistance was soon overcome. During this action Major Rodgers killed at least four of the defenders, captured 12 prisoners and wounded several other.
>
> Unable to contact battalion headquarters by wireless, he quickly completed the reorganization of his company to hold the position in the event of counterattack and proceeded on foot to headquarters to report details.
>
> On reaching the area which had been chosen for battalion headquarters he found that the battalion commander had been killed and the intelligence officer severely wounded by artillery fire, the whole headquarters pinned down by intense fire from strong enemy

positions which had been bypassed by the main assault, and communications destroyed. The artillery representative who had taken charge explained the situation, pointing out a building from which the enemy were sweeping the area with fire from automatic weapons. . . .

Appreciating that the success of the entire operation might well be prejudiced without headquarters functioning, Major Rodgers, accompanied by his batman, went forward through a barn on the near side of the road coming into the open within 25 yards of the house held by the enemy. Firing their automatic weapons from the hip they raced across the open to the front door of the house. Kicking open the door Major Rodgers charged into the nearest room. His automatic weapon now empty and no time to reload, he fired his pistol wounding two of the occupants and the remainder surrendered. Then room by room he cleared the entire house himself, killing or wounding at least nine and again capturing twelve prisoners.

Rodgers then reorganized the headquarters, established communications with brigade and set out on foot to visit the companies whose situation was as yet unknown. At the first, the commander pointed out enemy troops and tanks forming up for a counterattack. He raced back to battalion headquarters and called down artillery fire which dispersed the enemy.

Although the area was being subjected to intense artillery and mortar fire . . . he visited each company in turn, encouraging the men and assisting the commanders. After satisfying himself that each company was in proper position and prepared for any counterattack which might develop he returned to battalion headquarters remaining in command of the battalion until the arrival of the second in command, some time later.[1]

The intensity of the fighting left signs which the veteran 4th Somerset Light Infantry recorded in their history:

On the 27th the Battalion moved up to take over the Canadian positions overlooking Calcar. The scene was one of incredible devastation, and many burnt-out vehicles, corpses and traffic jams all added to the final impression. The Canadians had 'everything in the shop window' at this stage.[2]

By 8:30 a.m. the 2nd Division's objectives were sufficiently under control for the second phase of Blockbuster to be launched by the 4th Armoured Division.
Meanwhile, on the right, the attack of the 3rd Division had begun with the Queen's Own Rifles of the 8th Brigade advancing up a mile-long slope of open farmland to secure a portion of the ridge from which the enemy could fire on the approaches to Keppeln. Plodding forward through fields so sodden that they were impassable to tanks, the leading platoon of D Company soon found their progress barred by paratroops fighting from three fortified farm buildings on the outskirts of the village of Mooshof. The cost in casualties began to mount alarmingly in the face of the enemy's withering fire. After they had beaten off a savage counterattack, the platoon was reduced to five men huddled close to the ground, their position laced by machine-gun fire. At that moment Sergeant Aubrey Cosens saw the welcome sight of a Sherman of the 1st Hussars grinding its way forward. With bullets plucking at his clothes, he ran to it and hauled himself to sit in front of the turret. From there he directed the gunner's fire on to the enemy, then ordered the tank to charge a group of paratroops forming up for another counterattack. They fled and Cosens returned to the problem of capturing the German position.
Still on the tank, he ordered the driver to ram the first of the three defended buildings and, while his men covered him, broke into it and killed or captured the defenders. From it he ran into the next building to find it abandoned. The third, a two-storied building defended by several enemy, lay beyond a road. Ordering the tank to cover him, he raced across to it alone, as bullets sparked and whined off the cobbles. From the building came the sound of a grenade exploding, followed by bursts of automatic fire; then Cosens emerged with a group of prisoners. In all he killed more than 20 Germans and captured as many more. Having given orders for its defence, he left the position to

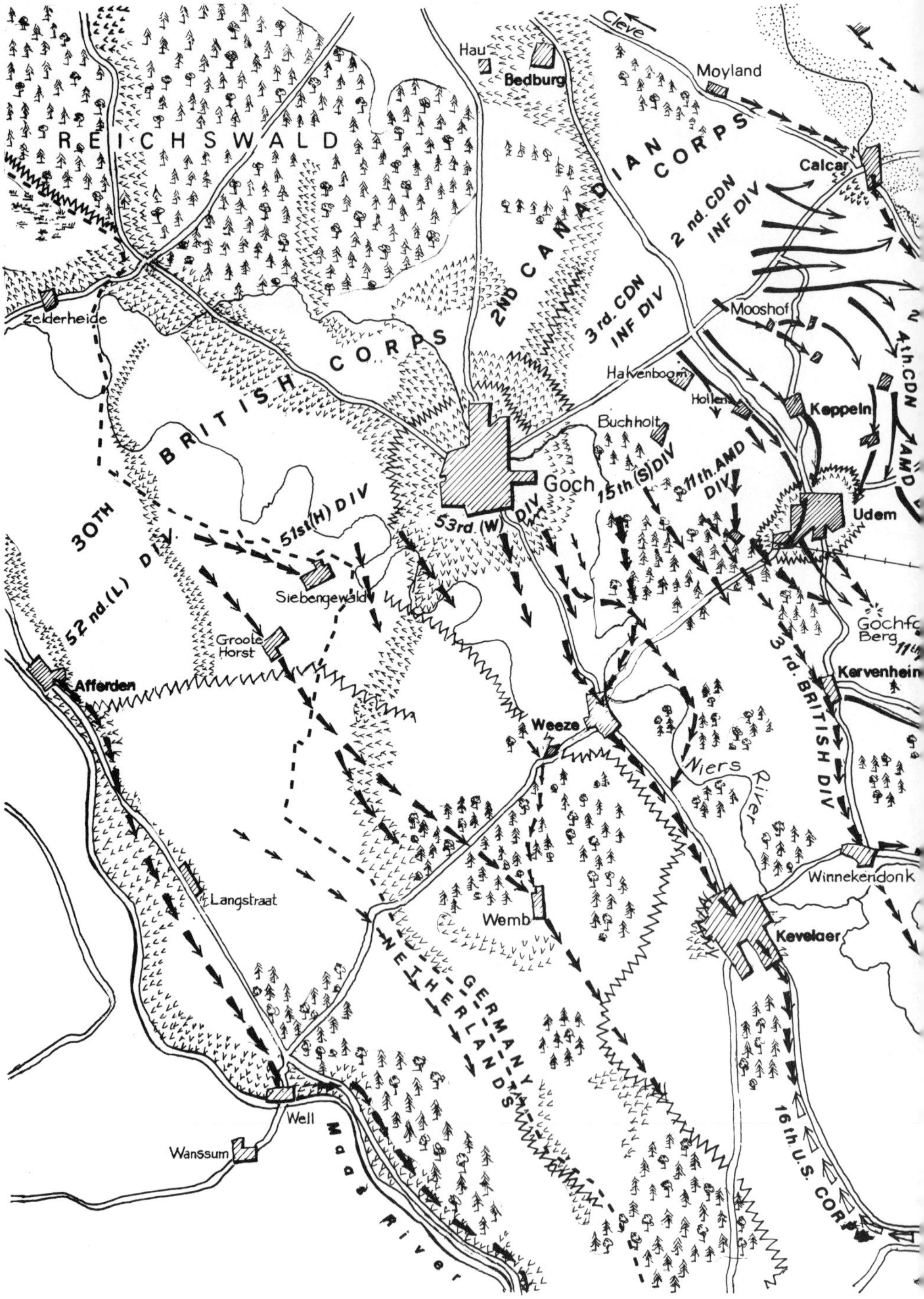
REICHSWALD
Cleve
Hau
Bedburg
Moyland
Calcar
2ND CANADIAN CORPS
2 nd. CDN INF DIV
3 rd. CDN INF DIV
Mooshof
4th. CDN AMD
Zelderheide
BRITISH CORPS
30TH
Halvenboom
Hollen
Keppeln
Buchholt
Goch
15th.(S) DIV
11th. AMD DIV
Udem
51st(H) DIV
53rd.(W) DIV
52 nd.(L) DIV.
Siebengewald
Groote Horst
Gochfort Berg
Afferden
3 rd. BRITISH DIV
Kervenheim
Weeze
Niers River
Winnekendonk
Langstraat
Wemb
Kevelaer
NETHERLANDS
GERMANY
Well
Wanssum
Maas River
16th. U.S. COR

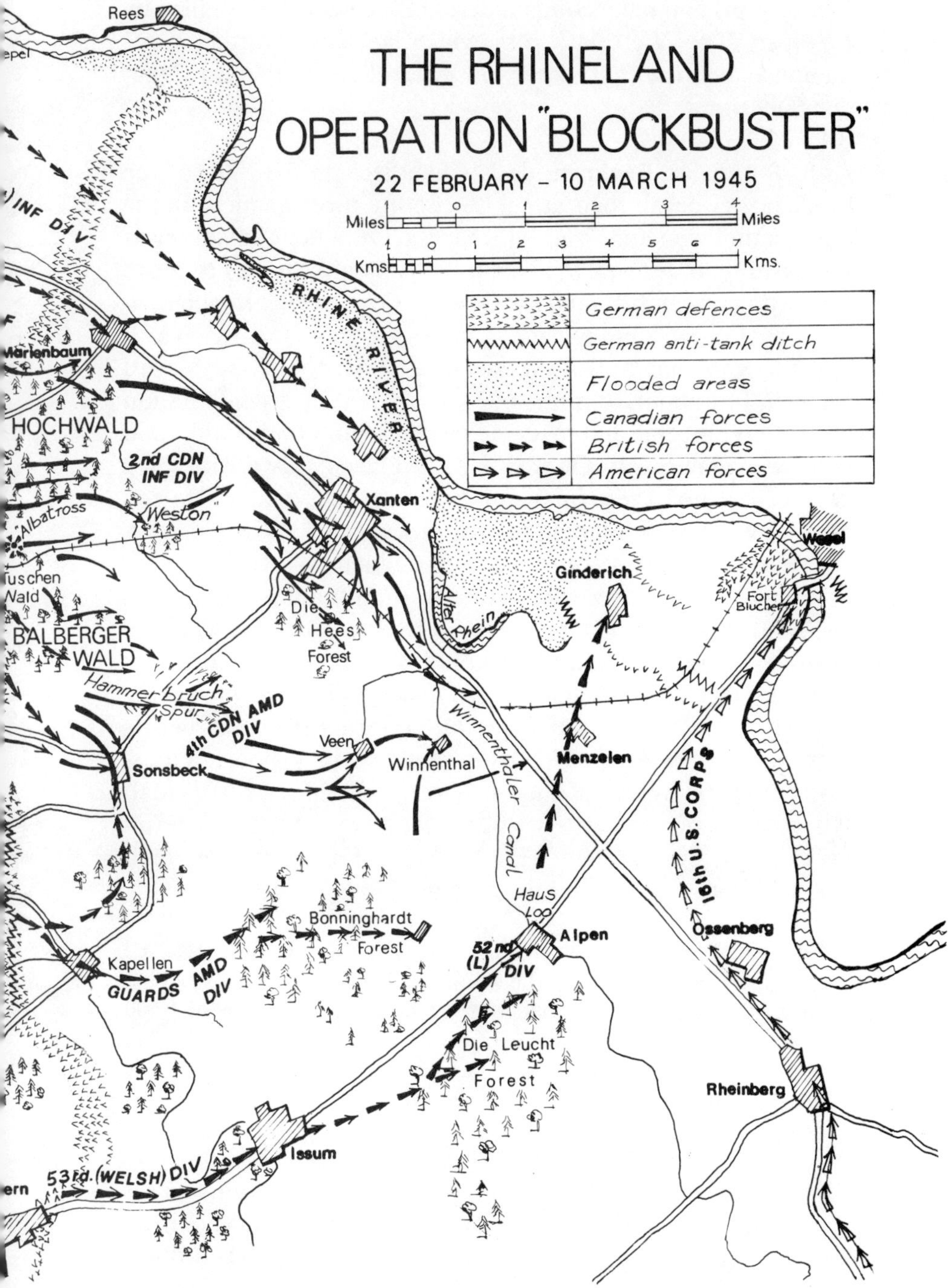
THE RHINELAND
OPERATION "BLOCKBUSTER"
22 FEBRUARY – 10 MARCH 1945
Miles 1 0 1 2 3 4 Miles
Kms 1 0 1 2 3 4 5 6 7 Kms.
German defences
German anti-tank ditch
Flooded areas
Canadian forces
British forces
American forces
Rees
RHINE RIVER
Marienbaum
HOCHWALD
2nd CDN INF DIV
"Albatross"
"Weston"
Xanten
BALBERGER WALD
Hammerbruch "Spur"
4th CDN AMD DIV
Sonsbeck
Veen
Winnenthal
Die Hees Forest
Alter Rhein
Ginderich
Wesel
Fort Blucher
Menzelen
Winnenthaler Canal
16th U.S. CORPS
Haus Loo
Alpen
52nd (L) DIV
Bonninghardt Forest
Kapellen
GUARDS AMD DIV
Ossenberg
Die Leucht Forest
Rheinberg
Issum
53rd. (WELSH) DIV

report to his company commander. On the way he was killed by a sniper. The Victoria Cross which he was awarded posthumously was the first to be won by a soldier of the 3rd Canadian Division.[3]

At 8:30 a.m. Le Régiment de la Chaudière on the right of the 8th Brigade, began their attack to capture three hamlets on the high ground west and south of Keppeln. Once their advance was successfully under way the North Shore Regiment was to move forward between them and the Queen's Own to take Keppeln.

At first the Chaudière made good progress and the North Shore began their mile-long advance down the slope toward Keppeln but about 10 a.m. they were halted by a combination of artillery, mortar and machine-gun fire from both flanks and from the village itself. On their left the Queen's Own Rifles had not yet reached their final objectives and the Chaudière too were blocked by fire from the area of Keppeln in which at least 10 enemy tanks and self-propelled guns had been seen.

Brigadier Jim Roberts was faced with an unpleasant tactical decision. Though their progress had been slow, the Queen's Own were confident that they would capture their final objectives that day, but that implied an unacceptable delay in taking Keppeln. The only possible way of capturing the town before then was to provide the North Shore with tank support. To Lt-Colonel Frank White of the 1st Hussars the idea was suicidal. His account of the battle written later concealed the forcefulness of his disagreement with Roberts who, as an armoured corps officer, was equally aware of the risks.

> Brigadier J. Roberts discussed the situation with me and suggested the use of tanks to relieve the situation. I pointed out the seeming hopelessness of sending tanks down a bare forward slope of 1,500 yards against AFVs in cover, which he agreed, but as no other plan was possible it was decided to withdraw C Squadron from the Queen's Own Rifles and attempt to displace the enemy armour by using heavy artillery (7.2s) on the town.[4]

Major Jake Powell had already lost six of the 19 tanks in his squadron that morning in supporting the Queen's Own Rifles. When White explained his next task to him, he replied, 'I don't think it's on, sir, but at least we should cause enough of a diversion for the infantry to get forward.'[5]

Powell reported to Lt-Colonel John Rowley of the North Shore and together they worked out a plan of attack making use of all available artillery. Then at 1:20 p.m. the 13 tanks of the squadron, carrying two platoons of infantry, swung into line and, with all guns blazing, charged down the slope toward Keppeln. Following them came two companies on foot and the battalion's Wasp flamethrowers. Within 30 seconds of crossing the startline, one tank was hit by an 88 and burst into flames. Moments later two more went up on mines. As they neared the village more were hit and Powell's tank bogged down in a shell hole.

Concealed among houses on the outskirts, two German panzers concentrated their fire and their full attention on the Canadian Shermans. Apparently they ignored, or did not see, the three low-slung tracked carriers racing toward the village. Suddenly flame from the Wasps enveloped them and they were on fire. Escorted by infantry, the five remaining Shermans now broke into Keppeln and engaged several enemy self-propelled guns which promptly retired toward Üdem.

By 5 p.m. the North Shore Regiment had cleared the last of the German paratroops from the village and four hours later the 9th Brigade passed through the 8th to begin their assault on Udem.[6]

Since early morning five regimental battle groups of the 4th Canadian Armoured Division had waited near the Goch road, south of Calcar, their tanks belly-deep in wet clay. At 9:30 a.m., after the 2nd Division had reported that the way was clear, they began to churn forward through the clinging mud toward firmer ground on top of the Calcar ridge. Moving in two columns they headed east, then south, toward Üdem.

At the outset progress was painfully slow. In the first two hours the leading squadrons had advanced barely 500 metres against determined Panzerfaust teams, mines, 88s and German armour. But gradually the well-trained teams of infantry and tanks cleared enemy strong points and anti-tank weapons from their path and the momentum of the advance picked up.

Unmarked minefields were the cause of many casualties in the attacking force, one being the scout car from which the C.O. of the Argyll and Sutherland Highlanders of Canada was commanding his battalion's attack on the nearby village of Follingshof.

> Lt-Col Wigle, temporarily out of communication with his companies, took refuge in the co-driver's seat of Major Hale's tank which had a second wireless set on the infantry net. This arrangement persisted for no more than thirty seconds when the Colonel, a hardy six-foot two-inch Scot, climbed out onto the back deck proclaiming, 'Be damned if I can command my regiment from that rat hole — pass me the microphone up here and let's go!' This was satisfactory; the village was taken in the late afternoon.[7]

The Ridge by then had been cleared to a point north-east of Keppeln.

As dusk fell the reserve battle group — the Governor General's Foot Guards and the Lake Superior Regiment (the division's motor battalion) — thrust further along it to seize its two highest points in what has been described as 'an armoured classic.'[8] Well-planned and executed on schedule, his night attack by tanks took the Germans by surprise. By morning the entire Ridge from Calcar to Üdem was clear of enemy and the 9th Brigade were driving the 7th Parachute Regiment from that town.

On the left of 2nd Corps the 43rd Wessex Division relieved the 5th and 6th Brigades, while their reconnaissance regiment began sweeping down the river flats between the Goch-Xanten railway and the Rhine. On that day, the 27th, the 5th Wiltshires entered Calcar unopposed.

Despite the loss of more than 100 tanks and 1,000 casualties, Guy Simonds could view the events of the 26th with satisfaction. The complex of attacks had intermeshed into a single operation whose momentum had given the enemy no chance to disrupt it. Twenty-four hours after it had begun, the assaulting brigades had been relieved and were in position for their next task, the thrust through the Hochwald.

21

The Hochwald

EAST OF THE CALCAR RIDGE, across an open valley 1,000 metres wide, rises another eight kilometres long, crescent-shaped and surmounted by two state forests. In the gap between the northernmost, the Hochwald, and the Balberger Wald, runs the Goch-Xanten railway whose capture was vital to 2nd Corps' advance to the east. For the Germans it was the last defensive barrier before the Rhine bridges at Wesel and they were prepared to defend it to the death. Along it the remnants of four parachute divisions, amply supported by anti-tank weapons, waited in prepared defences.

In the cold hours before dawn on 27 February, battalions of the 2nd Infantry and 4th Armoured Divisions prepared to advance down the slopes of the high ground captured the day before, toward the Schlieffen defences at the edge of the Hochwald. On the left the Calgary Highlanders were to break into the wood half-way along its face while the Algonquin Regiment, supported by tanks of the South Albertas, seized Point 73, nicknamed 'Albatross,' a round-topped hill which blocked the entrance to the Hochwald Gap.

There had been no opportunity for ground observation of the Hochwald position before the Highlanders began their advance well before first light. In the lead was C Company commanded by Capt Bill Lyster, one of the two officers of the Regiment who had won the Sword of Honour at Sandhurst, leading his first company attack.

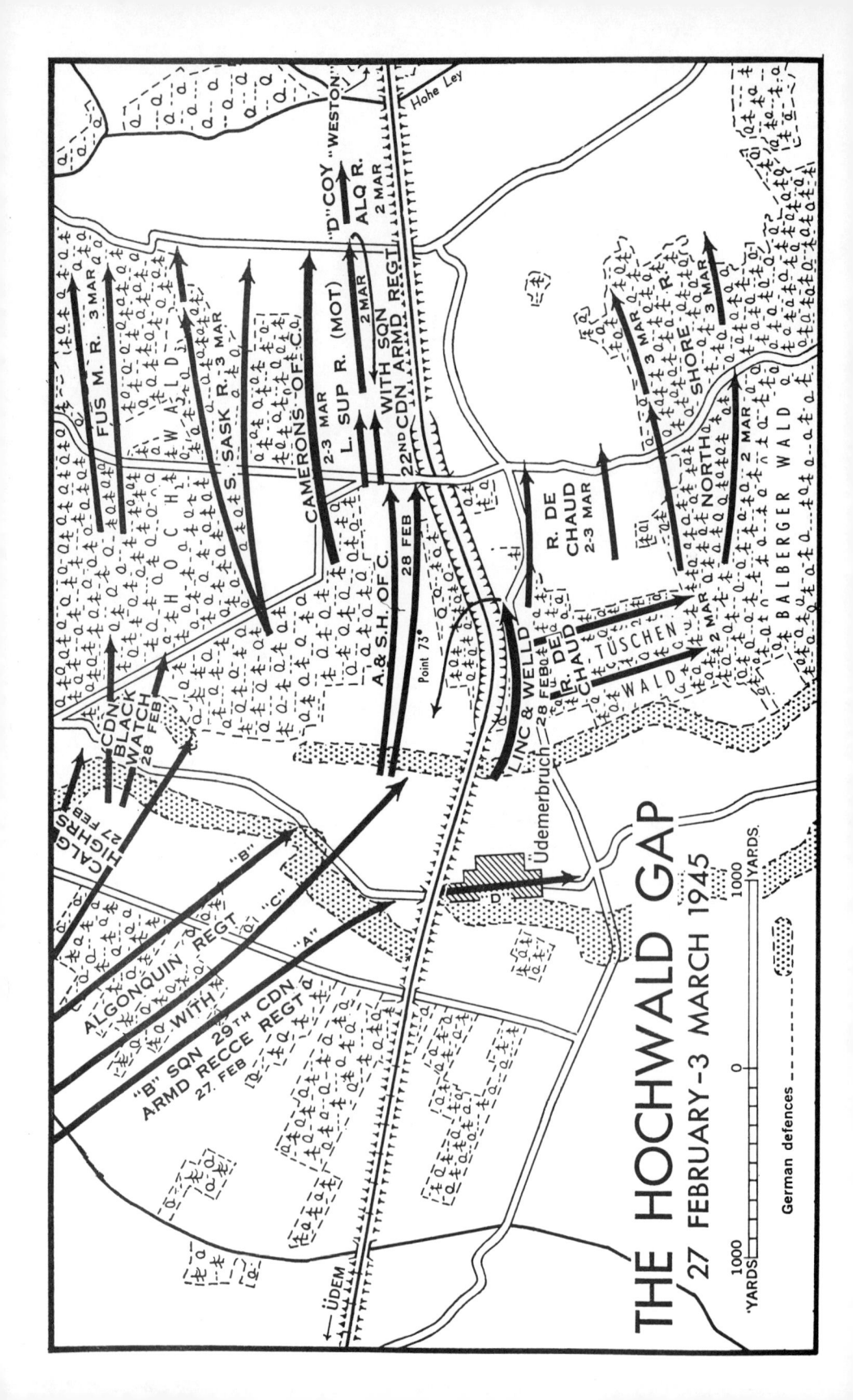

THE HOCHWALD GAP
27 FEBRUARY – 3 MARCH 1945

It was a gorgeous moonlight night. I decided on the old formation we had learned at Hillhurst Park in Calgary in 1939, arrowhead — one platoon up, two back with company headquarters in the centre, well spread out. We went down the slope across open ground for quite a distance then spotted some farm buildings on the edge of what we determined was the Hochwald. As we got close to them, all hell broke loose. Our company went to ground but bounced up and the lead platoon rushed the farmhouse. The others came in on the flanks in a pincer. An MG42 had company HQ pinned down, firing from the loft of the barn but was soon silenced — the Gerries had been killed or had fled, all but two who hid on the property and made their escape after killing a sentry who was exhausted and not on his toes.

I contacted Battalion HQ and, it now being daylight, was ordered to move into the forest covered by smoke from our tanks.

Later Ross Ellis with his artillery battery commander, Major Nixon, came up to where we were being shelled and mortared near some buildings inside the forest. The three of us were standing in the doorway of a battered old house planning a push up a trail which we had found, when a shell burst outside the open door. I grabbed my face because a piece of shrapnel had hit me in the nose and when my vision cleared, I saw a blue hole in Major Nixon's forehead. He was dead of course and Ross and I had concussion.

I was ordered back to the RAP where the MO put me to sleep with a shot of Morphine. The next day I went back to C Company which by now had a firm grip on the edge of the Hochwald.[1]

Not since Normandy had the Highlanders met such heavy German mortar and artillery fire but by making the most of the accuracy of their own supporting guns, all their companies had broken through the network of fortified houses and concealed machine gun positions of the main Schlieffen position and were established in the Hochwald before 9 o'clock. Their casualties had been heavy, particularly in officers. Major Sherwin Robinson, wounded, was carried on to B Company's objective by his sergeant-major where he controlled its reorganization before agreeing to be evacuated. All of C Company's officers were knocked out and, not for the first time, its command passed to CSM 'Swede' Larson who commanded it with such skill and gallantry that he was awarded a Military Cross, a rare decoration for a warrant officer. By the end of the afternoon the

Calgaries were dug in on all their objectives and, despite incessant pounding by enemy mortars and artillery, were not about to be shifted by the counterattacks of the German paratroops.[2]

Their success was not simply the result of guts and determination. Like the 4th Brigade on the Goch-Calcar road and the 6th on the Calcar Ridge, they had become battlewise veterans more than able to compete with the soldiers of the Wehrmacht on their home ground.

It is a rule of war that, even in the most professional of armies, something always goes wrong in a battle. On the right, when the Algonquins and B Squadron of the South Alberta Regiment were due to begin their advance, one rifle company and half of another were missing because the tanks carrying them had bogged down. At 5:15, less than an hour before dawn, Lt-Colonel R.A. Bradburn knew that he could wait no longer for his missing troops. To cross the open ground in front of the German defences in daylight would be suicidal for tanks. As the artillery began to place red marker shells on to the objectives and Bofors guns fired tracers to mark the way, he gave the order to advance.

So unpromising was the approach across the boggy farmland that the German defenders, sheltering from the artillery, never suspected that the Canadians would attack with tanks at night. Before the sun appeared over the dark wall of the forest, the two leading Algonquin companies had crossed the enemy's anti-tank ditch and the minefield and low wire entanglements behind it and were clearing his first line of trenches. A third company passed through them and, before 10 a.m., sized the final entrenchments at the base of 'Albatross.' They had broken through the last German prepared positions before the Rhine but there they were stopped. The fourth company which might have leapfrogged through had not arrived.

The German reaction to what they recognized as a most serious threat to their bridgehead was immediate and violent. From every quarter guns and mortars poured a stream of shells and bombs on to the Algonquins' positions and laid a curtain of fire behind them to prevent help getting through. From north of the Rhine the shells of the enemy's heaviest guns raised enormous eruptions while machine guns swept the approaches to 'Albatross.'

With the help of B Squadron's tanks and their own very effective artillery, the Algonquins beat off a succession of counterattacks. Their numbers dwindled and it was virtually impossible to remove casualties through the storm of fire which blocked the way to the rear.

The options open to Brigadier J.C. Jefferson of the 10th Brigade to counter the deadly threat to the Algonquins and to exploit their successes were limited — partly as the result of a disaster suffered by his supporting armoured regiment.

Before the attack it appeared likely that B Squadron of the South Albertas might bog down in the sodden fields which lay in front of the German defences. To secure tank support on the objective, Jefferson ordered the Regiment to send its A Squadron with the Algonquins' carrier platoon around the right flank, south of the railway. The Regiment protested that the route lay through enemy-held territory. The order was confirmed. As they moved through a cutting south of the tracks, the little force was trapped in an ambush by 88s and infantry Panzerfaust teams. Every tank and all but one of the carriers was destroyed. Not only was this a serious loss of fighting power, their destruction left the Algonquins' right flank wide open.

Late in the afternoon of the 27th Jefferson ordered the Argyll and Sutherland Highlanders of Canada to move forward through the Algonquins, across the summit of 'Albatross' to the far side of the 'Gap.' From the moment their advance began they were met by heavy shellfire which so increased in intensity that they were forced to dig in 500 metres short of the gap.

A mile to the north the Calgary Highlanders had been joined by Le Régiment de Maisonneuve in the western fringe of the Hochwald, but the enemy shelling was so heavy that an attempt by the Canadian Black Watch to advance south-eastward toward the gap had to be postponed until morning. No help could be expected yet from the 3rd Division who were still engaged in Üdem.[3]

The 10th Brigade's attempt to burst through the gap had failed. It was obvious both to Jefferson and to Major-General

Chris Vokes, commanding the 4th Division, that a much greater effort would be needed to clear the enemy from it and from the adjacent fringes of the woods — just how much greater they did not then realize.

Ahead, about 1,500 metres east of the western edge of the Hochwald, a north-south lateral road divided the forest in two. Another lay along its eastern edge. Beyond that, by about the same distance, was an isolated wood which was given the codename 'Weston.' The western end of the gap itself was constricted by a spur of the Balberger forest, known as the Tuschen Wald.

Vokes ordered the 10th Brigade to clear the Tüschen Wald, open the gap as far as the first lateral road and secure the railway from Üdem into the forest. The 4th Armoured Brigade would then send a battle group through to seize 'Weston.'

It was obvious that the Germans now had brought an unprecedented weight of artillery into the battle (later found to amount to 717 mortars, 1,054 guns and an unknown number of self-propelled guns).[4] Montgomery commented that 'the volume of fire from enemy weapons was the heaviest which had been met so far by British troops in the campaign.' To reinforce the defenders of the gap on the 27th Lüttwitz brought in a fresh parachute battalion and more tanks of the 116th Panzer Division.

About midnight an uneasy stillness settled over the Hochwald, broken only by the occasional nervous stutter of a Bren or a tearing burst of Spandau fire. Waiting to advance once more up the slopes of 'Albatross,' otherwise known as 'Point 73,' at the entrance to the gap, the depleted Argylls checked their ammunition and equipment and cursed the mud and the cold.

Three hours before dawn the first shells of a heavy artillery barrage screamed overhead and the leading companies climbed from their slits and moved up the slope. Before the first glow of morning began to show on the eastern horizon, 'Albatross' was theirs, 70 prisoners were on the way to the rear and they were digging in on the first lateral road. Counterattacks by tanks and infantry began almost immediately, while the enemy artillery pounded the whole of the battalion area. To the already deafening noise of the battle were added the explosions of Canadian heavy-calibre shells seeking out German panzers and the tearing bursts and ear-splitting cracks of the Brownings and 75mm guns of the South Alberta's Shermans. All day the battle went on. One of the Argyll's companies was reduced to 15 men. Tanks carried ammunition and supplies to the hard-pressed companies and evacuated their casualties.

Near the entrance to the gap, German artillery observers spotted the Lincoln and Welland Regiment moving up for their attack on the railway and the Tüschen Wald. Mortar, artillery and rocket fire bursting in the tree tops caused so many casualties that the attack had to be abandoned until the unit could be reorganized.

All morning tanks of the Canadian Grenadier Guards with the Lake Superior Regiment had been working forward to attack through the Argylls toward 'Weston.' Of their normal strength of 63 tanks, the Guards had only 31 left after the fighting on the Calcar-Üdem ridge. Their C.O. had been severely wounded and Major Ned Amy was promoted to replace him. Forty-five minutes before the assault was to begin Amy too was wounded by shellfire and turned over command of the attack to Major George Hale while he had his wound dressed.[5]

The start line was the first lateral road held by the Argylls. Only 10 tanks of the two leading squadrons reached it — the rest had bogged down in heavy mud and on slopes so steep that even with new 'extended-end-connectors' fitted to their tracks, the Shermans could not make the grade. Of the 10, three were put out of action by anti-tank guns firing from high ground south of the railway. The remainder manoeuvred along the left side of the gap and succeeded in advancing another 600 metres. There, four more were lost to the guns on their right while two of the enemy guns were knocked out by one of the surviving tanks.

Next morning the Grenadiers had 21 tanks available for action. Major Hale had been wounded and command passed to Major Curt Greenleaf.

Until the enemy anti-tank guns could be cleared from the high ground to the south and the fringes of the woods were secure, it was highly unlikely that armour could pass through the gap. Simonds directed the 2nd Division to clear the Hochwald and relieve the tired battalions in the gap while the 3rd captured the woods to the south. In the meantime the 4th Armoured Brigade was to continue attempts to break through.

On the right of the Corps the 11th British Armoured Division had passed south of Üdem, stormed the high Gochfortz Berg on the 27th, then ploughed their way through forest and bog to the Schlieffen defences south of the Balberger Wald. Beyond them, to the south, 30 Corps were advancing on a broad front and were beginning to make faster progress. The 3rd British Division, which relieved the 15th, had crossed the Üdem-Weeze road and was closing on Kervenheim. The 53rd Welsh were in the final stages of their hard battle for the fortified town of Weeze while the 52nd were picking up speed in their advance to the south-east down the Maas.

Further to the south, after six days of building up its forces and some hard fighting in taking the towns east of the Roer, the U.S. Ninth Army's armoured divisions were beginning to roll northwards toward the Canadian front.

With every day Schlemm's position was becoming more hopeless. To stem the American advance, he now was forced to bring down forces from the north, but not from the front of 2nd Canadian Corps where a breakthrough would threaten the existence of his army. In the first two days of March he reinforced the Hochwald front with two independent parachute units, the strongest left in his reserve, one of which was the Parachute Army Assault Battalion.

On 1 March Major-General Bruce Matthews of the 2nd Division sent his 4th Brigade into the Hochwald on the left of the 5th Brigade with orders to clear the northern half of the forest. Leading the assault were the Essex Scottish, supported by artillery and a troop of tanks of the Sherbrooke Fusiliers. In a particularly vicious battle, the Essex fought their way into the edge of the forest and seized a foothold for a further advance. On the left C Company lost three-quarters of its strength and its commander, Major Fred Tilston, was twice wounded leading the assault. Before they could consolidate, the Germans counterattacked. Through a hail of fire, Tilston moved from platoon to platoon, organizing the defence. Soon ammunition began to

The road to Cleve, the Army's main supply route, 13 February, 1945. (Photo by C.C. McDougall / Public Archives Canada / PA 143946)

Cleve: 'A pathetic heap of rubble, roofs and radiators...sagging, crazy skeletons of homes.' (Imperial War Museum)

Churchill AVREs with fascines and a bridgelayer in the Reichswald. (Imperial War Museum)

Bren carrier, scout car and Sherman tank of the 43rd Wessex Division moving through Bedburg toward Goch. (Imperial War Museum)

'Land Mattress' of 1st Canadian Rocket Battery being re-loaded. (Imperial War Museum)

Queen's Own Cameron Highlanders of Canada opening a parcel from home in the Hochwald. (Photo by K. Bell / Public Archives Canada / PA 137458)

Major-General Chris Vokes (4th Canadian Armoured Division) General Crerar, Field-Marshal Montgomery, Lt-General Brian Horrocks (30th British Corps) Lt-General Guy Simmonds (2nd Canadian Corps) Major-General Dan Spry (3rd Canadian Division) in the Rhineland. (Imperial War Museum)

In sight of the enemy, a British soldier forces two Dutch children to take cover. (Imperial War Museum)

Montgomery with Brigadier John Rockingham of the 9th Brigade near Cleve, 16 Feburary, 1945. (Imperial War Museum)

Company Sergeant-Major 'Swede' Larson, MC, Calgary Highlanders, searching German prisoners near Doetinchem, 1 April, 1945. (Photo by Lt. M.M. Dean / Public Archives Canada / PA 131699)

North Shore Regiment crossing canal near Zutphen under fire, April, 1945. (Photo by Lt. D.I. Grant / Public Archives Canada / PA 130059)

A platoon of the South Saskatchewan Regiment meets opposition at the Oranje Canal, 12 April, 1945. (Photo by D. Guravich / Public Archives Canada PA 138284)

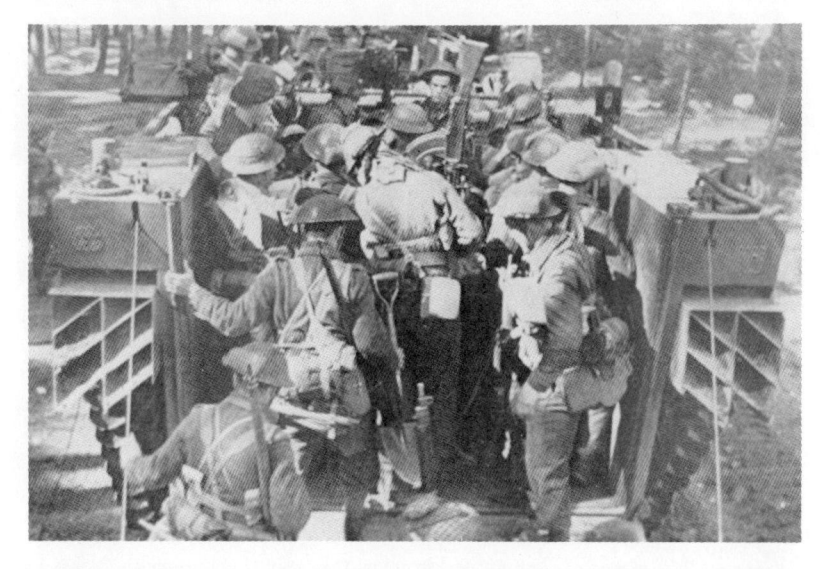

Veterans of Scily and Italy prepare for first action in Holland. A rifle platoon of Princess Patricia's Canadian Light Infantry boarding a Buffalo before attacking across the River Ijssel.

Lt-General Charles Foulkes of 1st Canadian Corps orders the German forces in the Netherlands to lay down their arms, 5 May, 1945. Lt.-General Paul Reichelt (2nd left) Brigadier George Kitching, Foulkes, staff officer, Prince Bernhard. (Photo by Alex Stirton / Public Archives Canada / PA 133321)

The German platoon which confronted Brigadier Jim Roberts on 4 May, 1945, marching into barracks at Aurich next day to surrender. (Photo by D.I. Grant / Public Archives Canada / PA 143950)

run low; the only source was the adjoining company. Six times he crossed the open bullet-swept ground which separated them to fetch bandoliers and grenades. Eventually he was hit again, so badly that he could not move, but before agreeing to take a morphine injection he insisted on giving orders for the defence of his position to another officer and made sure that the need to hold it was clearly understood. For his gallantry in securing a base for the further advance of his brigade, he was awarded the Victoria Cross but the action cost him the loss of both his legs.[6]

Next morning the fury of the battle erupted anew when the RHLI pushed north-eastwards through the Essex in the direction of Marienbaum. Further to the right, the 6th Brigade was attempting to clear the southern half of the Hochwald and, on the fringe of the gap, worked forward to within 500 metres of the eastern face of the forest. To the south, the Chaudières who had been stopped by overwhelming fire on the 1st, succeeded in reaching the eastern end of the Tuschen Wald. Passing through them, the remainder of the 8th Brigade began clearing the Balberger Wood.

In the gap itself, Brigadier Robert Moncel's 4th Armoured Brigade made another attempt to break through to 'Weston,' the wood a mile to the east of the exit. Three companies of the Lake Superior Regiment, mounted in Kangaroos instead of their usual half-tracks, with a composite squadron of 10 tanks of the Canadian Grenadier Guards, were to advance from the first lateral road which crosses the gap to capture a group of buildings on the second lateral by the east face of the Hochwald. A company of the Algonquins carried on tanks of the Governor-General's Foot Guards would then drive beyond them to the edge of 'Weston.' Moncel believed that the enemy's resistance was almost finished and that a determined thrust would crack his will. Unfortunately his own units were sadly depleted — the strongest Lake Superior company had only 44 men — and they were very tired.

To avoid the deadly enemy anti-tank fire which had proved so costly, the attack was to begin at 2 a.m. but the Kangaroos were late, held up in the morass near the entrance to the gap. Dawn was nearly breaking when the attacking force started down the slope and reached their first objective, a group of buildings halfway to the second lateral. From all sides the Germans poured machine-gun and anti-tank fire at the Canadian tanks and personnel carriers advancing through a storm of bursting artillery shells. Six of the Grenadier's tanks bogged down in mud during the advance; the remainder were knocked out by Tiger tanks and 88s from south of the railway. With no armour left to support them, C Company of the Lake Superiors fought their way to their final objective on the road where they were pinned down in the buildings of a farm which were rapidly disintegrating under incessant shelling.

In the growing light of dawn, the remains of two platoons of the Algonquin Regiment now arrived and pushed forward toward 'Weston.' Five of the eight tanks of the Foot Guards on which they had been riding had been knocked out. Three hundred metres beyond the road the heavy enemy fire forced them to dig in, their objective plainly in view. Two Shermans stopped in flames and a counterattack by five Tigers was repulsed by artillery and the fire of the tanks mired in the gap.

Desperately, two companies of the Algonquins tried to get forward through the intense fire to reach their beleaguered comrades, but without success. Then late in the afternoon, a survivor brought the news that their two platoons had been surrounded by tanks and overrun. Of the leading company of the Lake Superiors only eight men came back. They brought tales of great gallantry, of panzers knocked out by PIATs, of counterattacks against enemy inside their position and of Sergeant C.H. Byce who took command when all his officers were down, had extricated the survivors and had then killed seven Germans and wounded 11 more as they attempted to follow. Nothing more could be done that night.[7]

Early next morning the Canadian Black Watch relieved the weary battalions on the first lateral road and the 5th Brigade prepared to renew the attack. During the day the 4th and 6th Brigades advanced further into the Hochwald until by nightfall they controlled much of the forest.

At 3 a.m. on 4 March the Watch and the Maisonneuve advanced east to the second lateral road without meeting resistance. As morning broke reports came in from across the front that the enemy was pulling back. By nightfall 2nd Canadian

Corps reported the Hochwald and the Balberger Wald cleared of enemy, the 43rd Division on the left were within two miles of Xanten, while the 11th Armoured were on the outskirts of Sonsbeck.

22

THE WESEL BRIDGEHEAD

AT LAST the effect of the American drive toward First Canadian Army was being felt. By the time they crossed the Roer only four weak German infantry divisions remained to face the U.S. Ninth Army — the reserves held in rear to counter such an attack had been drawn north to the Reichswald front. Now Simpson's three corps were surging ahead toward the Rhine. By 2 March they had reached the river at Neuss, opposite Düsseldorf and had taken Venlo on the Maas.

With its back to the Rhine, the First Parachute Army was encircled on the west. Schlemm was quite certain as to what would happen next — having reached the Rhine, the Americans would turn north, down the left bank to Wesel and cut off his retreat. To him, withdrawal across the Rhine was inevitable. Instead he received orders, originating with the Führer, to hold the west bank of the Rhine at all costs — it was vital to protect the passage of coal barges from the Ruhr to the Lippe canal near Wesel which carried them inland to the North Sea ports.

Schlemm ordered his battered army to defend a bridgehead from Krefeld north through Geldern and the Hochwald to Marienbaum. At the same time he began preparing a shorter line from the Rhine opposite Duisburg along the western edge of the Bonninghardt forest, south of Veen, to Xanten.

As he tried desperately to deal with a situation growing worse with every hour, he received a series of orders from Hitler which in tone and content reflected a state of mind bordering on hysteria. The first made him personally responsible to ensure that none of the nine Rhine bridges in his area was captured by the Allies. If he failed to do so he would pay with his life. Furthermore, none of the bridges was to be destroyed until it was under direct threat so that as much industrial machinery as possible could be moved to the east bank.

This was followed by another instruction which forbade him to move a single man or piece of military equipment across the Rhine without Hitler's personal permission. As a result, the contracting bridgehead was soon clogged with a welter of vehicles, guns and tanks needing repair or for which there was no fuel or ammunition. Hapless rear echelon troops, without arms or equipment, their depots overrun, crowded close to the crossing at Wesel where they were pounded by the unremitting Allied bombardment. Finally, after an intervention by Blaskowitz, Schlemm was allowed to send back some specified equipment, and those who were physically unfit for fighting, each of whom must carry a certificate to that effect, signed by a commander.

Yet he did not lose his nerve or his finely tuned ability to 'read' a battle. Hours before an inevitable breakthrough on the Hochwald front, he ordered a withdrawal to a tighter bridgehead to prevent the Allies reaching the Wesel escape route before his own troops.[1]

On Crerar's right 30 Corps were moving rapidly ahead against diminishing resistance. On 3 March the 52nd and 53rd Divisions met American reconnaissance units south of Kevelaer and by next morning there were no organized German units west of Geldern. Closer to the inter-corps boundary, the 3rd British Division reached the deserted Schlieffen defences in front of Kapellen.

Crerar now directed Horrocks to swing his attack to the north-east with his right on the road from Geldern, through Issum and Alpen, to Wesel, while Simonds drove down the Rhine through Xanten and east from the Balberger Wald, through Veen, into the heart of the German bridgehead.[2]

By midday on the 4th the Welsh Division had taken Issum, but, beyond it, ran into strong opposition. On their left, the Guards Armoured, fighting as a division for the first time in the Rhineland battles, overcame a stubborn group of paratroopers east of Kapellen. Next morning their infantry and tank battle groups drove forward into the woods which lay between them and their next objective, Bonninghardt. It took them two days of hard fighting, much of it hand-to-hand, to make their way through the surrounding woods to reach the village and the high ground which surrounds it. The significance of their success was soon apparent. Before them, plainly in view, lay the entire German bridgehead around Wesel. Nothing that moved within it would now be safe from observed artillery fire.

To their right the Welsh were fighting hard and taking heavy losses in the Die Leucht Forest on the outskirts of Alpen. Beyond them, troops of the U.S. 16th Corps were about to enter Rheinberg. To the left of the Guards, patrols of the two 3rd Divisions, Canadian and British, met south of Sonsbeck which was taken by the Regina Rifles. Further north, Rockingham's 9th Brigade were driving the last German rearguards from the Hammerbruch Spur south and east of the Balberger Wald. That afternoon, 6 March, company-size battle groups of the 4th Armoured Division moved east through Sonsbeck toward Veen, while, closer to the Rhine, the 2nd Division's first battalion-strength probe toward the defences of Xanten proved only that a major effort would be needed to take the town. Nowhere on the Army front was there any sign of a weakening in the enemy's determination to hold the ring around Wesel.

But the German High Command had accepted the inevitable — that day they gave Schlemm permission to evacuate the bridgehead by the 10th. Before midnight on the 6th, a day when weather prevented air attacks, three corps headquarters and the remnants of several divisions streamed back across the Rhine. Remaining on the left bank with their army commander were the remains of the 6th, 7th, and 8th Parachute, 116th Panzer and 346th Infantry Divisions strengthened by a considerable force of anti-tank and anti-aircraft guns.

On 7 March, while the 2nd and 43rd Divisions prepared for a deliberate attack on Xanten, the 4th Armoured Division was engaged in a struggle of unexpected bitterness for the town of Veen. A breakthrough there would cut the already narrow escape route of the 6th Parachute Division at Xanten.

The 4th's leading battle group, Argylls and South Albertas,

had been halted on the 6th by heavy fire from Veen's defenders, amongst whom were the formidable Parachute Army Assault Battalion. Next day a full-scale attack by the Algonquin and Lincoln and Welland Regiments, supported by tanks of the South Alberta and British Columbia Regiments, made slow progress against fanatical resistance, which took a heavy toll in men and tanks. Not until the morning of the 9th were the 10th Brigade firmly in control of Veen.

A mile to the east a company of Algonquins and a squadron of Canadian Grenadier Guards were by then fighting for the village of Winnenthal. By noon the Algonquins were half-way into the town where they faced a heavily defended monastery, 'with a bazooka in every window.' Late in the afternoon a company of the Lake Superiors arrived to help with flamethrowers but they failed to break into the building. Early next morning a white flag appeared above its roof and 125 paratroopers led by a medical officer filed out to surrender. Their combatant officers had abandoned them during the night.[3]

On the 4th Division's right, the Guards Armoured, too, were attacking over the dead flat country below the Bonninghardt hills. On the 9th, in what their history describes as 'one of the stiffest battles ever fought by troops of the division,' the 5th Battalion Coldstream Guards, supported by their armoured 1st Battalion, cut the road between Xanten and Rheinberg near Menzelen, the last main lateral route across the German bridgehead.[4]

At Alpen the 52nd Lowland Division, who had relieved the Welsh, met the same fanatical resistance as the Canadians at Veen. Encircling the town to the west and north, and under heavy fire, they were not amused to hear on the 9 o'clock BBC news that Alpen had fallen to the Americans. Not until noon next day were the Scots able to overcome the Germans in the town. The 4th King's Own Scottish Borderers then went on to capture the Haus Loo farm close to the junction of Schlemm's main lateral and the road to Wesel. As an example of the type of enemy they had faced, the Borderer's regimental history told of C Company finding 'one young German still firing his M.G. with his jaw shot off and standing in a trench on the body of a dead comrade.'[5] The Lowlanders' losses had been heavy, one battalion, the 6th Cameronians, suffering 173 in a day's fighting.

The Americans too could vouch for the stubbornness of the opposition. They took Rheinburg on the 6th but were unable to capture nearby Ossenberg, whose defenders 'made a strongpoint of every house,' until the 9th.[6]

On the left of the Army front preparations for the attack on Xanten were completed on the 7th. Using the road and railway from Calcar as the axis of their advance, the 129th Brigade was to seize the main part of the town and the villages of Lüttingen and Beek which lie between it and the Rhine. On their right the 4th Canadian Infantry Brigade would capture the western side of Xanten and establish a start line from which 5th Brigade would attack the high ground south and east of the town.

In driving rain before sunrise on the 8th both brigades advanced behind powerful artillery barrages, followed by Flails, Crocodiles and, in the case of the Canadians, a squadron of the Sherbrooke Fusiliers.

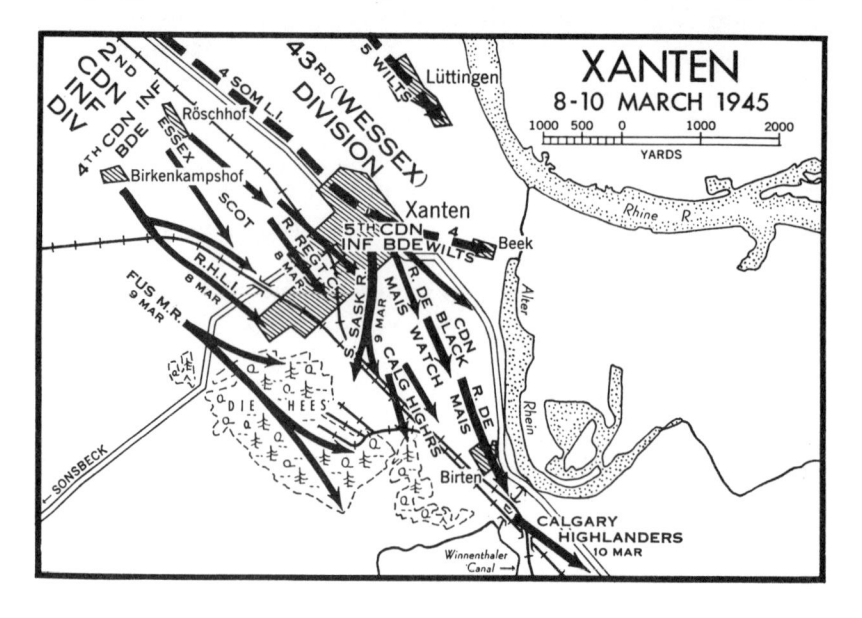

The 4th Somerset Light Infantry knew that the first obstacle in front of them on the Calcar road was a wide anti-tank ditch. Relying on flame-throwing Crocodiles to cover them, they hoped to cross it in the dark. Engineers would then throw across a prefabricated Bailey bridge over which Crocodiles and AVREs would follow to support them in the town.

At the ditch they were met by intense Spandau fire which the Crocodiles could not smother. The artillery barrage moved on, leaving the infantry without support. There was no alternative but for each section of the leading company, small groups of riflemen, to work forward to the ditch and cross it covered by the fire of their light machine guns. This they proceeded to do, then attacked and destroyed each of the enemy machine-gun teams in turn — classic infantry fighting.

Once the crossing place was clear of the enemy, the Bailey bridge arrived. It was 20 feet too short — the gap had been underestimated from an indifferent air photograph. Just as they were facing the unpleasant prospect of street fighting without the support of their 'specialized armour,' a tank-borne scissors bridge, borrowed ahead of time by a prudent General Ivor Thomas, arrived and spanned the ditch, and the Crocodiles lumbered across into the town.

South of the main road and railway, the 4th Brigade's attack began well. From their start line some 2,000 metres west of the road from Sonsbeck the Essex Scottish on the left and the Royal Hamilton Light Infanty moved steadily forward, pausing only to clear groups of paratroops from farms on the outskirts of Xanten. By noon the Essex had reached the outskirts of the town but the Rileys had run into trouble.

Moving up a secondary road, they found it blocked for vehicles by a crater 55 feet wide. Beyond it a well-concealed enemy allowed the two leading companies to pass by unchallenged, then opened fire into their backs. Artillery, mortar and machine-gun fire swept the area as casualties mounted. Two company commanders were killed and a third was taken prisoner when his company was cut off.

At midday Cabeldu sent the Royal Regiment of Canada through the Essex Scottish into Xanten to ease the pressure on the RHLI and to assist the advance of the Somersets. By late afternoon fighting in the town was nearly ended and the Somersets were pushing on to Beek. On their left the 5th Wiltshires advanced over open fields to Lüttingen where they found themselves engaged in a costly house-to-house battle with an enemy who was able to bring in reinforcements from the east.

South-west of the town, the RHLI had taken only part of their objective across the Sonsbeck road. Two of their companies were pinned to the ground by heavy fire, much of it coming from the Die Hees forest which crowns the hills to the south of Xanten.

Major-General Bruce Matthews of the 2nd Division sensed that the critical moment of the battle had arrived. Although the situation in Xanten was not clear, the time had come to strike for the enemy's most vulnerable point, the road and rail crossings of the Winnenthaler Canal at the edge of the Alter Rhein. He ordered the 5th Brigade to attack through Xanten as soon as they could move into position.[7]

At 10:45 p.m. Le Régiment de Maisonneuve, in Kangaroos and supported by tanks and Flails, drove down the Calcar road through Xanten, brushing aside opposition and capturing 118 prisoners, to seize a base on the wooded hills south of Beek shortly after midnight. Moving on foot, the Black Watch passed through them to capture a road junction a kilometre further down the road.

Brigadier Megill then sent the South Saskatchewan Regiment to occupy the near side of the Die Hees woods while the Calgary Highlanders moved forward to the high ground overlooking the village of Birten and the crossings of the Winnenthaler Canal. Against light opposition but under considerable shelling they seized their objectives before dawn broke on the 9th.

With the heights thus secured, the Maisonneuve moved down through the Black Watch toward the crossings over the canal. Resistance was stiffening and a prisoner, captured in a brush with paratroops, told of a force of 300 enemy forming up in a nearby wood with the intention of cutting off one of the Canadian companies.

Calling for the support of tanks and Crocodiles, the Maisonneuve quickly organized an attack. While two troops of tanks moved to isolate the wood by the fire of their guns, Crocodiles and Wasps crossed the open fields to set trees and buildings alight. Then the infantry attacked. The battle was soon over and a further 200 prisoners began their long march to the rear.[8]

The Calgary Highlanders now took the lead and, during the night, crossed the canal without opposition and sent patrols up the shortest route to Wesel.

While they were moving forward, Lt-Colonel Ross Ellis was thinking hard about their next operation. The fertile mind of Lt-General Guy Simonds had conceived a plan for 'bouncing' one of the last bridges over the Rhine. The Calgaries, mounted in Kangaroos, with tanks, anti-aircraft guns and engineers, were to drive headlong across the railway bridge at Wesel, followed by the rest of the 5th Brigade.[9]

Early in the morning of 10 March Ellis and his company commanders were on a hill attempting to see their next objective through the early morning mist and drizzle. Kangaroos and the rest of their supporting arms were expected at any moment. Then, suddenly, the operation was 'off.' From the direction of Wesel came two loud explosions as the Germans blew the last bridges over the Rhine.[10]

The Rhineland battles were over. The few German soldiers left on the west bank gave little trouble. Patrols of the Calgary Highlanders met troops of the 52nd Division near Ginderich during the 10th and next day the garrison of old Fort Blücher opposite Wesel surrendered to the Americans.

First Canadian Army's battles in the Rhineland had lasted one month — grim struggles to the end. During the last seven days the Army's casualties were almost as high as in any previous week. Its victory had cost 15,634 officers and men, of whom 10,330 were British, 5,655 Canadian. It had taken 22,000 German soldiers prisoner and had killed or seriously wounded 22,000 more. In the seventeen days of Operation Grenade the American Ninth Army suffered slightly less than 7,300 battle casualties, captured 29,000 prisoners and caused the death or serious injury of 16,000 of the enemy. In total the two armies inflicted a loss of 90,000 men on the Germans, losing 23,000 themselves.

On 26 March General Eisenhower wrote to Crerar:

> 'to express to you personally my admiration for the way you conducted the attack by your Army beginning on February 8 and end-

ing when the enemy had evacuated his last bridgehead at Wesel. Probably no assault in this war has been conducted under more appalling conditions of terrain than was that one.'[11]

To 'terrain' might have been added 'and weather.' Flying conditions were so bad that only on one day, 28 February, were 2nd Tactical Air Force able to give support on a large scale during the last two weeks of the battle.

Mud deprived Crerar of the speed and mobility of his armour which paid a heavy price to enemy anti-tank guns for its loss of agility. The weight of the battle had fallen upon the infantry who had to contend with the growing power of the German artillery and enemy soldiers of the highest quality. A British brigadier, an infantryman throughout the 1914-18 War, took over from Canadians near the Hochwald and found 'the wrack of a battle fought to the bitter end by both sides. The sodden, featureless fields presented a scene of ruin comparable only to Ypres in the First World War.'[12]

In these conditions there was no opportunity to cut the enemy's line of retreat. The resourceful and experienced Schlemm withdrew the remnants of his forces across the Rhine in good order and, at the end, there was no great haul of tanks and guns to be counted by the victor on the west bank.

Yet the Germans had suffered a deadly blow. Along the whole Western Front Hitler had decided to fight west of the Rhine. In doing so, he lost the equivalent of 20 divisions which, east of that formidable barrier, might have prolonged the War.

Two actions by the enemy changed what might have been a lightning armoured thrust through the Reichswald front into a bitter slugging match. Their Ardennes offensive delayed the opening of Crerar's attack from early January when the ground was frozen hard, until a month later, when a thaw had begun. Their jamming open of the sluices in the Roer dams delayed the American offensive by two weeks. The first slowed the pace of First Canadian Army's advance and gave the Germans time to reinforce. The second freed their reserves from the American front. The result was a situation like Normandy where the weight of the German armour was drawn to the front of 21st Army Group easing the way for the Americans to attack.

It does not belittle the achievement of Simpson's Ninth Army to say that they met less resistance than they would have done if their attack had begun on 10 February. Nor does it diminish those of the American First and Third Armies further south who met few armoured reserves in their swift advance to the Rhine. By the fortunes of war, the British and Canadians had had to fight harder and their losses were higher. Against them the Germans concentrated the best divisions left in their army. When their defeated remnants retreated over the Rhine at Wesel, they had lost the last major battle of the War in the West.

Part Four

The Final Six Weeks

23

THE RHINE TO THE NORTH SEA

IN MAY, 1944, before 1st Canadian Corps had fought its first battle in Italy, Ottawa requested the British Government to arrange for it to rejoin First Army as soon as it conveniently could. On 9 February, 1945, the day after 'Veritable' began, the Combined Chiefs of Staff meeting in Malta agreed that it should return to North-West Europe.

Operation 'Goldflake' began almost at once. The Corps was lifted by sea from Leghorn to Marseilles, from whence it motored up the Rhone valley, its armoured units to re-equip in Belgium, the 1st Division to concentrate in the Reichswald.[1]

On 15 March, Lt-General Charles Foulkes, commanding 1st Canadian Corps, took over the responsibility for the Arnhem 'island' and for planning operations across the river lines into Holland. For the present the British 49th (West Riding) Division was the only formation under his command. The future employment of the 1st and 5th Divisions would depend upon the development of Allied operations beyond the Rhine.

Planning for the Rhine crossing began well before the Rhineland offensive was launched on 8 February. The 21 Army Group attack would be led on the right by the Ninth U.S. Army, crossing in the vicinity of Rheinberg, while Second British Army crossed at Xanten and Rees. 2nd Canadian Corps would be under General Dempsey's command during the initial stages of the operation (as 30 Corps had been under Crerar's in the Rhineland), although it would not take part in the initial assault.

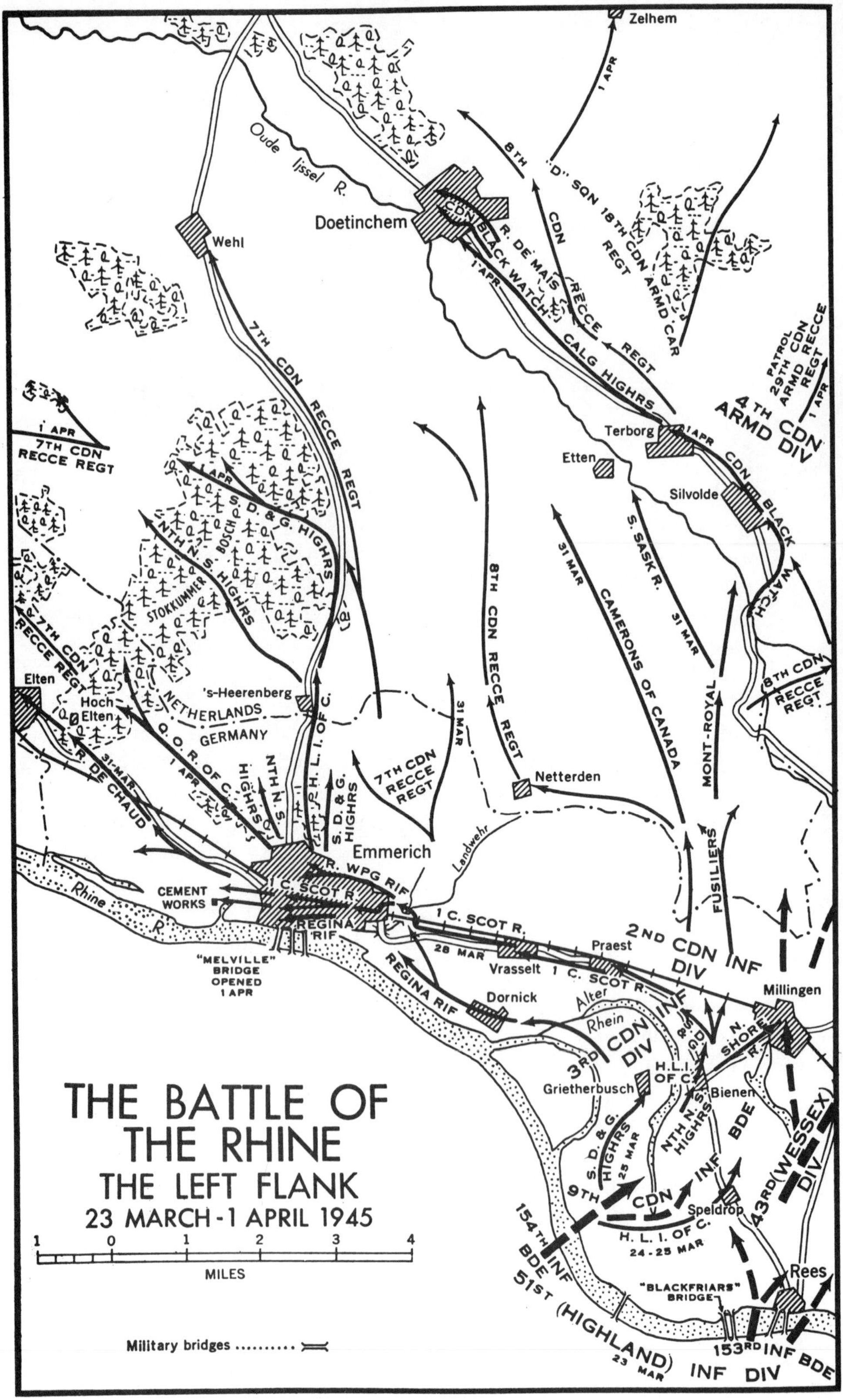
THE BATTLE OF THE RHINE
THE LEFT FLANK
23 MARCH - 1 APRIL 1945
MILES
Military bridges
Zelhem
Doetinchem
Wehl
Oude Ijssel R.
Terborg
Etten
Silvolde
Elten
Hoch Elten
's-Heerenberg
NETHERLANDS
GERMANY
STOKKUMMER BOSCH
Netterden
Emmerich
Landwehr
Rhine R.
CEMENT WORKS
"MELVILLE" BRIDGE OPENED 1 APR
Praest
Vrasselt
Dornick
Millingen
Alter Rhein
Griétherbusch
Bienen
Speldrop
Rees
"BLACKFRIARS" BRIDGE
4TH CDN ARMD DIV
2ND CDN INF DIV
3RD CDN INF DIV
9TH CDN INF BDE
154TH INF BDE
51ST (HIGHLAND) INF DIV
153RD INF BDE
43RD (WESSEX) DIV
8TH "D" SQN 18TH CDN ARMD CAR REGT
CDN BLACK WATCH
R. DE MAIS
CDN RECCE REGT
CALG HIGHRS
PATROL 29TH CDN ARMD RECCE REGT
7TH CDN RECCE REGT
8TH CDN RECCE REGT
S. D. & G. HIGHRS
NTH N. S. HIGHRS
Q. O. R. OF C.
R. DE CHAUD
H. L. I. OF C.
CAMERONS OF CANADA
S. SASK R.
MONT-ROYAL
FUSILIERS
R. WPG RIF
1 C. SCOT R.
REGINA RIF
N. SHORE R.
1 APR
31 MAR
28 MAR
25 MAR
24-25 MAR
23 MAR

Once Emmerich and the Hoch Elten ridge beyond it were captured, Crerar was to bridge the Rhine there and take command of operations on the northern flank.

Before that time 2nd Corps would cross the river and be deployed on the left flank to facilitate their coming under Crerar's command. Specifically, the 3rd Division was directed to take Emmerich, whose capture was a prerequisite to First Canadian Army's entering the battle.

For the crossing near Rees, Rockingham's 9th Brigade of three Canadian Highland battalions were under command of the 51st (Highland) Division. Before the dawn following the initial assault, which began at 9 p.m. on 23 March, the Highland Light Infantry of Canada crossed the river in Buffaloes. Soon they were heavily engaged with enemy paratroops in the village of Speldrop where parties of the 7th Black Watch had been cut off and surrounded. It took two days of house-to-house fighting before the HLI overcame resistance in the village and relieved the British.

On the left of the Allied advance, to quote the Official History, 'the Canadians had, in fact, drawn in the lottery the area on the British front where resistance was fiercest.'[2] During the 24th, the remainder of the 9th Brigade crossed the river and began expanding the bridgehead so that the 3rd Division could move down the right bank toward Emmerich.

Inland from Rees, the initial attack of the North Nova Scotia Highlanders on the 25th was stopped by intense shelling and automatic fire laid down by the 15th Panzer Grenadier Division defending the little town of Bienen. There the road along the Rhine passes through a bottleneck between swamp and open water. Early in the afternoon Lt-Colonel Don Forbes organized a second attack with the help of armour and Wasps. As the light began to fail the Maritimers fought their way into the town at a cost of 114 casualties, 43 of which were fatal. The HLI now passed through and overcame the last resistance. During the morning of the 26th, as their diarist commented 'Progress was very slow as the enemy fought like madmen.'

Later the same day the Brigade pushed further inland making room for the remainder of the 3rd Division. On the 27th General Keefler, with two brigades across the river, took over the left sector of 30 Corps' front and at noon next day, 2nd Canadian Corps (still under command of Second Army) assumed control.

In the meantime the attack on the eastern approaches to Emmerich had begun on the night of 27/28 March when the Canadian Scottish and the Regina Rifle Regiments began clearing villages on its outskirts in the face of units of the 6th Parachute and 46th Infantry Divisions.

Vicious street fighting followed in which the 7th Brigade were supported by tanks of the Sherbrooke Fusiliers and Crocodiles of the Fife and Forfar Yeomanry. Emmerich had been heavily bombed ('completely devastated,' according to the 2nd Division; 'only Casino in Italy looks worse,' according to the 1st which passed through the town nine days later).[3] Fortified houses and hidden tanks formed the framework of the enemy defences. As the attack moved into the centre of the town, supporting tanks found it almost impossible to manoeuvre in the rubble-choked streets. As expected, the Wehrmacht were not content simply to fight hard, then fall back. On the 30th they mounted a fierce counterattack, supported by tanks and SP guns, against the Royal Winnipeg Rifles. When it failed, resistance began to slacken and by next morning Emmerich was clear of the enemy.

Beyond the town, some three miles to the north-west, the Hoch Elten ridge dominates the river and no bridge could possibly be built at Emmerich until the Germans were driven from it. For several days the enemy positions on it had been pounded by artillery and the Air Force. When the Queen's Own Rifles and Le Régiment de la Chaudière attacked on the night of 30/31 March they met little resistance. Major Armand Ross commented that the ground was 'peut-être le plus bombardé dans l'histoire de la guerre.'[4]

Bridging began next day and by 8 p.m. on 1 April the first of three bridges across the Rhine at Emmerich was open for traffic. One minute before midnight that night Headquarters First Canadian Army took control of 2nd Corps operations east of the Rhine.

On 27 March Montgomery issued orders to his army commanders for their future operations. His intention was to drive hard for the line of the River Elbe between Magdeburg and Hamburg with the Ninth U.S. Army on the right and Second British Army on the left. Meanwhile First Canadian Army would open up the supply route to the north through Arnhem, then clear north-east Holland, the coastal belt eastward to the Elbe, and west Holland. The Ninth U.S. Army was also to assist the American 12th Army Group in mopping up the Ruhr.

When he received a copy of Montgomery's directive, Eisenhower informed the Field-Marshal that he was changing the main target of the Allies' eastward thrust from Berlin to Leipzig and, that after the Ruhr had been encircled, the Ninth U.S. Army would no longer be under 21st Army Group. This abrupt change in strategic direction was to have little effect on speeding the end of the war, but it resulted in the Russians capturing every major capital of eastern Europe, including Berlin, Prague and Vienna, and altering, irretrievably, the political complexion of post-war Europe.

During the last three days of March the 2nd Infantry and 4th Armoured Divisions had crossed into the bridgehead. Next day 1st British Corps, which had served in First Canadian Army since Normandy were returned to Second Army. The lower Maas front and the Scheldt islands now came under a new organization known as Netherlands District, which took under its command the 1st Polish Armoured Division and the 4th Commando and 116th Royal Marine Brigades. From its boundary some 30 kilometres west of Nijmegen, the front to the east was covered by 1st Canadian Corps, with the 1st Armoured Brigade south of the river and the 5th Armoured and 49th British Infantry Divisions on the Arnhem island.

The immediate task of the Army as defined by Montgomery was to liberate Holland and to clear the North Sea coast of Germany. The advance into western Holland, that part of the country bounded on the east by the Ijssel river, would take second priority to the operations in Germany.

Resulting from that instruction, Crerar's plan was for Simonds to advance northward into Holland from the Emmerich bridgehead. South of Deventer he was to launch the 1st Division across the Ijssel river to take Apeldoorn, where it

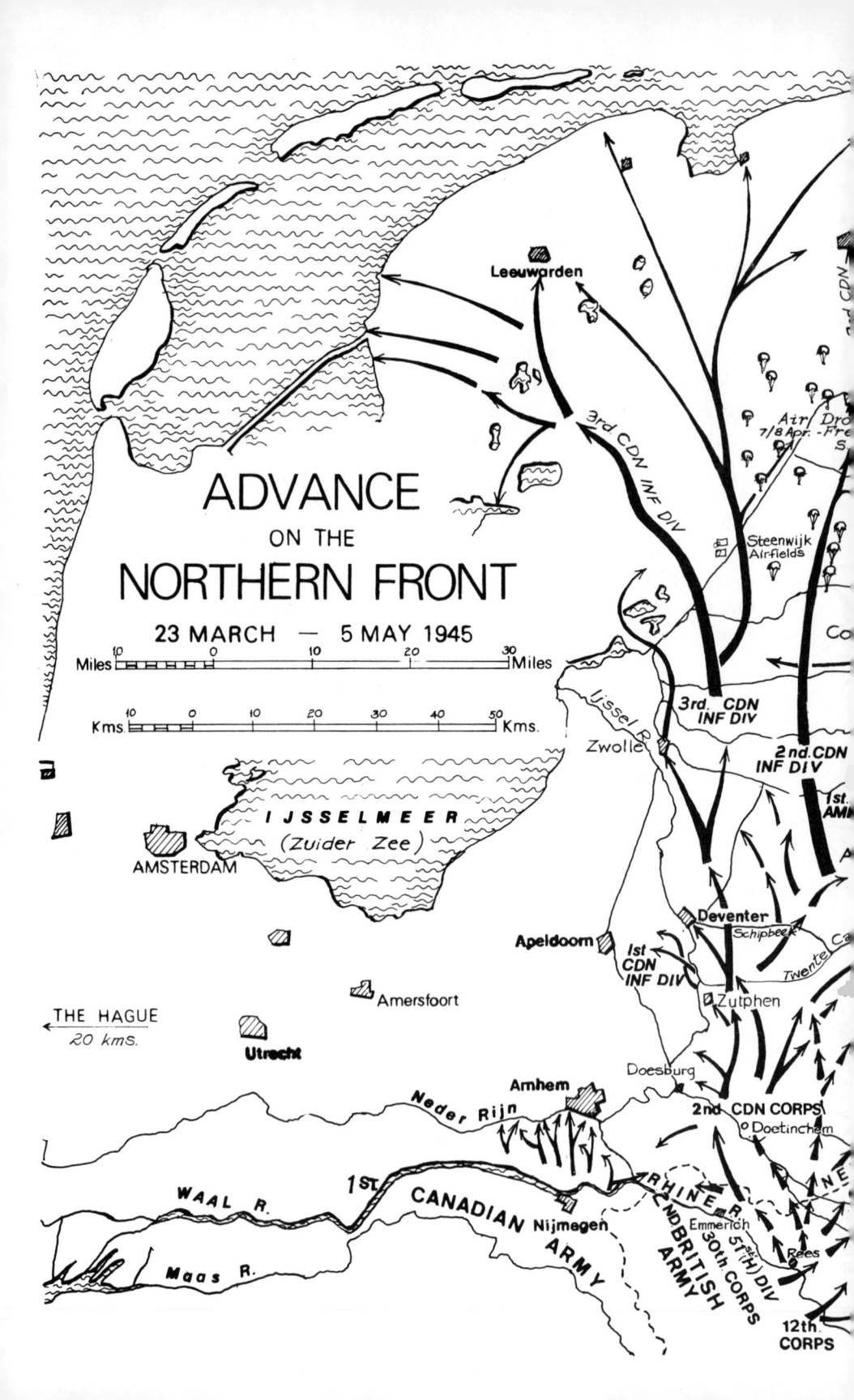

ADVANCE ON THE NORTHERN FRONT
23 MARCH — 5 MAY 1945

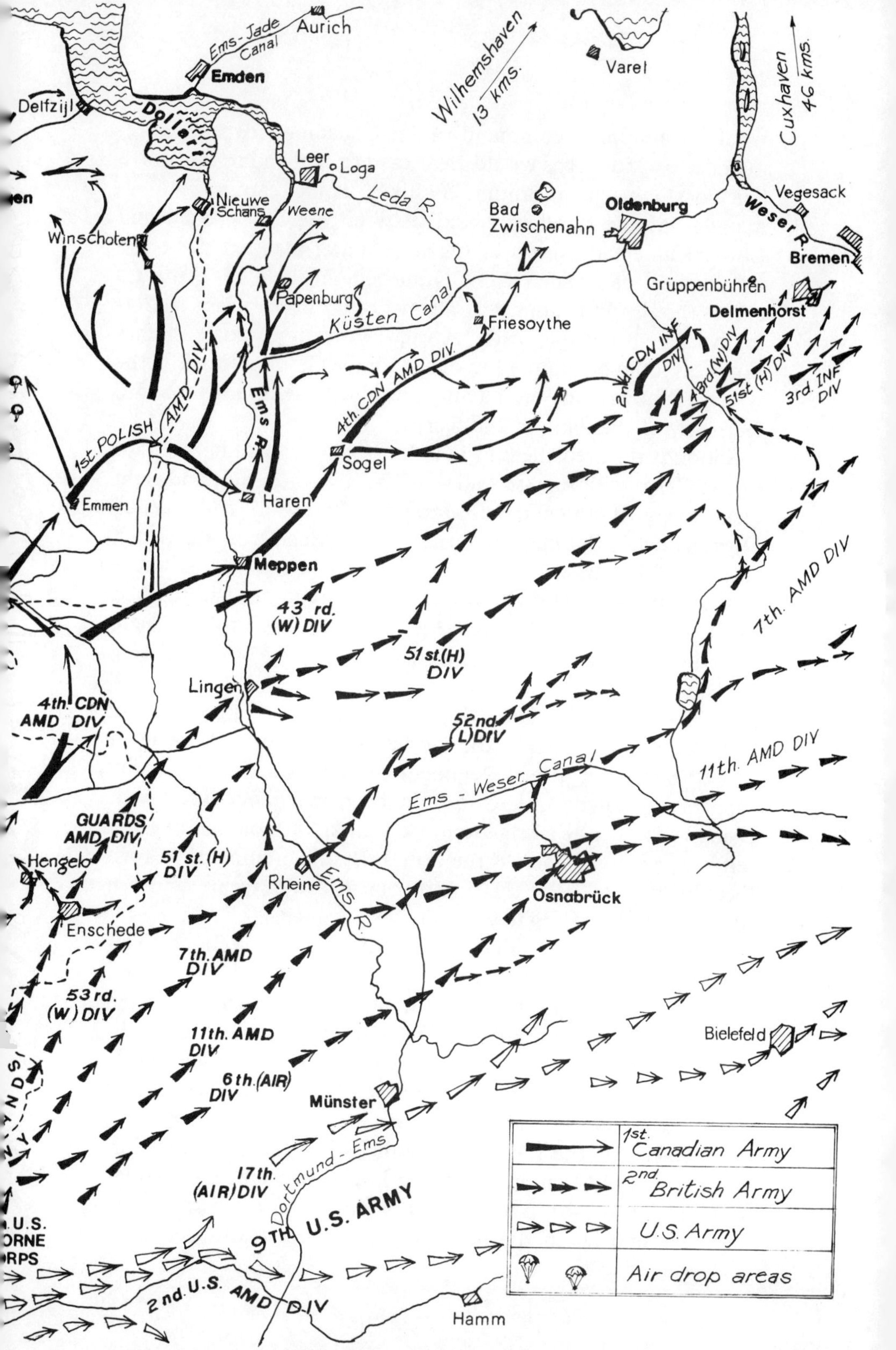

Aurich
Ems-Jade Canal
Emden
Delfzijl
Dollart
Wilhemshaven 13 kms.
Varel
Cuxhaven 46 kms.
Leer
Loga
Leda R.
Nieuwe Schans
Weene
Winschoten
Bad Zwischenahn
Oldenburg
Vegesack
Weser R.
Bremen
Grüppenbühren
Delmenhorst
Papenburg
Küsten Canal
Friesoythe
1st. POLISH AMD. DIV
Ems R.
4th. CDN AMD DIV.
2nd. CDN INF DIV.
43rd (W) DIV
51st. (H) DIV
3rd. INF DIV
Sogel
Emmen
Haren
Meppen
43 rd. (W) DIV
51 st.(H) DIV
7th. AMD DIV
Lingen
4th. CDN AMD DIV
52 nd. (L) DIV
Ems - Weser Canal
11th. AMD DIV
GUARDS AMD DIV
Hengelo
51 st. (H) DIV
Rheine
Ems R.
Osnabrück
Enschede
7th. AMD DIV
53 rd. (W) DIV
11th. AMD DIV
6 th. (AIR) DIV
Bielefeld
Münster
17th. (AIR) DIV
Dortmund - Ems
9TH. U.S. ARMY
U.S. ORNE RPS
2 nd. U.S. AMD DIV
Hamm
1st. Canadian Army
2nd. British Army
U.S. Army
Air drop areas

would come under command of 1st Canadian Corps. The remainder of 2nd Corps would clear eastern Holland to the North Sea coast. In the meantime Foulkes would capture the remainder of the Arnhem island between the rivers Waal and Lower Rhine and capture Arnhem. A major maintenance route would then be opened from Nijmegen through Arnhem and across the Ijssel to support 21 Army Group's operations in Germany. At this stage, early April, it was uncertain whether Foulkes would be required to deal with the German forces in the western Netherlands or, having contained them, advance into Germany on the flank of 2nd Corps.

Simonds directed the 2nd Division to spearhead the advance of the Corps with the 3rd and 4th Divisions on its left and right respectively. It moved on 30 March and by 1 April had reached Doetinchem, 15 kilometres north of Emmerich across the Dutch frontier. Moving behind them, the 4th Armoured Division headed north-eastward. By 2 April both formations had reached the Twente Canal which runs east from the Ijssel to Enschede near the German border. It was defended by the 6th Parachute Division.

The speed of the 2nd Division's attack that night after a 20-mile advance, caught the Germans off guard. Crossing in assault boats, the Royal Regiment of Canada captured enemy sappers preparing positions for infantry who had not yet arrived. Using rafts, the 4th Brigade moved tanks, armoured cars and self-propelled guns across the Canal. By the evening of 3 April their bridgehead over this major obstacle was secure and 5th Brigade was preparing to continue the advance.

Thirty kilometres to the east, the Lincoln and Welland Regiment had a much stiffer battle in crossing against an enemy who held the far bank in some strength. While the enemy's attention was concentrated on driving them back, the Lake Superior Regiment made a diversionary attack across some lock gates about a thousand metres to the west. Here they discovered a 30-foot gap suitable for bridging. As soon as the Germans were driven away on the far side, the 9th Field Squadron came forward and, in little more than two hours, had erected a bridge and tanks of the 4th Armoured Brigade began to cross. By next day they had taken the important communications centre of

Almelo, 12 kilometres north of the Canal, and were racing toward the Ems river at Meppen across the German border.

Meanwhile on the left flank, the 3rd Division advanced steadily northward, clearing the enemy from the right bank of the Ijssel, their objectives Zutphen and Deventer, the main road and rail crossing points on the river.

On 5 April the 7th Brigade advancing astride the Twente Canal closed in on the eastern outskirts of Zutphen while the 9th moved in from the south and east. In fighting their way across the old water defences of the ancient town, the latter was strongly opposed by young soldiers of a parachute training battalion. When the leading brigades reached the inner perimeter of the town, General Keefler gave the task of clearing it to the 8th Brigade. The 7th was to take Deventer and the 9th to cross the Schipbeek Canal east of that town and continue the advance to the north.

The enemy resistance in Zutphen itself was uneven. In places they pinned our infantry down with sniper and machine-gun fire and were prepared to fight hand-to-hand for their positions. Elsewhere they lacked the tenacity our troops had come to expect. Nonetheless it was not until the morning of the 8th that Roberts' men, supported by Crocodiles, extinguished the last resistance in the factory area of the town.

Next day the 7th Brigade began their attack on Deventer. Like Zutphen the town lay on the east bank of the Ijssel and its defences were based on a network of canals, streams and drainage ditches for which the Germans were prepared to fight. By noon on the 10th the Brigade had crossed the two main canals which radiated from the town and began to advance toward the outskirts from the north-east and south.

The enemy attempted to hold the line of an encircling anti-tank ditch but failed. Some fell back to be trapped in the town and killed or captured by the advancing Canadians and the Dutch Underground. Others tried escaping to the west, across the Ijssel through a curtain of fire laid down by guns of the 1st Canadian Division, being heard for the first time in North-West Europe.

With Zutphen and Deventer in this hands, Simonds was ready to launch the 1st Division westward to join 1st Corps. Mean-

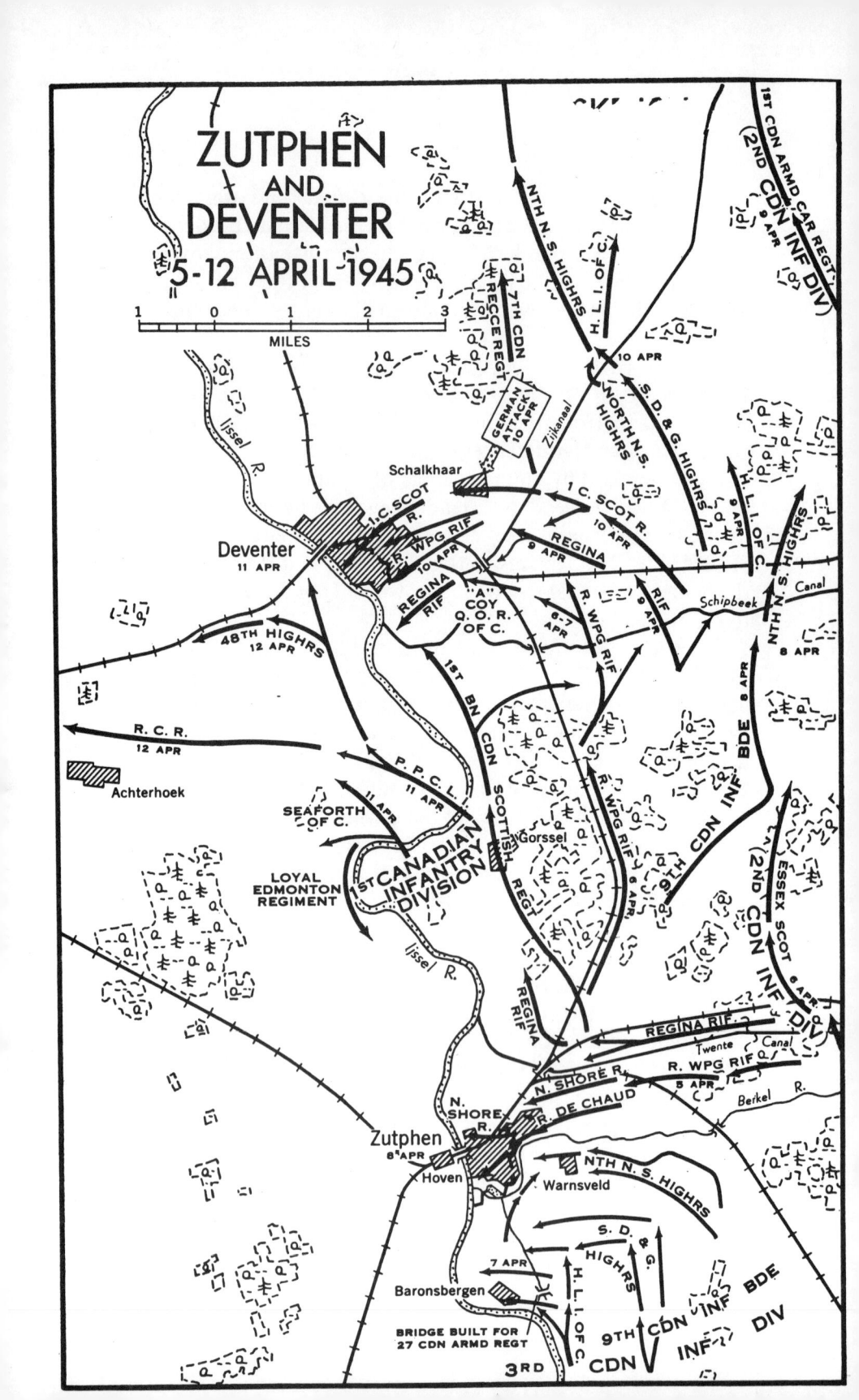

ZUTPHEN AND DEVENTER
5-12 APRIL 1945

while his other three divisions, which had been joined by the Poles on the 8th, were fanning out to the north and east as they drove the enemy from the eastern Netherlands.

Intelligence reports showed that approximately three German divisions faced 2nd Corps. Crerar had no wish to trap them, since doing so would pin down forces which could better be used in advancing into Germany. He therefore planned to sweep northward and force them to retreat to the east. Montgomery, too, was well aware of the bitter price the Army had paid in reducing the trapped enemy garrisons of the Channel ports and the Scheldt. He approved of Crerar's strategy.

To help speed the advance, units of the Special Air Service were made available to First Canadian Army early in April. On the night of the 7th two French units, the 2nd and 3rd Régiments de Chasseurs Parachutistes, were dropped in a wide area some 50 to 100 kilometres in front of 2nd Corps. Organized in small detachments of an officer and a dozen men, their task was to prevent the demolition of bridges and of the two airfields at Steenwijk, to cooperate with the Dutch Underground and to provide information on the enemy. Contact with some detachments was made as early as the 9th, but others fought for nearly a week before ground forces reached their area. The small force of less than 700 men killed or captured 350 Germans and added considerably to the confusion of the enemy. Simonds was delighted with their work and reported to Crerar that as well as preventing the destruction of bridges, 'it was largely through their help that we were able to capture Steenwijk airfield intact.'[5]

In the centre the 2nd Division was driving hard toward Groningen. Lt-Colonel Peter Bennett, its GSO 1, later commented that the enemy had been unable to muster any significant support from guns or mortars. As a result, his tactics were to hold important crossroads and villages and to defend every water line. When these were breached, he would withdraw, generally at night. However, in the last nine days before the Canadians reached Groningen, the Germans seemed to lose their old skill in fighting rearguard actions. Co-ordinated direction disappeared and he seemed disposed to withdraw at any hour of the day, generally leaving it too late to be successful.[6]

No sooner had the Germans departed than every village along the route turned out to greet their liberators. Within minutes, fear and repression gave way to carnival. Orange flags waved from every window and, bathed in the warm spring sunshine, the crowds waved and cheered, sang and wept for joy. No one who took part in that advance could fail to be moved by the almost overwhelming gratitude of the Dutch. It was a very emotional time.

On the 13th the 4th Brigade drove back the last German rearguards before Groningen. That evening as they moved toward the southern outskirts they — and the rest of the Division — anxiously waited the first German reaction. In infantry parlance, would the city be 'soft' or 'hard'? If it were strongly held, the battle would be particularly unpleasant.

Any house-to-house fighting is costly in casualties, but here the streets of four-storey apartment blocks would be particularly difficult to clear. To make matters worse, the Dutch Underground reported that most of the population of 140,000 were still in the city. Despite the probability of additional casualties, the Canadians were not prepared to increase the suffering of the Dutch by blowing the Germans from their positions with aircraft bombs or artillery shells.

The answer was not long in coming. The leading company of the RHLI had barely reached the first street when it came under fire. Machine-gun positions, well-protected in basements, covered the roadways while snipers infested the upper storeys. When the Canadians smashed their way into apartment buildings, they met an enemy who was not prepared to give an inch. The bloody hand-to-hand battles which followed were a new experience in this part of Holland and were an ominous indicator of what the battle for Groningen might prove to be. It gradually became apparent that most of the enemy who fought with such ferocity were from SS units raised in Holland. Death in battle or at the hands of their outraged countrymen was their inevitable fate.

Fortunately it was soon found that most of the city was defended by German troops who had easier options open to them.

Next day the 6th Brigade joined the 4th in clearing the city from the south, while the 5th moved in from the west. It took four days before Groningen could be declared free from enemy units but still the Dutch SS, in civilian clothes, lay hidden waiting for an easy kill. Orders were issued to shoot them on sight.

Groningen had suffered little physical damage from the war and its people had continued to go about their business, albeit under the ruthless restraints of the Germans, since 1940. It was also a major supply centre for the Wehrmacht with warehouses of warlike stores and food and a hospital filled with wounded German soldiers. Throughout the city members of the Dutch Underground joined in the battle. 'In spite of the severe fighting . . . great crowds of civilians thronged the streets — apparently more excited than frightened by the sound of nearby rifle and machine-gun fire.'[7] But the euphoria of the first hours of their liberation soon changed to thoughts of retribution against the hated Nazis, collaborators and the traitors of the SS.

Into this stew of conflicting emotions came the Canadians. For most it had been months since they had seen an undamaged city. The people were friendly and their sympathies were with them, yet the tensions and danger of battle were not over. Every battalion of the 2nd Division had experiences which varied from the bizarre to the ludicrous.

'We came into Groningen from the west,' reported Captain Sandy Pearson of the Calgary Highlanders:

> I was commanding B Company and we carried portable lifebuoy flamethrowers for the first time. We had pretty heavy house-to-house fighting and used the flamethrowers several times. By evening we had consolidated within reach of the city centre. Sometime during that day, another company had captured a warehouse full of Dutch gin, all marked 'Reserved for the Wehrmacht.' Before a guard could be put on, the boys had their blouses bulging with bottles and that night all hell broke loose. Someone tried to shoot RSM Bowen, a Bren carrier was driven into a canal, and in general it was a bad night.
>
> In the early evening, I had a visit from the postmaster, a distinguished man in a morning coat, silk hat, etc. He explained that the Germans were concentrated in the post office which he did not want burned. He wanted me to walk to the post office with a

white flag and to persuade them to surrender peacefully. I told him I'd much sooner burn the post office than risk any Canadian lives and he left in a bad mood. Next morning we attacked and the Germans tumbled out in a hurry to surrender.[8]

The fighting in Groningen ended late on 16 April. The day before, the Royal Canadian Dragoons, who had been protecting the Division's left flank during the advance, swept on to the North Sea coast and to the town of Leeuwarden, some 50 kilometres west of Groningen. That afternoon they were joined there by the 17th Duke of York's Royal Canadian Hussars, the reconnaissance regiment of the 3rd Division. With only demolitions to delay them, Rockingham's 9th Brigade had led the 70-mile advance from Deventer. The garrisons of the North Sea coastal towns were quickly overcome and on the 18th the Queen's Own Rifles, with tanks and the help of RAF Typhoons, seized the eastern end of the causeway across the Zuider Zee which the Canadians were now learning to call the Ijssel Meer.

To the east the 1st Polish Armoured Division struck northward from Almelo on 8 April, clearing broad areas on the flank of the 2nd Division's thrust. On the 10th they widened their advance by moving eastward across the German border and the Ems river near Haren, then turned north to advance astride it to its mouth. As they did so, they began closing the escape routes of the Germans in the Dutch province of Groningen. To the west of the river the Poles, and the 1st Belgian Parachute Battalion operating under their command, ran into increasing resistance as they approached the coast. On the 15th they reached the Dollart, the bay at the mouth of the Ems. Between it and Groningen were several thousand German troops, the last of their forces remaining in north-east Holland. Their only route of escape now was by boat from the Dutch port of Delfzijl to the German coast near Emden. For the next four days the Poles worked forward against strong resistance toward the Dutch port.

On the 20th the 3rd Division relieved their Allies of their commitments west of the Ems. Next day the Canadian Scottish Regiment with tanks of the Sherbrooke Fusiliers, closed the noose tighter at the cost to the Scottish of 64 casualties. That day General Keefler learned that his division, in turn, would be relieved by the 5th Canadian Armoured Division, now completing its operations in western Holland.

With the exception of the pocket around Delfzijl, 2nd Corps had cleared the enemy from north-east Holland and would now throw its full strength into a familiar task, clearing the coastal belt eastwards to the Elbe. The Canadian role on the Allied flank promised to produce many of the difficulties they had faced before — crossing canals and fighting over boggy ground too soft for armour. But there was a difference. To the south and east the Russians and the western Allies were crushing the life out of the German Army.

24

INTO GERMANY

ON 6 APRIL, Vokes's 4th Armoured Division, beginning its thrust into Germany, reached the Ems opposite Meppen. The east bank was held by the enemy and the next day was spent preparing for an assault crossing.

On the 8th the Argyll and Sutherland Highlanders of Canada stormed across the river and overran the town. By a seeming miracle, they suffered only one casualty. The reason may have been the inexperience of the enemy. Most of the many prisoners were 17-year-olds who had been in the army for fewer than eight weeks.

East of the river, the Division resumed its drive towards 2nd Corps' next objective, the city of Oldenburg, 80 kilometres to the northeast.

The low-lying, boggy country effectively restricted tank movement to the roads and, as in the Scheldt estuary, the brunt of the fighting fell to the infantry. Mines and demolitions slowed the advance more often than did direct opposition by the enemy.

At Sögel, 25 kilometres beyond Meppen, the Lake Superior Regiment ran into unusually strong opposition from German infantry who counterattacked several times after the town had been cleared. German civilians joined in the fighting and cost the lives of several Canadian soldiers. This was a new experience with unpleasant implications. The Germans had to be taught a lesson — keep to the rules of war or suffer reprisals.

In comparison to the murderous behaviour of the Nazis when faced with resistance in the countries they occupied, the Canadian reaction was comparatively mild. Major-General Chris Vokes ordered his engineers to destroy several houses in the centre of the town to provide rubble for road work. The Division met with little trouble from civilians until, two-thirds of the way to Oldenburg, they came to the town of Friesoythe.

In a skillful operation the Argylls outflanked the town while the Lake Superiors made a diversionary attack from the front. Sadly it cost the Argylls their popular and very competent commanding officer, Lt-Colonel F.E. Wigle. A report reached Vokes which said that he had been shot in the back by a civilian. The General's reaction was typical and forthright:

> I was enraged. Not a few days earlier, during the fighting for the town of Sogel, civilians had taken part and inflicted casualties on soldiers of mine in both the Lincoln and Welland Regiment and the Lake Superior Regiment. I had caused a few houses in the centre of the town to be levelled by way of retribution and as a lesson to the populace to stand aside from direct participation in the war between my soldiers and the German soldiers.
>
> Apparently they had not learned their lesson.
>
> I summoned my GSO 1, Lt-Colonel W.G.M. Robinson. . . .
>
> 'Mac,' I roared at him, 'I'm going to raze that goddamn town.'
>
> 'All right.'
>
> 'Get out some proclamations.' I didn't want to kill or injure civilians, no matter the provocation. 'Tell them we're going to level their goddam place. Get the people the hell out of their houses first.'
>
> 'That's all right, sir,' Mac agreed partly, 'but you can't put it in writing.'
>
> He was right. I retracted that part of the order. It is fortunate perhaps that there was no voice-activated tape recorder at hand.
>
> Friesoythe was levelled. We used the rubble to make traversable roads for our tanks. The ground around was overly soggy. The local roads were brick and torn up quickly by tank traffic.
>
> Unfortunately it was verified later . . . that a party of fifty bypassed soldiers had accidentally come on Freddie and his outnumbered little group.
>
> Freddie [Wigle] got it in the back all right, but from a German soldier with a Schmeisser who burst through a door in a building in which the Argyll's had taken refuge. Freddie and the German both died right away, the German from Sten slugs from the weapons of

WESTERN NETHERLANDS
1ST CANADIAN CORPS OPERATIONS
2-25 APRIL 1945

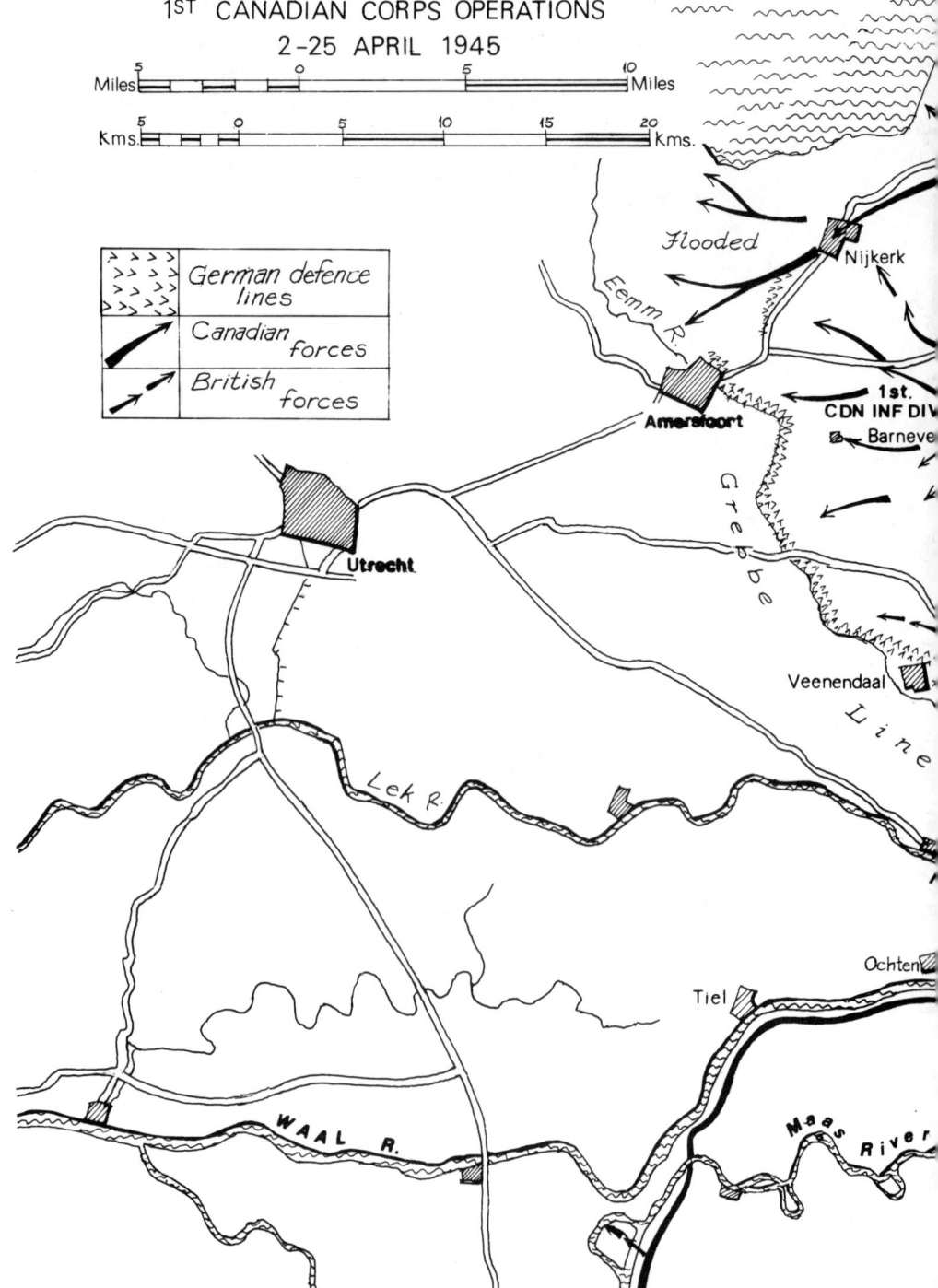

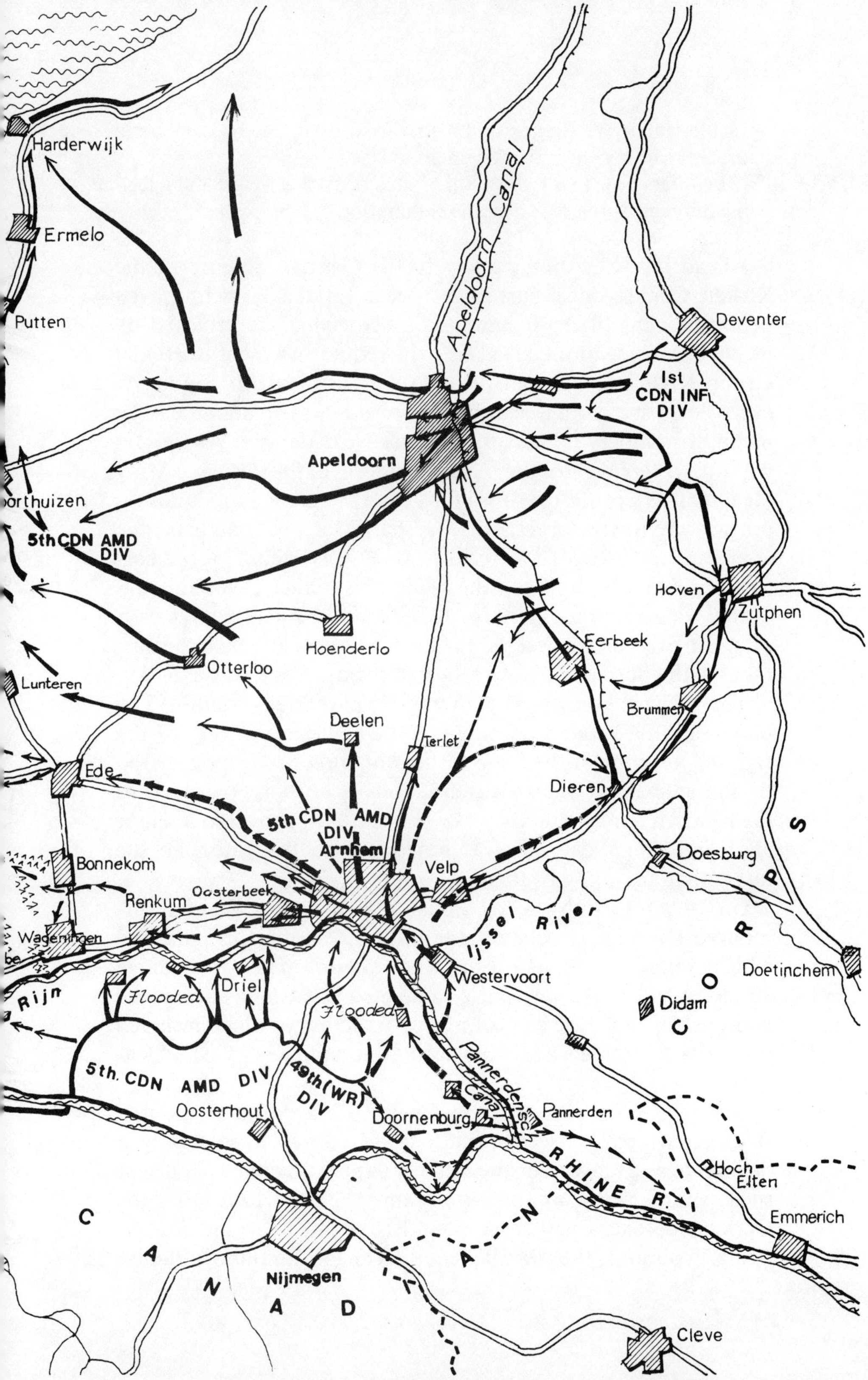
Harderwijk
Ermelo
Putten
Apeldoorn Canal
Deventer
1st CDN INF DIV
Apeldoorn
orthuizen
5th CDN AMD DIV
Hoven
Zutphen
Hoenderlo
Otterloo
Eerbeek
Lunteren
Brummen
Deelen
Terlet
Ede
Dieren
5th CDN AMD DIV
Arnhem
Bonnekom
Velp
Doesburg
Oosterbeek
Renkum
Ijssel River
Wageningen
Westervoort
Doetinchem
Rijn
Flooded
Driel
Flooded
Didam
5th. CDN AMD DIV
49th (WR) DIV
Pannerdensch Canal
Oosterhout
Doornenburg
Pannerden
RHINE R.
Hoch Elten
Emmerich
CANADA
Nijmegen
CORPS
Cleve

Lieutenant R.W. Roscoe and a Private Fraser, one of the several Frasers who served in the Regiment.

I confess now to a feeling still of great loss over Wigle and a feeling of no great remorse over the elimination of Friesoythe.[1]

Ahead lay Oldenburg, a key to the German defence of the Küsten Canal which barred the great Emden-Wilhelmshaven peninsula. On 14 April Simonds asked that it be attacked by heavy bombers. In the usual way the request was sent to HQ 84 Group RAF and through them to 2nd Tactical Air Force. At every level it was agreed, but on the basis of an attack by medium bombers instead of heavies. Next day the Air Force, without reference to the Army, cancelled the attack. Army Headquarters protested. Two days later, with medium bombers on the way to the target, Air Marshal 'Mary' Coningham, the commander of 2nd TAF, recalled them, his excuse — the barracks in Oldenburg, now full of German soldiers, would be required for accommodation for Allied troops! Finally, three days after the original request, 60 medium bombers attacked the barracks with good results, and repeated the process next day.[2]

The officers concerned at Army Headquarters continued to be among the keenest admirers of the skill and bravery of the fighting air crew of their supporting air forces, a feeling shared by the soldiers at the sharp end. But too often, it seemed to them, when a major target was referred for approval to a senior air marshal, his decision was based less on the nature of the target than his mood of the day.

On 14 April both the 1st Polish and the 4th Canadian Armoured Divisions reached the 90-kilometre-long Küsten Canal which joins the Rivers Ems and Weser. This formidable 30-metre-wide waterway, only completed in 1936, lay across the approaches to a large area of northern Germany which included the ports of Emden and Wilhelmshaven and the city of Oldenburg.

Near the Ems two attempts by the 10th Polish Armoured Brigade to cross it were repulsed with heavy losses. Only a deliberate assault with heavy artillery support had any chance of success, and that took time to organize. On the 19th, after the German defences had been pounded by artillery and rocket-firing Typhoons, the assault went in. The 9th Infantry Battalion seized a bridgehead and, while engineers were rushing a bridge to completion, General Maczek completed his detailed plans for a breakout to the north. At that moment a large German force advanced to counterattack through the target area already registered by the 4th Medium Regiment RCA to support Maczek's attack. They opened fire and the counterattack 'ended right away with white flags waved all over the place.'[3]

From the canal the Poles met little resistance as they drove northwards toward the Leda River and the port of Leer. No Allied troops carried the war into Germany with more enthusiasm than did the Poles and the ruthless drive of their advance reflected it.

Next day, in the operations tent at HQ First Canadian Army, reports began coming in that the Poles had been halted by unexpected resistance, yet they seemed to be doing little about it. They refused offers of air support.

The 'resistance' turned out to be unusual — one of the more poignant episodes of the war. Within hours the story spread through the Army, often much garbled.

Dick Payan, the staff officer in charge of ammunition supply at Army Headquarters, had a direct telephone line to his opposite number, Joe Sarantos, at 2nd Corps Headquarters. The distance between them was now so great that even with a high-power phone Payan had to shout at the top of his voice to make himself heard. Work was impossible during their conversations as Payan bellowed, 'What's that you say, Joe? Three thousand rounds of 5.5?' That day the whole Headquarters stopped work to listen, fascinated.

'Yes, I got that Joe. What's that first item again? 250 brassieres?'

The list went on, articles of women's clothing, sheets, pillows, all items rarely found in a field army forward of its hospitals.

As he put down the phone, someone said, 'What's that about, Dick?'

The sympathetic Payan's face was a picture of wonder, bordering on disbelief, his eyes moist. He blew his nose. 'The Poles have overrun a concentration camp and it's full of Polish women. Some of them are the wives and daughters of men in the Division.'[4]

Already 2nd Corps had sent doctors, nurses, food and

medical supplies to the camp at Niederlangen. On 22 April 1st Polish Armoured Division resumed its advance.

The ground over which the two armoured divisions were now operating was difficult — boggy, intercepted by streams and drainage canals, and with limited roads. Vokes decided that the best approach to Oldenburg would be to cross the Küsten Canal north of Friesoythe to Bad Zwischenahn where the ground leading to the city was higher and drier. There was only one possible crossing place of the canal and it was defended by two battalions of a German marine regiment.

In the early hours of 17 April the Algonquin Regiment crossed in assault boats, supported by the fire of the divisional artillery, the tanks of the British Columbia Regiment and the machine guns of the New Brunswick Rangers firing from the south bank of the canal. By dawn the Algonquins were digging in and bridging had begun. The German marines, supported by a self-propelled gun, counterattacked with such speed and force that they penetrated almost to the canal. For a time the bridgehead was in danger.

Heavy enemy shelling and mortaring made the crossing of the wide and open canal difficult and dangerous. During the following night the Argylls and some of the Lincoln and Welland Regiment managed to cross, while the Royal Canadian Engineers worked steadily at building a long Bailey bridge. Under frequent, heavy and accurate mortaring and shelling and repeatedly swept by machine-gun fire, the bridging site was an uncomfortable place to work. Erecting the girder bracing with bullets whining as they ricocheted off the steel work was the most nerve-wracking and dangerous job of all. But brave men led by Sergeant Schell of the 9th Field Squadron worked on. By dawn on the morning of the 19th the bridge was completed and armour began crossing the canal. Gradually the enemy was forced back.

With the 4th Division moving north, a gap began to develop between the Canadians and Second Army's left-hand division, the 43rd Wessex, advancing on Bremen. Montgomery instructed Crerar to shift an infantry division from north-eastern Holland to close the gap. The 2nd Division, which had almost finished with Groningen, was ordered to take on the task.

Transport was limited but the more mobile elements left on the 18th and, within two days, the entire division had moved 250 kilometres and were in position to the south of Oldenburg.

On the 21st the 3rd Division moved east of the Ems to relieve the Poles and then began preparing yet another amphibious operation — to capture the port of Leer before advancing on the naval base of Emden. The Poles were to drive northeastward to Varel where they would relieve the pressure on the 4th Division and sever communications between Oldenburg and Wilhelmshaven.

At the beginning of the last week of April, the stage was set for the final operations in Germany.

25

1st Corps in the Netherlands

WEST OF THE IJSSEL and north of the Maas, the most densely populated area of Holland, the Dutch people waited in quiet desperation for the arrival of their liberators. They were hungry and their inadequate rations were being steadily reduced. Each cut brought starvation closer. Tens of thousands had been shipped to Germany to concentration camps or as forced labour and those who remained were at the mercy of the ruthless Nazi occupiers of their country.

Their hatred for the 'Rot-moffen,' as they called the Germans, had been honed to killing point. Everywhere, underground groups waited for the moment to rise and strike the enemy, yet everywhere there were collaborators who cooperated with the Germans.

There was little that the underground could do but plan, identify traitors and make life uncomfortable for the Germans. They took terrible risks to commit small acts of sabotage — the cutting of telephone lines or the polluting of enemy rations.

The Dutch could understand the military logic which called for the Allies to throw their full strength behind a drive into Germany, but with every day which passed during the last long winter of the war their positions had grown worse, even more so since the Rhine was crossed on 23 March. Surely the Allies must realize how desperate was their situation and come to their rescue before it was too late. Until then there was little but hope to sustain them.

Mercifully they did not know that the Allies had no immediate plans to liberate western Holland with its great cities of Rotterdam, Amsterdam and the Hague. Montgomery's orders to First Canadian Army on 28 March were to 'open up the supply route to the north through Arnhem and then to operate to clear north-east Holland, the coastal belt eastwards to the Elbe, and west Holland.' But he made it plain to Crerar that he hoped that the last task, which he regarded as a diversion from defeating the German armies in north-west Europe, would be unnecessary.[1]

To open the supply route north to Arnhem would involve both Canadian Corps (see above — 'Rhine to North Sea,' p. 000). The 2nd, having taken Zutphen and Deventer, was to launch the 1st Division west across the Ijssel. Twenty-four hours later, the 49th Division of 1st Corps would take Arnhem. Then these two divisions, operating together under Foulkes, would clear the road from Arnhem to Zutphen and seize enough territory to the west to secure it from German interference. As late as 2 April Crerar envisaged them using both corps in the advance into Germany.

In the meantime, before these operations could begin, the so-called Arnhem island must be cleared.

Following its deliberate flooding by the Germans in December, the 49th Division held about half of this tongue of land between the lower Rhine and the Waal, in the form of a semi-circular bridgehead north of Nijmegen. During the last week of March, the 5th Canadian Armoured Division took over the western half of the perimeter from the 49th. Then on 2 April the two divisions swept forward together and met unexpectedly light resistance. For the most part artillery, tanks and fighter-bombers blew the opposition from the path of the advancing infantry. Everywhere mines, craters and road blocks gave trouble. The only real show of fight on the part of the Germans occurred in the 5th Division's sector after the Perth Regiment had taken Driel. There the veterans from Italy beat off two counterattacks 'without much trouble.'[2]

Early on 3 April men of the 146th Brigade crossed the Pannerdensch Canal (that stretch of the lower Rhine between its junctions with the Waal and the Ijssel) and seized Westervoort which lies east of the Ijssel less than two kilometres from Arnhem.

Preparations now began in earnest for the 49th Division's attack on the town. It could not begin for at least a week until the 1st Canadian Division had crossed into western Holland.

In the past few months the problem of taking Arnhem had been studied by every headquarters concerned, by none more carefully than that of Major-General Rawlins' 49th (West Riding) Division. The consensus was that the attack should begin with a crossing of the lower Rhine at one of two sites, 6 and 12 kilometres west of the town, followed by an advance up the north bank. When 1st Canadian Corps became responsible for the operation on 15 March, Foulkes and his staff agreed to this concept and the day after the Arnhem island was cleared, the briefing of the battalions chosen for the assault began.

Then things began to go wrong.

From the high ground on the north bank of the river, the Germans had a clear view over much of the island. A large smoke screen similar to those used for the Rhine crossing was laid along the river but air currents and shifting winds made it ineffective. At one point near Driel several infantry battalion commanders on reconnaissance were pinned down in the open by German machine-gun fire when the smoke shifted. When the town was later plastered by artillery fire, it was obvious that the enemy had spotted trucks dumping stores for the assault.

To Foulkes and his experienced staff it seemed likely that the enemy would now expect an attack west of Arnhem. The current plans were a recipe for disaster. On 7 April he ordered Rawlins to prepare to attack Arnhem from the east.

To regimental officers in the 49th Division, who had so recently been briefed on two alternative plans, the introduction of a third indicated that the Canadian commander could not make up his mind. When the grumbling reached the ears of veterans of the battles of the Italian river lines, the reactions varied from amusement to indignation. The most polite comment was that of the Chief Engineer: 'Crossed more rivers than they've had hot breakfasts.'[3]

Thirty kilometres to the north-east, at 4:30 p.m. on 11 April, Princess Patricia's Canadian Light Infantry and the Seaforth Highlanders of Canada crossed the hundred-metre-wide Ijssel river in Buffaloes of the 4th Royal Tanks. They met little opposition and within 90 minutes both battalions had landed on the west bank. Behind them the Royal Canadian Engineers suffered more casualties than the infantry as they built bridges and rafts under enemy shell fire. Next day the remainder of the Division crossed the river. By the morning of the 13th when it once more came under command of 1st Corps, its leading elements were moving west toward the city of Apeldoorn and attempting to open a route southward toward Arnhem.

There the 49th Division's attack had begun at 10:40 p.m. the previous evening.

All day on the 12th RAF Spitfires and Typhoons strafed and rocketed the Arnhem defences. West of the city, enemy positions near the river were shelled by the Corps artillery, whereupon German guns retaliated on Driel and other nearby villages where an assault force might be concentrating. As darkness fell, the full weight of the Corps artillery switched to the south-east outskirts of Arnhem. When the 56th Brigade — South Wales Borderers, Glosters and Essex Regiment — crossed the Ijssel in Buffaloes, they had little difficulty in seizing a bridgehead in the fringes of the town.

Early next morning soldiers near the crossing site at Westervoort were astonished to see a complete Bailey pontoon bridge being towed toward them from the direction of the lower Rhine. It had been prefabricated eight kilometres away near Doornenburg by the 12th Field Company, Royal Canadian Engineers. Rafts were already in operation when it arrived, carrying Crocodiles and the tanks of the Ontario Regiment. During the day the remainder of the Division crossed into the town.

The second battle of Arnhem was not like the first. The enemy was neither as strong, as determined, nor as skilled this time and the British victory seemed easy by comparison. But street fighting of any kind is a dangerous and nerve-wracking business and no one who saw the wounded of the 49th Division or counted its dead would use the word 'easy' to describe their battle.

By the 14th Arnhem was free of the enemy.

In the meantime, the suffering of the Dutch population began at last to affect military plans. It was learned that in parts of western Holland the daily ration for a civilian was less than that of a concentration camp inmate in Germany. This disquieting news had resulted in Montgomery's instructions to Crerar, on 5 April, to clear western Holland of the enemy. The orders were passed to 1st Corps.

On the 12th, while the 49th Division was crossing into Arnhem, Foulkes relieved the 5th Armoured on the island, with a mixed force under the 1st Armoured Brigade. From there it moved across the Rhine at Emmerich where it concentrated, ready to break out to the west through either of his two infantry divisions. As soon as these had cleared the Arnhem-Zutphen road, the Corps would strike westward to the Hague, Rotterdam and Amsterdam.

While this regrouping was taking place, another change in orders was imposed by the Allied governments. Montgomery had pointed out that if the Germans chose to offer more than token resistance, the attack into densely populated western Holland must inevitably result in heavy civilian casualties. At the same time there were indications that Seyss-Inquart, the Reichskommissar in Holland, might be prepared to allow relief supplies into the country. Foulkes' orders were changed. He was to advance no further west than the Grebbe Line, a system of old Dutch field fortifications running from the south shore of the Ijsselmeer, east of Amersfoort to the Lower Rhine. On 14 April he passed on these new instructions to his divisional commanders.

To the east of Apeldoorn, the 1st Division met unexpectedly strong resistance from the 361st Volksgrenadier Division. Both the 1st and 3rd Brigades were able to make only slow progress against its rearguards of infantry and self-propelled guns. Air reconnaissance and intelligence reports showed that the enemy intended to defend the line of the Apeldoorn Canal which runs roughly north and south through the city. During the night of 13/14 April an attempt to cross by a company of the Royal Canadian Regiment and a squadron of the 1st Hussars failed with the loss of two Shermans.

Major-General Harry Foster had no intention of making a direct assault on Apeldoorn. 'It was a friendly city, filled with refugees and I was not prepared to use artillery on it.'[4] He planned to hold the enemy garrison in its prepared positions by threatening an attack by the 1st Brigade while the 3rd crossed the Canal to the south and swung around to isolate the city.

During the afternoon of the 14th Charles Foulkes saw that the 49th Division's rapid success at Arnhem and the Germans stubborn resistance at Apeldoorn had presented him with an unexpected tactical opportunity. He ordered the 5th Armoured Division to advance at once with all speed through Arnhem, north to the Ijsselmeer, thereby cutting the escape route to the west of the forces facing Foster at Apeldoorn. By early morning next day the Division had moved to the northern outskirts of Arnhem and was ready to attack. Their first task would be to break through the enemy's 346th Division and seize the high ground north of the town.

At first light, 6:30 a.m., the British Columbia Dragoons and the 8th Princess Louise's (New Brunswick) Hussars roared forward into the densely wooded sand hills. Tanks crashed through the trees, by-passing road blocks as they sped toward their first objectives. The speed and direction of the advance took the Germans by surprise. At Deelen the Hussars captured the commander of the 858th Grenadier Regiment and his staff. Swinging toward the north-west Lord Strathcona's Horse passed through, heading for Otterloo. By nightfall they were on the outskirts of the town with the 8th Hussars harboured to the south-west. Late the next afternoon the Strathconas and the British Columbia Dragoons, having by-passed Barneveld, were at Voorthuizen, threatening to cut the Apeldoorn-Amersfoort highway, the enemy's escape route to the west. Here the Germans were prepared to fight.

In failing light the Dragoons attacked and, despite slow going across the surrounding marshy ground, succeeded in cutting the vital highway.

To the east, near the Ijssel, brigades of the 1st and 49th Divisions were advancing toward each other along the Arnhem-Zutphen road. Near the start the Seaforths of Canada and the Loyal Edmonton Regiment had to break through the young fanatics of a parachute training regiment who fought to the death, even when attacked with flame-throwers. Flanking them to the west, the Patricias swept southward, rounding up groups of wandering Germans: 'A patrol, wearying of foot-slogging, borrowed bicycles from the Dutch Resistance and rode in carefree fashion into the south. Out of the ditch beside the road a balaclaved head rose and in broad East Anglian shouted "Close." As one man the Patricias replied "Shave." It was the joint password and the gap between the 1st Canadian and 49th British Divisions had been closed.'[5]

At Dieren the Edmontons crossed the Apeldoorn Canal and turned north up the west bank. The right flank of the enemy defending the city had been turned.

West of Arnhem, the 49th Division moved down the north bank of the Lower Rhine toward the Grebbe Line and by nightfall on the 16th were half-way to Ede and Renkum.

Except for a narrow corridor between Voorthuizen and the Ijsselmeer, the German escape routes to the west were virtually closed and as yet there was no sign of them attempting to pull back. Next day the ring should close as the 1st Division began their attack on Apeldoorn from the south.

At noon on the 16th Charles Foulkes might have been pleased at the development of his tactical plan but for an order he had just received from Crerar. Within 48 hours he would lose his blocking force. In two days' time the 5th Division was to move to 2nd Corps near Groningen. There was little he could do but urge his divisions to speed their operations.

At about the same time General Philipp Kleffel, commanding the German 30th Corps, became aware of the deadly threat to his 361st Division at Apeldoorn and his 6th Parachute Division north of the city. He ordered them to withdraw that night to the Grebbe Line. Conscious of the danger that might lie in their path, the German infantry were moving in tactical formation when, shortly after midnight, they met the Canadian road blocks.

At Voorthuizen paratroops tried repeatedly to break through the British Columbia Dragoons but made no progress against the withering crossfire of the tanks. Their efforts finally ceased when the Dragoons brought a tank-mounted Badger flamethrower into action.

South-west of Apeldoorn, Headquarters of the 5th Armoured Division was in the village of Otterloo. Warned by a radio intercept that enemy might attempt to move through the village, they had halted the Irish Regiment of Canada, who were following the Armoured Brigade, and ordered them to block the Apeldoorn road. Three hundred metres north of the village, two batteries of the 17th Field Regiment RCA were deployed, with a third to the south of the village alongside a battery of the 3rd Medium Regiment Royal Artillery.

Shortly after midnight a German patrol burst into Otterloo, shouting wildly and spraying the street ahead with automatic fire. They were the vanguard of a group of some 800 enemy commanded by the colonel of the 952nd Volksgrenadier Regiment. Using tracks parallel to the main road, the Germans probed forward trying to find routes through or around the village. When they ran into opposition they called down artillery and mortars and attempted to burst through with every weapon firing. Soon the forward batteries of the 17th Field were in action, firing over open sights, fuses set at 'zero' so that their high explosive shells exploded as they left the muzzle. In F Troop, Lieutenant Alexander Ross issued orders that rifle ammunition would only be used for a sure hit, 'as a result when the enemy arrived in strength, only visible targets were engaged, that is at about four yards.'[6] Within minutes the troop was completely surrounded and cut off as the enemy attack swept on towards the left battery position.

In the rear the 60th Battery's guns were growing hot as they answered calls for fire from their hard-pressed sister batteries. Soon they themselves came under mortar fire, then Sergeant Edward Knight saw enemy soldiers appearing out of the dark. He shot the first to approach his gun, then his pistol jammed. He grabbed the next and strangled him with his bare hands while one of his men dispatched a third with his rifle butt. 'While all this was going on he still continued to pass fire orders to his gun which remained in action the whole time.'[7]

At divisional headquarters everyone from the General down was involved in the battle. Matthew Halton of the CBC, who was there, compared it to an Indian attack on a wagon train even to the extent of saying, 'Nearly everybody in the headquarters has at least one notch to carve on his gun. Some have as many as ten.'

For more than six hours the confused battle went on. There

was little the Canadians could do in the darkness but stand their ground. At daybreak the enemy made a final attempt to break through and this time the Canadian reaction was violent. Major-General Bert Hoffmeister brought the four tanks of his protective troop into action with the Wasp carriers of the Irish Regiment and obliterated a final enemy thrust.

Soon the fighting was over and the Canadians began to count the cost. A patrol from the 17th Field Regiment approached the site where F Troop had been surrounded, expecting it to have been wiped out. They found Ross and his men cleaning their guns and having breakfast. For six-and-a-half hours the troop had beaten off attack after attack and had not lost a gun to the enemy.

In all the Canadians had suffered less than 50 casualties while three guns and several vehicles were destroyed. Some 300 Germans had been killed or wounded, another 250 captured. To quote Matthew Halton, 'Man for man, those gunners and headquarters soldiers had out-fought the Germans. They killed more of the enemy than I have ever seen in such a small area.'[8]

A warrant officer of the 17th Field Regiment later remarked, 'The remaining action in North-West Europe was really dull after Otterloo.'[9]

Further north the Germans fought hard to keep open an escape route near the shores of the Ijsselmeer. On the morning of 17 April, while the British Columbia Dragoons and a company of the Westminster Regiment were clearing the last of the enemy from Voorthuizen, the remainder of the 5th Armoured Brigade struck north. On the left the Strathconas, advancing toward Nijkerk, ran into dug-in infantry with anti-tank weapons which knocked out three of their Shermans. They were probing for a way around when they received orders to break off the engagement and support the 8th (New Brunswick) Hussars who were making better progress towards Putten.

Moving through close country, the Hussars were fighting a difficult battle against paratroops who as usual were handling their anti-tank and self-propelled guns and their aggressive Panzerfaust teams with skill and obstinacy. During the afternoon of the 17th they knocked out 14 of the Hussars' tanks and halted them about one kilometre south of Putten. During the night much of the 6th Parachute Division escaped to the west.

Early next morning the 8th Hussars, supported by a company of the Westminsters and members of the Dutch Resistance, smashed their way into Putten. Bypassing the town, the Strathconas headed for Harderwijk, 10 kilometres to the north. With the help of the British Columbia Dragoons, the Perth Regiment and the Resistance, they occupied it that afternoon. Arriving at the shore of the Ijsselmeer, their tanks opened fire on boats carrying the last escaping Germans westward across the sea toward Amsterdam.

With all of their escape routes blocked, 1st Corps completed the round-up of the enemy and closed up to the Grebbe Line. On 22 April Field-Marshal Montgomery confirmed that, pending further instructions, 1st Corps 'will not for the present operate further westward than the general line now held east of Amersfoort.'

The Army's attention now turned to the urgent problem of feeding the starving Dutch. Already thousands of refugees in Apeldoorn were being supplied by its Civil Affairs organization. Further west, troops reported signs of malnutrition bordering on starvation among the people. Many a Canadian and British ration was shared, particularly with the young and the very old.

On 27 April Seiss-Inquart, the evil Reichskommissar of the Netherlands, agreed to discuss the entry of food into western Holland. That night verbal instructions were circulated within 1st Corps that from 8 o'clock next morning, the enemy would not be fired upon unless he was seen to be taking offensive action.

Negotiations with the Germans began next day, but two more meetings were needed before the noticeably hostile enemy officers agreed to procedures for the Canadian Army's road convoys to enter their area. On May 2, Canadian and British Army Service Corps units began delivering some 1,000 tons of food per day into distribution depots inside the enemy lines. Farther west, aircraft of Bomber Command and the United States 8th Air Force were already dropping millions of rations close to

Rotterdam and the Hague. After the war it was estimated that mass starvation had been avoided by only a matter of two or three weeks.

The war for 1st Canadian Corps was over. Referring to its final offensive operation, the Official History commented:

> Not a particularly formidable task by the standards of the war in Italy from which the Corps had come, it had nevertheless not been simple. Since entering the new theatre, the Corps had taken 8,860 prisoners. It was now to sit out the final fortnight of the war in front of the Grebbe Line.[10]

26

END OF THE WAR IN EUROPE

BY THE BEGINNING of the last week in April the end of the war in Europe was in sight. To the east Soviet Armies were approaching Berlin; Leipzig and Nuremberg had fallen to the Americans; the British had reached the Elbe and were closing in on Hamburg and Bremen. Germany was being torn apart but still its armies fought on. There were rumours of them retreating to a great redoubt in the Alps for a last stand which would cost the Allies dear.

Although they did not know it at the time, the two divisions of 1st Canadian Corps halted in front of the Grebbe Line had fought their last offensive battle of the war.

For the rest of the Army there was more fighting ahead. 2nd Corps was advancing on a front which ranged from north-east Holland to the left bank of the Weser near Bremen when, on 22 April, General Crerar returned to England for a week of consultations and medical check-ups. Lt-General Simonds took command of the Army but remained at his own headquarters to control operations.

With its task in the west completed, the 5th Armoured Division was now ordered to clear the Germans from the remaining corner of north-east Holland, centred on the port of Delfzijl. The remainder of the Corps, 2nd, 3rd, 4th and Polish Divisions, were to capture the great Emden-Wilhelmshaven promontory.

On the Army's eastern flank the 2nd Division, operating on the left of the 43rd Wessex, drove north-eastward toward Vegesack on the Weser some 15 kilometres downstream from

Bremen. At first, apart from mines and trees felled across the roads, they met little opposition, but on the 23rd, the leading brigades discovered that the enemy still could fight.

On the left of the Division, the 6th Brigade were obliged to mount a full scale attack supported by tanks, artillery and aircraft to deal with a battle group formed from a German NCO's school near Hanover. They were well dug-in and when the Queen's Own Cameron Highlanders of Canada drove them from their positions, they promptly counterattacked in traditional Wehrmacht style.[1]

On the right, the 4th Brigade — Royals and RHLI — were slowed by a mixed collection of infantry, engineers, marines and paratroops in their advance to the Oldenburg-Delmenhorst highway.

On 26 April the 5th Brigade took up the advance. Its actions that day were typical of the final stages of the war.

Moving north-west from Delmenhorst the Black Watch met no opposition during the morning. Le Régiment de Maisonneuve then passed through them to occupy a succession of objectives. Key crossroads, farms, hamlets, all had to be checked. Again there was no opposition. In front lay the village of Grüppenbühren and it was defended.[2]

At 6 p.m. A and B Companies of the Calgary Highlanders, led by Majors Nobby Clarke and Sandy Pearson, attacked across open ploughed fields toward it. Despite heavy shelling and the fire of 20mm anti-aircraft guns, their advance, covered by smoke, went well. Then about halfway across the fields, the wind changed and they lost their smoke cover. Immediately men began to fall; in Clarke's company, a platoon commander and two sergeants were hit. Knowing that it would be fatal to stop in the open, the Highlanders raced to their objectives where they captured an '88', three 20mm guns and several machine guns, killing or capturing their crews.

From his new position Clarke could see that the enemy was totally disorganized and that a further immediate attack would result in taking the battalion's final objectives with, ultimately, fewer casualties.

Obtaining permission from the commanding officer by radio, Clarke and Pearson urged their weary companies forward and seized the main road junction in Grüppenbühren. Both companies lost heavily, not knowing that they had overcome the last serious opposition which the battalion would encounter in the war.[3]

Far to the west, on the Corps' other flank, the 11th Brigade of the 5th Armoured Division was attacking the German defenders of Delfzijl.

The problem of taking the busy little Dutch port was similar to capturing one on the Scheldt estuary. The low-lying ground around it, much of it flooded, was criss-crossed by ditches and canals, and vehicle movement was confined to the roads. A continuous belt of trenches and barbed wire surrounded the town, backed by batteries in concrete emplacements. The garrison of some 1,500 fighting troops was supported by heavy guns of the German navy at Emden.

The outer perimeter of the enemy's defences was anchored on villages lying some six to ten kilometres from the centre of the port. Brigadier Ian Johnston's plan was to drive them in simultaneously, until a break came, giving the opportunity for a direct assault on the town.

From the north and west the Perth Regiment and the British Columbia Dragoons, partly dismounted, met heavy shelling and stubborn resistance. Moving in from the south, the going was somewhat easier for the Irish Regiment of Canada and the Westminsters, but mines and road demolitions slowed their advance. Using artillery, close air support and the fire of tank guns and mortars wherever possible to save the lives of his infantry, Johnston's advance was like the deliberate closing of a fist around the port.

On the 30th the Cape Breton Highlanders launched the assault on Delfzijl itself. Progress was slow through wire and mine fields overlooked by enemy positions dug in on the dykes. Bunkers the size of bungalows, constructed of four-foot thick reinforced concrete, barred the path of one company, but another, supported by tanks of the New Brunswick Hussars, broke through to seize the railway station on the northern outskirts of the town.

Immediately the enemy's resistance faltered and boats filled with German soldiers were seen heading out across the estuary.

Next day, 2 May, the last of the enemy in north-east Holland were killed or captured. In its final operations of the war, the 5th Armoured Division had captured 4,143 prisoners and liberated one of the last areas occupied by the Nazis beyond the borders of the Reich.[4]

Over the border in Germany the 3rd Division was preparing to capture the port of Leer preparatory to advancing northward, east of the Ems. On 22 April the Poles, whom they had relieved, were directed north-eastward in the hope of weakening the strong opposition facing Vokes' 4th Armoured Division on the Kusten Canal.

The small port of Leer could only be taken by a water assault. Lying on the Leda River, near its junction with the Ems, it was a key centre of the road system of north-west Germany. General Keefler's plan was for the 9th Brigade to storm across the two rivers into the town, whereupon the 7th would clear the north bank of the Leda as far as Loga, some two miles to the east. A base would thus be established for the division's drive northward toward Emden and Aurich.

There was little information about the enemy but it seemed unlikely that they were well supplied with supporting arms. John Rockingham of the 9th Brigade reckoned that a simultaneous attack by his three battalions would prevent the enemy from concentrating enough force to stop any one of them. He ordered the North Nova Scotia Highlanders and the Highland Light Infantry of Canada to attack from the south across the Leda, while the Stormont Dundas and Glengarry Highlanders crossed the estuary of the Ems in storm boats. Both rivers were formidable obstacles being 200 to 400 metres wide.[5]

The assault began at 3 o'clock in the afternoon of 28 April. The two battalions attacking from the south were supported by heavy and very accurate artillery fire and they crossed without loss, to find enemy troops cowering in their trenches, not having fired a shot. They were soon advancing into Leer.

The assault by the Glengarrians was a different matter. Accurate machine-gun fire swept the 400-metre-wide Ems from both flanks. Boats were sunk and several men drowned before the leading companies fought their way ashore. On the far bank was a much more stubborn enemy than faced the assault from the south. Indeed by now the Germans were fighting with renewed resolution and there was heavy street fighting before the 9th Brigade cleared the town.

In the last two days of April the 7th Brigade completed the capture of Leer and the town of Loga to the east. On 1 May Keefler directed the 8th Brigade toward Aurich, the 9th, on their left, to Emden.

North of the Küsten Canal and east of the Ems, 2nd Canadian Corps found themselves under fire from the heavy guns of naval ships in Emden and Wilhelmshaven, one of which, the cruiser *Köln*, was firing as she rested on the bottom of the harbour. A far greater hazard came from the air defences of the naval ports and of the cities of Bremen and Hamburg, which were concentrated in the area. A mass of 88s had been converted to the anti-tank role and covered every approach.

Fighting hard to contain the advance of the 4th Armoured Division, German Marines and remnants of the 7th Parachute Division inflicted 402 casualties on the 10th Brigade in the period 17-25 April.

On the 25th the 4th Armoured Brigade entered the action on the left of the 10th and, with the help of close support aircraft, began blasting their way toward Bad Zwischenahn. It was a grinding process. The condition of the roads was such that no more than two troops of tanks could bring their fire to bear at any time. Self-propelled guns, mortars and machine guns covered the mines and craters which had to be shifted before the armour could advance.

Two days later Simonds reinforced the left flank of the 4th Division (where only the armoured cars of the 12th Manitoba Dragoons were operating), with the 2nd Canadian Armoured Brigade, another armoured car regiment, the Royal Canadian Dragoons, and the 1st and Belgian Special Air Service Regiments. He ordered them to fan out to the north and west to make contact with the Poles.

At this stage of the war it was not only the infantry who were weary and under strain. Reconnaissance regiments of the infantry divisions and the corps armoured car regiments began losing an increasing number of men and vehicles. When an armoured car ran over an anti-tank mine there were casualties, but usually some men escaped uninjured or with minor wounds. But as the advance neared the air and naval bases of the North Sea coast, Germany marines and Luftwaffe personnel brought the resources of their own services into the fight. Sea mines or 1,000-pound aerial bombs were linked to conventional anti-tank mines. When one of these exploded an armoured car and its occupants were obliterated. The nervous strain was increased by the knowledge that some were fired by a ratchet device set to allow up to thirty vehicles to pass over it before it detonated the mine or bomb.

On 30 April infantry operating under the command of the 4th Armoured Brigade practically surrounded Bad Zwischenahn and next day the enemy withdrew.

By now the 2nd Division on the right was making such good progress that Simonds directed them to take Oldenburg and ordered Vokes to swing north toward Varel. By 4 May the Canadian Grenadier Guards and the Lake Superior Regiment (Motor) were nearly 20 kilometres north of Oldenburg. At the same time, 50 kilometres to the west, Brigadier Jim Roberts, commanding the 8th Infantry Brigade, was having an interesting day.

At nightfall on the 3rd his leading troops were close to the Ems-Jede Canal south of Aurich. At midnight Roberts had just gone to sleep when Lt-Colonel Gus Taschereau of Le Régiment de la Chaudière arrived with a German colonel, the Burgomaster of Aurich and another civilian. They had come through his lines under a white flag and wanted to discuss the conditions under which Aurich could be surrendered undamaged.

It soon evolved that none of the party had the authority even to discuss the surrender of the German forces defending the town. Roberts sent them away saying that they should return by noon next day with the authority to agree to a military surrender. In the meantime his brigade would withhold their fire. If they did not appear by 12 o'clock, Aurich would be attacked and heavily shelled and bombed. The Germans agreed and he reported to General Keefler, who approved his initiative.

Shortly before the deadline the German colonel returned with the news that the garrison commander in Aurich, a naval officer, was ready to discuss the Allied surrender terms pending contact with the overall military commander of East Friesland, General Erich von Straube. They had not yet been in touch because of a complete breakdown of communications.

Roberts and Keefler moved out of earshot, where they agreed that now was the time to seize the initiative and force the German commander to agree to the unconditional surrender of his forces and to an immediate takeover of Aurich by Canadian troops. Shortly before 1 p.m. Roberts, with a staff officer, an interpreter and a motorcycle dispatch rider, set out on foot with the German colonel for Aurich.

Picking their way past booby traps, they moved into the enemy lines under a white flag. German soldiers, heavily armed, stood silent as they passed.

About 500 metres further along the road, a young German lieutenant with several infantrymen behind him stood in front of a shed. 'He was,' Roberts said:

> ... very alert, very nervous, and obviously very upset by the white flag under which we were marching into Aurich. . . . The German Colonel spoke a few words to the young lieutenant which seemed to defuse the atmosphere a bit, but suddenly some distance to our left the familiar rhythm of a Bren gun broke out. The German lieutenant began to shout at me angrily and I was unable to understand him or to reply. Keeping my voice as steady and as calm as I could I asked Captain Pootmans (Roberts' interpreter) to explain that I had issued orders for the withholding of fire but that it was possible that it had not yet reached the forward Canadian posts. . . . I asked the young German to be calm and patient, that the firing was a mistake.[6]

Beyond the bridge over the Ems-Jede Canal a German jeep awaited them, in which they drove through the deserted streets of Aurich. In a conference room in Blücher Barracks they were met by the garrison commander, Captain Jahnke of the German navy, the Burgomaster of Aurich and the Gauleiter of the East Friesland peninsula. In Roberts' words: 'The atmosphere was highly charged and very formal and correct.' Jahnke stated that he had heard that negotiations were now taking place between Grand Admiral Doenitz, who had taken the place of the Führer after his suicide, and General Eisenhower. No formal decision could be made until the result of these negotiations was known and orders were received through von Straube to stop fighting.

Roberts said that he knew of no negotiations and was there on the understanding that Jahnke was prepared to discuss the surrender of Aurich. If that was not the case he would return to his lines and inform himself of the negotiations. If these were not taking place, the temporary ceasefire would be cancelled and the Canadians would attack.

This blunt statement caused consternation among the civilians. They said they were prepared to declare Aurich, Emden and Wilhelmshaven open cities and do all possible to influence a surrender. Jahnke shouted that he could do nothing without orders and that it was his duty as a naval officer to hold his position. Roberts interrupted the argument between the Germans to say that he would remain in the barracks long enough for one of his officers to discover whether or not surrender negotiations were taking place.

Some three hours later his staff officer, Major Arthur McKibbin, returned from Brigade Headquarters with the news that negotiations were indeed in progress at Lübeck between Montgomery and Doenitz' representatives. The meeting with Jahnke was reconvened and Roberts announced the arrangements which would apply for separating the opposing troops if a German surrender was confirmed. If the negotiations at Lübeck were satisfactorily completed, he would come back to Aurich the following morning.

At his headquarters he learned that the Germans had been negotiating with Montgomery since early on 3 May and that hostilities would cease at 8 o'clock next morning, the 5th. The first official news that First Canadian Army received of the negotiations was at 12:55 p.m. on 4 May, more than 28 hours after they had begun, when Brigadier Belchem of Montgomery's staff telephoned General Crerar. That evening the news of the unconditional surrender reached the Army Commander at 8:35 p.m. through a news broadcast on the BBC, followed shortly afterwards by an official signal from 21 Army Group.

The news was received with little emotion by the soldiers of First Canadian Army. 'We were near Oldenburg when the war ended,' wrote Sandy Pearson. 'I remember calling the Company together to tell them and it was a quiet affair. There were no cheers or celebration, just great relief.'[7]

Next day, in a near-derelict hotel at Wageningen in the Netherlands, General Johannes Blaskowitz surrendered the German forces in the Netherlands to General Foulkes. There was a noticeable difference in the atmosphere from the conferences of the previous week to arrange for food for the Dutch, when the arrogance and hostility of the Germans was so marked.

> The terms of surrender were read over by General Foulkes, and Blaskowitz hardly answered a word. Occasionally he would interpose with a demand for more time to carry out the orders given to him, otherwise nothing was said from the German side. They looked like men in a dream, dazed, stupefied and unable to realize that for them their world was utterly finished.[8]

On that same day Brigadier Roberts returned to Aurich with a military police motorcycle escort to fetch von Straube to Bad Zwischenahn where he would surrender the German forces facing 2nd Corps to General Simonds. While waiting for von Straube to arrive,

> ... standing near the big iron gate at the barracks entrance I heard marching feet approaching and saw that it was the young German lieutenant of yesterday's near unpleasantness leading his even younger soldiers into the barracks to concentrate and to disarm, as ordered. The approaching German unit, which had fought us well, was marching proudly toward the entrance, heads high and in good order. Almost every man (or boy) was carrying either a *panzerfaust* or a Schmeisser as they marched in to end their war. They looked neither defeated nor dispirited.[9]

Von Straube and his adjutant rode with Roberts in his jeep to meet Simonds. There was no conversation. At Bad Zwischenahn they entered a conference room and took their seats. Then Simonds entered. He read the document of surrender. Von Straube agreed and signed it. After some photographs, the return journey to Aurich began.

After driving for perhaps 20 minutes in silence, the German staff officer tapped Roberts on the shoulder and said that the General wished to know what he had done before the war.

The Brigadier found the question strangely unsettling. It suddenly opened a door in his mind, not to the past but to the new life which soon would begin. As for many soldiers, the war had been his world — existence beyond it an improbable dream. To think of a future which so many would never see was to tempt fate.

The German spoke again: 'Were you a professional soldier?'

In the welter of thoughts which flooded his mind, Jim Roberts looked only at the surface of the question. It did not occur to him until later that von Straube was desperately seeking a shred of solace to bind his shattered professional pride.

Remembering his last impermanent job, he answered, 'No, I wasn't a regular soldier. Very few Canadians were. In civilian life I made ice cream.'

APPENDICES

Glossary

AVRE – Assault Vehicle Royal Engineers Tank. Churchill tank with mortar (petard) instead of gun which fired 40-pound H.E. charge for use against concrete.
Badger – 'Ram' personnel carrier fitted with 'Wasp' flame-thrower.
Buffalo – Tracked lightly armoured amphibian.
Churchill – 37-ton tank with 75mm gun.
Crocodile – Churchill tank with flame gun in place of bow machine gun.
88 – German 88mm anti-aircraft gun used as anti-tank and high-velocity field gun.
Kangaroo – Armoured Personnel Carrier: A Canadian improvisation based initially on a self-propelled gun chassis (Priest) subsequently on a turretless Ram tank.
LVT – Landing Vehicle Tracked: see **Buffalo**.
Panzerfaust – German infantry shoulder-controlled anti-tank weapon.
Panther – 45-ton German tank with 75mm high-velocity gun.
PIAT – (Projector, Infantry Anti-Tank): Infantry shoulder-controlled anti-tank weapon.
Sherman – 30-32-ton tank with 75mm or 17-pounder gun.
Spandau – Nickname for German machine gun.
Tiger – 54- or 68-ton German tank with 88mm guns.
Wasp – Universal (or Bren) tracked carrier with flame-thrower.

Military Organization

Canadian and British military units were similar in structure and equipment, except that many items such as clothing and vehicles differed in details of design. During the Second World War there were considerable differences in organization and equipment in the various theatres of operations. The following notes outline the structure of most of the fighting units of First Canadian Army in 1944-45.

The basic military 'formation' was the division, either infantry, armoured or airborne.

An *infantry division* consisted of three infantry brigades of three battalions each. To support them, it contained a reconnaissance regiment, the divisional artillery of three field regiments, an anti-aircraft and an anti-tank regiment, engineers, signals, a machine-gun battalion and supply, transport, medical, ordnance, workshop and military police units.

An *armoured division* had one armoured brigade of three regiments and an infantry motor battalion, an infantry brigade of three battalions, an armoured reconnaissance regiment and two artillery field regiments. Its other arms and services were similar to those for an infantry division.

A corps consisted of two to five divisions, supported by an independent armoured brigade and an AGRA (Army Group Royal Artillery) of four or five regiments of medium, field and heavy artillery. In its 'corps troops' were an armoured car regiment, anti-tank and anti-aircraft regiments, a survey regiment, engineers and signals.

Basic units, commanded by lieutenant-colonels, were organized as follows:

Armoured and armoured reconnaissance regiments: 61 Sherman tanks organized in three squadrons of 19 plus a headquarters of 4 tanks and a reconnaissance troop of 11 Stuart light tanks.

Artillery regiments:
Field - 24 25-pounder guns organized in three batteries of two troops of 4 guns each

Medium – 16 5.5-inch guns organized in two batteries of two troops of 4 guns each

Anti-Tank – 48 17-pounder guns organized in four batteries of three troops of 4 guns each

Light Anti-Aircraft – 54 40-mm Bofors guns organized in three batteries of three troops of 6 guns each.

Infantry Battalions:
Rifle – *Support company:* four platoons; mortar (six 3-inch mortars), carrier (13 Bren carriers), anti-tank (six 6-pounder guns) and assault pioneer.
Four rifle companies: each three platoons of three sections. The section contained 10 men with one light machine gun; the platoon one officer and 36 men with one 2 in. mortar, and the company five officers and 122 men with three PIATs at company headquarters.
Strength: 36 officers and 809 Other Ranks.

Machine Gun – *Heavy mortar company:* 16 4.2-inch mortars in four platoons of 4 mortars each. Three machine gun companies: each of 12 Vickers .303-inch machine guns organized in three platoons of 4 guns each — total 36.
Strength: 35 officers and 662 Other Ranks.

Motor – *Support company:* five platoons; three anti-tank (total 12 6-pounder guns) and two medium machine guns (total 8 guns). Three motor companies: each three rifle platoons in armoured trucks and one platoon in Bren carriers.
Strength: 37 officers and 782 Other Ranks.

Commandos (Royal Marines and British Army) – Organized in troops of 3 officers and 60 men, lightly armed and equipped with a minimum of transport.
Strength: 24 officers and 440 Other Ranks.

Fighting Organization:
Close co-operation in battle was ensured by integrating units of the supporting arms and services of the division into its brigades. Thus each had, in effect, its own artillery field regiment, anti-tank battery, field company of engineers, machine-

gun company, medical unit and so on and were referred to as brigade groups. In turn, each infantry battalion had its own supporting field artillery battery whose commander lived at the battalion headquarters. Supporting tank units were integrated in the same way. Rarely did infantry fight without the close support of its team of guns, mortars, tanks and engineers.

Order of Battle

Including British and Allied units temporarily under command.

FIRST CANADIAN ARMY

General Officer Commanding-in-Chief
Lieut-General H. D. G. Crerar

Chief of Staff
Brigadier C. C. Mann

G.H.Q. AND ARMY TROOPS

79th Armoured Division —
Major-General Sir Percy C. S. Hobart

1st Tank Bde.	11th, 42nd† and 49th Royal Tank Regt. (C.D.L.)
30th Armoured Bde.	22nd Dragoons (Flails)
	1st Lothians and Border Horse (Flails)
	2nd County of London Yeomanry (Westminster Dragoons) (Flails)
31st Armoured Bde.	1st Fife and Forfar Yeomanry (Crocodiles)
	4th Royal Tank Regt. (L.V.T.s)
	7th Royal Tank Regt. (Crocodiles)
	49th Armoured Personnel Carrier Regt. (Kangaroos and C.D.L.)
	1st Canadian Armoured Personnel Carrier Regt. (Kangaroos)

33rd Armoured Bde.	The Staffordshire Yeomanry (D.D. tanks) 1st Northamptonshire Yeomanry (L.V.T.s) 1st East Riding Yeomanry (L.V.T.s) 11th Royal Tank Regt. (L.V.T.s)
1st Armoured Engineer Bde.	5th, 6th and 42nd Armoured Engineer Regts. (A.V.R.E.s and L.V.T.s)
Divisional Troops	R. Signals — 79th Armoured Divisional Signals

Netherlands District — Major-General A. Galloway (from 2.4.45) R. Signals — No. 5 Wireless Group

C.D.L. = Searchlight; L.V.T. = Landing Vehicle Tracked; D.D. = Duplex Drive (Amphibian); AVRE = Assault Vehicle, Royal Engineers.

Independent Brigades

1st Canadian Armoured Bde.	11th Armoured Regt. (The Ontario Regt.) 12th Armoured Regt. (Three River Regt.) 14th Armoured Regt. (The Calgary Regt.)
2nd Canadian Armoured Bde.	6th Armoured Regt. (1st Hussars) 10th Armoured Regt. (The Fort Garry Horse) 27th Armoured Regt. (The Sherbrooke Fusiliers Regt.)
6th Guards Armoured Bde.	4th Armoured Grenadier Guards 4th Armoured Coldstream Guards 3rd Armoured Scots Guards
8th Armoured Bde.	4th/7th Royal Dragoon Guards 13th/18th Royal Hussars The Nottinghamshire Yeomanry 12th Bn. The King's Royal Rifle Corps (Motor)

34th Armoured Bde.   9th Royal Tank Regt.
                            107th and 147th Regts. R.A.C.
4th Commando Bde.   No. 4 Commando
                            Nos. 41, 47 and 48 (Royal Marine) Commandos
                            No. 10 (Inter-Allied) Commando†

Other Formations and Units Armoured

25th Canadian Armoured Delivery Regt. (The Elgin Regt.)

Artillery

1st Army Group, Royal Canadian Artillery: 11th Field, 1st, 2nd, 5th Medium Regiments

2nd Army Group, Royal Canadian Artillery: 19th Field, 3rd, 4th, 7th Medium and 2nd Heavy Anti-Aircraft Regiments

3rd, 4th, 5th and 9th Army Groups, Royal Artillery

74th and 106th Anti-Aircraft Brigades, Royal Artillery

Infantry

First Canadian Army Headquarters Defence Bn. (Royal Montreal Regt.)

Special Air Service

1st Special Air Service Regt.
The Belgian Special Air Service Regt.
2nd and 3rd French Parachute Bns.

CORPS

1st Canadian Corps — Lieut-General C. Foulkes

Corps Troops   C.A.C. — 1st Armoured Car Regt. (The Royal Canadian Dragoons)
                      R.C.A. — 7th A/Tk., 1st L.A.A. (Lanark and Renfrew Scottish) and 1st Survey Regts.
                      R.C.E. — I Corps Troops Engineers
                      R.C. Signals — I Corps Signals

2nd Canadian Corps — Lieut-General G. G. Simonds

Corps Troops   C.A.C. — 18th Armoured Car Regt.
(12th Manitoba Dragoons)
R.C.A. — 6th A/Tk., 6th L.A.A. and
2nd Survey Regts.
R.C.E. — II Corps Troops Engineers
R.C.Signals — II Corps Signals

1st British Corps — Lieut-General J. T. Crocker

Corps Troops   R.A.C. — Inns of Court Regt.
(Armoured Car)
R.A. — 62nd A/Tk., 102nd L.A.A.
and 9th Survey Regts.
R.E. — I Corps Troops Engineers
R. Signals — I Corps Signals

30th British Corps — Lieut-General B. G. Horrocks

Corps Troops   R.A.C. — 11th Hussars (Armoured Car)
R.A. — 73rd A/Tk., 27th L.A.A. and
4th Survey Regts.
R.E. — XXX Corps Troops Engineers
R. Signals — XXX Corps Signals

A/Tk. = Anti-Tank; L.A.A. = Light Anti-Aircraft.

ARMOURED DIVISIONS

4th Canadian — Major General H. W. Foster (to **30.11.44**)
Armoured Division — Major General C. Vokes
(from 1.12.44)

4th Canadian   21st Armoured Regt. (The Governor
Armoured Bde.   General's Foot Guards)
22nd Armoured Regt. (The Canadian
Grenadier Guards)
28th Armoured Regt. (The British
Columbia Regt.)
The Lake Superior Regt. (Motor)

10th Canadian Infantry Bde.	The Lincoln and Welland Regt. The Algonquin Regt. The Argyll and Sutherland Highlanders of Canada (Princess Louise's)
Divisional Troops	C.A.C. — 29th Recce Regt. (The South Alberta Regt.) R.C.A. — 15th and 23rd Field, 5th A/Tk. and 8th L.A.A. Regts. R.C.E. — 4th Canadian Armoured Divisional Engineers R.C. Signals — 4th Canadian Armoured Divisional Signals

Recce. = Reconnaissance

5th Canadian Armoured Division —
Major-General B. M. Hoffmeister

5th Canadian Armoured Bde.	2nd Armoured Regt. (Lord Strathcona's Horse (Royal Canadians)) 5th Armoured Regt. (8th Princess Louise's (New Brunswick) Hussars) 9th Armoured Regt. (The British Columbia Dragoons) The Westminster Regt. (Motor)
11th Canadian Infantry Bde.	The Perth Regt. The Cape Breton Highlanders The Irish Regt. of Canada
Divisional Troops	C.A.C. — 3rd Armoured Recce Regt. (The Governor General's Horse Guards) R.C.A. — 17th and 8th Field, 4th A/Tk. and 5th L.A.A. Regts.

R.C.E. — 5th Canadian Armoured Divisional Engineers
R.C. Signals — 5th Canadian Armoured Divisional Signals

Guards Armoured Division — Major-General A. H. S. Adair

5th Guards Armoured Bde.
2nd (Armoured) Grenadier Guards
1st (Armoured) Coldstream Guards
2nd (Armoured) Irish Guards
1st (Motor) Grenadier Guards

32nd Guards Bde.
5th Coldstream Guards
2nd Scots Guards
3rd Irish Guards

Divisional Troops
2nd Armoured Recce. Welsh Guards
R.A. — 55th and 153rd Field, 21st A/Tk. and 94th L.A.A. Regts.
R.E. — Guards Armoured Divisional Engineers
R. Signals — Guards Armoured Divisional Signals

7th British Armoured Division — Major-General G.L. Verney

22nd Armoured Bde.
5th Royal Inniskilling Dragoon Guards
1st and 5th Royal Tank Regt.
1st Bn. The Rifle Brigade (Motor)

131st Infantry Bde.
1/5th, 1/6th and 1/7th Queen's Royal Regt.
2nd Devonshire Regt. (ex-50th Division)
9th Durham Light Infantry (ex-50th Division)

Divisional Troops	R.A.C. — 8th King's Royal Irish Hussars
	R.A. — 3rd and 5th Regts. R.H.A.; 65th A/Tk. and 15th L.A.A. Regts.
	R.E. — 7th Armoured Divisional Engineers
	R. Signals — 7th Armoured Divisional Signals

11th British Armoured Division —
Major-General G. P. B. Roberts

29th Amoured Bde.	23rd Hussars
	2nd Fife and Forfar Yeomanry
	3rd Royal Tank Regt.
	8th Bn. The Rifle Brigade (Motor)
159th Infantry Bde.	1st Cheshire Regt. (ex-115th Bde.)
	4th King's Shropshire Light Infantry
	1st Herefordshire Regt.
Divisional Troops	R.A.C. — 15th/19th King's Royal Hussars
	R.A. — 13th Regt. R.H.A.; 151st Field, 75th A/Tk. and 58th L.A.A. Regts.
	R.E. — 11th Armoured Divisional Engineers
	R. Signals — 11th Armoured Divisional Signals

1st Polish Armoured Division — Major-General S. Maczek

10th Polish Armoured Bde.	1st and 2nd Polish Armoured Regts.
	24th Polish Armoured (Lancer) Regt.
	10th Polish Motor Bn.
3rd Polish Infantry Bde.	1st (Highland), 8th and 9th Polish Bns.
Divisional Troops	10th Polish Mounted Rifle Regt.
	1st and 2nd Polish Field, 1st Polish A/Tk. and 1st Polish L.A.A. Regts.

1st Polish Armoured Divisional
Engineers
1st Polish Armoured Divisional Signals

INFANTRY DIVISIONS

1st Canadian Division — Major-General H. W. Foster

1st Canadian Bde.	The Royal Canadian Regt. The Hastings and Prince Edward Regt. 48th Highlanders of Canada
2nd Canadian Bde.	Princess Patricia's Canadian Light Infantry The Seaforth Highlanders of Canada The Loyal Edmonton Regt.
3rd Canadian Bde.	Royal 22e Regt. The Carleton and York Regt. The West Nova Scotia Regt.
Divisional Troops	C.A.C. — 4th Recce. Regt. (4th Princess Louise Dragoon Guards) R.C.A. — 1st (R.C.H.A.), 2nd and 3rd Field, 1st A/Tk. and 2nd L.A.A. Regts. R.C.E. — 1st Canadian Divisional Engineers R.C. Signals — 1st Canadian Divisional Signals Machine Gun — The Saskatoon Light Infantry

2nd Canadian Division —
Major-General C. Foulkes (to 9.11.44)
Major-General A. B. Matthews (from 10.11.44)

4th Canadian Bde.	The Royal Regiment of Canada The Royal Hamilton Light Infantry The Essex Scottish Regt.
5th Canadian Bde.	The Black Watch (Royal Highland Regt.) of Canada Le Régiment de Maisonneuve The Calgary Highlanders

6th Canadian Bde.	Les Fusiliers Mont-Royal
	The Queen's Own Cameron Highlanders of Canada
	The South Saskatchewan Regt.
Divisional Troops	C.A.C. — 8th Recce Regt. (14th Canadian Hussars)
	R.C.A. — 4th, 5th and 6th Field, 2nd A/Tk. and 3rd L.A.A. Regts.
	R.C.E. — 2nd Canadian Divisional Engineers
	R.C. Signals — 2nd Canadian Divisional Signals
	Machine Gun — The Toronto Scottish Regt.

3rd Canadian Division —
Major-General D. C. Spry (to 22.3.45)
Major-General R. H. Keefler (from 23.3.45)

7th Canadian Bde.	The Royal Winnipeg Rifles
	The Regina Rifle Regt.
	1st Bn. The Canadian Scottish Regt.
8th Canadian Bde.	The Queen's Own Rifles of Canada
	Le Régiment de la Chaudière
	The North Shore (New Brunswick) Regt.
9th Canadian Bde.	The Highland Light Infantry of Canada
	The Stormont, Dundas and Glengarry Highlanders
	The North Nova Scotia Highlanders
Divisional Troops	C.A.C. — 7th Recce. Regt. (17th Duke of York's Royal Canadian Hussars)
	R.A.C. — 12th, 13th and 14th Field, 3rd A/Tk. and 4th L.A.A. Regts.
	R.C.E. — 3rd Canadian Divisional Engineers

R.C. Signals — 3rd Canadian Divisional Signals
Machine Gun — The Cameron Highlanders of Ottawa

BRITISH INFANTRY DIVISIONS

3rd Division — Major-General L. G. Whistler

8th Bde.	1st Suffolk Regt.
	2nd East Yorkshire Regt.
	1st South Lancashire Regt.
9th Bde.	2nd Lincolnshire Regt.
	1st King's Own Scottish Borderers
	2nd Royal Ulster Rifles
185th Bde.	2nd Royal Warwickshire Regt.
	1st Royal Norfolk Regt.
	2nd King's Shropshire Light Infantry
Divisional Troops	R.A.C. — 3rd Recce. Regt.
	R.A. — 7th, 33rd and 76th Field, 20th A/Tk. and 92nd L.A.A. Regts.
	R.E. — 3rd Divisional Engineers
	R. Signals — 3rd Divisional Signals
	Machine Gun — 2nd Middlesex Regt.

15th (Scottish) Division — Major-General C. M. Barber

44th (Lowland) Bde.	8th Royal Scots
	6th Royal Scots Fusiliers
	6th King's Own Scottish Borderers
46th (Highland) Bde.	9th Cameronians
	2nd Glasgow Highlanders
	7th Seaforth Highlanders
227th (Highland) Bde.	10th Highland Light Infantry
	2nd Gordon Highlanders
	2nd Argyll and Sutherland Highlanders
Divisional Troops	R.A.C. — 15th Recce. Regt.
	R.A. — 131st, 181st and 190th Field, 97th and 102nd (ex-50th Division) A/Tk. and 119th L.A.A. Regts.

R.E. — 15th Divisional Engineers
R. Signals — 15th Divisional Signals
Machine Gun — 1st Middlesex Regt.

43rd (Wessex) Division — Major-General G. I. Thomas

129th Bde.
4th Somerset Light Infantry
4th and 5th Wiltshire Regt.

130th Bde.
7th Hampshire Regt.
4th and 5th Dorsetshire Regt.

214th Bde.
7th Somerset Light Infantry
1st Worcestershire Regt.
5th Duke of Cornwall's Light Infantry

Divisional Troops
R.A.C. — 43rd Recce. Regt.
R.A. — 94th, 112th and 179th Field, 59th A/Tk. and 110th L.A.A. Regts.
R.E. — 43rd Divisional Engineers
R. Signals — 43rd Divisional Signals
Machine Gun — 8th Middlesex Regt.

49th (West Riding) Division —
Major-General E. H. Barker (to 29.11.44)
Major-General G. H. A. MacMillan (to 24.3.45)
Major-General S. B. Rawlins (from 28.3.45)

56th Bde.
2nd South Wales Borderers
2nd Gloucestershire Regt.
2nd Essex Regt.

146th Bde.
4th Lincolnshire Regt.
1/4th King's Own Yorkshire Light Infantry
Hallamshire Bn. York and Lancaster Regt.

147th Bde.
1st Leicestershire Regt.
11th Royal Scots Fusiliers
7th Duke of Wellington's Regt.

Divisional Troops
R.A.C. — 49th Recce. Regt.
R.A. — 69th, 74th (ex-50th Division), 143rd and 185th† Field, 55th A/Tk. and 89th L.A.A. Regts.

R.E. — 49th Divisional Engineers
R. Signals — 49th Divisional Signals
Machine Gun — 2nd Princess Louise's Kensington Regt.

50th (Northumbrian) Division —
Major-General L. O. Lyne (to 21.11.44)
Major-General D. A. H. Graham (from 27.11.44)

69th Bde.   5th East Yorkshire Regt.
6th and 7th Green Howards

151st Bde.   6th, 8th and 9th Durham Light Infantry

231st Bde.   2nd Devonshire Regt.
1st Hampshire Regt.
1st Dorsetshire Regt.

Divisional Troops   R.A.C. — 61st Recce. Regt.
R.A. — 74th, 90th and 124th Field, 102nd A/Tk. and 25th L.A.A. Regts.
R.E. — 50th Divisional Engineers
R. Signals — 50th Divisional Signals
Machine Gun — 2nd Cheshire Regt.

51st (Highland) Division — Major General T. G. Rennie

152nd Bde.   2nd and 5th Seaforth Highlanders
5th Queen's Own Cameron Highlanders

153rd Bde.   5th Black Watch
1st and 5th/7th Gordon Highlanders

154th Bde.   1st and 7th Black Watch
7th Argyll and Sutherland Highlanders

Divisional Troops   R.A.C. — 2nd Derbyshire Yeomanry
R.A. — 126th, 127th and 128th Field, 61st A/Tk. and 40th L.A.A. Regts.
R.E. — 51st Divisional Engineers
R. Signals — 51st Divisional Signals
Machine Gun — 1/7th Middlesex Regt.

52nd (Lowland) Division — Major-General E. Hakewill-Smith

155th Bde.	7th/9th Royal Scots
	4th King's Own Scottish Borderers
	6th Highland Light Infantry
156th Bde.	4th/5th Royal Scots Fusiliers
	6th Cameronians
	1st Glasgow Highlanders
157th Bde.	5th King's Own Scottish Borderers
	7th Cameronians
	5th Highland Light Infantry
Divisional Troops	R.A.C. — 52nd Recce. Regt.
	R.A. — 79th, 80th and 186th Field, 1st Mountain, 54th A/Tk. and 108th L.A.A. Regts.
	R.E. — 52nd Divisional Engineers
	R. Signals — 52nd Divisional Signals
	Machine Gun — 7th Manchester Regt.

53rd (Welsh) Division — Major-General R. K. Ross

71st Bde.	1st Oxfordshire and Buckinghamshire Light Infantry
	1st Highland Light Infantry
	4th Royal Welch Fusiliers
158th Bde.	1st East Lancashire Regt.
	7th Royal Welch Fusiliers
	1/5th Welch Regt.
160th Bde.	6th Royal Welch Fusiliers
	2nd Monmouthshire Regt.
	4th Welch Regt.
Divisional Troops	R.A.C. — 53rd Recce. Regt.
	R.A. — 81st, 83rd and 133rd Field, 71st A/Tk. and 25th L.A.A. Regts.
	R.E. — 53rd Divisional Engineers
	R. Signals — 53rd Divisional Signals
	Machine Gun — 1st Manchester Regt.

AIRBORNE DIVISIONS

6th Airborne Division — Major-General R. N. Gale

3rd Parachute Bde.	8th and 9th Parachute Regt.
	1st Canadian Parachute Bn.
5th Parachute Bde.	7th, 12th and 13th Parachute Regt.
6th Airlanding Bde.	12th Devonshire Regt.
	2nd Oxfordshire and Buckinghamshire Light Infantry
	1st Royal Ulster Rifles
Divisional Troops	R.A.C. — 6th Airborne Armoured Recce. Regt.
	R.A. — 53rd Airlanding Light and 2nd Airlanding A/Tk. Regts.
	R.E. — 6th Airborne Divisional Engineers
	R. Signals — 6th Airborne Divisional Signals

UNITED STATES DIVISIONS

82nd Airborne Division — Major-Gen James M. Gavin

101st Airborne Division — Major-Gen Maxwell D. Taylor

104th Infantry Division — *Major-Gen Terry Allen*

European Allies

1st Belgian Bde.	I, II and III Belgian Bns.
Royal Netherlands Bde. (Princess Irene's)	Composite force of infantry, artillery and reconnaissance sub-units
Czechoslovakian Armoured Bde.	1st, 2nd and 3rd Czechoslovakian Armoured Regts.
	The Czechoslovakian Field Arillery Regt.
	The Czechoslovakian Motor Bn.

A Note on Casualties

The Second World War followed the First by fewer than 21 years and those who took part in it were, in a sense, the offspring of the soldiers of the earlier conflict. The memories of its appalling casualties and of the horror of trench warfare on the Western Front were etched into the consciousness of the generation who fought it. Historians, school text books, Remembrance services, poets, military writers and veterans' tales all played their part in transferring them to the soldiers of First Canadian Army. They in turn saw more than enough of death and misery but they rarely accepted that their war and their performance in it could match the experience of their fathers.

In one respect it did. A Canadian infantryman in North-West Europe in 1944-45 stood a greater chance of becoming a 'battle casualty' than his father had in an equivalent period on the Western Front in the First World War.

The average casualty rate for an infantry battalion, Canadian or British, over the periods they were in France and Belgium in the 1914-18 War was about 100 per month. In North-West Europe, Canadian battalions, and many British, lost a minimum of that figure. For some it reached an average of 175 per month over the whole period of their service on the Continent ending on 8 May, 1945.

The equivalent rates for the North African and the Italian campaigns were about seventy per month.

In order to compare like with like, to the extent that that is possible, the calculations in the following table are for standard rifle battalions in infantry brigades in both wars. Machine-gun, parachute and motor battalions are not included. A 'battle casualty' means a soldier who is killed, wounded or missing in action. Those incurred in the Dieppe raid of 1942 have not been included in the totals of the 2nd Division's battalions.

Average Monthly Battle Casualty Rate

Infantry rifle battalions calculated from date of landing in France, First World War

(Random selection of battalions	Total Casualties	Months in Theatre	Monthly Average
PPCLI	4076	46	89
2 Bn (Toronto Regt)	4773	45	106
10 Bn	4276	45	95
58 Bn	3114	33	94

The total battle casualties of all arms and services of the 1st Canadian Division for 45 months of the First World War was 59,055 or 1,312 per month. If this figure is divided by 12, the number of infantry battalions, it gives an average of 109. The true average is less, suggesting that the accepted figure of 100 casualties per month is about right.

Second World War[1]

	Total Casualties	Months in Theatre	Monthly Average
a. Battalions with highest & lowest monthly rate:			
Black Watch (RHR) of Canada	1772	10	177
Régt de la Chaudière	1014	11	92
b. All battalions of 2nd Division	1445 (average)	10	144
3rd "	1270 "	11	115
4th "	1387 "	9.5	146
All battalions of 15th Scottish Division[2]	1147 "	10.5	109

1. Canadian figures are derived from 'Battle Casualties by Units Showing Theatre of Operations' — Crerar Papers, MG30 E, 157 Vol 29
2. 'Fifteenth Scottish Division 1939-1945' by Lt-General H.G. Martin, pp. 347-354

While no part of an infantry battalion was immune to casualties, the largest proportion, inevitably, occurred in the rifle companies. In World War 1 these contained 908 of the 1012 officers and men of a battalion. In the Second World War, out of a total of 845, only 508 were in the four rifle companies which consequently bore a proportion of losses considerably higher than those in the 1914-18 War.

There are many reasons why the losses in 1944-45 were comparatively so high. In the earlier war, after units suffered heavily, they were, if possible, rested and placed in quiet sectors for some months. It was common for most battalions to have fought only some 22 major engagements in nearly four years at the front. In the Second World War, a proportion of men were 'Left Out of Battle' so that a battalion was never 'wiped out.' With an efficient reinforcement system, casualties were quickly replaced, so that the unit could continue fighting. With a high proportion of automatic weapons, infantry companies could, and did, continue to do their operational jobs with severely depleted strengths.

By 1944, weapons technology and tactical methods had progressed considerably from 1918. Armies had become more efficient at killing each other. Since 1945, progress has been even greater, a sobering thought for anyone contemplating the possibility of a major non-nuclear war.

This comparison of infantry casualties does not prove that the Northwest Europe Campaign was as terrible as the Western Front in 1917. What it does show is that, faced with a formidable enemy, the infantry suffered appalling losses and that for the period of the campaign, a rifleman in First Canadian Army ran a higher risk of death or injury than if he had fought for an equivalent period in the First World War.

ENDNOTES

Abbreviations:

PARC – Public Archives of Canada, Ottawa
PRO – Public Records Office, Kew

The term 'Official History' refers to *The Official History of the Canadian Army, Volume 3: The Victory Campaign* by Colonel C.P. Stacey, 1960.

'British Official History' refers to *The History of the Second World War, Volume 2: Victory in the West* by Major L.F. Ellis, 1962.

Foreword

1. *The Canadians in Italy* by Col G.W.L. Nicholson, p. 343.

Chapter 1 — Pride and Prejudice

1. *Monty: Master of the Battlefield* by Nigel Hamilton, p. 796.
2. *Crerar Papers* – Speech to War Correspondents before 'Veritable.'
3. *Monty: The Making of a General* by Nigel Hamilton, p. 129.

4. *McNaughton: Vol. 2* by John Swettenham, p. 346.
5. *Crerar Papers:* Vol. 30.
6. ibid.
7. *Arms, Men and Governments* by C.P. Stacey, p. 214.
8. *Monty: The Making of a General*, p. 501.
9. *Crerar Papers:* Vol. 30.
10. *Monty: Master of the Battlefield*, p. 780.
11. *Official History*, p. 612.
12. Interview with Commodore William Hayes, 12 May, 1985.
13. *A Date with History* by C.P Stacey, p. 135.
14. *Crerar Papers:* Vol. 7.
15. ibid.
16. *Crerar Papers:* Vol. 30 – Message COS 641 — Crerar to CGS Ottawa, 5 July, 1945.
17. Interview with Colonel C.P. Stacey, 21 May, 1985.
18. *Crerar Papers* – Message C143 Crerar to CMHQ, 8 November, 1944.
19. After the war Simonds continued to be regarded with a respect which bordered on awe by the officers and men whom he had commanded. Few could believe their eyes when, after a regimental dinner in Calgary in the 1950s, they saw Simonds, seated at a piano, singing 'Ragtime Cowboy Joe' to a circle of delighted subalterns.

Chapter 2 — To the Seine

1. *History of The Calgary Highlanders* by Roy Farran, p. 164.
2. Interview with Lt-Colonel Mark Tennant, 23 October, 1986, and *Toronto Star* 12 September, 1944.
3. *Official History*, pp. 285-86.
4. ibid, p. 280.
5. ibid, p. 292.
6. ibid, pp. 284-85.

Chapter 3 — Escape of the German Fifteenth Army

1. *Crerar Papers:* Vol. 7 – CMHQ message A6300 of 2 September, 1944.

2. *Official History*, pp. 303-06.
3. *Tug of War* by Denis Whitaker and Shelagh Whitaker, p. 69.
4. ibid, pp. 69-70.
5. *Official History*, p. 310.
6. *Corps Commander* by Lt-General Sir Brian Horrocks, pp. 80-81.
7. *Official History*, p. 309.
8. ibid, p. 302.

Chapter 4 — The Cinderella Army

1. War Diary and Regimental History, 12 Manitoba Dragoons; *The Canadian Summer* by James Alan Roberts; interview with Colonel E.F. Bastedo, May 1985.
2. *Official History*, p. 324.
3. Brigadier Churchill Mann at operations briefing, 4 September 1944 – author's notes.

Chapter 5 — Dunkirk-Ostend

1. War Diary, Calgary Highlanders.
2. Interview with Lt-Colonel Mark Tennant.
3. *Legion* magazine, October 1984.
4. *History of The Calgary Highlanders*, p. 172.
5. War Diary, Calgary Highlanders.
6. War Diary, HQ 4th Canadian Armoured Division.
7. *The Canadian Summer* by J.A. Roberts, pp. 85-87.

Chapter 6 — Le Havre

1. Log, HMS *Erebus*.
2. *British Official History*, pp. 13-15.

Chapter 7 — Boulogne

1. *Dampier Papers:* Interrogation report, Lt-General Heim.
2. *Dampier Papers:* Operation Order, 3 Cdn Inf Div.
3. Interview with Maj-General J.M. Rockingham, December 1984.
4. *Dampier Papers:* 3 Div Historical Record, Operation 'Well Hit.'
5. ibid.
6. *The Stormont, Dundas and Glengarry Highlanders, 1783-1951* by Lt-Colonel W. Boss, p. 216.
7. *Dampier Papers:* 3 Div Historical Record.
8. Interview with Maj-General J.M. Rockingham.
9. *Official History*, p. 342.
10. *SDG Highlanders,* p. 218.
11. ibid, p. 384.
12. Interview with Maj-General E.K.G. Sixsmith, 1982.

Chapter 8 — Calais

1. War Diary, 3 Med Regt. RCA.
2. *Le Gestes du Régiment de la Chaudière* by Ross and Gauvin, pp. 63-64.
3. War Diary, 141 RAC.

Chapter 9 — The Fortress

1. *British Official History*, p. 5.
2. *Official History*, p. 329.
3. ibid, p. 331.
4. ibid, pp. 359-61.
5. ibid, p. 362.

Chapter 10 — Outflanking Antwerp

1. War Diary, Calgary Highlanders; and interview with P.S. Brain.

2. V.C. Citation Sgt Crockett; and interview with Lt-Colonel Tennant.
3. *British Official History*, p. 80 footnote.
4. ibid, p. 12.
5. Major H.J.S. Pearson in a letter to the author, 24 March, 1986.
6. Interview with Lt-Colonel Tennant.
7. V.C. Citation Cpl Harper — PARC RC24, Vol. 10572.

Chapter 11 — Woensdrecht

1. War Diary, HQ 5 Cdn Inf Bde.
2. War Diary, Calgary Highlanders.
3. Conversation with Lt-Colonel R.L. Ellis 1945; author's note, confirmed by Lt-Colonel Tennant.
4. War Diary, Calgary Highlanders.
5. Conversation with Lt. Colonel Ellis, 1945; author's note.
6. Battle report MS/B 798 — Imperial War Museum. Translated by Capt Westra and quoted in *Tug of War*, p. 170.
7. War Diary, HQ 5th Cdn Inf Bde.
8. War Diary, RHC (Black Watch).
9. *Tug of War*, p. 195.
10. War Diary, HQ 4 Cdn Inf Bde.
11. C in C West Diary, 16 October 1944.
12. *Dampier Papers:* 3 Div Historical Record.

Chapter 12 — Water Enough for Drowning

1. DCM Citation – Sgt Gri.
2. DSO Citation – Lt (A/Capt) V.R. Schjelderup.
3. *Dampier Papers:* 3 Div Intelligence Summary No. 63 of 27 January 1945.
4. War Diary, R Wpg R.
5. ibid.

Chapter 13 — Breskens Pocket — The Braakman Approach

1. Major F.A. Sparks quoted in *Tug of War*, p. 298.
2. *Tug of War*, p. 295.
3. Interview with Maj-General Roger Rowley, 13 November 1984.
4. *Dampier Papers:* 3 Div Historical Record.
5. ibid.
6. *Official History*, p. 400; and interview with Lt-Colonel M.K. Reed, May 1985.

Chapter 14 — South Beveland

1. War Diary, 5 Cdn Inf Bde.
2. ibid.
3. *Mountain and Flood* by George Blake, p. 85.
4. 1:25,000 sheet — author's papers.
5. War Diary, HQ 4 Cdn Inf Bde.
6. War Diary, HQ 5 Cdn Inf Bde.
7. War Diary, HQ 4 Cdn Inf Bde.
8. War Diaries of HQ 5 Cdn Inf Bde, R.H.C. and Calgary Highlanders.
9. War Diary, HQ 5 Cdn Inf Bde.
10. Lt-Colonel F.H. Clarke — letter to author, 26 July 1987.
11. War Diary, R.H.C.
12. War Diary, H.Q. 5 Cdn Inf Bde.
13. War Diary, Calgary Highlanders.
14. Conversation with Lt-Colonel R.L. Ellis 1944 – author's notes.
15. Interview with P.S. Brain.
16. Lt-Colonel F.H. Clarke, letter 26 July 1987.
17. Interview with Hon George Hees, 6 June 1985.
18. Lt-Colonel F.H. Clarke, letter 26 July 1987.
19. War Diary, Calgary Highlanders.
20. *Tug of War*, pp. 337-38.
21. ibid, p. 341.
22. *Mountain and Flood*, p. 92.

23. ibid, pp. 93-98.
24. Conversation with Lt-Colonel R.L. Ellis 1944 – author's notes.

Chapter 15 — Walcheren Island

1. 2 Cdn Corps – GOC 5 – 1 of 21 September 1944.
2. *Official History*, p. 374.
3. Brig-General W.K. Lye in a letter to the author, 12 February 1888.
4. *Crerar Papers:* Vol 8 – Bomber Command message AC361.
5. ibid, AC 359.
6. *Official History*, p. 411.
7. *Tug of War*, p. 356; and History of 5 KOSB.
8. *Official History*, p. 418.
9. ibid, p. 417.
10. *Eleven Men and a Scalpel* by Lt-Colonel J.B. Hillsman.
11. *Mountain and Flood*, pp. 106-10.
12. *Official History*, p. 422.

Chapter 16 — The End of the Affair

1. Conversations with Maj-General Terry Allen, El Paso, September, 1961 – author's notes.
2. War Diary, HQ 10 Cdn Inf Bde.
3. p. 128.
4. Diary quoted in *Triumph in the West* by Arthur Bryant, p. 232.
5. p. 297.
6. *Struggle for Europe* by Chester Wilmot, p. 545.

Chapter 17 — Winter on the Maas

1. Interview with Maj-General Roger Rowley.
2. Interview with J.L. Dampier, December 1984.
3. *March of the Prairie Men* by Lt-Colonel G.B. Buchanan, p. 46 and conversation Major W.S. Edmondson 1946, author's notes.

4. Interview with Maj-General Roger Rowley.
5. *Official History*, p. 42.
6. Author's notes.

Chapter 18 — The Reichwald

1. *British Official History*, p. 256.
2. *The Canadian Summer*, pp. 106-08.
3. *Corps Commander*, pp. 182-83.
4. ibid, p. 183.
5. War Diary, Calgary Highlanders, 8 February 1945.
6. *Ready for the Fray* by R.H. Roy, p. 369.
7. ibid, p. 370.
8. *The Canadian Summer*, pp. 112-13.
9. C in C West Daily Intelligence Report No. 854 of 6 February 1945.
10. *Official History*, p. 375.
11. The 6th (Border) Battalion, KOSB, by Capt J.R.P. Baggaley MC, pp. 80-81.
12. The 15th Scottish Division by Lt-General H.G. Martin, p. 240.
13. *Corps Commander*, pp. 186-87.
14. *The Story of the 7th Battalion Somerset Light Infantry* by Capt J.L.J. Meredith, p. 132.
15. pp. 77-78.
16. *History of the 51st Highland Division* by J.B. Salmond, p. 219.
17. Interview with Maj-General Roger Rowley.

Chapter 19 — Beyond the Forest

1. Author's notes.
2. *The 43rd Wessex Division at War* by Maj-General H. Essame, p. 216.
3. *History of the 4th Battalion Somerset Light Infantry*, p. 82.
4. *Mountain and Flood*, pp. 153-54.
5. *The 15th Scottish Division*, pp. 255-56.

6. *Dampier Papers:* 3 Div Historical Record.
7. DSO Citation Lt-Colonel W.D. Whitaker.
8. *Struggle for the Goch-Calcar Road* by Brig F.N. Cabeldu, recorded by Historical Officer 2 Cdn Inf Div.
9. ibid.
10. DSO Citation Major K.W. MacIntyre.
11. *British Official History*, p. 269.
12. MC Citation Lt David Heaps.

Chapter 20 — Operation Blockbuster

1. PARC RG 24 vol. 10572.
2. *History of 4th SLI*, p. 84.
3. VC Citation Sgt Aubrey Cosens.
4. Statement by Lt-Colonel F.E. White, April 45 – author's notes.
5. ibid.
6. *The Canadian Summer*, p. 117.
7. *History of the Canadian Grenadier Guards* by Colonel A.F. Duguid, p. 320.
8. *Official History*, p. 501.

Chapter 21 — The Hochwald

1. Major W.L. Lyster in a letter to the author, 14 July 1987.
2. War Diary, Calgary Highlanders.
3. War Diary, HQ 5 Cdn Inf Bde.
4. *Official History*, p. 507.
5. *History of Canadian Grenadier Guards*, p 322.
6. VC Citation Major F.A. Tilston.
7. *Official History*, p. 312.

Chapter 22 — The Wesel Bridgehead

1. *Official History*, pp. 509-10.
2. ibid, p. 515.

3. ibid, pp. 520-21.
4. *The Story of the Guards Armoured Division* by Rosse and Hill, pp. 211-14.
5. *War History of 4th KOSB*, p. 143.
6. *Official History*, p. 521.
7. ibid, p. 518.
8. War Diary HQ 5 Cdn Inf Bde.
9. ibid.
10. Conversation with Lt-Colonel R.L. Ellis 1945 – author's notes.
11. *Crerar Papers:* Vol. 6.
12. Brigadier H. Essame in *43rd Wessex Division at War*, p. 226.

Chapter 23 — The Rhine to the North Sea

1. Official History, p. 529.
2. ibid p. 538.
3. War Diaries HQs 1st and 2nd Canadian Divisions.
4. La Geste du Régiment de la Chaudière, p. 116.
5. HQ 2 Cdn Corps letter GOC 30 of 15 April 1945.
6. 2 Cdn Inf Div from the Rhine to the North Sea by Lt Col P.W. Bennett 10 May 1945.
7. *Official History*, p. 555.
8. Major H.J.S. Pearson in a letter to the author, 1 October 1986.

Chapter 24 — Into Germany

1. *Vokes, My Story* by Maj-General C. Vokes, p. 194.
2. *Official History*, p. 558.
3. War Diary, 4 Med Regt RCA.
4. Author's notes.

Chapter 25 — 1st Corps in the Netherlands

1. *Crerar Papers:* Diary 27 March, 1945.
2. War Diary, Perth Regt.
3. Author's notes.
4. Quoted in *Official History*, p. 575.
5. War Diary, PPCLI.
6. MC Citation Lt A.M. Ross.
7. DCM Citation Sgt E.A. Knight.
8. CBC Broadcast.
9. *The Gunners of Canada:* Vol. II by Colonel G.W.L. Nicholson, p. 434.
10. *Official History*, p. 587.

Chapter 26 — End of the War in Europe

1. War Diary, Camerons of Canada.
2. War Diary, HQ 5 Cdn Inf Bde.
3. Major H.J.S. Pearson in a letter to the author, 1 October 1986.
4. War Dairy GSHQ 5 Cdn Armd Div.
5. Interview with Maj-General J.M. Rockingham.
6. *The Canadian Summer*, p. 134.
7. Major H.J.S. Pearson in a letter to the author, 1 October 1986.
8. War Diary, GSHQ 1 Cdn Corps Appx 43, 16 May 1945.
9. *The Canadian Summer*, p. 142.

BIBLIOGRAPHY

Unpublished Sources

British Army of the Rhine, *Battlefield Tour — Operation Veritable.*

Crerar Papers — Gen H.D.G. Crerar's files in Public Archives of Canada, Ottawa, reference no. MG 30 E157.

Dampier Papers — collection of operational records and maps related to the 3rd Canadian Infantry Division in possession of J. Lawrence Dampier, Vancouver.

Historical Section, Canadian Military Headquarters, London, *The Strategic Role of First Canadian Army, 1942-1944.*

Official Histories

British:

Ellis, Major L.F. *History of the Second World War, Vol. 2 — Victory in the West.* 1962.

Canadian:

Nicholson, Col G.W.L. *The Canadian Expeditionary Force, 1914-19, 1964.*

————, *The Canadians in Italy.* 1957.

Stacey, Col C.P., *The Canadian Army 1939-1945.* 1948.

————, *Six Years of War — The Army in Canada, Britain and the Pacific.* 1955.

————, *The Victory Campaign,* 1960.

————, *Arms, Men and Governments — The War Policies of Canada 1939-1945.* 1970.

Public Documents

At the Public Record Office, Kew:
  War Diaries of British units which served in First Canadian Army.
  Logs of HM Ships and reports of naval actions.

At the Public Archives of Canada:
  War Diaries and operations files, units of First Canadian Army.

Published Sources

Baggaley, Capt J.R.P *The Sixth (Border) Battalion, King's Own Scottish Borderers.* 1945.
Barclay, Brig C.N. *The 53rd Welsh Division.* 1956.
Blake, George. *Mountain and Flood.* 1950.
Boss, Lt Col W. *The Stormont, Dundas and Glengarry Highlanders 1783-1951.* 1952.
Bryant, Arthur. *Triumph in the West.* 1959.
Buchanan, G.B. *The March of the Prairie Men.* 1957.
Chalmers, R Adm W.S. *The Biography of Admiral Sir Bertram Home Ramsay.* 1959.
Essame, Maj Gen H. *The 43rd Wessex Division at War 1944-45.* 1952.
Farran, Major Roy. *History of The Calgary Highlanders 1921-54.* 1954.
Goodspeed, Major D.J. *Battle Royal — Royal Regiment of Canada.* 1962.
Gunning, Capt Hugh. *Borderers in Battle.* 1947.
Hamilton, Nigel. *Monty: The Making of a General, 1887-1942.* 1981.
_____. *Monty: Master of the Battlefield, 1942-44.* 1983.
_____. *Monty: The Field-Marshal, 1944-1976.* 1986.
Hillsman, Lt Col J.B. *Eleven Men and a Scalpel.* 1948.

History of the 4th Bn The Somerset Light Infantry in the Campaign in North-West Europe, June 1944-May 1945.

Horrocks, Sir Brian. *Corps Commander.* 1977.

Martin, Lt Gen H.G. *History of the 15th Scottish Division* 1948.

Meredith, Capt J.L.J. *The Story of the Seventh Battalion, The Somerset Light Infantry.* 1945.

Montgomery, F.M. Viscount. *Memoirs.* 1958.

Nicholson, Col G.W.L. *The Gunners of Canada, Vol. II.* 1972.

Roberts, James Alan. *The Canadian Summer.* 1981

Ross and Gauvin, Majors Armand and Michel. *Le Geste de la Régiment de la Chaudière.* 1945.

Rosse & Hill. *The Story of the Guards Armoured Division.* 1956.

Roy, R.H. *Ready for the Fray — History of the Canadian Scottish Regiment.* 1958.

Salmond, J.B. *History of the 51st Highland Division.* 1953.

Shulman, Milton. *Defeat in the West.* 1973.

Sixsmith, E.K.G. *Eisenhower as a Military Commander.* 1973.

Stacey, C.P. *A Date with History.* 1984.

Swettenham, John. *McNaughton, Vol 1.* 1968.

_____. *McNaughton, Vol 2.* 1969.

_____. *The Campaign in N.W. Europe (5th Bn KOSB).* 1945.

XII Manitoba Dragoons Regimental History. 1945.

Vokes, Maj Gen C. with John P. Maclean. *My Story.* 1985.

War History 1939-1945, The Fourth Battalion King's Own Scottish Borderers. 1945.

Whitaker, Denis & Shelagh. *Tug of War.* 1984.

Wilmot, Chester. *The Struggle for Europe.* 1953.

Woolcombe, Robt. *Lion Rampant.* 1955.

INDEX

Aardenburg, 125
Abbeville, 34, 42
Afferden, 213
Albert Canal, 37, 42, 92-3, 95, 97-8, 102
Allen, Major-Gen Terry de la M., 160
Almelo, 265
Alpen, 245-7
Alter Rhein, 207
Alway, Lt-Col M., 131
Amersfoort, 284-5, 289
Amiens, 33, 42
Amy, Lt-Col E.A.C., 239
Anderson, H/ Capt J.M., 124
'Angus', Operation, 107, 109, 135
Antwerp, 17, 37, 40-3, 46, 48, 53, 81-3, 86-7, 90-3, 95-8, 101-2, 111, 129, 132, 142, 147, 152, 158-9, 164-5
Antwerp-Turnhout Canal, 95, 98, 105
Apeldoorn, 170, 261, 283-7, 289
Appeln, 102
Ardennes: German offensive, 175-7, 184, 252
Armée Blanche, 40, 55
Arnhem, 17, 40-1, 46, 61, 82-3, 86, 97, 112, 165, 170-1, 173, 181, 257, 261, 264, 281-6
Asperden, 186
'Astonia', Operation, (Le Havre), 56
Aurich, 294-9

Baarle Nassau, 101
Bad Zwischenahn, 278, 295-6, 299
Balberger Wald, 185, 221-3, 238, 240-1, 243, 246-6
Barber, Major-Gen C.M., 194, 201-2, 204
Barker, Major-Gen E.H., 95
Barneveld, 285
Battery Todt, 78
Beales, Capt Donald, 205
Beckhurst, Major V.W., 212
Bedburg, 210, 213
Beek, 248, 250
Belchem, Brig R.F.K., 298
Belgian Resistance - see Armée Blanche
Bell, Sgt Ross, 44-6
Belle Vue Ridge, 74

Bennett, Lt-Col P.W., 267
Bergen op Zoom, 92, 96, 104, 111, 113, 161, 165
Beveridge, Lt, 157
Bergues, 50, 52, 54
Bernay, 27
Beveland - see South Beveland
Beveland Canal, 83, 129-30, 133
Bienen, 259
Bierville, 44
Biervliet, 123
Birten, 250
Blaskowitz, Col-Gen Johannes, 198-200, 245, 299, photo
Bletchley Park, 37
'Blockbuster', Operation (Hochwald), 221-2, 227
Bonninghardt, 244-5, 247
Boulogne, 39, 42, 46, 48-9, 61-2, 64, 66-7, 71-3, 75, 78, 83, 86-7, 95, 149, 164
Bourbourg, 50-1
Braakman Inlet, 87, 90, 115-6, 122, 124-5
Bradburn, Lt-Col R.A., 236
Bradley, Gen Omar, 35, 111, 147, 166
Brasschaet, 102
Bray Dunes, 50
Brecht, 98-9, 105, 111
Breda, 42-3, 102, 111-2, 161
Bremen, 278, 291, 295
Brereton, Lt-Gen Lewis H., 147
Breskens, 37, 43, 87, 90, 115, 122-6, 129-30, 144, 147, 150-2, 155, 159, 166
Bresserberg, 202-3
Brionne, 28
Brooke, Field Marshal Sir Alan, 19, 20, 22-3, 165
Bruges, 32, 48-9, 53-4, 61, 82
Brussels, 17, 41, 46, 97
Buchholt, 213
Byce, Sgt C.H., 242
Byng, Field Marshal the Viscount, 188

Cadzand, 127
Cabeldu, Brig F.N., 130, 133-4, 219-20, 249
Calais, 39, 42, 46, 48, 50, 61-2, 72-5, 77-8,

82-3, 86-7, 116, 164
Calcar, 186, 202, 205, 209, 211, 213, 217-20, 222, 224-6, 231-3, 235, 239, 248, 250
Canal de Dérivation de la Lys, 87-8, 90
Cap Blanc Nez, 62, 72-5, 77-8, 122
Carrière, Pte J.-C., 140
Casualties: Scheldt, 164; Rhineland, 251; comparison with First World War, 18, 164, 318-320; *see also* formations, units *and* operations by name
Caudebec-en-Caux, 29
Causeway, Walcheren, 132-4, 136-7, 139-43, 146, 157-8.
Chill, Lt-Gen Kurt, 97, 101
Churchill, Rt Hon W.S.C., 126, 150
Clarke, Major F.H., 136-9, 292
Cleve, 186, 189, 192-6, 200-5, 207, 209-10, 213, 221-2
Coningham, Air Marshal Sir Arthur,
Coquelles, 74-5
Corbyn, Lt-Col J.E.L., 203
Cosens, Sgt Aubrey, VC, 227, 230
Crerar, Gen H.D.G.: 18, 27; relations with Montgomery, 19-24, 33-6; with corps commanders, 24-6, 188; with Bomber Command, 149; at Channel ports, 37-9; at Le Havre, 56; at Boulogne, 61, 65, 71; at the Scheldt, 82-3, 86-7, 92, 95, 144, 146-7, 166; sick, 96; returns from hospital, 170; promoted General, 170; Kapelsche Veer, 177; Operation 'Veritable' 171, 175-6, 184-6, 188, 190, 192, 198, 209, 216, 221, 245, 251-2; congratulations from Eisenhower, 251; Rhine crossings, 259; operations in Holland, 261, 267, 278, 281, 284, 286; leaves command, 291; German surrender, 298; photo
Crocker, Lt-Gen Sir John, 23-4, 27, 56-7, 95-6, 98-9, 102, 111-2, 161, 171, 177, 179; photo
Crockett, Sgt Clarence, 94-5
Crofton, Lt-Col Desmond, 197
Cuijk, 171
Cumming-Bruce, Brig H.C.T., 200-1
Currie, Gen Sir Arthur, 20, 188

Dailley, Major G.D., 207
Dampier, Major J.L., 128
Daser, Lt-Gen Wilhelm, 144, 158
Deelen, 285
Delfzijl, 270, 291, 293

Delmenhorst, 292
de Merlis, Lt Guy, 140
Dempsey, Gen Sir Miles, 34-5, 82, 92, 111, 257
Den Heuvel, 193
Depot de Mendicité, 99, 101
Deventer, 261, 265, 270, 281
Die Hees Forest, 250
Die Leucht Forest, 246
Dieppe, xii, 32-6, 39, 46, 48-50, 164
Dietrich, Col-Gen Sepp, 29
Doetinchem, 264
Doenitz, Grand Admiral Karl, 297-8
Dollart, 270
Domburg, 155
Donsbrüggen, 207
Doornenburg, 283
Dore, Capt C., 104
Driel, 281-3
Duclair, 29
Duffelward, 207
Dunkirk, 39, 42, 48-50, 52-4, 61, 83, 87, 115, 164
Dutch Resistance, 120, 131, 265, 267-8, 289
Dutch S. S., 268-9

Eberding, Major-Gen Kurt, 115-6, 123-4, 126-7
Ede, 286
Edmondson, Major W.S., 172-3
Eeckeren, 102
Eindhoven, 97
Eisenhower, Gen of the Army Dwight. D.: and escape of German 15th Army, 39; commands land operations, 41; and the Scheldt battles, 40-1, 81-3, 111, 142, 148-9; neglect of Canadian operations, 165-6; on shortage of infantry, 170; visits Canadians, Rhineland, 184, 251; other refs: 261, 298; photo
Elbeuf, 27, 31
Ellis, Lt-Col R.L., 53, 105, 136-9, 193-4, 235, 251
Emden, 270, 276, 279, 291, 293-5, 298
Ems, R., 265, 270, 272, 276, 294-5
Ems-Jade Canal, 296-7
Emmerich, 186, 192, 202, 259-61, 264, 284
Enschede, 264
Escalles, 74
Escaut Canal, 97
Eselsberg, 205

Essame, Brig Hubert, 211
Esschen, 112
Ewing, Major W., 108

Falaise, 18, 23, 27, 29, 54
Fiebig, Major-Gen Heinz, 184, 203
Field, Pte, 53
Flushing, 42-3, 106, 123-4, 138, 144, 148, 150-2, 155-8
Follingshof, 232
Fontaine, River, 59
Forbes, Lt Charles, 140
Forbes, Lt-Col D.F., 77-8, 259
Forêt de La Londe, 30-1
Forêt de Montgeon, 59
Forman, Major J., 174
Fort Cataraqui, S.S., 159
Fort de la Crèche, 62, 67, 69, 71-2
Fort de Tourneville, 59
Fort Frederik Hendrik, 125, 127, 150
Fort Lapin, 77
Fort Nieulay, 77
Fort Ste. Addresse, 59
Foster, Major-Gen H.W., 88, 284-5
Foulkes, Major-Gen Charles: and Simonds, 26; at Seine, 30; Channel ports, 50; Antwerp, 93; ; temporary commander of 2nd Corps, 96, 141; commands 1st Corps in Italy, 170; in Holland, 257, 264, 281-2, 284-6, German surrender, 299; photo
Franks, Comd R.D., 130
Frasselt, 195-6, 200, 206
French Resistance, 'FFI', 46
Friesoythe, 273, 276, 278
Furnes, 53-4

Gauvreau, Brig J.G., 131
Gavin, Major-Gen James, 172
Geldern, 186, 221, 244-5
Gennep, 96, 186, 205
Ghent, 48-9, 54, 61, 82, 87-8, 122
Gilsa, Gen Inf Werner, Freiherr von und zu, 88
Ginderich, 251
Goch, 186, 189, 202, taken 213, 221, 232-3, 236
Goch-Calcar Road, battle of, 211, 217-20, 236
Gochfortz Berg, 240
Goes, 129, 132, 134
'Goldflake', Operation, 257
Grave, 97

Gravenpolder, 132
Grebbe Line, 284, 289-91
Greenleaf, Major C.A., 239
'Grenade', Operation, 199, 251
Gri, Sgt Armando, 119-20
Groesbeek, 171-2, 185, 195
Groningen, 267-70, 278, 286
Grüppenbühren, 292-3

Haig, Field Marshal the Earl, 20, 166
Hakewill-Smith, Major-Gen E., 141
Hale, Major G.R., 232, 239
Halton, Matthew, 287-8
Halvenboom, 213
Hammerbruch Spur, 246
Harderwijk, 289
Haren, 270
Harfleur, 59
Harper, Cpl John, VC, 100-1
Harris, Marshal of the RAF Sir Arthur, 63, 149
Hasselt, 205, 213
Hau, 204, 210
Hayes, Commodore William, 23
Heaps, Lt David, 220
Hees, Major George, 139
Heim, Lt-Gen Ferdinand, 62, 71
Hekkens, 192, 205-6
Herenthals, 92, 95
Heydte, Lt-Col Frederich von der, 102, 105-6, 109, 210
Hillsman, Major J.B., 156
Hitler, Adolf, 37, 42-3, 61-2, 82-3, 97, 161, 163, 181, 244-5, 252, 297
Hobart, Major-Gen Sir Percy, 75
Hoch Elten Ridge, 259-60
Hochstrasse, 193
Hochwald, 185-6, 190, 221-2, 224, 232-3, 235, 237-45, 252
Hoedekenskerke, 130
Hoffmeister, Major-Gen B.M., 288; photo
Hoofdplaat, 123
Hoogerheide, 103, 105-6
Horrocks, Lt-Gen Sir Brian, 24, 40, 97, 186-8, 190, 192, 200, 202, 209, 221, 245; photo
Hulst Canal, 90
Humphrey, Sgt, 142

Ijssel, R., 170, 261, 264-5, 280-3, 285
Ijsselmeer, 270, 285-6, 288-9
'Infatuate', Operation, (Walcheren), 144, 152
Isabella, 115, 125
Issum, 245

Jahnke, Capt Reichsmarine, 297-8
Jefferson, Brig J.C., 55, 237
Jefferson, Lt Kenneth, 55
Jodl, Col-Gen Alfred, 101
Johnston, Brig I.S., 293
Johnston, Major R.H.B. 158

Kamperland, 131-2
Kapellen, 245-6
Kapelsche Veer, 177, 179-80, 216
Kastel Blijenbeek, 213
Keefler, Major-Gen R.H., 96, 105, 107, 133-4, 224, 259, 265, 271, 294, 296-7
Kekerdom, 196
Keller, Major-Gen R.F.L., 63
Keppeln, 222, 227, 230-2
Kerfoot, Capt. R.J., 108
Kervenheim, 222, 240
Kevelaer, 209, 245
Kiggell, Lt-Gen S.E., 166
King, Capt, 74
Kitching, Brigadier George; photo
Kleffel, Gen Philipp, 286
Knight, Sgt Edward, 287
Knocke, 116, 127
Korteven, 105, 112
Krabbendijke, 130
Kranenburg, 192-3, 195, 201, 208
Krefeld, 244
Küsten Canal, 276, 278, 294-5

La Caucherie, 66
La Hève, 59
Laloge, Sgt E.J., 138-9
Lamb, Capt H.S., 136
La Panne, 53
Larson, CSM H.O., 104, 235, photo
Lasher, Major Winfield, 104, 139
La Trésorerie, 62, 67, 69
Le Havre, 18, 32, 42, 46, 48-9, 56-7, 61, 71-2, 78, 86
Le Portel, 63, 70-2
Leda R., 277, 294
Leer, 277, 279, 294-5
Leeuwarden, 270
LeFroy, Lt W., 136
Leicester, Brig B.W., 150, 152-3, 155
Leigh-Mallory, Air Chief Marshal Sir Trafford, 148-9
Leopold Canal, 83, 87-8, 90-1, 93, 115-6, 123
Leuth, 196
Lewis, Lt-Col T.A., 131
Liane, R., 62, 64, 66-7, 69, 70

Lipscomb, Lt-Col C.G., 211
Lisieux, 27
Lochtenberg, 95, 98, 102
Loga, 294-5
Loon Plage, 50-2
Louisendorf, 214, 218
Lübeck, 298
Lüttwitz, Gen Heinrich Freiherr von, 205, 219, 224, 238
Lyster, Major W.L., 233

Maas, R., 111-3, 160-1, 163-4, 169, 171, 175-7, 184-5, 189-90, 199, 201, 206, 208, 213, 221, 240, 244, 261, 280
MacDonald, Pte, 53
MacIntyre, Major K.W., 220
MacKenzie, Major Bruce, 138
MacLauchlan, Lt-Col D.G., 51, 104
Maczek, Major-Gen Stanislaw, 90, 277; photo
Maldegem, 87
Mardick, 50, 52
Maren, 171
Marienbaum, 241, 244
Mark, River, 161
Marks, Major, 198
Materborn, 194, 201-6
Matthews, Major-Gen A.B., 150, 170, 240; photo
McKibbin, Major H.A., 298
McLaren, Brig J.F.S., 157-8
McNaughton, Gen A.G.L., xii, 20-1, 48
Megill, Brig W.J., 50, 93, 104, 107-8, 133, 135, 137, 139, 141
Meindl, Gen Para Tps Eugen, 224
Melville, Lt-Col, 157
Menzelen, 247
Meppen, 265, 272
Merxem, 92, 102
Merxplas, 99
Meuse, R., 170, 176
Middelburg, 133, 140, 157-8
Model, Field Marshal Walter, 29, 41-2
Moerbrugge, 54, 87
Moerdijk, 161, 163, 175
Moerkerke, 88
Moershoofd, 118
Moffat, Lt John, 136
Moncel, Brig R.W., 241
Monpetit, Capt Camille, 140
Mont Lambert, 62-6, 69

Montgomery, Field Marshal Sir Bernard:
record, 19; opinion of Canadians,
19-21; of Crerar, 22-4, 33-6; of
Simonds, 23; and Channel ports, 56,
61, 71 and Scheldt battles, 40-1, 46,
81-3, 86, 96, 98, 111, 144, 148-9;
failure of judgement on Antwerp, 142,
165-6; and Rhineland battles, 170, 175,
181, 184, 199, 238; in final phases of
war, 260-1, 267, 278, 281, 284, 289;
German surrender, 298
Montgomery, Major Donald, 19
Montivilliers, 59
Mook, 205
Mooshof, 227
Morgan-Deane, Lt R., 29
Moyland, 209, 213-4, 216-7, 220

Nauts, Doctor E.L., 158
Neder Rhine, 170
Netherlands: food relief, 289-90
Newman, Capt Walter, 139
Niederlangen, 278
Niel, 197
Niers, R., 205, 213
Nieuport, 53
Nijkerk, 288
Nijmegen, 41, 96-8, 101, 169-71, 173-5,
190, 192, 194, 196, 202, 207, 261,
264, 281
Nixon, Major, 235
Nocquet, 62
Noires Mottes, 74-5
Nutterden, 201, 203

Octeville, 59
Oldenburg, 272-3, 276, 278-9, 296, 298
Oorderen, 92
Oost-Cappel, 52
Oostburg, 125, 127
Oosthoek, 119
Orbec, 27-8
Ossenberg, 248
Ossendrecht, 105
Ostend, 50, 53-4, 130, 150-1, 154, 156,
164
Otterloo, 285, 'Battle of', 286-8
Outreau, 63, 70

Pangman, Lt-Col J.E.C., 219
Pannerdensch Canal, 281
Passchendaele, 18, 20, 164-6
Patton, Gen George S., 166, 184

Payan, Major C.R., 277
Pearson, Major H.J.S., 99, 269, 292, 299
Pfalzdorf, 211
Phelps, Lt Charles, 55
Pigott, Major J.M., 109, 219
Pont de L'Arche, 31
Pont Remy, 34
Pootmans, Capt, 297
Poperinghe, 54
Porteous, Major C.H.R., 131
Powell, Major J.W., 230-1
Ptak, Capt Lew, 156
Pugsley, Capt A.F., 150, 153-4
Putte, 102
Putten, 288-9

Quer Damm, 196-7

Ralston, Col J.L., xii
Ramsay, Admiral Sir Bertram, 81, 159
Rawlins, Major-Gen S.B., 282
Reed, Major L.M.K., 127
Reichswald, 171-2, 181, 184-6, 189-92,
194, 199-201, 204-6, 208-10, 244,
252, 257
Reinforcements, infantry: 30-1, 169-70;
NRMA (National Resources
Mobilization Act) conscripts, 169
Renkum, 286,
Retranchement, 127
Rheinberg, 246-8, 257
Rhine, R., 17, 41, 81-2, 129, 170-1,
173-5, 184-6, 222, 244-6, 251-3, 257,
259, 282 ; crossing, 257-60
Rhineland, Battles of, 175, 181-253
Richardson, Lt-Col C.W.P., 195, 200
Rindern, 207
Ritchie, Lt-Col B.R., 108, 135
Roberts, Brig J.A., 54-5, 186, 198, 230,
265, 296-300
Roberts, Major-Gen G.P.B., 40
Robinson, Lt-Col W.G.M., 273
Robinson, Major Sherwin, 235
Rockingham, Brig J.M., 31, 63-4, 69, 71,
77, 122-3, 125, 207, 246, 259, 270,
294; photo
Rodgers, Major D.M., 225-6
Roer, R., 184, 199, 205, 208, 221-2,
240, 244, 252
Roesbrugge, 52
Rommel, Field Marshal Erwin, 52
Roosendaal, 92, 96, 112, 161
Roscoe, Lt R.W., 276

Rose, Major H., 157
Ross, Lt Alexander, 287-8
Ross, Major J.A., 260
Rowley, Lt-Col J.W.H., 231
Rowley, Lt-Col R., 66, 70, 126, 174, 207
Ruhr, 111
Rundstedt, Field Marshal Gerd von, 101, 111-2, 161, 175-6, 189, 199, 200, 205
Russell, Brig J.D., 141-2

St. Cyr de Salerne, 28
St. Etienne, 62
St. Germain-la-Campagne, 28
St. Leonard, 98
St. Martin, 62, 66
St. Nicolas, 90
St. Omer, 54, 62
St. Valéry-en-Caux, 57
Sander, Lt-Gen Erwin, 88
Sangatte Battery, 75
Sarantos, Major L.E., 277
Sas van Gent, 122
Schell, Sgt Henry, 278
Schipbeek Canal, 265
Schjelderup, Major J.R., 119-20
Schlemm, Gen Alfred, 185, 190, 192, 198-9, 201, 204-5, 222, 224, 240, 244-7, 252
Schlieffen Position, 221, 224, 233, 235, 240, 245
Schoondijke, 125, 127
Schouwen, 163, 175
Schroeder, Lt-Col Ludwig, 74, 77
Schwalbe, Lt-Gen Felix, 176
Sellar, Comdr K.S., 153-4
Seyss-Inquart, Reichscommissar Arthur, 284, 289
s'Hertogenbosch, 96, 101, 161, 171
Sicily, xii
Siegfried Line or 'West Wall', 17, 41, 82, 170, 181, 185, 192, 192, 194-6, 200-1, 205-7
Simonds, Lt-Gen G.G: relations with Crerar, 24-6; with Montgomery, 23; with Foulkes, 26; pursuit to Seine, 27; ULTRA, 37; escape of German 15th Army, 37-41; south of the Scheldt, 48, 54; Boulogne, 63-4; at Scheldt, 87, 90, 95; acting Army Commander, 96, 111, 116, 129; Walcheren Island, 146-50, 159-61; returns to 2nd Corps, 170; in Rhineland, 186, 188, 209, 216, 221, 232, 239, 245, 251; in Germany, 261, 264-5, 267, 276; commands Army, 291, 295-6; German surrender, 299; photo
Simpson, Lt-Gen W.H., 199, 222, 244, 253
Slooe Channel, 142
Sluis, 125, 127
Smith, Cpl J.A.M., 52
Sogel, 272-3
Somme, R.18, 33, 41-2, 46
Sonsbeck, 243, 246, 249-50
South Beveland, 40, 43, 83, 86, 92, 95-6, 103, 105, 107, 111-3, 116, 129, 132, 134, 142, 144, 146-7, 151, 159
Speldrop, 259
Spitzbergen, xii
Sponheimer, Gen Inf Otto, 95
Spoy Canal, 207
Spragge, Brig J.G., 77, 119, 216-7
Spry, Major-Gen D.C., 48-9, 62-3, 75, 77, 115, 123, 127, 171, 207, 217
Spycker, 50
Stacey, Col C.P., 24
Standdaarbuiten, 161
Steenbergen, 161, 163-4
Steenwijk, 267
Steinmuller, Lt Gen Walter, 29, 30
Stothart, Major J.G., 67
Straube, Gen Inf Erich von, 297-300
Strooibrug, 121
Student, Gen Kurt, 171, 185
'Switchback', Operation, (Scheldt south), 114 - 128, 206

Taschereau, Lt-Col G.O., 296
Tedder, Marshal of the RAF Sir Arthur, 150
Tennant, Major Mark, 28, 51, 99
Terneuzen, 43, 90, 122-3, 130, 150
Terneuzen Ship Canal, 87, 122
Thomas, Major-Gen Ivor, 210, 249
Tilburg, 96, 101, 161, 176-7
Tilston, Major F.A., VC, 240
Tipple, Pte H.A., 204
Trun, 27
Turner, Lt F., 142
Turnhout, 98, 101
Tuschen Wald, 238-9, 241
Twente Canal, 264-5

Üdem, 186, 202, 205, 209 222, 224-5, 231-2, 237, 239-40
Uitwaterings Canal, 127

ULTRA, 37, 39, 40
'Undergo', Operation, (Calais), 73-8

Varel, 279, 296
Veen, 244-7
Vegesack, 291
'Veritable', Operation, (Rhineland), 175, 181-253
Vieux Coquelles, 74-5
Vimoutiers, 27-8
Visiting Forces Act, 21
'Vitality', Operation, (South Beveland), 129-143
Vokes, Major-Gen Christopher, 26, 237- 8, 272-3, 294, 296, photo
Voorthuisen, 285-6, 288
Vossendaal, 193

Walcheren Island, 37, 39, 42-3, 83, 91, 97, 107, 111, 113, 115-6, 123, 125-6, 129, 131-5, 137-8, 140-2, 144, 146-8, 150-2, 158-9, 164-5, 170-1, 175
Walker, Bdr John, 152
Walsh, Brig Geoffrey, 148
Wardhausen, 207
Weeze, 186, 202, 209, 222, 224, 240
Welberg, 163
'Wellhit', Operation, (Boulogne), 61-72
Wesel, 46, 82, 184, 192, 222, 233, 244-7, 251-3
Weser, R., 276, 291
West, Capt R.C., 148
Westervoort, 281, 283
Westkapelle, 147-8, 151-2, 154-6
'Weston' (objective), 238-9, 241
Whitaker, Lt-Col W.D., 109-10, 219-20
White, Lt-Col F.E., 230
Wigle, Lt-Col F.E., 232, 273, 276
Wildermuth, Col Eberhard, 57, 59
Wilhelmshaven, 276, 279, 291, 295, 298
Wilmarsdonck, 92
Wimereux, 62, 69
Wimille, 69
Winnenthal, 247
Winnenthaler Canal, 250
Woensdrecht, 83, 102-3, 105-7, 109-10, 112-3, 124, 129, 135, 142, 165, 210, 219
Wolfsberg, 201
Wouwsche Plantage, 112
Wrightman, Earl, 51
Wuestwezel, 111-2
Wyler, 192-4, 196

Wyneghem, 94

Xanten, 186, 222, 232-3, 243-50, 257

Ypres, 19, 52, 103, 252

Zandvoort, 103
Zand Kreek, 131
Zangen, Gen Inf Gustav von, 41-3, 86, 98
Zeebrugge, 87
Zijpe, 163
Zuider Zee (see also Ijsselmeer), 270
Zuidzande, 127
Zundert, 161
Zutphen, 265, 281, 284
Zyfflich, 196-7

MILITARY UNITS
(see also 'Order of Battle' in Appendix)
Canadian Forces

Air Force
Royal Canadian Air Force:
squadrons in RAF 83 Group, 18, 189

Army
Army, First Canadian: Organization, xii, 18,(*see also* Order of Battle, 304-17); Seine, 27-32; Channel ports, 48- 78; Antwerp and the Scheldt, 81- 166; on the Maas, 169-180; Rhineland, 181-253; Eastern Holland and into Germany, 259-279; Western Holland, 280-90; Final operations, 291-6

Brigades, Armoured -
- 1st: xii, 261, 284
- 2nd: 161, 199, 209, 295
- 4th: 31, 90, 112, 238, 240-1, 264, 295-6
- 5th: 287-8

Brigades, Infantry -
- 1st: 284-5
- 3rd: 284-5
- 4th: 30, 53, 92, 102-3, 105, 109, 113, 129-32, 134, 218-9, 224, 240, 242, 248-9, 264, 268, 292
- 5th: 28, 50, 53, 93, 98, 103-4, 129, 131-5, 137, 140-1, 192, 220, 224, 232, 240, 242, 248, 250-1, 264, 269, 292
- 6th: 20, 28, 30, 53, 95, 102, 105, 112,130-1, 224, 232, 236,241-2, 268, 292
- 7th: 49, 73, 75, 77, 116, 118-20, 122-23, 125, 127, 197, 214, 216, 218, 260, 265, 294-5
- 8th: 62, 66-7, 69, 123-5, 127, 131, 187, 197, 227, 230-1, 241, 265, 295-6
- 9th: 31, 62-3, 69, 71, 77, 121-5, 127, 206-7, 231-2, 246, 259, 265, 270, 294-5
- 10th: 88, 112-3, 163, 237-8, 247, 295
- 11th: 293

Corps -
- Canadian (1914-18): 20, 164, 188
- 1st: xii, 18, 20-2, 24, 26, 170, 257, 261, 264,-5, 280-4, 289-91
- 2nd: 18, 24-5, 27, 29, 48, 92, 95-6, 102, 141, 146, 150, 170, 173, 186, 206, 209, 214, 221-2, 232, 240, 242, 257, 259-60, 264, 267, 271-2, 277, 286, 291, 293, 295, 299

Divisions, Armoured -
- 4th: 31, 34, 42, 48-9, 54, 82, 87-8, 92, 107, 111-3, 115-6, 125, 161, 163, 175, 179, 209, 221-2, 224, 227, 231, 233, 238, 246-7, 261, 264, 272, 276, 278-9, 291, 294-5, 319
- 5th: 24-5, 257, 261, 271, 281, 284-6, 291, 293-4

Divisions, Infantry -
- 1st: xii, 24-5, 257, 260-1, 265, 281-2, 284-6, 319
- 2nd: 27, 30-31, 33-5, 48-50, 61, 73, 87, 92, 95-6, 98, 102, 105, 107, 109-13, 132-3, 142, 144, 146, 164-5, 170, 187, 189, 191, 199, 209, 217, 220-2, 224, 227, 231, 233,239-40, 246, 250, 260-1, 264, 267, 269-70, 278, 281, 291-2, 296, 319

3rd: 30-1, 33, 48-9, 61, 63, 72-3, 75, 78, 87, 115-6, 124-5, 127, 146, 150, 171, 187, 191-2, 196, 199, 206-7, 209, 214, 217, 221-2, 227, 230, 237, 240, 246, 259, 264-5, 270, 279, 291, 294, 319

Units, Armoured -
  The British Columbia Dragoons (9th Armd Regt): 285-6, 288-9, 293
  The British Columbia Regiment (28th Armd Regt): 121, 163, 247, 278
  The Canadian Grenadier Guards (22nd Armd Regt):239, 241-2, 247, 296
  8th Princess Louise's (New Brunswick) Hussars (5th Armd. Regt.): 285, 288-9, 293
  1st Armd. Personnel Carrier Regt: 195
  1st Hussars (6th Armd. Regt.): 75, 227, 230, 284
  The Fort Garry Horse (10th Armd. Regt.): 65, 75, 98, 106, 218-20, 225
  14th Canadian Hussars (8th Recce. Regt.): 51, 131-2
  The Governor General's Foot Guards (21st Armd. Regt.): 232, 241-2
  Lord Strathcona's Horse (Royal Canadians) (2nd Armd.Regt.): 285, 288-9
  The Ontario Regiment (11th Armd. Regt.): 283
  The Royal Canadian Dragoons (1st Armd. Car Regt.): 270, 295
  17th Duke of York's Royal Canadian Hussars (7th Recce. Regt.): 285, 288-9, 293
  The Sherbrooke Fusiliers Regiment (27th Armd. Regt.): 101, 217, 225, 240, 248, 260, 270
  The South Alberta Regiment (29th Armd. Recce. Regt.): 54, 180, 233, 236-7, 239, 246-7
  12th Manitoba Dragoons (18th Armd. Car Regt.): 46, 53-4, 175, 295

Units, Artillery -
  Batteries :18th Anti-Tank, 220; 60th Field, 287; 112th Light Anti-Aircraft, 151; 1st Rocket, 212
  Regiments:
    12th Field, 175
    14th Field, 175
    15th Field, 180
    17th Field, 287-8
    3rd Medium, 73-4
    4th Medium, 277

Units, Engineers -
  Field Squadrons: 9th, 264, 278
  Field Companies: 7th, 94-5; 12th, 283; 18th, 66

Units, Infantry -
  The Algonquin Regiment : 88, 90, 93, 116, 163, 233, 236-7, 241-2, 247, 278
  The Argyll and Sutherland Highlanders of Canada (Princess Louise's): 54, 163, 180, 232, 237-9, 246, 272-3, 278
  The Black Watch (Royal Highland Regiment of Canada): 28, 93, 98-9, 105, 107-8, 110, 124, 135-8, 237, 242, 250, 292, 319
  The Calgary Highlanders: 28, 50-3, 93-5, 98-9, 103-6, 108, 112-3, 134-40, 192-4, 233, 236-7, 250, 269, 292
  The Cameron Highlanders of Ottawa (M.G.): 123
  The Canadian Scottish Regiment, 1st Bn:77,

116-7, 119-20, 197, 214, 217-8, 260, 270
The Cape Breton Highlanders: 293
The Essex Scottish Regiment: 102, 218-20, 240-41, 249
Les Fusiliers Mont-Royal: 28, 30, 130-31, 225
The Highland Light Infantry of Canada: 31, 69, 70, 77-8, 123-5, 127, 207, 259, 294
The Irish Regiment of Canada: 287-8, 293
The Lake Superior Regiment (Motor): 163, 232, 239, 241-2, 247, 264, 272-3, 296
The Lincoln and Welland Regiment: 54, 179-80, 239, 247, 264, 273, 278
The Loyal Edmonton Regiment: 285-6
New Brunswick Rangers, 278
The North Nova Scotia Highlanders: 65, 70, 77, 123-5, 127, 207, 259, 294
The North Shore (New Brunswick) Regiment: 65, 75, 117, 198, 230-1
The Perth Regiment: 281, 289, 293
Princess Patricia's Canadian Light Infantry: 282, 285-6, 319
The Queen's Own Cameron Highlanders of Canada: 102, 130-1, 219-20, 225, 292
The Queen's Own Rifles of Canada: 67, 69, 127, 187, 227, 230, 260, 270
Le Régiment de la Chaudière: 67, 69, 75, 127, 198, 230, 241, 260, 296, 319
Le Régiment de Maisonneuve:28, 30, 50-1, 95, 98-9, 103-5, 135, 137, 139-42, 250,
292
The Regina Rifle Regiment: 75, 77, 116, 118-20, 196, 214, 216, 246, 260
The Royal Canadian Regiment:284
The Royal Hamilton Light Infantry: 53, 63, 102, 109-10, 218-20, 224-1, 249-50, 268, 292
The Royal Montreal Regiment: 118
The Royal Regiment of Canada: 102, 107, 130, 133, 218-20, 249, 264, 292
The Royal Winnipeg Rifles: 75, 77, 119-20, 214, 217-8, 260
The Seaforth Highlanders of Canada: 282, 285
The South Saskatchewan Regiment, 31, 102, 130-1, 172-3, 225, 250
The Stormont, Dundas and Glengarry Highlanders: 65-7, 70, 123, 125-7, 174, 207, 294
The Toronto Scottish Regiment (M.G.): 73, 109, 131, 218
The Westminster Regiment (Motor): 288-9, 293

Units,Infantry, First World War - Princess Patricia's Canadian Light Infantry, 319
2nd Battalion (Toronto Regiment) 319,
10th (Canadians) Battalion,, 319
29th (Vancouver) Battalion, 19, 20
58th Battalion, 319
Royal Canadian Army Medical Corps: 156
Royal Canadian Army Service Corps: 289

British and Allied Forces

British Forces

Air Force

Royal Air Force: 63, 69, 75, 105, 124, 152, 270, 283
Bomber Command: 56-7, 77, 144, 147-50, 153, 189, 289
2nd Tactical Air Force: 39, 150, 189, 252, 276
Groups -
  No.2: 151
  No.83: 18, 189
  No.84: 18, 101, 131, 151, 154, 163, 189, 213, 217, 276
Squadron, No.183: 154

Army

Armies -
  Second: 18, 33-5, 46, 48, 61, 82, 86, 96-7, 111, 161, 184,189, 199, 206, 257, 260-1, 278
  Eighth: 18, 19, 40, 114

Army Group, 21st: 19, 60, 86, 96, 111, 159, 175, 184, 252, 257, 261, 264, 298

Brigades, Armoured -
  6th Guards: 191, 194
  8th: 191
  34th: 191

Brigades, Commando & Special Service-
  4th Commando, 261
  4th Special Service, 53, 146, 150-1

Brigades, Infantry-
  8th: 191
  44th: 195, 200-1, 212
  46th: 195, 209, 213-4, 220
  56th: 57, 283
  129th: 203-4, 210, 248
  130th: 210, 212
  146th: 99, 281
  152nd: 205
  153rd: 205
  154th: 206

155th: 151, 157
156th: 129—31, 157
157th: 125, 140-1, 157
159th, 40
160th, 192
214th: 204, 210, 212
227th: 195, 202, 204

Corps -
  1st: 18, 23-4, 27, 29, 31, 49, 56-7, 59, 61, 71, 86, 92, 95-6, 101-2, 111, 113, 160-1, 165, 171, 175-6, 179, 189, 261
  30th: xii, 24, 97, 171, 175-7, 186-7, 190, 193, 196,200, 204-6, 208-9, 213-4, 221, 240, 245, 257, 260

Divisions, Airborne-
  1st, 97
  6th: 27

Divisions, Armoured -
  Guards: 97, 200, 209, 221, 245-7
  7th: xii, 27, 54, 102
  11th: 34, 41-2, 81-2, 209, 221-2, 240, 243
  79th: 75, 125, 129-30, 152, 195

Divisions, Infantry -
  3rd: 221-2, 240, 245-6
  15th (Scottish): 191-4, 200, 202, 204, 207, 209, 212-3, 221-2, 240
  43rd (Wessex): 200, 202-5, 209, 213, 243, 246, 278, 291
  49th (West Riding): 27, 56-7, 59, 86, 95-6, 99, 101, 111-2, 161, 163, 174, 257, 261, 281-6
  50th (Northumbrian): 171, 173
  51st (Highland): 57, 59, 86, 102, 166, 174, 191-2, 199, 205-6, 208, 212-3, 221, 259
  52nd (Lowland): 111, 125, 129-30, 132-4, 141, 146, 150, 152, 156, 175, 208, 213, 221, 240, 245, 247, 251
  53rd (Welsh): 92, 191, 195, 199, 205-6, 208, 212-3, 221-2, 240, 245-7

Netherlands District: 261

Units, Armoured -
  Coldstream Guards: 1st Bn, 247
  Fife and Forfar Yeomanry: 260
  4/7th Dragoon Guards: 211
  Grenadier Guards: 1st Bn, 202; 4th Bn, 195
  Royal Armoured Corps: 141st Regiment, 78
  Royal Tank Regiment: 4th, 282; 7th: 59
  Scots Guards, 3rd Bn: 214
  13/18th Royal Hussars: 196
  22nd Dragoons: 57

Units, Artillery -
  3rd Medium Regiment, 287
  452 Mountain Battery: 152

Units, Commando (*See also* Royal Marines)-
    No. 4: 151, 155
    No. 10 (Inter-Allied): 155

Units, Engineers -
  Assault Regiment, 5th: 122
  Assault Squadrons, 87th: 65
  Field Company, 202nd: 142

Units, Infantry and Foot Guards-
  Argyll and Sutherland Highlanders (Princess Louise's):2nd Bn, photograph
  Black Watch: 5th Bn, 205; 7th Bn: 259
  Cameronians: 6th Bn, 130, 142, 248; .7th Bn, 130; 9th Bn, 214
  Coldstream Guards: 5th Bn, 247
  Dorsetshire Regiment: 4th Bn, 210; 5th Bn, 211
  Duke of Cornwall's Light Infantry: 5th Bn, 211
  East Lancashire Regiment: 1st Bn, 206
  Essex Regiment: 2nd Bn, 57, 283
  Glasgow Highlanders: 1st Bn, 140-2;2nd Bn, 214
  Gloucestershire Regiment: 2nd Bn, 57, 283
  Gordon Highlanders: 2nd Bn, 195, 201, 207
  Highland Light Infantry: 5th Bn, 142, 158
  King's Own Scottish Borderers: 4th Bn, 151, 158; 6th Bn, 195, 200-2, 247
  King's Own Yorkshire Light Infantry: 1/4th Bn, 59
  Lincolnshire Regiment: 4th Bn, 59
  Royal Hampshire Regiment: 7th Bn, 210
  Royal Scots:.7/9th Bn, 157-8; 8th Bn, 195
  Royal Scots Fusiliers: 4/5th Bn,130; 6th Bn, 195
  Royal Welch Fusiliers: 6th Bn, 206
  Seaforth Highlanders: 7th Bn, 214
  Somerset Light Infantry: 4th Bn, 203, 210-3, 226, 248-9; 7th Bn, 211-2
  South Wales Borderers: 2nd Bn, 57, 283
  Welch Regiment: 1/5th Bn, 206
  Wiltshire Regiment: 4th Bn, 203, 210; 5th Bn, 210, 232, 249
  Worcestershire Regiment: 1st Bn, 211
  York and Lancashire Regiment: Hallamshire Bn, 59, 99

Special Air Service:1st Regiment, 295; other ref. 267

Navy and Marines

Royal Navy: 18, 130, 159;
  Force "T", 150
  H.M. Ships -
    Erebus, 57, 153
    Kingsmill, 154
    Roberts, 153, 155
    Warspite, 57, 153
  Support Squadron, Eastern Flank: 153-4

Royal Marines -
  Brigades: 116th, 261
  Commandos:
    No.41, 152, 155
    No.47, 152, 155-6, 179
    No.48, 152, 155

Allied Expeditionary Force

Allied Expeditionary Force, 17, 40
Supreme Headquarters (SHAEF), 59, 150, 159
1st Allied Airborne Army, 147

United States Forces

Air Force
8th Air Force: 144, 148-9, 289

9th Air Force: 189

Army
Army Groups: 12th, 111
Armies-
   First: 35, 46;.Third: 253;.Ninth: 184, 199, 205, 208-9, 222, 240, 244, 251, 253, 257
Corps - 16th, 246
Divisions -
   Airborne: 82nd, 171-2; 101st, 171, 173
   Infantry: 1st, 161; 104th, 111, 160-1, 163

Belgian Forces

Belgian Special Air Service Regiment: 295
1st Belgian Infantry Brigade: 48
1st Belgian Parachute Battalion: 270

French Forces
2nd Régiment de Chasseurs Parachutistes 267
3rd Regiment de Chasseurs Parachutistes:

Netherlands Forces

Royal Netherlands Brigade (Princess Irene's): 48

Polish Forces

10th Polish Armoured Brigade: 276
1st Polish Armoured Division:18, 48-9, 82, 87, 90, 92, 95-6, 101, 111, 161, 163, 169, 175, 179, 270, 276-9, 294-5
3rd Polish Infantry Brigade: 90

Units -
   9th Polish Infantry Battalion, 179, 276
   10th Dragoons (10th Polish Motor Battalion): 90

German Forces

Air Force
"Hermann Göring" units and Parachute Divisions - see under 'Army'

Army
Armed Forces High Command (*Oberkommando der Wehrmacht - O.K.W.*): 101, 114

Armies -
  First Parachute: 97, 171, 224, 244; Fifth Parachute: 185, 198; Fifth Panzer: 29, 42, 175; Sixth Panzer: 175; Seventh: 29, 42, 82; Fifteenth: 40-3, 82, 86, 97, 114-5, 161, 163, 171

Army Groups -"B": 41; "H": 171, 176-7, 199

Battalions -
  Infantry: 276th (Magen) Bn: 184
  Parachute Army Assault Bn: 240, 247
  12th Parachute Reconnaissance Bn: 218

Battle Groups - Chill: 97, 101, 105, 107; Hutze, 210

Corps -
  Infantry-30th: 286; 63rd: 224; 67th: 42, 95, 101; 86th:42, 224; 88th:176; 89th:42-3, 88
  Panzer - 47th: 199, 205, 219, 224
  Parachute - 2nd: 224

Divisions, Infantry - 46th: 260; 64th: 62, 115,123-4, 158; 70th: 107, 123, 144; 84th: 184-5,188-90, 201, 203, 205, 224; 85th: 101; 89th:101; 180th: 192; 245th: 88, 112; 331st, 29;346th: 246, 285; 361st: 286; 719th: 101

Divisions, Panzer - 2nd SS: 30; 9th SS: 30; 116th: 30, 200, 216, 219-20, 224, 238, 246; Lehr: 219-20, 222

Divisions, Panzer Grenadier -15th: 200, 210, 259

Divisions, Parachute - 2nd: 190; 6th: 174, 179-80, 203, 216, 222, 224, 246, 260, 262, 286; 7th: 199, 201-2, 216, 224, 246, 295; 8th: 101, 216, 222, 224, 246

Divisions, Volksgrenadier - 361st: 284

Regiments-
  Grenadier: 858th, 285
  Parachute: 6th: 101, 105-6, 113, 163; 7th: 224, 232; Hermann Göring Replacement Training Regt: 101, 107, 163
  Volksgrenadier: 952nd, 287

Navy and Marines

Ships: *Köln*, 295
Marine Infantry, 278, 295